Dog Training

FOR

DUMMIES®

3RD EDITION

by Jack and Wendy Volhard

WILEY

Wiley Publishing, Inc.

Dog Training For Dummies®, 3rd Edition

Published by
Wiley Publishing, Inc.
111 River St.
Hoboken, NJ 07030-5774
www.wiley.com

WILEY

About the Authors

Jack and Wendy Volhard are best-selling authors of many dog training books, which have been translated into ten languages. They also have produced a two-set DVD called "Living with your Dog," which shows the Volhard method of developing a mutually inspiring relationship with man's best friend.

Jack is the recipient of five awards from the Dog Writers Association of America (DWAA) and was an American Kennel Club obedience judge for 33 years. He's the author of more than 100 articles for various dog publications and the senior author of *Teaching Dog Obedience Classes: The Manual for Instructors,* which is known as "the bible" for trainers, and *Training Your Dog: The Step-by-Step Manual,* which was named Best Care and Training Book for 1983 by the DWAA.

Wendy is the recipient of four awards from the DWAA. She's the author of numerous articles, a regular columnist for the *American Kennel Gazette,* and co-author of five books, including the *Canine Good Citizen: Every Dog Can Be One,* which was named Best Care and Training Book for 1995 by the DWAA, and *The Holistic Guide for a Healthy Dog,* which is now in its second edition.

Wendy, whose expertise extends to helping owners gain a better understanding of why their pets do what they do, developed the *Canine Personality Profile,* and her two-part series, "Drives — A New Look at an Old Concept," was named Best Article in a Specialty Magazine for 1991 by the DWAA. She also developed the most widely used system for evaluating and selecting puppies, and her film, *Puppy Aptitude Testing,* was named Best Film on Dogs for 1980 by the DWAA. Wendy specializes in behavior, nutrition, and alternative sources of health-care for dogs, such as acupuncture and homeopathy, and she has formulated a balanced homemade diet for dogs. The February/March 2010 issue of *Bark Magazine* included Wendy in its list of Best and Brightest 100 for developing the Puppy Aptitude Test and the Drives Profile.

The Volhards share their home with two Labrador Retrievers, two Standard Wirehaired Dachshunds, and two cats. The dogs are more or less well-trained, and the cats do their own thing. All are allowed on the furniture, but they do get off when told. The Volhards are true practitioners — they have obtained more than 50 conformation and performance titles with their German Shepherds, Labrador Retrievers, Landseer Newfoundlands, Wirehaired Dachshunds, and Yorkshire Terriers.

Through their classes, lectures, seminars, and training camps in the United States, Bermuda, Canada, England, and Puerto Rico, the Volhards have taught countless owners how to communicate more effectively with their pets. Individuals from almost every state and 15 countries have attended their training camps. Internationally recognized as "trainers of trainers," Jack and Wendy were inducted into the Hall of Fame of the International Association of Canine Professionals in 2006.

Visit their Web site at www.volhard.com.

Dedication

This book is for those who like their dogs and who have them first and foremost as pets and companions.

Authors' Acknowledgments

All of us are the product of our life experiences. Our life experiences with dogs started in the 1960s, when we were exposed to many of the famous behaviorists of the day. Being avid readers, we absorbed as much information as we could from individuals such as Konrad Most, Konrad Lorenz, and Eberhard Trummler. We discovered why dogs do what they do and how to apply a behavioral approach to training, one that copies how dogs interact with each other. John Fuller's work in Bar Harbor, Maine, and Clarence Pfaffenberger's with Guide Dogs for the Blind, as well as the experiments done in Switzerland by Humphrey and Warner to indicate the working abilities of German Shepherds, all went into the mix that eventually became our *Motivational Method* of training.

Our sincere thanks to those who contributed to this book and shared their insights: Sheila Hamilton-Andrews, Steve Brown, Emily Emmet, Patty Ferrington, Merry Foresta, Diane Kramer, Carolyn Noteman, Desmond and Lise O'Neill, Ginny Padgette, Theresa Richmond, Diana Rockwell, Peggy Toms, Mary Ann Zeigenfuse, Sandy Stokes, and Dr. Regina Schwabe, DVM. Special thanks to Pauline and Danny Scott for their help with the illustrations.

Finally, we thank our editors at Wiley Publishing — Acquisitions Editor Tracy Boggier, Senior Project Editor Alissa Schwipps, Copy Editors Jessica Smith and Krista Hansing, and Technical Editor Michael Eldridge. They have demonstrated the two most important qualities of a good dog trainer — patience and persistence.

Publisher's Acknowledgments

We're proud of this book; please send us your comments at http://dummies.custhelp.com. For other comments, please contact our Customer Care Department within the U.S. at 877-762-2974, outside the U.S. at 317-572-3993, or fax 317-572-4002.

Some of the people who helped bring this book to market include the following:

Acquisitions, Editorial, and Media Development

Senior Project Editor: Alissa Schwipps
(Previous Edition: Natalie Harris)

Acquisitions Editor: Tracy Boggier

Copy Editor: Jessica Smith
(Previous Edition: Chad Sievers, Trisha Strietelmeier)

Assistant Editor: Erin Calligan Mooney

Senior Editorial Assistant: David Lutton

Technical Editor: Michael Eldridge

Senior Editorial Manager: Jennifer Ehrlich

Editorial Assistants: Rachelle Amick, Jennette ElNaggar

Art Coordinator: Alicia B. South

Cover Photos:
© iStockphoto.com / Adam Hester

Cartoons: Rich Tennant
(www.the5thwave.com)

Composition Services

Project Coordinator: Lynsey Stanford

Layout and Graphics: Timothy C. Detrick, Mark Pinto

Proofreader: Susan Hobbs

Indexer: Glassman Indexing Services

Special Help
Krista Hansing

Publishing and Editorial for Consumer Dummies

Diane Graves Steele, Vice President and Publisher, Consumer Dummies

Kristin Ferguson-Wagstaffe, Product Development Director, Consumer Dummies

Ensley Eikenburg, Associate Publisher, Travel

Kelly Regan, Editorial Director, Travel

Publishing for Technology Dummies

Andy Cummings, Vice President and Publisher, Dummies Technology/General User

Composition Services

Debbie Stailey, Director of Composition Services

Contents at a Glance

Table of Contents

Introduction

....

*B*oth of us have had dogs of one kind or another since we were children. Although neither one of us was the primary caregivers of those dogs, we did have the responsibility of walking them.

Children have entirely different expectations of their dogs than adults do. For one thing, children don't believe in leashes. And because both of us were brought up in a city, we had to train our respective dogs to stay close by during our walks. Neither one of us remembers exactly how we did that. No doubt our dogs were smarter than we were and viewed their daily outings as having to keep an eye on us rather than the other way around.

Not until 1968 did we get involved in a more structured way of training. We had a Landseer Newfoundland and were encouraged to join the local training club. Before we knew it, a pleasant pastime turned into a hobby and then an avocation. Before long, we were conducting seminars and week-long training camps, which have taken us to almost every state in the United States, Bermuda, Canada, England, and Puerto Rico.

More than 30 years later we're still sharing what we have learned along the way. Every one of our dogs has been more of a teacher than a pupil, and we have discovered much more from our dogs than we could ever have hoped to teach them. This book is our attempt to pass on to you what our dogs have taught us.

Without help, few people can become proficient, much less an expert, in a given field. We certainly have had plenty of help. A well-trained dog is the result of education, more yours than your dog's. You need to know what makes a dog a dog, how he thinks, how he reacts, how he grows, how he expresses himself, what his needs are, and most important, why he does what he does. When you understand your dog fully, you can achieve a mutually rewarding relationship. A dog isn't a homogenous commodity. Each one is a unique individual, and in their differences lies the challenge.

About This Book

We truly want this book to be a useful tool for you. And we don't want dog training to feel like a chore that you have to slog through step by step. So we've structured this book in such a way that you can jump in and out of the text as it interests you and applies to your situation. For instance, is your dog partially trained but needs to learn a few things? If so, consult the table of contents or index and go directly to the chapters you need.

Nor do we expect you to internalize every bit of information in this book. Throughout the text, we include reminders of key points and cross-references to more information about the topic at hand. Remember, dog training is fun! It isn't a series of tests that you have to pass — unless, of course, you and your dog enter the world of competitive events.

In this newest edition, we bring you three chapters devoted to puppies. Because training starts the moment you bring your little bundle of fur home, we tell you about behavioral development and what to expect during the few weeks and months. We even tell you what to do the day you come home with young Buddy. We guide you with tips on training, tell you about up-to-date training equipment, and help you to establish a daily schedule. We devote a whole chapter to housetraining and crate training.

We consider our older dogs our friends as well and have included in this edition a chapter on keeping your old dog young. We offer exercises that can be used to limber up the old joints, tips on feeding, information on the latest supplements, and much more. Finally, we've included up-to-date information on rescue dogs, dog parks, doggie day care facilities, and traveling successfully with Buddy. We even have tips on staying overnight with Buddy at a friend's house.

All in all, this is a practical book that we hope will make your relationship with Buddy the very best it can be.

Conventions Used in This Book

We use the following conventions throughout the text to make everything consistent and easy to understand:

- ✔ All Web addresses appear in monofont.
- ✔ New terms appear in *italics* and are closely followed by a definition.
- ✔ **Bold** text indicates keywords in bulleted lists or highlights the action parts of numbered steps.

✔ When referring to a specific dog training command or signal, we capitalize it. For example, we may tell you to use the Come command. When we tell you to give a certain command to your dog, we capitalize it and put it in quotation marks. When referring to a position, we capitalize the term. For example, we may tell you to put your dog into the Heel position.

✔ No matter what your dog's name (or gender) is, in this book we refer to your dog as Buddy. And isn't he your best bud?

When this book was printed, some Web addresses may have needed to break across two lines of text. If that happened, rest assured that we haven't put in any extra characters (such as hyphens) to indicate the break. So, when using one of these Web addresses, just type in exactly what you see in this book, pretending as though the line break doesn't exist.

What You're Not to Read

We've written this book just like any other *For Dummies* book so you can easily find the information that you need. For instance, you may have had a dog for years, and you just want a few pointers to help with your training. No matter your circumstance, chances are you don't have time to read every single word in this book. In that case, we simplify it so you can identify "skip-pable" material. Although the following information is interesting and related to the topic at hand, it's not essential for you to know:

✔ **The text in sidebars:** The sidebars are the shaded boxes you see here and there. They share fun facts and interesting stories but nothing that's essential to the success of training your dog.

✔ **Anything with a Technical Stuff icon attached:** This information is interesting, but if you skip it, you still can train your dog successfully.

✔ **The stuff on the copyright page:** Hey, you may find the Library of Congress numbers and legal language enthralling, but feel free to skip over them if you want.

Foolish Assumptions

In writing this book, we assume a few things about you:

✔ You have a dog or plan to get one.

✔ You want your dog to be well behaved — for his sake as well as yours.

✔ You're self-motivated and ready to make training a priority.

✔ You're looking for an inexpensive guide that gives you the freedom to train your dog what and when you want.

✔ You know little about training a dog, or have tried it on your own with limited success.

Even if you do have training experience, you'll find this book helpful. Through our many years of working with a wide variety of dog breeds and personalities, we have picked up many tricks that are sure to prove useful even to experienced dog trainers.

How This Book Is Organized

In structuring this book, we went from basic to intermediate and finally to advanced training. Each part contains the respective training progressions you need, plus some supplementary information to ensure success. You can apply all of it to your dog — or just the parts you want.

Part I: Setting the Stage for Successful Training

This part helps you prepare yourself for the task of training your dog. Here you find chapters on recognizing the importance of training, understanding canine psychology (including why your dog does what he does), and developing training savvy. Your dog's nutritional needs and health contribute a great deal to his behavior, so this part talks about the importance of good nutrition and quality healthcare. This part also includes a chapter on selecting the training equipment you need, such as collars and leashes.

Part II: Performing Puppy Preliminaries

In this part, we help you navigate your puppy's developmental periods and show you how they influence his behavior. We also help you start out on the right foot with advice on what to do with your puppy once you get him home. We include special training tips that are easy to implement. We also provide a chapter on housetraining and crate training.

Part III: Tackling Training Basics

In this part, you get down to training your dog to become a well-mannered pet. Each chapter details the basic commands and how to teach them to your dog. Chapter 9 provides the lowdown on Sit, Down, Stay, and Leave It, while Chapter 10 covers walking on lead and teaching Buddy the Come command. This part also includes a chapter on how to deal with the most common doggie don'ts, including jumping and barking.

Part IV: Taking Training to the Next Level

This part introduces you to the world of organized dog activities in which you and your dog can participate. The introduction to such events can be the American Kennel Club's enormously popular S.T.A.R. Puppy and Canine Good Citizen programs. These are forums where you can demonstrate your commitment to a well-behaved dog. In this part, we spell out the requirements for participating and the basic exercises your dog needs to know. We also include a chapter about retrieving on command, which can be helpful if you want Buddy to bring you the morning paper.

Part V: Dealing with Special Situations

Here we introduce some not-so-uncommon problems — such as aggressive behaviors, separation anxiety, and fear of thunder and loud noises — and how to deal with them. We also include a chapter on the special needs of the older dog and how to keep him young with specific exercises. We round out this part with a chapter on seeking outside training help and the options that are available to you.

Part VI: The Part of Tens

Every *For Dummies* book has a Part of Tens. Here in this part, you find lists of ten items each — bits of handy information about dog training and other related topics that you can read through in a flash. We include chapters on training traps, sporting activities, and reasons why dogs do the things they do. For fun and games, check out the final chapter on tricks.

Icons Used in This Book

To help you navigate your way through the text, we have included some high-lights of important material, some hints, some cautions, and some true stories of success. This key information is marked with little pictures (or icons) in the margins. Here's what the icons tell you:

This icon draws your attention to ways to save time, money, energy, and your sanity.

This icon raises a red flag; your safety or your dog's may be at risk. It also tells you about the don'ts of dog training. Proceed at your own risk!

This icon directs you to information that's important to remember — key points that you want to focus on.

This icon highlights in-depth information that isn't critical for you to know but that can enhance your knowledge of dog training and make you a better teacher.

This icon points out stories of successful dog training techniques and strategies.

Where to Go from Here

The important thing about dog training is getting started *today*. The sooner you train your dog to behave the way you want him to, the sooner the two of you can live in peace together, and the more problems you can prevent down the road. So turn the page (or use the table of contents or index to get to the information you need the most) and get going! Your dog will thank you for it.

Part I

Setting the Stage for Successful Training

The 5th Wave   By Rich Tennant

"I think he's just displaying normal pack instincts."

In this part . . .

Of course you want your dog to succeed at training. After all, a well-trained dog is a happy dog, and happy dogs have happy owners. However, you can't expect a dog to do what you want him to do (or don't want to do) unless you show him what your expectations are. And your dog won't learn properly or be willing to heed your commands unless you use effective training methods.

In this part, we describe how to prepare yourself for training, including how to choose the right approach, how to adapt your methods to your particular dog, and how to become your dog's teacher. Also, because feeding your dog foods that keep him physically healthy contributes to his overall well-being and behavior, we provide a chapter that explains everything you need to know. We round out the part with a chapter on training equipment.

Chapter 1

Dog Training: The Key to Your Dog's Safety and Your Sanity

In This Chapter

▶ Taking a look at what training truly is

▶ Recognizing a well-trained dog

▶ Reviewing the training models

▶ Understanding the five basic commands

▶ Becoming familiar with factors that influence success

▶ Exploring additional training

▶ Getting started

As a gift to yourself and your dog, as well as your family and your friends and neighbors, train your dog. Doing so means sanity for you, safety for your dog, and compliments from people you meet. Make him an ambassador of goodwill for all dogs. Your dog has a life expectancy of 8 to 18 years, depending on his breed and how well you take care of him. So now is the time to ensure that these years are mutually rewarding for you and your dog.

Some dogs don't need much training, if any. They seem to just naturally fall into step with their owners' daily routines. Most, however, need at least some basic training, especially with coming when called. After all, a trained dog is a free dog. Rather than being condemned to a life on leash, he can be taken for romps in the woods and accompany his owner to many public places.

You should start training your dog the day after you bring him home, and puppies are included in this rule. Just because puppies are cute and cuddly doesn't mean they can't learn. They not only can learn, but they also learn much more quickly than an older dog. That's because they haven't acquired any bad habits.

This chapter gets you started on how to teach your dog to be the well-trained pet you want him to be. Believe us when we say it's well worth the investment.

What Exactly Does Training Mean?

Before you get started with training your dog, you first need to understand what training really is. The term *training* is used to describe two separate and distinct concepts:

- ✔ **To teach Buddy to do something that you want him to do, but that he wouldn't do on his own:** For example, Buddy knows how to sit and sits on his own, but you want him to sit on command, something he doesn't do on his own without training.

  This concept is called *action training.* This type of training relies mainly on using pleasant experiences, such as inducing your dog to sit with a treat. Teaching Buddy the commands Sit, Down, Stand, and Come are examples of action training.

- ✔ **To teach Buddy to stop doing something he would do on his own, but that you don't want him to do:** For example, Buddy chases bicyclists, something he does on his own that you want him to stop doing.

  This concept is called *abstention training.* This type of training typically relies on unpleasant experiences, although it doesn't have to. In other words, the dog learns to avoid the unpleasant experience by not chasing the bicyclist or doing what you don't want him to do. For example, to teach Buddy not to pull on the leash, you can use a check. A *check* is a crisp snap on the leash with an immediate release of tension. In order to be effective, the leash must be loose before the check is made. Buddy can avoid the check by not pulling.

Dogs already know that avoiding unpleasant experiences is advantageous, because that's how they deal with each other. The training begins with the mother dog. When the puppies reach about 6 weeks old, she begins the weaning process. At that point in time, the puppies have sharp little teeth, which aren't very pleasant for the mother when she feeds them. She begins to growl at the puppies to communicate to them not to bite so hard. She snarls and snaps at those who ignore her growls until they stop. An offending puppy may scream to high heaven and roll over on its back, having learned its lesson. The mother dog usually follows the disagreeable experience with an agreeable one — nuzzling the puppy.

The later section "Selecting a Training Model" focuses on the different models of dog training, from traditional training to operant conditioning and clicker training. Although dogs (as a species) haven't changed, the approach to training them has been refined.

The Quasi training of Cece

For more than 40 years, we've had a multi-dog household and at least one cat and have witnessed the abstention training phenomenon countless times (see the section "What Exactly Does Training Mean" for more information on abstention training). Our current menagerie consists of two Standard Wirehaired Dachshunds, two Labrador Retrievers, and Quasi, a male cat who was left on our doorstep when he was 6 weeks old. Quasi is an expert at abstention training.

For instance, when we got our Dachshund, Cece, she was 8 weeks old. Naturally, she was quite respectful of the older dogs, but treated Quasi as though he were a stuffed toy. Quasi, who had brought up a number of puppies, was amazingly tolerant of Cece. When Cece got too rough with him, he would growl, hiss, and hit her with his paw. When Cece didn't get the message, Quasi finally let her have it — he hauled off, all claws extended, and swiped her across the nose. Cece screamed and jumped back in horror, her nose dripping with blood.

Was Cece psychologically scarred for life? Did Cece take offense? Did she go away and sulk? Did she hold a grudge against Quasi? Nothing of the kind. Cece didn't hold any hard feelings; in fact, she gained a little more respect for Quasi. They still play together, and they sleep together. The only difference is that Cece discovered an important lesson — unacceptable behavior results in unpleasant experiences. Incidentally, all the other dogs received the same treatment at one point or another.

Identifying a Well-Trained Dog

A well-trained dog is a joy to have around. He's welcome almost anywhere because he behaves around people and other dogs. He knows how to stay, and he comes when called. He's a pleasure to take for a walk because he doesn't pull and can be let loose for a romp in the park. He can be taken on trips and family outings. He's a member of the family in every sense of the word.

The most important benefit of training your dog is safety: your safety, the safety of others, and his own safety. A dog that listens and does what he's told rarely gets into trouble. Instead of being a slave to a leash or a line, a trained dog is a free dog — he can be trusted to stay when told, not to jump on people, to come when called, and not to chase a cat across the road.

For more than 30 years, we have taught dog training classes, seminars, and weeklong training camps. We listen carefully when our students tell us what a well-trained dog should be. First and foremost, they say, he has to be house-trained (Chapter 7 can help you with that task). After that, in order of importance, a well-trained dog is one who

- Doesn't jump on people
- Doesn't beg at the table
- Doesn't bother guests
- Comes when called
- Doesn't pull on the leash

Note that these requirements, with one exception, are expressed in the negative — that is, *dog, don't do that.* For purposes of training, we express these requirements in the positive — teach your dog exactly what you expect from him. Here's what the new list of requirements for a well-trained dog looks like:

- Sit when I tell you.
- Go somewhere and chill out.
- Lie down when I tell you and stay there.
- Come when called.
- Walk on a loose leash.

The Sit and Down-Stay commands are the building blocks for a well-trained dog; if Buddy knows nothing else, you can still live with him (see Figure 1-1). Of course, your Buddy may have some additional wrinkles that need ironing out, some of which are more matters of management than training.

For instance, he may enjoy *landscaping,* as do our Dachshunds, who delight in digging holes in the backyard with amazing speed and vigor. Unless you're willing to put up with what can become major excavation projects, the best defense is to expend this digging energy with plenty of exercise, training, and supervision (see Chapter 11 for more). Another favorite pastime of some dogs is raiding the garbage. Prevention is the cure here: Put the garbage where your dog can't get to it.

One of our Dachshunds learned to open the refrigerator by yanking on the towel we kept draped through the door handle, so he could help himself to anything he could reach. Prevention was the answer: We removed the towel.

What is an untrained dog?

The untrained dog has few privileges. When guests come to visit, he's locked away because he's too unruly. When the family sits down to eat, he's locked up or put outside because he begs at the table. He's never allowed off leash because he runs away and stays out for hours at a time. Nobody wants to take him for a walk because he pulls, and he never gets to go on family outings because he's a nuisance.

Dogs are social animals, and one of the cruelest forms of punishment is to deprive them of the opportunity to interact with family members on a regular basis. Isolating a dog from contact with humans is inhumane. Spending quality time with your dog by training him will make him the beloved pet he deserves to be.

Figure 1-1: Well-trained dogs.

Selecting a Training Model

You have many ways to train a dog, ranging from rather primitive to fairly sophisticated. Even technology has had its impact on dog training. For example, rather than fenced yards, people often now have invisible fences, which contain dogs within their confines by means of an electrical shock.

A brief history of dogs

Dogs were originally bred for specific functions, such as guarding, herding, hauling, hunting, and so on. Before 1945, most dogs worked for a living, and many still do. The popularity as a household pet is a relatively recent phenomenon, fueled in part by the heroic exploits of the dogs used in World War II as well as the fictional Rin Tin Tin and Lassie. The upshot of this popularity has been a demand for the "family" dog who's easy to train, good with children, a little bit protective, and relatively quiet.

Our approach to training is for people who like their dogs and have them first and foremost as pets and companions. The training involves three phases: the teaching phase, the practicing phase, and the testing phase.

In the teaching phase, the dog is taught specific commands in an area free of distractions so he can focus on his owner and can be successful. When the dog reliably responds to the commands he has learned, distractions are introduced. As the dog progresses in this practice phase, the distractions become increasingly more difficult in order to simulate real life situations. In the testing phase, the dog is expected to demonstrate that he's a well-mannered pet around other dogs and people.

The method of training, or combination of methods, you ultimately choose depends on which one works best for you and your dog. Our goal in this section is to provide you with the options so you can select one that suits your personality and needs as well as those of your dog.

The ultimate object of any training is to have your dog respond reliably to your commands. Ideally, he responds to the first command. Telling your dog to do something only to have him ignore you is frustrating. Think of Buddy's response in terms of choices. Do you want to teach Buddy to think he has a choice of responding to you? We don't think so. We think you want a dog that understands — after you have taught him — that he has to do what you tell him.

First things first: Considering your dog's breed

Before you embark on your training program, consider what you want your dog to master, and then compare your answer to the task for which he was bred. Many people typically select their dogs based on appearance and without regard to breed-specific functions and behaviors. The results are frequently all too predictable — the cute little puppy becomes a grown dog that no longer fits into the scheme of things.

Although most dogs can be trained to obey basic obedience commands, breed-specific traits determine the ease or difficulty with which they can be trained. For example, both the Newfoundland and the Parson Russell Terrier can learn a Down-Stay command, but we suspect you'll need a great deal more determination, patience, and time to teach this exercise to the Parson Russell Terrier than you will to the Newfoundland.

According to the statistics of the American Kennel Club (AKC), the Labrador Retriever is first in registrations, with almost three times the number of registrations as the second most popular breed, the German Shepherd — about 150,000 to some 50,000. We're not questioning the quality of the breed — we have two ourselves. Labs are a fine breed and tend to be healthy, good with children, and more or less easy to train. They also have an average protectiveness trait and require little grooming. What prospective buyers frequently don't consider, however, are a Lab's activity level and exercise requirements, both of which are high. Moreover, as the name implies, a Labrador Retriever is, well, a retriever, which means he likes to retrieve anything and everything that isn't nailed down and doesn't necessarily belong to him.

An excellent resource for breed-specific behavior and traits is *The Roger Caras Dog Book: A Complete Guide to Every AKC Breed,* by Roger Caras and Alton Anderson (M. Evans & Company), now in its third edition. For each breed, the book lists on a scale from 1 to 10 the three characteristics you should pay attention to: the amount of coat care required, the amount of exercise required, and the suitability for urban/apartment life. Thirteen breeds in this group are considered unsuitable for urban/apartment life. The remaining 11 breeds, which include the Labrador, are considered suitable, but *only* if the dog's exercise requirements are being met. Another excellent source is *Paws to Consider: Choosing the Right Dog for You and Your Family* by Brian Kilcommons and Sarah Wilson (Warner Books).

Traditional training

We use the term *traditional training* to describe the most widely used training method for the last 100 years. The first comprehensive written record of traditional dog training is based on the principle that unacceptable behaviors result in unpleasant consequences and that acceptable behaviors result in pleasant consequences.

Konrad Most, a German service dog trainer, developed this method in the early 1900s; he also wrote *Training Dogs: A Manual.* (Dogwise Publishing has republished the book, and it's available at www.dogwise.com.) Most's method was introduced in this country in the early 1920s, when several of his students immigrated to the United States and became the teachers of future dog training instructors.

Most explains that training a dog consists of primary and secondary inducements. *Primary* inducements result in the behavior you want to elicit from the dog, and *secondary* inducements are commands and signals. By pairing the two, you can condition the dog to respond solely to commands and signals, the ultimate goal of any training.

Primary inducements can be pleasant or unpleasant experiences for the dog. Here's a rundown of each type:

- **Pleasant experiences:** These experiences, called *rewards,* consist of an object the dog will actively work for — such as food, an inviting body posture, verbal praise, or physical affection like petting — to induce the desired behavior. A common example is the owner who encourages his puppy to come to him by squatting down and opening his arms in an inviting fashion. Another example is to use a treat to induce the dog to sit or stay.

- **Unpleasant experiences:** These experiences are called *corrections,* and examples can be a check on the leash, a harsh tone of voice, a threatening body posture, or the act of throwing something at the dog. In order to extinguish the undesired behavior, the correction must be sufficiently unpleasant for the dog so that he wants to avoid it and change his behavior. Moreover, you must administer the correction immediately *before* or *during* the undesired behavior.

What constitutes an unpleasant experience varies from dog to dog and depends on his Personality Profile (head to Chapter 2 for more information). In other words, what's perceived as a sufficiently unpleasant experience to inhibit the unwanted behavior by one dog may be perceived as just an annoyance by another dog.

B.F. Skinner, the famous theoretical behaviorist, used the term *operant conditioning* to describe the effects of a trainer's particular action on the future occurrence of an animal's behavior. Four quadrants make up *operant conditioning,* and we show them in Table 1-1.

Table 1-1	The Four Quadrants to Operant Conditioning	
	Add Something	**Remove Something**
Pleasant	**Quadrant 1 – Positive reinforcement:** Following a behavior with something the dog perceives as pleasant will increase the behavior.	**Quadrant 2 – Negative punishment:** Following a behavior with removing something the dog perceives as pleasant will decrease the behavior.
Unpleasant	**Quadrant 3 – Positive punishment:** Following a behavior with something the dog perceives as unpleasant will decrease the behavior.	**Quadrant 4 – Negative reinforcement:** Following a behavior with the removal of something the dog perceives as unpleasant will increase the behavior.

Behaviorists have the tendency to use language that confuses the layman. If you think that "negative punishment" is a redundancy and "positive punishment" is an oxymoron, you're not alone.

To help you understand the differences among the Four Quadrants, here are some examples:

✔ **Quadrant 1 — positive reinforcement:** When one of our Dachshunds, Diggy, was still quite young, she assumed the begging position by sitting up on her haunches. She did this spontaneously and on her own, without any coaxing on our part. Naturally, we thought it was cute, so we gave her a treat, which increased the behavior. We periodically reinforced the behavior with a treat. Fourteen years later, she still offered this behavior to get treats.

✔ **Quadrant 2 — negative punishment:** You're watching TV and your dog drops his ball in your lap hoping you'll throw it. You get up and leave, which will decrease the behavior.

✔ **Quadrant 3 — positive punishment:** Your dog jumps on you to greet you when you walk in the door; you spritz him with water, which will decrease the behavior.

✔ **Quadrant 4 — negative reinforcement:** You lift up on your dog's collar until he sits, and then you release the collar, which will increase the behavior of sitting.

So, what's the bottom line in all this information about traditional training and operant conditioning? It's actually rather simple:

- ✔ Acceptable behaviors result in pleasant experiences.
- ✔ Unacceptable behaviors result in unpleasant experiences.
- ✔ All behaviors have consequences.

To help you keep all the training terminology straight, we provide Table 1-2 to combine it all into a neat, small package.

Table 1-2	How Dog Training Terminology Fits Together	
Vernacular	*Traditional Training*	*Operant Conditioning*
Correction	Anything the dog perceives as unpleasant, such as a check on the training collar, yelling "no," a harsh tone of voice, a threatening body posture, or throwing something at the dog.	An *aversive,* such as negative punishment or positive punishment. An aversive is anything the dog perceives as unpleasant, such as a check on the training collar, yelling "no," a harsh tone of voice, a threatening body posture, or the act of throwing something at the dog.
Reward	Anything the dog perceives as pleasant, such as something the dog will actively work for, which can be a treat, a ball, a stick, praise, or physical affection in the form of petting.	*Positive reinforcement,* such as anything the dog will actively work for, which can be a treat, a ball, a stick, praise, or physical affection in the form of petting.

Clicker training

Keller and Marian Breland created the foundation for the clicker training movement. In the mid-1940s, the Brelands were the first to apply clicker training to training dogs. The movement didn't become popular, however, until the early 1990s when Karen Pryor began to give seminars on clicker training. *Clicker training* is based on the concepts of operant conditioning (which we discuss earlier in the chapter). The dog is first trained to associate the clicker sound (see Figure 1-2) with getting a treat, a pleasant experience. After the dog associates the click with getting a treat, the trainer has two options:

✔ **Option 1:** The trainer can wait until the dog voluntarily offers the desired behavior on his own, such as sit. When the dog sits, the trainer clicks, marking the end of the behavior, and reinforces the behavior with a treat. This option works well with extroverted dogs that offer a variety of behaviors in the hope that one of them will get them a treat. An introverted dog, on the other hand, may show little interest in the game. The "wait and see what happens" approach, depending on the dog, can be a lengthy process for the trainer and a stressful one for the dog — he may stop offering any behaviors and just lie down.

✔ **Option 2:** With this option, the trainer doesn't have the patience to wait for the desired behavior to happen, so he induces the behavior. Again, in the case of the Sit command, the trainer uses a treat to get the dog to assume the sitting position, and when the dog sits, the trainer clicks, marking the behavior, and gives the treat.

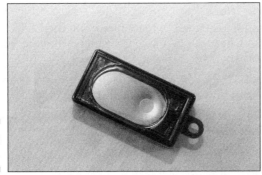

Figure 1-2:
A clicker.

With a clicker the trainer can mark the desired behavior with greater accuracy than he can with verbal praise, which means clearer communication with the dog. Clicker training is a wonderful tool; it does, however, require keen powers of observation and split-second timing. For more on clicker training, see Karen Pryor's *Reaching the Animal Mind: Clicker Training and What it Teaches Us About All Animals* (Scribner).

Five Basic Commands Every Dog Needs to Know

Every dog needs to know five basic commands: Sit, Down, Stay, Come, and Leave It. You can look at these as safety and sanity commands — your dog's safety and your sanity. Here's a look at each of these commands:

- ✔ **The Sit command:** You use the Sit command anytime you need your dog to control himself. You can use the command to teach your dog to do the following:

  - Sit politely for petting instead of jumping on people

  - Sit at the door instead of barging ahead of you

  - Sit when you put his food dish on the floor instead of trying to grab it out of your hand

- ✔ **The Down command:** You use the Down command when you want your dog to stay in one place for prolonged periods, such as when you're eating dinner.

- ✔ **The Come command:** You need to teach your dog the Come command so you can call him when you take him for a hike, when he wants to chase a squirrel, or whatever.

- ✔ **The Stay command:** When you want to teach your dog to remain in place without moving, you teach him the Stay command.

- ✔ **The Leave It command:** You teach your dog the Leave It command so he leaves stuff alone when you don't want him to have it.

Recognizing Factors that Influence Success

Of the many factors that influence success, you are the most important one. You're the one who decides how to approach training and what you want your dog to learn. Your dog is your responsibility and whatever your dog does — good or bad — is under your control.

Having a good relationship with your dog

The goal of training is to create a mutually rewarding relationship — you're happy and your dog is happy. To foster such a relationship, become aware of how many times you use your dog's name to change or control his behavior.

Your dog's name isn't a command and certainly isn't a reprimand. His name is used to get his attention and is then followed by a command.

Stop nagging and learn to communicate with your dog through training. Focus on teaching Buddy what you want him to do rather than on what you don't want him to do. Above all, limit negative verbal communications, such as "no," to emergencies. Repeatedly yelling "no" isn't the way to foster a good relationship.

A good relationship also requires spending quality time together. You can spend time with your dog by training, going for walks, playing ball, and so on. Chapter 21 provides some sporting activities you can do with Buddy.

Owning a healthy hound

Your dog's health has an enormous influence on his training success. A dog who doesn't feel well won't learn well either. First and foremost, his health depends on what you feed him. You need to feed him a high-quality food that provides the nutrients he needs (see Chapter 4).

Your dog also needs an annual checkup by your veterinarian, preferably with a blood test. Regular bathing and grooming are similarly important. If you live in an area where deer roam, you need to check him for ticks. Deer ticks spread Lyme disease, which can have debilitating effects on your dog. Ticks, heartworms, and internal and external parasites need to be diagnosed and treated by your veterinarian.

Making training time a priority

One of the most common complaints we hear is, "I just don't have the time to train my dog!" First, look at training as a fun game — something you and your dog enjoy doing together. It shouldn't be a chore. Then identify the times during the day when you interact most with your dog.

Here are some times when you can take advantage of training opportunities:

- ✔ **Feeding time:** If your dog is still a puppy, you feed him four, three and eventually two times a day. Each meal is a training opportunity — teach him to sit and stay before you put his dish down. Make him wait for a second or two, and then let him eat. You'll be surprised how quickly he catches on to this routine. You also can put the dish down first and follow the same procedure.

- ✔ **When exiting and entering buildings:** Because we have four dogs, we consider door manners an absolute must. It's equally important for the single-dog household, however. It usually takes about 30 seconds for the dog to catch on that he's supposed to wait before you tell him it's okay to exit (or enter). It's a matter of consistency on your part until the behavior becomes automatic.

✔ **While relaxing with your pooch:** The Leave It command can be taught while you're watching TV. Take a few treats to your favorite chair and have fun teaching the progressions to the exercise (see Chapter 9).

✔ **During walks:** Every time you take your dog for a walk is a training opportunity to teach him not to pull, to sit at the curb, and to heel when passing other dogs.

All four of these commands teach your dog to focus on you and look to you for direction — and they all happen as a part of your daily routine.

Oh, the Places You and Your Pooch Can Go: Beyond the Basics

Performance events for dogs date back to the early 1930s, and the first obedience trial under American Kennel Club (AKC) rules took place in 1936. The purpose of obedience trials, as stated in the AKC Obedience Regulations, is to "demonstrate the dog's ability to follow specified routines in the obedience ring and emphasize the usefulness of the purebred dog as a companion of man." Following are some of the options you can explore if you want to take training to the next level.

The Canine Good Citizen Certificate

In the early 1970s, the AKC developed the popular Canine Good Citizen (CGC) test, a program for both purebred dogs and mixed breeds. The CGC test uses a series of exercises that demonstrate the dog's ability to behave in an acceptable manner in public. Its purpose is to show that the dog, as a companion for all people, can be a respected member of the community and can be trained and conditioned to always behave in the home, in public places, and in the presence of other dogs in a manner that reflects credit on the dog. (For more details on this test, go to www.akc.org.)

In many areas you can find classes to help you train your dog and prepare the two of you for the CGC.

AKC S.T.A.R. Puppy program

The goal of the AKC S.T.A.R. Puppy program is similar to the Canine Good Citizen program, except that it's aimed at puppies. Just like the CGC program, the AKC S.T.A.R. Puppy program includes a *Responsible Dog Owner Pledge* as well as a basic training program in which puppies up to 1 year of age are eligible to participate. After you attend a basic training class locally, your puppy must take a test. Look in the phone book for information on dog training in your area. When the puppy passes the test, he receives a certificate and a medal. (For more details, go to www.akc.org.)

More than training: Understanding how dogs help people

Man and dog have been together for a long time. It didn't take man long to recognize the dog's potential as a valuable helper. Originally, the dog's main jobs were guarding, hauling, herding, and hunting. Over time, more jobs were added to the species' repertoire; now dogs perform an amazing variety of tasks. These tasks fall into four broad categories: service dogs, detection dogs, assistance dogs, and companion dogs.

You can head to Chapter 21 for more information regarding working dogs. Also, visit the Web sites for these organizations: Canine Companions for Independence (www.cci.org), Canine Assistants (www.canineassistants.org), Dogs for the Deaf (www.dogsforthedeaf.org), Assistance Dogs International, Inc. (www.assistancedogsinternational.org), Assistance Dogs of America, Inc. (www.adai.org), Guiding Eyes for the Blind (www.guidingeyes.org).

An Exercise to Get You and Your Pooch Started

Eager to get started with some training? We hope so! We begin with an exercise that shows you how to train your dog while you're feeding him. We chose this exercise because you're going to feed your dog two times a day (and even more frequently if he's a puppy), and each time you do so is a training opportunity. It's also a good exercise because the dog quickly figures out what is to his advantage, namely, he stays and he gets to eat.

If your dog is enthusiastic and bouncy, you'll have more success with this exercise when he's leashed rather than loose.

Follow these steps to successfully train your pooch to sit and stay before eating:

1. **Prepare his meal as you normally do.**

2. **Pick up his leash with your left hand and hold it as close to his collar as is comfortable for you, but without any tension on his collar.**

3. **Pick up his dish with your right hand, say "Stay," and then put the dish on the floor.**

   When he makes a dive for the bowl, pull up on the leash and pick up the dish. He doesn't have to sit; he just isn't allowed to dive for the dish.

4. **Repeat Step 3 until he holds his position when you put the dish on the floor; see Figure 1-3.**

5. **After he's successful at maintaining his position, say "Okay" and let him eat in peace.**

   "Okay" is a release term to tell the dog he's now free to move. If you don't like "Okay," you can choose a term to your own liking, such as "You're free."

As a general rule, it takes about three to five repetitions on the first try for the dog to get the message. Avoid the temptation to use negative communications, such a "no" or "ah-ah." Instead, use the leash to gently yet authoritatively control your dog. After several sessions, he'll more than likely sit on his own in anticipation of getting his meal.

Figure 1-3:
Teaching your dog the Stay command as a part of feeding him.

Chapter 2

Canine Psychology 101: Getting to Know Your Dog

*I*n this chapter, we discuss how your dog thinks. Discovering how your dog thinks isn't as complicated as it sounds. By observing his behavior and body posture, you can predict, based on what he has done before, what he's going to do next.

To help you in understanding what motivates *your* dog, we have devised a Personality Profile. Each dog is an individual, and your training efforts have to take his personality into account to succeed with his training.

Figuring Out How Your Dog Thinks

Does your dog think? Certainly. He thinks like a dog, but sometimes it's almost as though he can read your mind. But is he reading your mind, or has he simply memorized your behavior patterns?

Using your powers of observation, you can discover what goes through Buddy's mind. The direction of his eyes, his body posture, his tail position, the position of his ears (up or down), and the direction of his whiskers (pointed forward or pulled close to his muzzle) are all indicators of what he's thinking at the moment. The more the two of you interact, the better you'll get at knowing what Buddy thinks.

In the following sections, we provide you with information to help you to read your dog and what to do if you don't read him quickly enough to intervene in an unwanted behavior. We also discuss the influences of distractions on your dog's behavior.

Reading your dog

Just as your dog takes his cues from watching you, you can interpret what's on his mind by watching him. For instance, you know Buddy has the propensity to jump on the counter to see whether he can find any food to steal. Because he has done this a number of times, you begin to recognize his intentions by the look on his face — for example, you notice that his head and ears are up, his whiskers are pointed forward, and he carries an intent stare. The way he moves in the direction of the counter, with deliberate tail wagging, is the final giveaway.

What do you need to do? You interrupt Buddy's thought process by derailing the train. You can say, "Just a minute, young man, not so fast," in a stern tone of voice. You also can whistle or clap your hands — do anything to distract him. After that, tell him to go lie down and forget about stealing the food.

What if he has already started the objectionable behavior? Maybe he has his paws firmly planted on the counter and is just about to snatch the steak. Use the same words to stop the thought process, physically remove him from the counter by his collar, and take him to his corner and tell him to lie down.

Knowing what to do when you don't read your dog in time

What should you do if your dog has already managed to achieve the objectionable behavior — he has successfully surfed the counter and grabbed a nice snack, for instance? Absolutely nothing! Discipline after the fact is useless and inhumane. Your dog can't make the connection. The time to intervene is when your dog is thinking about what you don't want him to do.

Don't attempt any discipline after the offending deed has been accomplished. Your dog can't make the connection between the discipline and his actions. Your dog may look guilty, but not because he understands what he has done; he looks guilty because he understands that you're upset.

Imagine yourself preparing a piece of meat for dinner. You leave the counter to answer the phone, and when you return, the meat is gone. You know Buddy ate it; after all, no one else is home. Your first reaction is anger. Immediately, Buddy looks guilty, and you assume that he's guilty because he knows he has done wrong. However, Buddy knows no such thing. He's reacting to your anger and wonders why you're mad — and perhaps based on his prior experiences he expects to be the target of your wrath.

Your dog is already an expert at reading you. With a little time and practice, you, too, will be able to tell what's on his mind and read him like a book. His behavior is just as predictable as yours.

Try this experiment if you don't believe that your dog doesn't make the connection between discipline and bad behavior: Without Buddy's seeing you, drop a crumpled piece of paper on the floor. Call Buddy to you, point accusingly at the paper, and say in your most blaming voice, "What have you done, bad dog?" He'll reward you with his most guilty look without having a clue what it's all about.

If you attribute human qualities and reasoning abilities to your dog, your dealings with him are doomed to failure. He certainly doesn't experience guilt. Blaming the dog because "he ought to know better" or "he shouldn't have done it" won't improve his behavior. No matter what you think, he also doesn't understand every word you say, and he's able to interpret only your tone of voice and body language.

Moral of the story: Don't leave your valued belongings, such as shoes, socks, or anything else near and dear to your heart, lying about, where your dog can destroy them. Look at it this way — if you weren't a neat freak before you got your dog, you will be now.

Tackling distractions

Training your dog to respond to you in your backyard, with you being the center of his attention, is fairly simple. But then, the level of difficulty increases in relation to the distractions the dog encounters in real life, such as these headliners:

- ✔ Joggers and cyclists
- ✔ New locations
- ✔ Other dogs
- ✔ Other people
- ✔ Visitors to your home
- ✔ Wildlife

The ultimate goal of training is to have your dog respond to you under any and all circumstances. Your dog's Personality Profile can tell you how you have to train him to reach that goal. Refer to the later section "Determining Your Dog's Personality Profile" for more information.

Recognizing Your Dog's Instinctive Behaviors

Your dog — and every other dog — is an individual animal that comes into the world with a specific grouping of genetically inherited, predetermined behaviors. How those behaviors are arranged, their intensity, and how many components of each are at work determine the dog's temperament, personality, and suitability for a task. Those behaviors also determine how the dog perceives the world.

To give you a better understanding of your dog, we group instinctive behaviors into three drives:

✔ Prey

✔ Pack

✔ Defense

These drives reflect instinctive behaviors that your dog has inherited and that are useful to you in teaching him what you want him to learn. Each one of these drives is governed by a basic trait. We discuss all three in the following sections.

Prey drive

Prey drive includes those inherited behaviors associated with hunting, killing prey, and eating. The prey drive is activated by motion, sound, and smell. Behaviors associated with prey drive (see Figure 2-1) include the following:

✔ Air scenting and tracking

✔ Biting and killing

✔ Carrying

✔ Digging and burying

✔ Eating

✔ High-pitched barking

✔ Jumping up and pulling down

✔ Pouncing

✔ Seeing, hearing, and smelling

✔ Shaking an object

✔ Stalking and chasing

✔ Tearing and ripping apart

Can dogs reason?

As much as you want your dog to be able to reason, dogs can't reason in the sense that humans can. Dogs can, however, solve simple problems. By observing your dog, you learn his problem-solving techniques. Just watch him try to open the cupboard where the dog biscuits are kept. Or see how he works at trying to retrieve his favorite toy from under the couch. During your training, you'll also have the opportunity to see Buddy trying to work out what you're teaching him.

Our favorite story involves a very smart English Springer Spaniel who had been left on our doorstep. The poor fellow had been so neglected that we didn't know he was a purebred Spaniel until after he paid a visit to the groomer. He became a delightful member of the family for many years. One day, his ball had rolled under the couch. He tried everything — looking under the couch, jumping on the backrest to look behind it, and going around to both sides. Nothing seemed to work. In disgust, he lifted his leg on the couch and walked away. So much for problem solving.

Typically, chasing is the most common part of prey behaviors. It's triggered when Buddy is chasing a moving object, such as a toy, cyclist, jogger, or car. Buddy also may shake and rip up soft toys or bury bones in the couch. Failure to recognize the strength of prey behaviors in dogs is the most common reason for so-called behavior problems. For managing prey drive behaviors, see Chapter 16.

Figure 2-1:
Dogs showing the chase, a typical prey drive behavior.

Pack drive

Pack drive consists of behaviors associated with reproduction, being part of a group or pack, and being able to live by the rules. Dogs, like their distant ancestors the wolves, are social animals. To hunt prey that's mostly larger than themselves, wolves have to live in a pack. To ensure order, they adhere to a social hierarchy governed by strict rules of behavior. In dogs, this translates into an ability to be part of a human group and means a willingness to work with people as part of a team.

Pack drive is stimulated by rank order in the social hierarchy. Behaviors associated with this drive include the following:

- Being able to breed and to be a good parent
- Demonstrating behaviors associated with social interaction with people and other dogs, such as reading body language
- Demonstrating reproductive behaviors, such as licking, mounting, washing ears, and all courting gestures
- Exhibiting physical contact with people or other dogs
- Playing with people or other dogs

A dog with many of these behaviors follows you around the house, is happiest when with you, loves to be petted and groomed, and likes to work with you. (Check out Figure 2-2.) A dog with these behaviors may be unhappy when left alone too long, which is a feeling that can express itself in separation anxiety.

Figure 2-2:
A dog enjoying physical contact with a person, a typical pack drive behavior.

Defense drive

Defense drive is governed by survival and self-preservation and consists of both fight and flight behaviors. Defense drive is complex because the same stimulus that can make a dog aggressive (fight) can elicit avoidance (flight) behaviors, especially in a young dog.

Fight behaviors aren't fully developed until the dog is sexually mature or about 2 years old. You may notice tendencies toward these behaviors at an earlier age, and life experiences determine their intensity. Behaviors associated with fight drive include the following:

✔ Exhibiting hair (hackles) standing up from the shoulder forward

✔ Growling at people or dogs when he feels his space is being violated (see Figure 2-3)

✔ Guarding food, toys, or territory against people and dogs

✔ Lying in front of doorways or cupboards and refusing to move

✔ Putting his head over another dog's shoulder

✔ Showing aversion to being petted or groomed

✔ Standing tall, weight forward on front legs, tail high, and staring at other dogs

✔ Standing his ground and not moving

Figure 2-3:
A dog growling, a typical fight behavior.

Whoa! Buddy's got his hackles up

Hackles refer to the fur along the dog's spine from the neck to the tip of his tail. When a dog is frightened or unsure, the fur literally stands up and away from his spine. In a young dog, it may happen frequently because the dog's life experiences are minimal. When he meets a new dog, for example, he may be unsure of whether that dog is friendly, so his hackles go up. A dog's whiskers also are a good indication of his insecurity; in a frightened dog, they're pulled back, flat along his face. His ears also are pulled back, his tail is tucked, and he cringes, lowering his body posture and averting his eyes. All in all, he'd rather be somewhere else.

On the flip side, when the hackles go up only from the neck to the shoulders, the dog is sure of himself. He's the boss, and he's ready to take on all comers. His ears are erect, his whiskers are forward, all his weight is on his front legs, his tail is held high, and he stands tall and makes direct eye contact. He's ready to rumble.

Flight behaviors demonstrate that the dog is unsure. Young dogs tend to exhibit more flight behaviors than older dogs. The following behaviors are associated with flight drive:

- ✔ Demonstrating a general lack of confidence
- ✔ Disliking being touched by strangers
- ✔ Exhibiting hair (hackles) that stands up the full length of the body, not just at the neck
- ✔ Flattening the body, with the tail tucked, when greeted by people or other dogs
- ✔ Hiding or running away from a new situation
- ✔ Urinating when being greeted by a stranger or the owner (submissive urinating)

Freezing — not going forward or backward — is interpreted as inhibited flight behavior.

Understanding how the drives affect training

Because dogs were originally bred for a particular function and not solely for appearance, you generally can predict the strength or weakness of the individual drives. For example, the northern breeds, such as Alaskan Malamutes and Siberian Huskies, were bred to pull sleds. They tend to be low in pack drive, and training them not to pull on the leash can be a bit of a chore. Herding dogs were bred to herd livestock under the direction of their master. Although high in prey drive, they also tend to be high in pack drive and should be relatively easy to train not to pull on the leash. The guarding breeds, such as the German Shepherd, Doberman, and Rottweiler, were bred to work closely with man, so they tend to be high in fight drive with a desire to protect family and property. They easily can be taught to walk on a leash. The Retrievers tend to be high in both prey and pack drive and generally love to retrieve. They, too, easily learn to walk on a leash.

Many of the behaviors for which dogs were bred, such as herding and hunting, are the very ones that get them into trouble today. These behaviors involve prey drive and result in chasing anything that moves. A guard dog may guard your home against intruders and protect your children, but those "intruders" may include the children's friends.

Clearly, these are generalizations that don't apply to every dog of a particular breed. Today many dogs of different breeds were bred solely for appearance and without regard to function, so their original traits have become diluted.

Determining Your Dog's Personality Profile

To train Buddy, you need some insight into what's happening in his little brain at any given moment. Here your powers of observation can help you. In many instances, Buddy's behavior is quite predictable based on what he has done in similar situations. You may be surprised at what you already know. You can almost see the wheels turning when he's about to chase a car, bicycle, or jogger. If you're observant, Buddy will give you just enough time to stop him.

However, you don't have to rely on observation alone. To help you understand how Buddy's mind works and, in turn, understand how to approach your dog's training, we created *Volhards' Canine Personality Profile.* The profile catalogs ten behaviors in each drive that influence a dog's responses and that are useful in training. The ten behaviors chosen are ones that most closely represent the dog's strengths in each of the drives. The profile doesn't pretend to include all behaviors seen in a dog nor does it interpret the complexity of their interaction. For example, what drive is Buddy in when he's sleeping? For purposes of training, we don't care. Although our Personality Profile is an admittedly crude tool for predicting Buddy's behavior, you'll find it surprisingly accurate.

The results of the profile can give you a better understanding of why Buddy is the way he is and the most successful way to train him. You can then make use of his strengths, avoid needless confusion, and greatly reduce training time.

When completing the profile, keep in mind that we devised it for a house dog or pet with an enriched environment and perhaps even a little training, not a dog tied out in the yard or kept solely in a kennel — such dogs have fewer opportunities to express as many behaviors as a house dog. Answers should indicate behaviors Buddy would exhibit if he'd not already been trained to do otherwise. For example, before he was trained properly, did he jump on people to greet them or jump on the counter to steal food?

The possible answers and their corresponding point values are as follows:

✔ Almost always — 10

✔ Sometimes — 5 to 9

✔ Hardly ever — 0 to 4

For example, if Buddy is a Beagle, the answer to the question "When presented with the opportunity, does your dog sniff the ground or air?" is probably "Almost always," giving him a score of 10.

You're now ready to find out who Buddy really is. You may not have had the chance to observe all these behaviors, in which case you leave the answer blank.

When presented with the opportunity, does your dog

1. Sniff the ground or air?   7

2. Get along with other dogs?   10

3. Stand his ground or show curiosity in strange objects or sounds?   9

4. Run away from new situations?   1

5. Get excited by moving objects, such as bikes or squirrels?   5

6. Get along with people?   10

7. Like to play tug-of-war games to win?   9

8. Hide behind you when he feels he can't cope?   0

9. Stalk cats, other dogs, or things in the grass?   1

10. Bark when left alone?   5

11. Bark or growl in a deep tone of voice?   8

12. Act fearfully in unfamiliar situations?   1

13. Bark in a high-pitched voice when excited?   1

14. Solicit petting or like to snuggle with you? _8_
15. Guard his territory? _2_
16. Tremble or whine when unsure? _0_
17. Pounce on his toys? _8_
18. Like to be groomed? _5_
19. Guard his food or toys? _8_
20. Cower or turn upside down when reprimanded? _9_
21. Shake and "kill" his toys? _5_
22. Seek eye contact with you? _7_
23. Dislike being petted? _0_
24. Act reluctant to come close to you when called? _3_
25. Steal food or garbage? _2_
26. Follow you around like a shadow? _5_
27. Guard his owner(s)? _0_
28. Have difficulty standing still when groomed? _1_
29. Like to carry things in his mouth? _9_
30. Play a lot with other dogs? _4_
31. Dislike being groomed or petted? _0_
32. Cower or cringe when a stranger bends over him? _0_
33. Wolf down his food? _10_
34. Jump up to greet people? _5_
35. Like to fight other dogs? _0_
36. Urinate during greeting behavior? _0_
37. Like to dig or bury things? _2_
38. Show reproductive behaviors, such as mounting other dogs? _2_
39. Get picked on by older dogs as a young dog? _0_
40. Tend to bite when cornered? _0_

Score your answers by using Table 2-1.

Table 2-1		Scoring the Profile	
Prey	**Pack**	**Fight**	**Flight**
1.	2.	3.	4.
5.	6.	7.	8.
9.	10.	11.	12.
13.	14.	15.	16.
17.	18.	19.	20.
21.	22.	23.	24.
25.	26.	27.	28.
29.	30.	31.	32.
33.	34.	35.	36.
37.	38.	39.	40.
Total Prey 50	**Total Pack** 61	**Total Fight** 36	**Total Flight** 15

After you've obtained the totals, enter them in the appropriate column of the profile at a glance shown in Table 2-1. And check out Figure 2-4 to see your dog's profile at a glance. In the figure, simply shade in the columns to see your dog's profile at a glance.

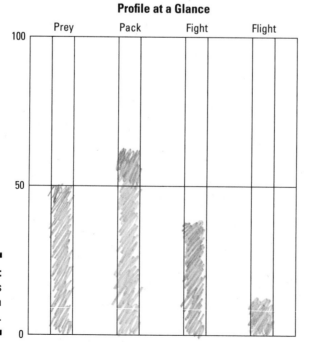

Profile at a Glance

Figure 2-4:
Your dog's
profile at a
glance.

To make best use of the concept of drives in your training, you need to know what you want Buddy to do or stop doing. Usually, you want him to be in pack drive and he wants to be in prey. When you've mastered how to get him out of prey and into pack, you have a well-trained dog.

Deciding How You Want Buddy to Act

Before you can use the results of the profile in the preceding section, you need to look at what you want Buddy to do or — and this is often more important — stop doing. For example, when you walk Buddy on leash and want him to pay attention to you, he has to be in pack drive. If Buddy, on the other hand, wants to sniff, maybe follow a trail, or chase the neighbor's cat, he's in prey drive.

For most of what you want Buddy to do, such as the following, he needs to be in *pack* drive:

- Come
- Down
- Sit
- Stay
- Walk on a loose leash

For most of what Buddy wants to do, such as the following, he's going to be in *prey* drive:

- Chase a cat
- Dig
- Follow the trail of a rabbit
- Retrieve a ball or stick
- Sniff the grass

You can readily see that those times when you want him to behave, you have to convince Buddy to forget about being in prey drive. Dogs high in prey drive usually require quite a bit of training. A dog with high pack and low prey drive rarely needs extensive training, if any. Such a dog doesn't do the following:

- Chase bicycles, cars, children, or joggers
- Chase cats or other animals
- Chew your possessions
- Pull on the leash
- Roam from home
- Steal food

In other words, he's a perfect pet.

Theoretically, Buddy doesn't need defense drive (fight) behaviors for what you want him to learn, but the *absence* of these behaviors has important ramifications. A very low defense drive determines how Buddy has to be trained. For example, our first Labrador, Bean, was low in defense drive. If we, or anyone else, would lean over him, he would collapse on the floor and act as though he had been beaten. Katharina, our German Shepherd, on the other hand, who was high in fight drive, would just look at you if you leaned over her, as though to say, "Okay, what do you want?"

Training each dog required a different approach. With Bean, a check on his leash caused him to literally collapse — he didn't have enough fight behaviors to cope with the check. A slight tug on the leash or a quietly spoken command was sufficient to get him to ignore chasing our proverbial rabbit. Katharina required a firm check to convince her to forget about the rabbit. The only difference between the two dogs was their score in fight drive on their Personality Profile. Refer to the following sections for the different profiles and how to deal with them.

The beauty of the drives theory is that, if used correctly, it gives you the necessary insight to overcome areas where you and your dog are at odds with each other over appropriate behavior. A soft command may be enough for one dog to change the undesired behavior, whereas a firm check is required for another.

Bringing out drives

When you grill hamburgers on the barbecue, the aroma stimulates your appetite as well as everyone else's in the neighborhood. In effect, it brings out your prey drive. The smell becomes a cue. Incidentally, the smell also brings out Buddy's prey drive.

Following is a short list of cues that bring out each of the dog's major drives:

- **Prey drive** is elicited by the use of motion (hand signals), a high-pitched tone of voice, the movement of an object of attraction (stick, ball, or food), and the act of chasing or being chased.

- **Pack drive** is elicited by calmly and quietly touching, praising and smiling, grooming, and playing and training with an erect body posture.

- **Defense drive** is elicited by a threatening body posture, such as leaning or hovering over the dog from either the front or the side, staring at the dog with direct eye contact (this is how people get bitten), leaning over and wagging a finger in the dog's face while chastising him, and checking the dog and using a harsh tone of voice.

Switching drives

Buddy can instantaneously switch from one drive to another. Picture this scene. Buddy is lying in front of the fireplace:

> He's playing with his favorite toy.
>
> The doorbell rings; he drops the toy, starts to bark, and goes to the door.
>
> You open the door; it's a neighbor, and Buddy goes to greet him.
>
> He returns to play with his toy.

Buddy has switched drives from prey into defense, into pack, and back into prey.

During training, your task is to keep Buddy in the right drive and, if necessary, switch him from one drive to another. For example, say you're teaching Buddy to walk on a loose leash in the yard when a rabbit pops out of the hedge. He immediately spots it and runs to the end of the leash, straining and barking excitedly in a high-pitched voice. He's clearly in full-blown prey drive.

Now you have to get him back into pack drive, where he needs to be to walk at your side. The only way you can do that is by going through defense drive. You can't, for example, show him a cookie in an effort to divert his attention from the rabbit. The rabbit is going to win out, unless you have a bigger rabbit.

The precise manner in which you get Buddy back into pack drive — you must go through defense drive — depends on the strength of his defense drive. If he has a large number of defense (fight) behaviors, you can give him a firm check on the leash, which switches him out of prey drive into defense drive. To then get him into pack drive, touch him *gently* on the top of his head (don't pat), smile at him, and tell him how clever he is. Then continue to work on your walking on a loose leash. If he's low in defense (fight) behaviors, a check may overpower him, and a voice communication such as "Let's Go" will be sufficient to get him out of prey drive into defense drive, after which you put him back into pack drive.

If your dog has few fight behaviors and a large number of flight behaviors, a check on the leash often is counterproductive. Body postures, such as bending over the dog or even using a deep tone of voice, usually are enough to elicit defense drive. By his response to your training — cowering, rolling upside down, not wanting to come to you for the training session — your dog will show you when you overpower him, thereby making learning difficult, if not impossible.

Here are the basic rules for switching from one drive to another:

- ✔ **From prey into pack:** You must go through defense drive.
- ✔ **From defense into pack:** Gently touch or smile at your dog.
- ✔ **From pack into prey:** Use an object (such as food) or motion.

Understanding which drive Buddy has to be in speeds up your training process. As you become aware of the impact your body stance and motions have on the drive Buddy is in, you can deliver clear messages to him. Your body language becomes congruent with what you're trying to teach. Because Buddy is an astute observer of body motions, which is how dogs communicate with each other, he'll understand exactly what you want.

Applying drives to your training

After looking at your dog's Personality Profile (see the questionnaire earlier in this chapter), you know the training techniques that work best and that are in harmony with your dog's drives. You now have the tools to tailor your training program to your dog. Here are the different categories your dog may be in:

- ✔ **Defense (fight) — more than 60:** A firm hand doesn't bother your dog much. Correct body posture isn't critical, although incongruent postures on your part can slow down the training. Tone of voice should be firm, but pleasant and nonthreatening.

- ✔ **Defense (flight) — more than 60:** Your dog won't respond to strong corrections. Correct body posture and a quiet, pleasant tone of voice are critical. Avoid using a harsh tone of voice and hovering — leaning over or toward your dog. Focus on congruent body postures and gentle handling.

- ✔ **Prey — more than 60:** Your dog will respond well to a treat or toy during the teaching phase. A firm hand may be necessary, depending on the strength of his defense drive (fight), to suppress prey drive when in high gear, such as when chasing a cat or spotting a squirrel. This dog is easily motivated but also easily distracted by motion or moving objects. Signals mean more to this dog than commands. Focus on using body postures, hands, and leash correctly, so as not to confuse the dog.

- ✔ **Prey — less than 60:** Your dog probably isn't easily motivated by food or other objects, but he also isn't easily distracted by or interested in chasing moving objects. Use verbal praise to your advantage in training.

- ✔ **Pack — more than 60:** This dog responds readily to praise and physical affection. Buddy likes to be with you and will respond with little guidance.

- ✔ **Pack — less than 60:** Start praying. Buddy probably doesn't care whether he's with you. He likes to do his own thing and isn't easily motivated. Your only hope is to rely on prey drive in training. Limited pack drive is usually breed-specific for dogs bred to work independently of man.

Consider some important hints to keep in mind when planning your training strategy:

- ✔ Dogs with a defense drive of less than 60 rarely get into trouble — in fact, they avoid it. Many young dogs without life experience fall into this category, and although their numbers may be quite low as pups, they may vary slightly with age. With such a dog, a straight body posture is more important; to greet him, you need to squat down — as opposed to bending at the waist — to the dog's level.

- ✔ Dogs that exhibit an overabundance in prey or pack drive also are easily trained, but you have to pay more attention to the strengths of their drives and exploit those behaviors most useful to you in training. You now have the tools to do it!

- ✔ If your dog is high in defense (fight) drive, you need to work diligently on your impulse control exercises and review them frequently.

- ✔ If your dog is high in prey drive, you also need to work on these impulse control exercises to control him around doorways, moving objects, and similar distractions.

- ✔ If your dog is high in both prey and defense (fight) drives, you may need professional help with your training — you may become exasperated with your lack of success. The dog may simply be too much for you to train on your own.

Following are the nicknames for a few of the profiles. See if you can recognize your dog:

- ✔ **The Couch Potato — low prey, low pack, low defense (fight):** This dog is difficult to motivate and probably doesn't need extensive training. He needs extra patience if training is attempted because he has few behaviors to work with. On the plus side, this dog is unlikely to get into trouble, doesn't disturb anyone, makes a good family pet, and doesn't mind being left alone for considerable periods of time.

- ✔ **The Hunter — high prey, low pack, low defense (flight):** This dog gives the appearance of having an extremely short attention span but is perfectly able to concentrate on what he finds interesting. Training requires channeling his energy to get him to do what you want. You need patience, because you have to teach the dog through prey drive.

- ✔ **The Gas Station Dog — high prey, low pack, high defense (fight):** This dog is independent and not easy to live with as a pet. Highly excited by movement, he may attack anything that comes within range. He doesn't care much about people or dogs and works well as a guard dog. Pack exercises, such as walking on a leash without pulling, need to be built up through his prey drive. This dog is a real challenge.

✔ **The Runner — high prey, low pack, high defense (flight):** Easily startled and/or frightened, this dog needs quiet and reassuring handling. A dog with this profile isn't a good choice for children.

✔ **The Shadow — low prey, high pack, and low defense (fight):** This dog follows you around all day and is unlikely to get into trouble. He likes to be with you and isn't interested in chasing much of anything.

✔ **Teacher's Pet — medium (50 to 75) prey, pack, and defense (fight):** This dog is easy to train and motivate, and mistakes on your part aren't critical. Teacher's Pet has a nice balance of drives. Figure 2-5 shows the graph for Teacher's Pet.

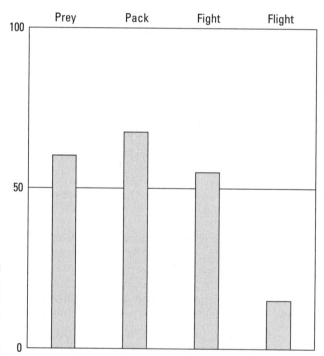

Figure 2-5:
A typical
Teacher's
Pet profile.

The easiest dogs are balanced among all drives. No matter what you do, the dog seems to be able to figure out what you want. If you're lucky enough to have such a dog, take good care of him. By applying the principles of drives, he'll be easy to turn into a well-trained pet.

People frequently ask us, "Can you change a dog's drives — either reduce or enhance a particular drive?" In a few instances you can enhance a drive through training. For example, after you've taught a dog with few prey behaviors to retrieve, he *may* be more inclined to participate in fetch games. As a general rule, however, you can't change a dog's drives. You see what you get and you get what you see.

Remembering Who's Training Whom

Training is a two-way street: Buddy is just as involved in training you as you are in trying to train him. The trouble is that Buddy is already a genius at training you — this is a skill he was born with. Put another way, a dog comes into the world knowing what is to his advantage and what isn't, and he'll do whatever he can to get what he wants. You, on the other hand, have to discover the skills of training him, just as we had to.

One of these skills is figuring out how to recognize when you're inadvertently rewarding behaviors you may not want to reinforce. Begging at the dinner table is a good example. When Buddy begs at the table and you slip him some food, he's training you to feed him from the table. You need to ask yourself, "Is this a behavior I want to encourage?" If the answer is no, then stop doing it.

Consider two more examples of how your dog may be training you:

- ✔ Buddy drops his ball in your lap while you're watching television, and you throw it for him.

- ✔ Buddy nudges or paws your elbow when you're sitting on the couch, and you absentmindedly pet him. When he has had enough, he walks away.

Buddy has trained you well. Is there anything wrong with that? Not at all, as long as you can tell him to go lie down when you don't feel like throwing the ball or petting him.

Become aware of the interactions between the two of you and who initiates them — you or Buddy. One of the quickest ways to gain your dog's respect is to follow this simple rule: Everything belongs to you, especially your attention, and Buddy has to earn what he wants. Buddy has to do something for you before you do something for him. Consider the following, for example:

- ✔ Before he gets a meal, he has to sit and wait until you give the okay that he may eat. (Chapter 1 gets you started with this exercise.)

- ✔ When he comes to you for some petting, ask for a sit, or any other behavior you have taught him, before you pet him.

- ✔ If he comes and drops a ball in your lap, you decide when to play, not Buddy. If you don't want to play, just ignore him.

Interact with your dog as often as you like, but remember that *you* initiate the interaction and *you* end it. (See Chapter 9 for more information.)

Are you spoiling your dog?

We hope so. We certainly spoil ours. We take them for their daily walk, play ball in the backyard, do some training, and on weekends go for outings with friends and their dogs.

Chapter 3

Developing Training Savvy

*Y*our dog's ability to learn and retain information — just like yours — is directly related to what goes on around him and how he feels. A noisy and distraction-filled environment makes it difficult for Buddy to concentrate on learning new commands. Strife in the household may cause Buddy to become irritable and even aggressive, which can impede the learning process. Even what you feed your dog has an effect on his ability to learn.

How Buddy feels, both mentally and physically, influences his ability to learn. If he feels anxious, depressed, or stressed, learning and retention decrease in direct proportion to the degree of the dog's distress. If he's physically ill or in pain, he can't learn what you're trying to teach him. These observations are stating the obvious — just think how you'd react under similar circumstances. Yet we need to point them out because some dog owners often seem to be oblivious to their effect on the dog's ability to learn.

As Buddy's teacher, you play a key role in his learning process — and not just because you're giving him the physical instruction. You also have to create a positive training atmosphere that maximizes his chances for success by easing any stress that can get in the way. Some of that stress comes from within Buddy, and you can alleviate that part by tending to his unique emotional and physical needs. The rest comes from you, so you have to examine what you bring to the table as a trainer. Setting realistic expectations and crafting a consistent training regimen go a long way toward creating a pleasant experience for both you and Buddy.

Managing the Dog Within

Even though some principal influences on your dog's ability to learn are under your control, some influences come from within your dog:

- Breed-specific behaviors
- Temperament
- Mental sensitivity

- Responses to visual stimuli
- Sound sensitivity
- Touch sensitivity

All these influences affect how the dog learns, what he finds difficult, and what comes almost naturally.

Breed-specific behaviors

Whether you have a designer dog, a dog of mixed origin, or a purebred, he comes with some breed-specific behaviors, such as hunting or herding, among others. These behaviors, in turn, have been further refined. Some dogs hunt large game, others hunt small game, and yet others hunt birds. Some hunt close by, and others hunt far away. Some herd and guard, and others just herd; some were developed to herd cows, and others, sheep.

By studying the task or tasks for which a particular dog was bred, you can get a pretty good idea of what's going to be easy and difficult for your dog to learn. Most terriers, for example, are lively little dogs because they were bred to go after little furry things that live in holes in the ground. Shetland Sheepdogs like to round up kids, because they were bred to herd. Pointers are bred to finger the game; Retrievers bring it back (see Figure 3-1); and Spaniels flush it. Each one has its own special talents.

Dog breeders of purebred dogs hardly ever select their breeding stock from working dogs these days. Instead, most dogs are bred to have correct ear or tail set or to have their eyes, faces, and bodies to look just so. Then there are the breeders who create designer dogs, such as Labradoodles, Goldendoodles, and Puggles, by purposefully breeding many breeds together. These dogs are very cute, but they have no predictable behavioral traits. The same is true of mixed breed dogs. However, you can begin to understand what makes your dog tick. To do so, head to Chapter 2 and take the Personality Profile of your dog. This profile will show the behaviors that define your dog.

Because most dogs were bred to work with or under the direction of man, these talents help with your training efforts. But sometimes the dog's instinct to do what he was bred for gets him into trouble. You may not want him hunting or herding or whatever, so you have to spent some of your training efforts redirecting these behaviors. Whenever you run into a roadblock in your training, ask yourself, "Is that what this dog was bred to do?" If so, it will take him more time to learn that particular exercise, and you have to be patient.

Figure 3-1:
A Labrador
Retriever
bred to
bring game
to hand.

Temperament

Most people readily agree that good temperament is the most important quality for pets. Unfortunately, the explanation of exactly what good temperament is often gets vague and elusive, and sometimes contradictory. The official breed standard of most breeds makes a statement to the effect that the dog you're considering is loyal, loving, intelligent, good with children, and easy to train. If only that were true!

Simply defined, *temperament* is made up of the personality traits suitable for the job you want the dog to do. If you want your dog to be good with children, and your dog has that personality trait, then he has good temperament. He may not do so well in other areas, such as guarding or herding, but that may not be what you were looking for.

Similarly vague and elusive have been attempts to define the dog's intelligence. Again, it goes back to function. We define a dog's *intelligence* as the ease with which he can be trained for the function the dog was bred.

You can better understand your dog's temperament if you have a sense of his drives (prey, pack, flight, and fight). See Chapter 2 to take the Personality Profile and find out your dog's strengths and limitations. You'll find which drive molds Buddy's behaviors.

You need to recognize your dog's strengths and limitations because they have a profound influence on the ease or difficulty of teaching your dog a particular task. Circus trainers have an old saying: "Get the dog for the trick and not the trick for the dog." Exploit your dog's strengths.

Mental sensitivity

Dogs, like people, vary in their ability to deal with negative emotions. No matter how they cope, most dogs are keenly aware of your emotions. Moreover, the more you work with Buddy, the greater bond you'll develop. It may seem as though he can read your mind. Okay, he may not be able to read your mind, but he certainly senses your emotions. If you're feeling frustration, disappointment, or anger, Buddy can sense it. Chapter 2 talks more about how your dog responds to your attitude and emotions.

Because dogs are ill-equipped to deal with these emotions, they tend to become anxious and confused, which then slows or even prevents the learning process. Your job in training Buddy is to maintain an upbeat and patient attitude. As your dog's teacher, you must teach him what you want and don't want him to do. Without your guidance, your dog simply does what comes naturally to him — he's a dog! Blaming Buddy for what you perceive to be a shortcoming on his part doesn't help and undermines the very relationship you're trying to build.

Responses to visual stimuli

Saying that a dog responds to *visual stimuli* is a fancy way of saying that a dog responds to moving objects. For purposes of training, it relates to the dog's distractibility when faced with something that moves. This, too, varies from breed to breed and depends on the nature of the moving object. Consider a few examples:

- ✔ Terriers are notoriously distractible. Our Yorkshire Terrier, although technically a member of the Toy Group, was convinced that he had to investigate every moving leaf or blade of grass. Although this made perfect sense to him, it made training him to pay attention a real challenge.

- ✔ In the Hound Group, some breeds, such as Afghan Hounds, Borzois, and Salukis, called *sight hounds,* aren't much interested in objects close by. Instead, they focus on items far away. Other breeds, such as the Basset Hound, Beagle, and Bloodhound, are more stimulated by scents on the ground or in the air than by moving objects. Training a Beagle to walk on a loose leash while paying attention to you and not sniffing the ground can be a Herculean task.

- ✔ The guarding breeds, such as the German Shepherd, Doberman Pinscher, and Rottweiler, were bred to survey their surroundings — to keep everything in sight, as it were. They, too, find it difficult to focus exclusively on you in the presence of distractions. Remember, their job is to be alert to what's going on around them.

✔ The weavers of the Canton of Berne used the Bernese Mountain Dog as a draft dog, drawing milk carts to the marketplace. As a breed, moving objects don't usually excite these dogs. After all, it would hardly do for the little fellow to chase a cat with his wagon bouncing behind him.

✔ The Newfoundland, an ordinarily sedate companion (see Figure 3-2), becomes a raving maniac near water with his instinctive desire to rescue any and all swimmers, totally disregarding the fact that they may not want to be rescued.

Figure 3-2: The Newfound-land, a large breed, is a laid-back dog except around water.

Sound sensitivity

Some dogs have a keener sense of hearing than others, to the point that loud noises literally hurt their ears. For example, our 5-month-old Dachshund puppy gets quite upset when the vacuum cleaner is turned on. He's not afraid of the machine itself; he's just upset by the noise. He finds it difficult to focus on his lessons if a machine is running at the same time. Similarly, one of our Landseers used to leave the room anytime the TV was turned on. Fear of thunder also can be the result of sound sensitivity.

Under ordinary circumstances, sound sensitivity isn't a problem, but it can affect the dog's ability to concentrate in the presence of moderate to loud noises. A car backfiring causes this dog to jump out of his skin, whereas it elicits only a curious expression from another dog.

Touch sensitivity – the adrenaline effect

A dog's threshold of discomfort depends on two things:

- ✔ His touch sensitivity
- ✔ What he's doing at the particular time

For purposes of training and for knowing what equipment to use, you need to have some idea of Buddy's touch sensitivity. For example, when a dog doesn't readily respond to the training collar, he's all too quickly labeled as stubborn or stupid. But nothing could be farther from the truth. The trainer has to select the right training equipment.

Discomfort thresholds tend to be breed specific. For example, we'd expect that a Labrador Retriever, who's supposed to be able to cover all manner of terrain, as well as retrieve in ice-cold water, would have a high discomfort threshold. Shetland Sheepdogs tend to be quite touch sensitive and respond promptly to the training collar. What one dog hardly notices makes another one change his behavior. And therein lies the secret of which piece of training equipment to use.

Touch sensitivity isn't size related. Small dogs can have just as high a discomfort threshold as large dogs. Nor is touch sensitivity age related. A puppy doesn't start out as touch sensitive and become touch insensitive as he grows older. Some increase in insensitivity may arise, but it's insignificant. A dog's touch sensitivity, however, is affected by what he's doing. In hot pursuit of a rabbit, his discomfort threshold goes up, as it would during a fight. We call this phenomenon the *adrenaline factor*.

When you have an idea of Buddy's discomfort threshold, you know how to handle him and the type of training equipment you need. See Chapter 5 for more on training gear.

Stressing the Effects of Stress

Stress is a byproduct of daily life and can result from many factors — health, family, your job, the state of the economy, the state of the country, or even the state of the world. Even pleasurable experiences, such as taking a vacation, can be a source of stress.

Stress is a physiological, genetically predetermined reaction over which the individual, be it a dog or person, has no control. Stress is a natural part of everyone's daily lives and affects each person in different ways. Dogs are no different. Just like people, they experience stress. As your dog's teacher, you must recognize the circumstances that produce stress and its manifestations and know how to manage it.

Your personal experiences with stress help you relate to what your dog is experiencing. Learning the signs and symptoms isn't difficult when you know what you're looking for.

Understanding stress

In both dogs and people, stress is the body's response to any physical or mental demand. That response prepares the body to either fight or flee. Stress increases blood pressure, heart rate, breathing, and metabolism, and it triggers a marked increase in the blood supply to the arms and legs.

Stress takes its toll on the body, be it a person's or a dog's. When stressed, the body becomes chemically unbalanced. To deal with this imbalance, the body releases chemicals into the bloodstream in an attempt to rebalance itself. The reserve of these chemicals is limited; you can dip into it only so many times before it runs dry and the body loses its ability to rebalance. Prolonged periods of imbalance then result in neurotic behavior and the inability to function. When the body's ability to counteract stress has been maxed out, stress is then expressed in more than just physical ways: It manifests behaviorally and physically. This is as true for your dog as it is for you.

Mental and physical stress ranges from tolerable all the way to intolerable — that is, the inability to function. Your interest here lies with your dog's stress experienced during training, whether you're teaching a new exercise, practicing a familiar one, or administering a test, like the Canine Good Citizen test (see Chapter 12). You need to be able to recognize the signs of stress and manage the stress your dog may experience.

Stress is characterized as both positive and negative. When stress is *positive,* it manifests itself in increased activity; when it's *negative,* it results in decreased activity. The following list explains both:

✔ **Help, I'm hyperactive!** Positive stress results in hyperactivity. Your dog may run around, not be able to stay still or slow down, not pay attention, bounce up and down, jump on you, whine, bark, mouth, get in front of you, anticipate commands, or not be able to learn. You may think your dog is just being silly and tiresome, but he's actually exhibiting coping behaviors.

> ✔ **Why am I so depressed?** So-called negative stress causes lethargy, with related behaviors such as lacking energy, being afraid, freezing, slinking behind you, running away, responding slowly to commands, showing little interest in exercise or training, or displaying an inability to learn. In new situations, Buddy gets behind you, seems tired and wants to lie down, or seems sluggish and disinterested. These aren't signs of relaxation; they're the coping behaviors for negative stress.

Recognizing the symptoms of stress

In dogs, signs of either form of stress — positive or negative — are muscle tremors; excessive panting and drooling; sweaty feet that leave tracks on dry, hard surfaces; dilated pupils; and, in extreme cases, urination, defecation (usually in the form of diarrhea), self-mutilation, and anxiety.

Anxiety is a state of apprehension and uneasiness. When anxiety is prolonged, two problems arise:

> ✔ The dog's ability to learn and think is diminished and ultimately stops. It also can cause a panic attack.

> ✔ Anxiety depresses the immune system, thereby increasing the dog's chances of becoming physically ill. The weakest link in the chain is attacked first. If the dog has structural flaws, such as weak *pasterns* (the region of foreleg between the wrist and digits), he may begin to limp or show signs of pain. Digestive upsets are another common reaction to stress.

In and of itself, stress isn't bad or undesirable. A certain level of stress is vital for the development and healthy functioning of the body and its immune system. Only when stress has no behavioral outlet — when the dog is put in a no-win situation — is the burden of coping borne by the body. The immune system then starts to break down.

Origins of stress — intrinsic and extrinsic

Intrinsic sources of stress are inherited and come from within the dog. They include structure and health. Dogs vary in coping abilities and stress thresholds. Realistically, you can't do much to change your dog — for example, you can't train him to deal better with stress. But you can use stress-management techniques to mitigate its impact (see the section "Managing Stress" later in this chapter).

Extrinsic sources of stress come from outside the dog and are introduced externally. They range from the diet you feed your dog to the relationship you have with him. Extrinsic sources include the following:

✔ Frustration and indecision on your part

✔ Lack of adequate socialization

✔ The dog's perception of his environment

✔ Training location

✔ Use of an appropriate training method

Fortunately, all these sources of stress are under your control (see the later section "Managing stress").

Relating stress to learning

In some instances, Buddy just doesn't seem to get the message. These situations can arise at any time, especially when you're working with distractions. Nothing you do works, and you feel that you're not making progress.

When you train Buddy, you can't prevent him from experiencing some stress, but you can keep it at a level at which he can still learn. If you find that your dog is overly stressed during a training session, stop the session. (One indicator of when Buddy has had enough is that he no longer takes a treat.) At that point, your dog's ability to learn is diminished, and neither of you will benefit from continuing.

"What can I do?" we're often asked. "If I stop, Buddy will think he has won and he will never do it for me." This line of thinking presumes that you and Buddy are adversaries, in some kind of a contest, such as, "You'll do it no matter what." Not exactly a "teacher/student" relationship!

Training Buddy has nothing to do with winning or losing, but with teaching. You can walk away from a training session at any time, whether or not you think you've been successful. When you see that no further learning is taking place, stop! If you don't and you insist on forcing the issue, you'll undermine both your dog's trust in you and the relationship you're trying to build.

Let Buddy rest for four hours and try again. You'll find that the light bulb suddenly seems to turn on. By having taken a break at that point, you give *latent learning* — the process of getting the point through time — a chance to work. Our advice is to quit training when you find yourself becoming irritable or when Buddy starts to show signs of stress.

Stress and distraction training

Prepare to be patient when you first introduce your dog to training with distractions. Naturally, Buddy is going to be distracted (that's the point!), but over time, he'll learn to respond correctly. If you feel yourself becoming distraught, it's time to take five.

Try to make every new exercise or distraction a positive experience for your dog. A favorable introduction will have a positive long-term impact. The first impression leaves the most lasting impact. Whenever you introduce your dog to a new exercise or distraction, make it as pleasant and as stress free as possible so that it leaves a neutral, if not favorable, impression.

Managing stress

Become aware of how Buddy reacts to stress, positively or negatively, and the circumstances under which he stresses. Something you're doing, or even a location, may cause him stress.

Understand that Buddy has no control over his response to stress — he inherited this behavior — and that it's your job to manage it as best as you can. Through proper management, Buddy will become accustomed, with every successful repetition, to coping with new situations like a pro.

Managing Your Dog's Environment

Your dog has a keen perception of his environment. Continuous or frequent strife or friction in your household can have a negative impact on your dog's ability to learn. Many dogs also are adversely affected by excessive noise and activity, and may develop behavior problems.

Look for the following signs that your dog has a negative perception of his environment:

- Aggression
- Aloofness
- Hyperactivity
- Irritability
- Lethargy

Under these circumstances, learning is reduced — if it takes place at all — and the dog won't retain the lesson. However, if you have a keen perception of how your dog responds to his environment, you'll more easily attain your training goals. This section provides some tips on creating for your dog the best possible environment for learning.

Starting on the right foot

You've heard the saying "You don't get a second chance to make a first impression." You also know that the first impression leaves the most lasting impact. The stronger that impression, the longer it lasts.

Introductions to a dog's new experiences need to be as pleasant as possible. For example, Buddy's first visit to the vet needs to be a pleasant experience, or he'll have an unpleasant association with going to the vet. Have the doctor give him a dog treat before his examination and another treat at the end of the visit.

The importance of making a good first impression applies to your dog's training as well. A particularly traumatic or unpleasant first experience can literally ruin a dog for life. The object is to make your dog's first impression of training as pleasant as you can.

Recognizing your dog's social needs

Dogs are social animals that don't do well when isolated. For example, if you work, you may have to leave your dog alone at home. Then when you get home, your dog is terribly excited and wants to play and be with you. But you also may need to go out in the evening, leaving your dog alone again.

If you simply don't have the time to give your dog the attention he craves, consider doggie daycare. Your dog will spend his day playing and interacting with other dogs and having a good time. Perhaps the best feature, depending on your perspective, is that when you pick up Buddy on your way home, he'll be too tired to make many demands on you. In addition to keeping Buddy entertained and amused, many doggie daycare facilities provide other services, such as bathing, grooming, and training.

A potential downside of doggie daycare is that Buddy may think it's playtime whenever he meets another dog, making him difficult to control around other dogs. Other potential downsides are possible exposure to disease and parasites, trauma due to inexperienced handling by daycare personnel, and personal liability for Buddy's actions.

As with any behavior, when it comes to exercise, your dog has a certain amount of energy. After Buddy has expended that energy, he is tired, and tired dogs have happy owners. If that energy isn't expended, it may redirect itself into barking, chewing, digging, house soiling, self-mutilation, and similar behaviors — clearly not what you have in mind for the well-trained pet.

Identifying your dog's emotional needs

Whether dogs have emotional needs depends on whether you accept that dogs have emotions. We believe they do, and here are some of them:

- ✔ Anger
- ✔ Apprehension
- ✔ Depression
- ✔ Fear

- ✔ Happiness
- ✔ Joy
- ✔ Sadness

You can see your dog exhibit some of these emotions, such as joy and happiness, on a daily basis, but what about sadness and depression? Dogs react with the same emotions that people have over the loss of a loved one, be it a member of the family or another dog.

For some 30 years, we've always had more than one dog, at times as many as ten. When one of them died, the dogs closest to that dog unquestionably experienced grief. One pair — Cato and his older sister, Cassandra — was particularly close. When Cassandra died, Cato showed all the signs of clinical depression.

At the time, Cato was 7 years old and had been retired from a successful dog-show career. Because Cato really enjoyed going to dog shows, we started showing him all over Canada to get him out of his depression. And it worked. He competed for another three years and finally retired for good at the age of 10.

How can you tell whether your dog is experiencing any of these negative emotions? Pretty much the way you can tell with a person. If your dog mopes around the house, doesn't seem to enjoy activities he previously enjoyed, is lethargic, isn't particularly interested in food, and sleeps a lot, chances are, he's depressed. Under those circumstances, he may not feel much like training.

We frequently see dogs with anxiety, apprehension, and fear — behaviors that can be hereditary or situational. Whatever the cause, training such a dog requires a great deal of patience and an understanding of how difficult it is for him to learn. On the other hand, the rewards are significant because, through the structure of training, the dog's confidence increases, sometimes to the point at which these behaviors disappear altogether.

Feeding your dog's nutritional needs

The most important influence on your dog's ability to learn, and the one under your most immediate control, is what you feed him. Because feeding is so important, we devote Chapter 4 to this topic. Nutrition is the fuel that runs Buddy's engine. Poor fuel provides a poor performance, so understanding how to feed Buddy correctly avoids stressing his system by providing enough nutrients for it to work properly.

So many dog foods are on the market today that making the best choice for Buddy can be a bewildering task. Just as you do when buying food for yourself or your family, you need to look at the ingredients. Dogs are carnivores and need animal protein. Select a food that lists an animal protein, such as chicken, beef, or lamb, in the first three ingredients. Avoid foods containing a lot of filler. When it seems that more comes out of your dog's rear end than went into the front end, you can safely bet that the food contains more filler than protein.

Understanding the "You" Factor

Several factors influence how successful you'll be in turning your pet into a well-mannered companion. Some of these are under your direct control, and others come with your dog or come from his surrounding environment. We discuss the factors that are out of your control in the earlier sections in this chapter. Here in this section, we explain those that are under your direct control. A direct relationship exists between your awareness and understanding of the following factors and your success as your dog's teacher.

Knowing your expectations

Most people have varying ideas of what to expect from their companions. Some of these expectations are realistic; others aren't. You've heard people say, "My dog understands every word I say," and perhaps you think yours does as well. If it were as easy as that, you wouldn't need dog trainers or training books.

Sometimes your dog may seem to really understand what you say. However, if a dog understands every word his owner says, why doesn't he do what he's told? Still, enough truth does exist to perpetuate the myth. Although dogs don't understand the words you use, they do understand tone of voice — and sometimes even your intent. Scientists have found that words used in the same tone of voice and inflection and with the same body motions allow a well-trained dog to learn to the capacity of a 2-year-old child.

Are your expectations realistic?

Do you believe your dog obeys commands because he

- Loves you?
- Wants to please you?
- Is grateful?

- Has a sense of duty?
- Feels a moral obligation?

We suspect that you answered yes to the first and second questions, became unsure at the third question, and then realized that we were leading you down a primrose path.

If your approach to training is based on moral ideas regarding punishment, reward, obedience, duty, and the like, you're bound to handle the dog in the wrong way. No doubt your dog loves you, but he won't obey commands for that reason. Does he want to please you? Not exactly, but it sometimes seems like he does. What he's really doing is pleasing himself.

Buddy is usually interested in only one thing: What's in it for me right now? Buddy certainly has no sense of duty or feeling of moral obligation. The sooner you discard beliefs like that, the quicker you'll come to terms with how to approach his education.

Are your expectations too low?

Do you believe your dog doesn't obey commands because he

- ✔ Is stubborn?
- ✔ Is hardheaded?
- ✔ Is stupid?
- ✔ Lies awake at night thinking of ways to aggravate you?

If you answered yes to any of these, you're guilty of *anthropomorphizing,* or attributing human characteristics and attributes to an animal. It's easy to do, but it doesn't help in your training.

Dogs aren't stubborn or hardheaded. To the contrary, they're quite smart when it comes to figuring out how to get their way. And they don't lie awake at night thinking of ways to aggravate you — they sleep, just like everybody else.

What should your expectations be?

So why does your dog obey your command? Usually for one of three reasons:

- ✔ He wants something.
- ✔ He thinks it's fun, like retrieving a ball.
- ✔ He has been taught specific behaviors.

When he responds to a command for either the first or the second reason, he does it for himself; when he responds for the third reason, he does it for you. This distinction is important because it deals with reliability and safety. Ask yourself this question: If Buddy responds only because he wants something or because it's fun, will he respond when he doesn't want something or when it's no longer fun? The answer is obvious.

The well-trained dog responds because he has been taught. This doesn't mean you and he can't have fun in the process; just make sure the end result is clearly understood. When you say, "Come," there are no options, especially when his safety or the safety of others is involved.

Knowing your attitude

Look at the following situation: Buddy has taken himself for an unauthorized walk through the neighborhood. You're late for an appointment but don't want to leave Buddy out on the streets. You frantically call and call. Finally, Buddy makes an appearance, happily sauntering up to you. You, on the other hand, are fit to be tied, and you let him know your displeasure in no uncertain terms by giving him a thorough scolding. Ask yourself, "Is this the kind of greeting that will make Buddy want to come to me?" If the answer is no, then stop doing it, no matter what.

Don't train your dog when you're irritable or tired. You want training to be a positive experience for your dog. If you ever get frustrated during training, stop and come back to it at another time. When you're frustrated, your communications consist of "No!" "Bad dog!" "How could you do this?" and "Get out and stay out!" You're unhappy, and Buddy is unhappy because you're unhappy. An unfriendly or hostile approach doesn't gain you his cooperation; it needlessly prolongs the teaching process. When you become frustrated or angry, Buddy becomes anxious and nervous and has difficulty learning. A better approach is to train Buddy when you're in a better frame of mind. You want training to be a positive experience for both of you.

One of the commands you want Buddy to master is to come when called. To be successful, remember this principle: Whenever your dog comes to you, be nice to him. Don't do anything the *dog* perceives as unpleasant. No matter what he may have done, be pleasant and greet him with a kind word, a pat on the head, and a smile. Teach your dog to trust you by being a safe place for him. When he's with you, follows you, or comes to you, make him feel wanted. (See Chapter 10 for more information.)

You may ask, though, "How can I be nice to my dog when he brings me the remains of one of my brand-new shoes, or when he wants to jump on me with muddy paws, or when I just discovered an unwanted present on the carpet?" We can certainly empathize with these questions, having experienced similar scenarios on many occasions. We know how utterly frustrating a dog's behavior can be. What we have discovered and accepted is that, at that moment in time, the dog doesn't understand that he did anything wrong. He understands only your anger — but not the reason for it. As difficult as it may be, you have to grin and bear it, lest you undermine the very relationship of mutual trust you're trying to achieve through training.

Being consistent with commands and tone of voice

If any magic is involved in training your dog, it's consistency. Your dog can't understand "sometimes," "maybe," "perhaps," or "only on Sundays." He can and does understand "yes" and "no." For example, you confuse your dog when you encourage him to jump up on you while you're wearing old clothes but then get angry with him when he joyfully plants muddy paws on your best suit.

Dogs often pick up consistent cues from unexpected sources. For example, before leaving for work, Mary always put Heidi in her crate. It wasn't long before Heidi went into her crate on her own when Mary was about to leave. "What a clever puppy," thought Mary. "She knows that I'm going to work."

Dogs often give the appearance of being able to read your mind. In actuality, by observing you and studying your habits, they learn to anticipate your actions. Because dogs communicate with each other through body language, they quickly become experts at reading yours.

What Heidi observed was that, immediately before leaving for work, Mary invariably put on her makeup and then crated her. Heidi's cue to go into her crate was seeing Mary putting on her makeup. Then one evening, before dinner guests were to arrive, Mary started "putting on her face." When Heidi immediately went into her crate, Mary realized the dog hadn't been reading her mind, but had learned the routine through observation.

Consistency in training means handling your dog in a predictable and uniform manner. If more than one person is in the household, everyone needs to handle the dog in the same way. Otherwise, the dog becomes confused and unreliable in his responses.

Most dogs eventually ignore commands that don't lead to tangible consequences. When Buddy responds to a command, praise him. When he chooses not to respond to a command he has been taught, correct him.

So does this mean that you can never permit your puppy to jump up on you (or do some other sometimes permissible behavior)? Not at all. But you have to teach him that he may do so only when you tell him it's okay. But beware: Training a dog to make this distinction is more difficult than teaching him not to jump up at all. The more black-and-white you can make it, the easier it will be for Buddy to understand what you want.

Outlasting your dog — be persistent

Training your dog is a question of who is more persistent — you or your dog. Some things he can master quickly; others will take more time. If several tries don't bring success, be patient, remain calm, and try again.

How quickly your dog will learn a particular command depends on the extent to which the behavior you're trying to teach him is in harmony with the function for which he was bred.

For example, a Labrador Retriever, bred to retrieve game birds on land and in the water, will readily learn how to fetch a stick or a ball on command. On the other hand, an Afghan Hound, bred as a coursing hound that pursues its quarry by sight, may take many repetitions before he understands the command to fetch and then responds to it each and every time. A Shetland Sheepdog, bred to herd and guard livestock, will learn to walk on a loose leash more quickly than a Beagle, bred to hunt hares.

Knowing to avoid "no"

As of right now, eliminate the word "no" from your training vocabulary. All too often, *no* is the only command a dog hears, and he's expected to figure out what it means. No exercise or command in training is called "no." At one of our training camps, one of the participants wore a T-shirt depicting a dog greeting another dog with "Hi. My name is 'No, No. Bad Dog.' What's yours?"

You need to avoid negative communications like "no" with your dog because they undermine the relationship you're trying to build. Also, don't use your dog's name as a reprimand. And don't nag your dog by repeatedly using his name without telling him what you want him to do. If you find yourself in a situation where it's imperative to interrupt Buddy's behavior, use the word "stop" instead.

Begin to focus on the way in which you communicate with Buddy. Does he perceive the interaction as positive or negative, pleasant or unpleasant, friendly or unfriendly? How many times do you use the word "no," and how many times do you say "Good dog" when interacting with your dog? Our experience has been that by the time we see the dogs, most have been no'ed to death. Everything the dog does brings forth a stern "Don't do this," "Don't do that," or "No, bad dog." Negative communications from you have a negative effect on your dog's motivation to work for you.

In dealing with your dog, ask yourself, "What exactly do I want Buddy to do or not to do?" Use a *do* command whenever possible so that you can praise your dog instead of reprimanding him. You'll notice a direct relationship between your dog's willingness to cooperate and your attitude. Get out of the blaming habit of assuming that Buddy's failure to respond is his fault. After all, *you* are his teacher! Your dog's conduct is a direct reflection of your teaching.

Does this mean you can never use the word "no"? Not exactly. In an emergency, you do what you have to do. But remember, do so only when in dire need.

Repeating commands

In training, use your dog's name once *before* a command to get his attention, as in "Buddy, Come." The quickest way to teach your dog to ignore you is to use his name repeatedly — and raising your voice doesn't help, either. When trying to communicate with someone who doesn't understand English, shouting doesn't improve their understanding.

Get into the habit of giving a command once and in a normal tone of voice — a dog's hearing is 80 times better than yours. By repeating commands, you systematically teach your dog to ignore you, and changes in inflections from pleas to threats don't help. Our experience has been that most people are unaware of how many times they repeat a command. Give the command, and if your dog doesn't respond, show him exactly what you want him to do.

Giving a dog a short name, or even changing his name can change his behavior, as strange as that sounds. We had a student who had a rescue dog named Trouble. She worked with Trouble for a long time and made a very good show dog out of him. Her complaint was that he always looked downtrodden and unhappy. We suggested renaming him — at first just when she worked him — and then gradually in his daily life. His name was changed to Puppy; he responded happily to his new name and perked right up. Hard to believe, but true. One-syllable names — Josh, Rex, Fritz, and so on — generally should be given to working dogs.

When training your dog, think of teacher and student — with you being the teacher. As every teacher knows, learning is a process of successive approximation. Children aren't born knowing how to read and write; they learn these skills in small increments. Similarly, a dog learns commands in small increments, one step at a time. Repetition enforces that incremental learning.

Chapter 4

Understanding the Vital Role Nutrition and Health Play in Training

In This Chapter

▶ Meeting your dog's nutritional needs with the right food

▶ Reviewing health problems that can affect training and behavior

*Y*our dog's behavior, training, happiness, health, longevity, and overall well-being are inextricably intertwined with what you feed him. Dogs, just like humans and all other animals, have specific nutritional requirements that need to be met. And to complicate matters, the needs of dogs vary. For example, even though your first dog may have done wonderfully well on one food, the same food may be completely wrong for Buddy. Every dog has his own nutritional needs that may be quite dissimilar to those of your neighbor's dog. What your dog eats has a tremendous impact on his health and his trainability.

We aren't trying to turn you into an expert on canine nutrition, but you do need to know some basic concepts. If you do want to become an expert on feeding your dog, see *The Holistic Guide for a Healthy Dog,* 2nd Edition, by Wendy Volhard and Kerry Brown, DVM (Howell Book House).

To get your dog's diet right, you also need to know the most common and most visible symptoms of nutritional deficiencies. Recognizing these deficiencies saves you a great deal of money in veterinary bills because you can make the necessary adjustments to your dog's diet.

In this chapter, we guide you through the overwhelming task of trying to find the right food for Buddy. These suggestions work for the vast majority of dogs and save you from the nerve-racking task of walking blind down the pet food aisles trying to make informed choices from the hundreds of choices offered. We discuss your dog's nutritional needs, show you how to find the right food to maintain your dog's health, and decipher how to interpret dog food labels. We also include a brief overview of how your dog's digestive system functions. This information helps you select the correct food. We also include several feeding options that meet both your lifestyle and your dog's needs. All the dogs photographed in this book were and are fed from the options mentioned in this chapter, so you have proof that they work.

The second part of this chapter deals with common health issues and our suggestions for dealing with them. We talk about the role your veterinarian has in your dog's health, when vaccines are necessary, and the expanding role of veterinary medicine into acupuncture, homeopathy, and chiropractic. We also explain when complementary medicine would be helpful for your dog, especially during the years when he's growing and being trained and as he ages. Training a dog that isn't feeling well is frustrating for both you and your dog.

When a dog's body is under stress — from poor health, vaccines, or poor nutrition — his brain doesn't have the ability to retain the information you're teaching. This explains why some dogs get stuck in their training and don't seem to progress.

Finding the Right Food for Your Dog

Not all dog foods are alike; enormous quality differences exist between the different types. Since the massive recall in 2008 of dog foods containing contaminated ingredients from China (which killed thousands of cats and dogs), the market has exploded with different types of food. Dry, freeze-dried, frozen raw, dehydrated, canned, semi-moist, and grain-free foods are available in a bewildering variety. With so many choices, trying to make an informed decision can become an overwhelming task. In this section, we help you tackle the job. If you want a really healthy dog like CJ (see Figure 4-1), the 2008 terrier group winner at Westminster, we show you how to do it in this section.

Figure 4-1:
A very
healthy dog.

Evaluating Buddy's current food

Following is a quick checklist to help you determine whether Buddy is getting what he needs from the current food you're feeding. Note that for each item Buddy, not an advertisement, is the source of your information.

❑ He doesn't want to eat the food.

❑ He has large, voluminous stools that smell awful.

❑ He has gas.

❑ His teeth get dirty and brown.

❑ His breath smells.

❑ He burps a lot.

❑ He constantly sheds.

❑ He has a dull coat.

❑ He smells like a dog.

❑ He is prone to ear and skin infections.

❑ He has no energy or is hyperactive.

❑ He easily picks up fleas and ticks.

❑ He has to be wormed frequently.

All these conditions happen occasionally with any dog — but only occasionally. When several of the items on the list occur frequently or continuously, you need to find out why.

Understanding the nutrients your dog needs

Since the 2008 pet food recall, pet owners have become more concerned about the ingredients in their pets' foods, and their demands for greater quality have been answered in the marketplace. The cliché "garbage in, garbage out" applies with terrifying validity.

Like yours, your dog's body consists of cells — a lot of them. Each cell needs 45 nutrients to function properly. The cells need the following nutrients:

✔ Protein

✔ Carbohydrates

✔ Fat

 ✔ Vitamins

 ✔ Minerals

 ✔ Water

All these nutrients need to be in the correct proportion for the necessary chemical reactions of digestion, absorption, transportation, and elimination to occur. If the cells are going to be able to continue to live, the exact composition of the body fluids that bathe the outside of the cells needs to be controlled from moment to moment, day by day, with no more than a few percentage points variation. So feeding a balanced diet daily is critical for Buddy's overall health.

These preceding nutrients are the fuel that's converted into energy. Energy produces heat, and the amount of heat your dog produces determines his ability to control his body temperature. Everything your dog does, from running and playing to working and living a long and healthy life, is determined by the fuel you provide and the energy it produces.

The term *calorie* is used to measure energy in food. Optimally, every dog will eat the quantity of food he needs to meet his caloric needs. The food you feed must provide the appropriate amount of calories so your dog's body can

 ✔ Produce energy to grow correctly

 ✔ Maintain health during adulthood

 ✔ Reproduce

 ✔ Grow into a quality old age

In the following sections, we start off by discussing a puppy's special nutritional needs, and then we move on to the nutritional needs of all dogs during their adult life. For information on older dogs (8 years old and older), see Chapter 18.

Meeting puppy's nutritional needs

In contrast to humans, dogs grow *fast*. During the first 7 months of Buddy's life, his birth weight increases anywhere from 15 to 40 times, depending on his breed. By 1 year of age, his birth weight increases 60 times and his skeletal development is almost complete. For strength and proper growth to occur, he needs the right food. He also needs twice the amount of food as an adult while he's growing, especially during growth spurts. Nutritional deficiencies at an early age, even for short periods, can cause problems later on. Some of the larger breeds continue to grow until they're 4 years of age.

The most critical period for a puppy is between 2 and 7 months, which is the time of maximum growth. His little body is being severely stressed as his puppy teeth drop out and his adult teeth come in. His adult coat also comes in at this time. He's growing like a weed, and at the same time his body is being assaulted with vaccines. During this time of growth, Buddy needs the right food so that his immune system can cope with all these demands and onslaughts.

Puppy foods contain more protein than adult or maintenance foods. Manufacturers know that puppies need more protein for growth. Nonetheless, you still need to know the source of the protein — that is, animal or plant. These foods also have to be carefully balanced with calcium, phosphorus, and magnesium. If you choose carefully, you can select a food that's suitable for a growing puppy (see Figure 4-2) as well as for an adult dog.

Figure 4-2:
Choose a
food that
can be fed
to all life
stages.

Look for a food that has two or three animal proteins in the first five ingredients — or better yet, one that lists animal protein as its first two or three ingredients. Check out foods that are listed for all growth stages or that are specifically designed for puppies.

If you're raising a giant breed puppy (one that will mature to weigh over 75 pounds), your choices are limited because little to no research has ever been done by the dog food companies on how to successfully raise these larger dogs. The research that has been done was on dogs weighing 25 to 75 pounds at maturity. In many dog foods, the ratio of calcium, phosphorus, and magnesium is insufficient in relationship to the protein content. So you'll often hear breeders of these large dogs tell their puppy owners to buy adult foods for their pups to make them grow more slowly. But this is a double-edged sword. Pups of these breeds don't get the amount of protein they need to develop correctly, and this malnutrition often leads to structural problems early in life. The later section "Making choices as to how to feed Buddy" can help you avoid this problem.

After you've selected a food for young Buddy on the basis of its protein percentage, your job isn't quite done yet. You also have to check the items we discuss in the following sections, which apply to both puppies and adults.

Keeping your dog's diet rich in protein

Your dog is scientifically categorized as a carnivore by the shape of his teeth. He isn't a vegetarian. He needs meat to be healthy and to maintain his proper protein levels. His teeth are quite different from yours — they're made for ripping and tearing meat. Also, his digestion starts in his stomach, not in his mouth as does a human. All the enzymes in his system are geared toward breaking down meat and raw foods.

The dog food packages tell you how much protein is in a specific food. The amount of protein is important, but the source of that protein is even more important. The manufacturer has choices as to what kind of protein to put into the food. The percentage of protein on the package generally is a combination of proteins found in plants or grains, such as corn, wheat, soy, and rice, plus an animal protein, such as chicken, beef, or lamb.

Different types of meat have different levels of protein, with beef being low and chicken and fish being high in protein. Lamb is in the middle. Venison has the highest protein content and should be fed sparingly. Feeding Buddy a food too high in protein is as dangerous as feeding a diet too low in protein. Long-term use of a high-protein food can damage the kidneys. We recommend beef-based foods for most dogs as a maintenance diet, chicken-based food for dogs that have had surgery or are healing from some disease, and lamb-based food if your dog doesn't like beef. Fish-based foods are too high in protein for regular use and make the kidneys work too hard.

By law, the heaviest and largest amount of whatever ingredient contained in the food has to be listed first. By looking at the list of ingredients, you can easily discover the protein's origin. For example, if the first five ingredients listed come from four grains, the majority of the protein in that food comes from grains. The more grains in a dog food, the cheaper it is to produce. We wonder what Buddy — the carnivore — thinks of such a food.

The activity level of your dog is likely to correspond with the amount of animal protein he needs in his diet. The majority of the Working breeds, Sporting breeds, Toys, and Terriers need a higher level of animal protein in their diets. For instance, the busy little Jack Russell is apt to need more animal protein than a pooch that spends his time lying around the house.

Amino acid is the name given to the building blocks of protein. When amino acids are heated, they're partially destroyed. All dry and canned commercial dog food is heated in the manufacturing process. So, commercial food contains protein that's chemically changed by heat and therefore deficient in amino acids. We show you how to compensate for that in the "Making choices as to how to feed Buddy" section later in this chapter. The freeze-dried, frozen, and dehydrated diets provide protein that's in a more natural form.

Animal protein: Getting to know the signs of deficiency and excess

The signs of a deficiency and an excess of protein (or any nutrient for that matter) are almost identical. In other words, both too much and too little protein have the same symptoms. When Buddy doesn't get enough protein or eats a food that's too high in animal protein, one or more of the following may occur:

- Aggression
- Chronic skin and/or ear infections
- Compromised reproductive system, heart, kidney, liver, bladder, and thyroid and adrenal glands
- Excessive shedding and poor, dull coat quality
- Gastrointestinal upsets, vomiting, or diarrhea

- Impaired ability to heal from wounds or surgery, such as spaying and neutering
- Kidney problems
- Lack of pigmentation
- Poor appetite
- Some kind of epilepsy or cancers
- Spinning or tail chasing
- Timidity
- Weakened immune system that can't properly tolerate vaccines

This is only a short list of the more common symptoms associated with animal protein deficiencies or excesses.

Going easy on the carbohydrates

Your dog needs the carbohydrates found in grains and most root vegetables for proper digestion. The digestive process first breaks down carbohydrates into starch and then into simple sugars and glucose, which are necessary for energy and proper functioning of the brain. Buddy also needs carbohydrates for stool formation and correct functioning of the thyroid gland.

Dogs don't need many carbohydrates to be healthy, however. A diet low in carbohydrates and high in protein is ideal. Oats, barley, wheat, and brown rice are carbohydrates that contain a lot of vitamins and minerals. They also contain protein and fat. Corn is a popular ingredient because of its low price; it's often used in lower-quality foods. Many grain-free foods are on the market, and it's difficult to know whether they're in fact good for your dog. If you want to feed Buddy a grain-free food, make sure the protein is balanced out with enough root vegetables.

Soy is another carbohydrate found in some of the cheaper foods. Soy is high in protein, but it binds other nutrients and makes them unavailable for absorption. We recommend that you stay away from dog foods containing soy.

Carbohydrates have to be broken down for the dog to be able to digest them. Dog food companies use a heat process to break them down, and therein lies a problem. The heat process destroys many of the vitamins and minerals contained in the carbohydrates. The question that immediately comes to mind is, "Where do dogs in the wild get the grains and vegetables they need?" The answer is from the intestines of their prey, all neatly predigested.

If you feed raw vegetables to a dog that has only been fed dry kibble, chances are he won't be able to break them down and you'll see them in his stool. His stomach acid and digestive juices are too weak to digest them. If you want to introduce your dog to a healthier diet by adding fresh vegetables and meat, our suggestion is to first lightly cook them, and then over a week, cook them less and less until the fresh foods are eaten raw. Doing so allows his stomach acid to come back to the proper pH for digestion.

Knowing the value of fats — in moderation

Fat is either *saturated* or *polyunsaturated,* and your dog needs both. Saturated fat (omega-3) comes from animal sources, and polyunsaturated fat (omega-6) comes from vegetable sources. Together they supply the essential fatty acids (EFA) necessary to maintain good health. Look for a dog food that contains both animal and vegetable oils.

In the manufacturing of the majority of kibbled dog foods, fat is sprayed on as the last ingredient. Fat makes the dog food palatable, like potato chips and French fries. This fat often is used by fast-food restaurants first and collected by the dog food manufacturer to spray onto dog food. Fat is highly palatable, and makes even poor-quality food taste good.

Saturated fat is used for energy. So, for dogs who get a great deal of exercise or participate in competitive events, the food they eat needs to contain 20 percent animal fat.

Not enough animal fat in your dog's diet can create:

- Cell damage
- Dry skin
- Growth deficits
- Heart problems
- Lack of energy

On the other hand, too much animal fat in the diet creates:

- Cancer of the colon and rectum
- Mammary gland tumors
- Obesity

Analyzing the healthfulness and safety of raw diets

Steve Brown, after attending one of our Training Camps in the late 80s, turned his passion for canine health into a career developing leading-edge products and educational programs to improve canine nutrition. Brown is an inveterate researcher and author of nutrition books for dogs. In his new book *Unlocking the Canine Ancestral Diet: Healthier Dog Food the ABC Way* (Dogwise Publishing), Brown states that many of the newer raw diets provide most of their calories from fat and may not have enough protein to meet the National Research Council's (NRC) standards for puppies.

He also notes that commercial raw diets often are given a 13-month shelf life even though the USDA says that ground meat only has a 3- to 4-month shelf life. Add in the ground vegetables, fish oils, and mineral amino acid chelates (that accelerate oxidation), and the shelf life of the foods is shortened ever further. In addition, the way many commercial raw diets are handled, with big temperature swings and freeze-defrost cycles, the oxidation of the fats is further accelerated.

Dry natural and organic foods are now adding DHA, EPA, and other fragile fats that don't remain stable enough after the bag is opened, so by the time the dog eats through to the food at the bottom of the bag, many of the fats are rancid.

If you choose one of the numerous natural or organic dry foods, raw, frozen, or dehydrated dog foods currently being offered, our advice is to refrigerate them when you get them home. And to be on the safe side, avoid buying in bulk and buy small, fresh quantities unless you can freeze the food.

Polyunsaturated fat is found in vegetable sources such as flaxseed oil, safflower oil, sunflower oil, wheat germ oil, olive oil, and corn oil. Your dog needs polyunsaturated fat for a healthy coat and skin. Lack of polyunsaturated fat in your dog's diet can cause

- Coarse, dry coat
- Extreme itching and scratching
- Horny skin growths
- Improper growth
- Poor blood clotting
- Skin lesions on the belly, on the inside of the back legs, and between the shoulder blades
- Skin ulcerations and infections
- Thickened areas of skin

Linoleic acid is one of the three essential fatty acids that have to be provided daily in your dog's food. Safflower and flaxseed oil provide the best source of this acid and are the least allergenic. Flaxseed oil is fragile and can become rancid quickly if not stored correctly, however. These oils are better than corn oil, which contains only a tiny amount of linoleic acid. We advise refrigeration after the oil has been opened.

Ensuring that your dog's diet is fortified with vitamins and minerals

Your dog needs vitamins and minerals in his food to release the nutrients and enzymes from the ingested food so his body can break down food and absorb its nutrients.

When researching our book *The Holistic Guide for a Healthy Dog,* 2nd Edition (Howell Book House), we called dog food manufacturers that produced kibble to ask them about their source of vitamins and minerals and how they protected them against destruction from the heat process. Their responses were astonishing. They acknowledged awareness of the problem and said that to overcome it, they added more vitamins to the food to make up the difference. Of course, doing so is nonsense. If vitamins are destroyed by heat, it doesn't make any difference how much you put in the food. They'll still be destroyed.

We also discovered that most of the finished products weren't tested as to their vitamin and mineral content after being made. This lack of testing also applies to many of the raw and frozen diets in the marketplace. In other words, vitamins and minerals go into the food, but what actually reaches your dog seems as much a mystery to some of the manufacturers as it is to us.

Two types of vitamins exist:

- **Water-soluble:** Vitamins B and C, which are water-soluble, are necessary for the breakdown of protein and many other chemical processes in the body. Any excess is filtered through the kidneys and urinated out between four to eight hours after ingestion. For this reason, these vitamins must be present in each meal.
- **Fat-soluble:** Vitamins A, D, E, and K are fat-soluble and stored in the fatty tissues of the body and the liver.

Your dog needs both types of vitamins. Your dog's overall health is dependent on the availability of both vitamins and minerals in a usable form. So, you need to add these to any kind of commercial kibble, to canned food, and to some of the frozen and raw diets. We recommend the all-in-one food supplement Endurance, which we discuss later in the chapter.

Minerals make up less than 2 percent of any formulated diet, and yet they're the most critical of nutrients. The minerals are needed to

- Correctly compose body fluids
- Form blood and bones
- Promote a healthy nervous system
- Function as coenzymes together with vitamins

Although your dog can manufacture some vitamins on his own, he isn't able to make minerals. So you need to add them to his diet with a product like the balanced, all-in-one supplement, Endurance. Trying to supplement your dog's food by using individual vitamins and minerals isn't a good idea. To do supplement properly, you would need to have a lot of experience in clinical nutrition. Instead, we suggest using Endurance. This product is available through www.volhard.com.

Vitamins and minerals begin to break down when you open a bag of dog food and expose the food to the elements. So make sure you close the food tightly and keep it away from light. Doing so helps to retain the quality of the contents. (Vitamins B and C are particularly sensitive to exposure.)

Don't forget to quench his thirst: Keeping fresh water around

Water is the most necessary ingredient for dogs. They need it on a daily basis. If a dog has adequate water, he can live for three weeks without food, but he can live only a few days without water.

Your dog uses water for the digestive processes, for breaking down and absorbing nutrients, and for maintaining his body temperature. Water helps to transport toxic substances out of the body through the eliminative organs. Water also keeps the acid levels of the blood constant.

Make sure your dog has access to fresh water in a clean bowl at all times. The exception is when the puppy is being housetrained. During that time, you need to limit access to water after 8 p.m. so the puppy can last through the night without having to go out. Use a heavy grade stainless steel or glass bowl — they keep the water fresh. Some ceramic bowls can leach lead out into the water.

The kind of food you feed Buddy determines how much water he needs. For example, kibble contains about 10 percent moisture, so your dog needs about a quart of water for every pound of food he eats. A dog fed only canned food, which is around 78 percent moisture, needs considerably less water. If fed raw foods, a dog may drink less than a cup of water a day because the food contains sufficient water.

What else is in this food? Paying close attention to preservatives

Dog food manufacturers have choices on how to preserve the fat in food to prevent it from becoming rancid. They can use the chemicals BHA, BHT, ethoxyquin, or propyl gallate. If a fat is preserved with these chemicals, it has a long shelf life and isn't significantly affected by heat and light. Even so, many dog owners prefer not to feed these chemicals to their dogs, especially ethoxyquin, which has been associated with chronic degenerative diseases, allergies, arthritis, and shortened life spans to name a few.

A manufacturer also can use natural preservatives, such as vitamins C and E and rosemary extract. Vitamin E is listed on packages as *tocopherol*. Most of the newer foods use these natural preservatives. The downside to natural preservatives is a shorter shelf life — no more than three to four months (provided the food is stored in a cool, dark place around 40 degrees, refrigerated or frozen).

Making choices as to how to feed Buddy

You have several options for feeding Buddy — from using commercial dry dog food (or beefing up a commercial food diet) to using the natural and raw diets to making your own. All the options have their pros and cons, so only you can decide which option is best for your lifestyle and comfort level.

Having bred, raised, and worked a lifetime with dogs as well as training thousands of people with different breeds has had a profound effect on our way of thinking about the best way to feed dogs. Even so, we're realists. You're probably a busy person and may not even cook for yourself, much less for your dog. Fortunately, you can take some shortcuts to safeguard your dog's health. Any of the options listed in this section will work and will keep your dog in balance nutritionally. Obviously some are better than others, but the choice is yours.

When choosing a food for your dog, be sure you forget about the following:

✔ **Advertising:** Disregard what the ads say about how good a particular food is for your dog. It may be okay for Buddy, but perhaps it isn't. You have to look at the food's ingredients.

✔ **Price:** This works both ways. Just because one brand of food costs more doesn't necessarily mean it's better than a less expensive variety. There's truth in the saying, "You get what you pay for." A correct and balanced raw food diet is going to cost more than commercial kibble. That's because the ingredients are a lot more costly. However, you save in the long run because your dog rarely gets sick. So no more expensive visits to the veterinarian — you just have to take Buddy to his annual health checkup.

As you can see, neither of the previous statements is a valid criterion for selection. You need to make the decision based on what's in the food and based on your dog's nutritional requirements.

Feeding Buddy commercial dry food

Your first option is, of course, feeding Buddy a commercial dry kibble diet that you buy at the pet store or grocery store. Dry kibble has been the staple of the dog food market. It is now being challenged by many of the natural or organic foods on the market. You have a huge variety from which to choose.

Digesting information

In a study done on gastric emptying time by the American Animal Hospital Association in 1992, it was found that raw, frozen, and dehydrated raw foods pass through a dog's stomach and into the intestinal tract in 4½ hours. After that time span, the dog is already receiving energy from that food. We recommend these diets, especially for performance dogs, because they're the most easily digested.

Semi-moist foods — canned food, the hamburger-shaped kind that you find in boxes on the supermarket shelf, and the ones in rolls like sausages — take almost nine hours to pass through the stomach.

Dry foods take between 15 and 16 hours to digest, so if you choose to feed Buddy any kind of dry processed dog food, it will be in his stomach from morning until night. This slow digestion isn't important for the average pet, but if you work or show your dog or want him to live a long life it becomes important. You don't want to work or jump Buddy when his stomach is full of food nor do you want him to die prematurely.

On the back of every dog food package is information that helps you decide which food is right for your dog. The information lists the ingredients in order of weight, in descending order. The package contains the guaranteed analysis for crude protein, fat, fiber, moisture, and often calcium, phosphorus, and magnesium ratios. The label also may state that the food is nutritionally complete or provides 100 percent nutrition for the dog. To make this claim, the food has to meet the nutrient requirements of the Association of American Feed Control Officers (AAFCO) — a guarantee that some form of testing, anywhere from two to six weeks, has been done on the product.

If Buddy doesn't eat the amount recommended on the package for his weight, he's not getting the minimum daily requirement of known nutrients that are necessary on a daily basis for good health. If Buddy is turning up his nose at his food, we recommend you change his food to something he's more tempted to eat. If you can't find a dry kibble that works for him, try one of the other options in this chapter.

A dog food company also must list its name and address and give its telephone number, plus provide the date of manufacture, the weight of the product in the package, and the life stage for which the food is intended. The life stage can be puppy, maintenance, adult, performance, old age, or lite food for overweight dogs. Some breed-specific foods are now popular, including Labrador food, Dachshund food, and so on. Some foods are designed specifically for those dogs with health-related issues, such as hip dysplasia. Organic and natural kibbles also are available.

The most important information to know is that you have to choose a kibble that lists two to three meat-based ingredients (animal proteins) in the first five ingredients on the label. This is true for dogs in all life stages, including over-weight and less active dogs. You'll find foods that advertise "grain free," which isn't necessarily a good thing (see the earlier section "Going easy on the carbohydrates"). Select a food that contains some grain (preferably oats, barley, wheat, or brown rice or one that has a large number of root vegetables), up to 25 percent of the total ingredients.

The levels of protein vary from 16 to 47 percent. Some of the newer brands of kibble have far too much protein in them, and dog owners are now seeing the result of long-term feeding of this food in the form of kidney problems because the kidneys get overworked trying to break down too much protein. Kibbles that are too low in protein, often advertised for senior or overweight dogs, cause your dog to get fat, don't provide enough protein to rebuild cells and maintain health, supply too many grains, and often contain soy, which isn't digestible by dogs. Choose a kibble that has 26 to 34 percent protein in it.

Stay away from foods that contain corn, rye, soy, spinach, bell peppers, tomatoes, trans fats, soy oil, artificial coloring and preservatives, or genetically altered grains. These are cheap ingredients with little, if any, nutritional value. Some actually stop the digestive tract from working properly. Most of these items can't be digested and make Buddy's digestive tract work too hard for no benefit.

Offering beefed-up commercial dry food

If you want to continue feeding your dog a commercial, dry kibble diet, or one of the grain-free kibbles, but you're concerned about the nutrients that he's getting, you can beef up that diet to give him what he needs. You can upgrade the diet in one of two ways: with an all-in-one supplement that contains all the food groups of protein, carbohydrates, vitamins, minerals, and oils or with a supplement plus fresh foods. We explain both options in the following sections.

Enhancing dry kibble with an all-in-one supplement

Feeding commercial kibble enhanced by an all-in-one supplement is the simplest method of adding the nutrients lost in the manufacturing of commercial cooked kibble. To apply this diet, choose a kibble according to our guidelines in the preceding section "Feeding Buddy commercial dry food" and then add a complete supplement to it. Follow the directions on the product as to how much to add.

The supplement we suggest is called Endurance. It has been clinically proven over many years and is dehydrated. It contains a small amount of liver, natural vitamins, minerals, herbs, dried fruit, fish oil, and ginger. It aids digestion by settling the stomach, reduces shedding, and increases vitality and longevity.

Endurance is available from www.volhard.com. This product is used by many police forces and professional trainers to keep their working dogs in good health. It is the supplement that CJ (see Figure 4-1), the 2008 Terrier group winner at Westminster, was fed when he was on the road being shown.

Adding a supplement plus fresh foods to dry kibble

With this option, you add a supplement such as Endurance plus fresh meats and vegetables to commercial kibble. The quantities of the respective ingredients listed in this section are for a 50-pound dog. You can adjust this recipe according to your dog's weight. This option offers digestive enzymes contained in the raw foods, which aids digestion and cuts down the time the food is in the stomach.

When calculating the amount for the weight of your dog, err on the side of too little, rather than too much. Some dogs eat more than their weight indicates, and some dogs eat less. Your dog's metabolism and the amount of daily exercise he gets determine the amount of food he needs. Use common sense and keep all ingredients in proportion.

To apply this diet, mix together the following ingredients and serve to your dog twice a day:

> High-quality dry kibble (follow the directions on the package as to how much to feed)
>
> ¼ teaspoon Endurance plus 2 tablespoons of water to rehydrate the supplement
>
> ¼ cup of ground beef (80 percent meat to 20 percent fat) lightly cooked for the first week, then cooked less and less over time until it's raw; rotate once a week with canned mackerel or cottage cheese; if your dog prefers chicken, serve it lightly cooked
>
> 2 tablespoons fresh vegetables (lightly cooked the first week, and then cooked less and less over time until they're raw)

For vegetables use carrots, parsnips, beets, sweet potatoes, broccoli, leeks, zucchini, squash, kale, cabbage, or any vegetable your dog likes. Chop the vegetables in a food processor or parboil them so it's easier for your dog to digest the cellulose. Whenever you can, use vegetables that are in season, because they have more nutrients. Vegetables that are shipped long distances contain fewer nutrients. For treats, try chopped carrots, broccoli, parsnips, sweet potatoes, rutabaga, lettuce, bananas, prunes, cucumbers, or any in-season fruit or vegetable that your dog likes.

Stay away from those fruits and vegetables that are commonly sprayed many times with pesticides before they reach the marketplace — for example, apples, bell peppers, carrots, celery, cherries, grapes, kale, lettuce, nectarines, peaches, pears, or strawberries. If you can find organic versions, they will be safe. However, grapes and onions have been associated with gastric problems and even death in dogs that already have underlying disease states. As always, a small amount isn't harmful, but too much can make Buddy feel sick.

Making major changes in Buddy's diet without keeping track of how these changes affect him isn't a wise idea. He may be out of balance nutritionally, which will have short- and long-term effects on his health. We recommend that you have a blood test done before making a dietary change and again six months later.

Trying a raw food or frozen diet

Our 40 years living with dogs have made it abundantly clear that feeding a balanced raw diet — which emulates what Buddy would eat in the wild — is the best and most efficient way to feed a dog. A correctly formulated raw diet provides all the known nutrients in a form the dog can quickly digest and turn into energy. Dogs fed this way tend to live longer and healthier lives than their counterparts who are fed commercial dry foods.

According to *Pet Business* magazine, which is the trade magazine for the pet food industry, one-third of all dog food sold now in pet stores and some supermarkets is in the form of "natural" or "raw" diets. This includes kibble with organic ingredients, frozen food, and dehydrated foods. Some of these foods are complete in themselves, but others suggest adding raw ingredients.

We have always felt that many disease states — including musculoskeletal disorders like hip dysplasia, skin diseases, and gastric upsets — certainly are exacerbated (if not actually caused by) poor nutrition. Our belief about this has since been confirmed by veterinarian Marc Torel and scientific journalist Klaus Dieter Kammerer in their book, *The Thirty Years War: 1966–1996* (Transanimal Publishing House). For more information on feeding raw diets, visit rawfed.com/myths/research.html.

Many natural and raw diets are available for you to choose from, but making the correct choice is even more difficult than comparing commercial dry foods. We apply the same criteria to the examination of natural and raw food diets as we do to commercial dry foods: Both need to be clinically tested and provide a balanced diet for a dog. Diets, especially homemade ones (raw or cooked), that don't meet these criteria can do more damage to your dog than dry dog food.

Many of the new raw and frozen diets aren't balanced and haven't had any long-term clinical testing. Some even use ingredients that are known to be canine allergens. Some use indigestible vegetables, and some lack fiber and the correct ratio of nutrients. Other diets suggest feeding raw chicken wings or backs; that sounds easy enough, but it's hardly a balanced diet. Just because a food's ingredients are advertised as human grade, organic, or whatever doesn't mean they're good for your dog. So, clearly you must be cautious when choosing your dog's raw or frozen diet. Write to the manufacturer and ask how many years of clinical testing have been done on a particular diet. You'll be surprised by the answers. Generally testing is done over a six-week period with dogs in a laboratory.

So are any of the available raw or frozen diets balanced? Of course. Just be vigilant in choosing the correct one for your dog. Read the label to make sure they're complete. If they aren't, read the guidelines as to what you should add to make them complete. Long-term feeding of an unbalanced diet can create a battery of new health problems not seen before in dogs.

Before changing Buddy's diet, we recommend that you take him to the vet for a baseline blood test. After Buddy has been on his new diet program for six months, have the vet perform another blood test and compare it to the previous one. The follow-up blood test will tell you whether his new diet is an improvement and whether he's in nutritional balance.

A dog's digestive system isn't the same as a human's — it's much shorter and food is processed more quickly. The dog's stomach acid is very strong, and in a healthy dog, this acid kills any bacteria that enter it. A sick dog, or a dog switching over to a raw diet from a kibble diet, needs a transition diet to rebuild that stomach acid to the point where it can deal with either E. coli or salmonella.

Feeding raw meat or raw chicken to a dog can cause digestive upsets if the meat contains high levels of bacteria in the form of E. coli or salmonella. Although a dog that has been fed raw foods for a long time can easily deal with both of these bacteria, a sick dog or a dog just being transferred over to a raw diet may experience digestive problems. We suggest you buy your meat or chicken from a good supermarket where the products are for human consumption.

After the transition diet is followed (see the later section "Transferring Buddy to his new diet"), you need to use a simple method of killing bacteria the first time uncooked meat is used: Put the meat or chicken into a sieve in the sink, pour boiling water over it, and cool it before feeding. Doing so kills the bacteria. After taking this step for a couple of weeks, the stomach acid will be strong enough to deal with the bacteria without problems, and you can introduce the raw meat.

Making your own food: Wendy Volhard's Natural Diet

Making one's own dog food is hardly a new idea. Every dog alive today can trace its ancestry back to dogs that were raised on homemade diets. The dog food industry, in comparison to dogs themselves, is young — maybe 60 to 70 years old — although canned meat for dogs was sold at the turn of the 20th century. Originally, the commercial foods were made to supplement a homemade diet.

A homemade diet allows you to tailor make it for your dog's nutritional needs, and it's ideal for all dogs. The drawback to this type of feeding is that it takes time to make and gather all the ingredients.

Many, but not all, present-day dogs are the beneficiaries of poor breeding practices, a lack of understanding of genetics on the part of many breeders, and 30 years of overvaccination and poor nutrition. Because of poor genetics (whether pure bred or a mixed breed), many can't thrive on commercially prepared rations. They exhibit disease states, which often are mistaken for allergies. These disease states can be deficiency diseases caused by feeding cereal-based foods or foods where the fat has turned rancid. Making the food from scratch often is the only available option for these dogs.

We began making our own dog food almost 40 years ago. Based on the pioneering work of Juliette de Bairacli Levy and the National Science Foundation's guidelines for dog food, our homemade diet was a 12-year labor of love to get the balance required. The results were amazing, as seen by Pavi, a Newfoundland who competed in both agility and obedience competitions until he was almost 12 years old. He garnered more than 20 titles. You can see Pavi in competition in Figure 4-3. The diet increases health and longevity, contains a lot of moisture in the natural ingredients, and produces more manageable stools. Plus dogs love to eat it. We're still seeing great results today with the newer dehydrated versions of the food. See the later section "Using the Natural Diet Foundation (NDF2)" for more information.

Figure 4-3:
Pavi, an 11-year-old Newfoundland, in Agility competition.

For more information on raising your dog holistically, transferring to a purely Natural Diet, making the diet and storing it, as well as a list of suppliers for ingredients, go to www.volhard.com. You also can look to the *Holistic Guide for a Healthy Dog,* 2nd Edition, by Wendy Volhard and Kerry Brown, DVM (Howell Book House).

The easiest way to travel with homemade or NDF2 diets is to make the required number of meals and freeze them in portion-control plastic bags. Keep the bags in a cooler, adding ice every day. You can travel safely up to 10 days using this method of packing the food.

Using the Natural Diet Foundation (NDF2)

The Natural Diet Foundation, or NDF2, is a dehydrated version of the original homemade Natural Diet discussed in the previous section. It came about because so many professional dog people asked us to come up with a diet to which they only needed to add one ingredient. These are busy people who train dogs for a living and travel a lot, so they don't have time to shop around for fresh ingredients for their dog food. They all wanted the benefits of feeding naturally but didn't have the time to do it. They also wanted to stay with our diet that had been clinically proven over so many years rather than experimenting with many of the new diets on the market.

So, six years ago we worked out the NDF2 diet, which is essentially the same as the original diet but in a dehydrated form. The only ingredients you have to add are meat and water. It has been an amazing success story, and we're now seeing 6-year-old dogs, raised from puppies on this food, who are in incredible health and whose structure is outstanding — a necessary trait for dogs being worked or shown.

NDF2 contains all the non-meat ingredients your dog needs for a healthy, vigorous, and long life. It's made every two weeks in small batches with whole human-grade foods and herbs that mostly come from Lancaster County, Pennsylvania. This recipe has been clinically tested for over 30 years. It's a food for all life-stages, from puppies to older dogs. It's also hypoallergenic and contains no genetically modified products. You can read more about this dehydrated diet and purchase this food at www.volhard.com.

Transferring Buddy to his new diet

When changing from dry kibbled foods to a higher-grade kibble and supplemented diet as those suggested earlier in the chapter, you must give your dog's system time to get used to the new ingredients. Your dog's intestinal tract needs about 6 to 11 days to be fully able to break down and digest a new diet.

When switching Buddy to a diet that is supplemented with raw foods, use the following transition diet. The transition diet allows time for the internal bacteria to adjust to a change in diet. (Transitioning your dog to a completely raw diet requires a different process. If you plan to feed your dog a raw diet, go to www.volhard.com for more info about the Natural Diet and a copy of the recipe as well as tips on making a smooth transition.)

What about table scraps?

There's nothing wrong with adding table scraps to Buddy's food, *provided* they don't exceed 10 percent of his total diet. Many dogs love leftover salad, meat scraps, and veggies. However, you do need to avoid certain foods, particularly those with a high sugar count, such as chocolate (which can be poisonous) and highly salted foods. Also avoid giving raw spinach, an ingredient that is found in so many of the newer raw food diets. It contains oxyalic acid that binds calcium and some minerals from being absorbed by the body. Avoid peppers, which are part of the deadly nightshade family, and can be allergenic. Processed human foods also aren't recommended for dogs.

Feeding a dog twice a day is the most efficient way to feed him. And always be sure to have fresh water available to him.

Here's how to transition your dog to a supplemented dog food diet:

Day 1: Add a small amount of your new food to each of Buddy's meals.

Day 2: Double the amount you fed on Day 1 of the new food and decrease Buddy's old diet by the same amount.

Days 3 through 6: Gradually increase the new diet and decrease the old diet until you have changed him over completely.

If at any time Buddy has loose stools, his digestive system needs more time to adjust to his new food.

After your dog has been introduced to the new additions in his diet for a couple of weeks, it's time to introduce bones. Once or twice a week, give your dog a bone as a special treat. They love beef (soup) bones, raw chicken necks, and the tips off chicken wings. If you're not sure about how long these items have been in the supermarket case, douse them with boiling water to kill any bacteria before feeding. One of the benefits of feeding bones is that your dog will have beautiful, pearly white teeth.

When you give your dog a bone, leave him alone (but not unattended) — dogs can get possessive about their bones. It's a special treat, and he wants to be in a place to relax and enjoy it. His crate is the perfect place. It also contains any soggy mess associated with gnawing on his bone. Give Buddy an hour or so to enjoy his bone and then pick it up and refrigerate it and give it to him the next day. Too much marrow in the bone's center may be a little rich for some dogs to digest all at once.

Feeding Buddy too many bones can give him constipation and hard, chalky stools. Only give your dog bones that can't splinter.

Sizing up supplements

As Bill Bookout, president of the National Animal Supplement Council says in the March 2010 *Pet Age* magazine, "The consumer wants to put all the pieces together — including diet, exercise, supplements and quality medical care — to create the best possible outcome, just like they are doing for themselves . . . Given huge lines of supermarket or pet store aisles devoted to the supplements, it's impossible for the average person to make the correct decision for his pet. Psychologically what happens when a consumer is given too much choice is that he walks away with nothing. Chances are if a consumer randomly buys a product, he'll make the wrong choice."

The reality is that if you're feeding correctly, you rarely need supplements of any kind. The nutrients should be in the food; they shouldn't have to be added as extras at high prices. The number of supplements available tells you a lot about the quality of the food on the market. If you're adding a lot of supplements to Buddy's food, it's time to think of changing to a balanced food that contains these ingredients.

You occasionally do need supplements. We have sorted through the thousands of products on the shelves and can recommend some that are known to work (we've used them ourselves, and our students have had good results as well). We mention a few supplements in the following health section, and we go into more detail regarding the supplements we recommend in Chapter 18, which focuses on older dogs. As dogs get older, they need supplementation.

Exploring Common Health Issues that Affect Behavior and Training

A dog that's fed correctly and given enough exercise and mental stimulation rarely exhibits behavior problems. He deals well with stress, hardly ever gets sick, and keeps his youthful characteristics into his teens. Also, a dog who's fed properly and is in good health, ages well and has few to no grey hairs. In fact, it's often difficult to tell this dog's age.

When your dog doesn't feel quite right, he won't act quite right. When he doesn't feel well, he doesn't have the ability to learn or retain information. When you're training him, it can be perplexing to know that you have properly taught a sequence of an exercise only to find that the dog shows no knowledge of what you have taught him. Not feeling well can manifest itself in many ways, but you as his owner, know he isn't acting as he did before. While it is always wise to check your dog out with his veterinarian, in the following sections, we provide information on some common health issues that affect behavior and training. We also discuss some supplements that may help Buddy feel better.

Prevention is the best policy when it comes to your dog's health. Here are some things you can do to prevent health problems later on and have a long and happy training career with Buddy:

- **Visit your veterinarian annually.** When you take Buddy to the vet, choose to have titers done (rather than vaccinations) to see Buddy's level of protection against parvovirus, distemper, and Lyme disease. (We explain what titers are in the later section "Looking at the problems with overvaccinating.") At the same time, have blood work done to see whether Buddy is in nutritional balance and whether all his organ systems are working properly. Signs of problems can show on blood work long before physical manifestations appear. Take in a fecal sample at least twice a year.

- **Provide an arthritis formula if necessary.** If your puppy's structure isn't perfect, or if he's in performance events of any kind, consider using an arthritis formula as a preventative. In the past, these products have been used after the dog was diagnosed with arthritis. Since then, however, it has been found that when structural problems become obvious in the young dog, the use of these products can be helpful in preventing arthritis later in life.

  The product we have recommended for years is called Myristin. We have used Myristin successfully with clients' dogs who were experiencing cruciate ligament problems as well as loose shoulders, loose hock joints, poor hips, and so on. This product works for 90 percent of dogs. The other 10 percent requires a different form of supplement. We recommend System Saver, which is an anti-inflammatory and works to build up the immune system. See www.volhard.com for more information on these products.

- **Keep his teeth healthy.** Dirty teeth can cause harmful bacteria buildup resulting in gingivitis, loose teeth, and bacterial infection of the gums. The bacteria drain into the system via the stomach and can, over a period of time, cause heart ailments. Clean teeth also prevent "doggy breath." To keep teeth clean, feed the correct diet with bones a couple of days a week. Or you can clean Buddy's teeth with a toothbrush and dog toothpaste or cleaning gel. We recommend Petzlife products, available through www.petzlife.com. See Chapter 18 for more information.

✔ **Choose an appropriate food for your dog.** Feeding the correct food helps to prevent internal and external parasites. External parasites, like fleas and ticks, are less likely to be attracted to a dog who's fed correctly, because his skin has a correct pH that deters external parasites. The acid/alkaline balance of his digestive tract makes a poor environment for internal worms to survive. Check out the earlier section "Making choices as to how to feed Buddy" for more information.

Here comes that needle again: Examining vaccination issues

Giving vaccines is a necessary part of owning a dog. The core vaccines are for distemper and parvovirus. Depending on where you live and the prevalence of other diseases, you may want to vaccinate against leptospirosis and hepatitis. In some instances, a Lyme disease vaccine may be necessary. Boarding kennels often require a bordatella (kennel cough) vaccine before they will accept a dog. It is very much a regional thing. The rabies vaccine is the only one that is mandatory. Every county in the country has a rabies vaccine requirement. The other vaccines are voluntary, so you don't have to give them if you don't want to.

Vaccines can disrupt a training program for your dog by making him feel unwell for a few days after they have been given. Sometimes vaccines interrupt the ability of the dog to do scent work like tracking or scent articles in obedience competition. The effects can last from three weeks to nine months. Some breeds of dogs have adverse reactions to vaccines and can experience swollen joints (as Great Danes can do with the rabies vaccine), some temporary paralysis (such as German Shepherds and Rottweilers from the parvovirus vaccine), seizures (such as Labradors from the rabies vaccine), and so on. Make a wise decision for you and your dog after you have researched all the facts.

To help you make a decision as to what is correct for your dog, check out *What Vets Don't Tell You About Vaccines* by Catherine O'Driscoll (Abbeywood Publishing). Catherine did a world-wide study of vaccines and reports of the long-term effects of overvaccinating. She charts diseases associated with overvaccinating and quotes the noted authorities in the United States, including Jean Dodds, DVM, and Ronald Schultz, MD, DVM, of the University of Wisconsin, on the current vaccine protocols recommended. For more information on Catherine and her research, visit www.canine-health-concern.org.uk.

Looking at the problems with overvaccinating

During the past 20 years, dog owners have seen a steady increase in the number of vaccinations that dogs receive each year. Sadly, instead of improving the dogs' health and longevity, the practice has frequently had the opposite effect.

Overvaccinating has created unintended and undesirable reactions to vaccinations, which result in *vaccinosis,* the term used to describe those undesirable reactions. The reactions can range from none or barely detectable to death. And they may occur as a result of one vaccine, several vaccines given at the same time, or repeated vaccinations given in a relatively short time frame.

Too many vaccinations too close together can cause a puppy's immune system to break down and can result in serious health problems. We aren't against vaccinations, but we're against random, repetitive, routine, and completely unnecessary vaccinations. Thank goodness in the last few years, vaccine protocols have changed and most up-to-date veterinarians are using vaccines more sparingly.

Where do annual booster shots fit into this picture? Actually, they don't. According to Kirk's *Current Veterinary Therapy* XI-205 (W.B. Saunders Co.) — the textbook used for many years by veterinary schools — no scientific basis or immunological reason necessitates annual revaccinations. Immunity to viruses can last for many years — even for a dog's lifetime.

When your dog already carries the antibodies against a particular virus, a revaccination can wreak havoc with his immune system. The many adverse reactions to unnecessary vaccinations have caused breeders, dog owners, and vets to begin questioning the need for boosters and to become more cautious in the way vaccines are administered. By law, your dog only needs a rabies vaccination and the rabies booster only every three years. Don't ever give your dog a rabies shot before he's 6 months of age.

Some breeds of dogs have extreme — even fatal — reactions to vaccines. Others develop odd behaviors and reactions such as the following:

- Aggression
- Anaphylactic shock
- Anxiety or fear
- Epilepsy and other seizure disorders
- Excessive licking
- Insomnia
- Snapping at imaginary flies
- Swelling of the whole body, cutting off air supply

A rabies vaccine given in conjunction with other vaccines can be responsible for aggression, epilepsy, and other seizure disorders. Labradors seems to be especially vulnerable.

How do you know if your dog will have a reaction to a vaccine? You don't, and that's the problem. Fortunately, you don't have to take the chance. When you take Buddy in for his annual checkup, you can ask your vet to do a *titer test,* a blood test that tells you whether Buddy has *antibodies* (or resistance) to the diseases for which he's already been vaccinated. If he has a high *titer,* or level of antibodies, to the disease, you don't need to have him revaccinated. Titering is becoming a more acceptable alternative to revaccinations. (Refer to the later section "Vaccinating for boarding or schooling" for information on whether businesses accept titering in place of revaccination.)

Whether you're rescuing a dog from the local humane society, adopting an "off-the-track" Greyhound, or buying a puppy from a pet store, be aware that the dog will probably have been vaccinated before you get him. Humane societies usually give you the dates when your rescue dog was vaccinated. Taking him to your veterinarian for a once-over health check is a good idea, but don't vaccinate again. Either titer the dog in the next six months or wait another year and titer before vaccinating, if necessary. However, remember that if your dog has reacted in the past to vaccination, the next time he's vaccinated, the reaction will be worse. So be careful! See how to deal with adverse reactions in the later section "Quelling fear, anxiety, and other conditions with homeopathy."

Vaccinating for boarding or schooling

Sometimes you have to vaccinate your dog. Many boarding kennels, obedience schools, and dog parks, for example, require proof of vaccination. However, titers are becoming more acceptable with these businesses and schools. The Pet Care Services Association (formerly known as the American Boarding Kennel Association) considers titers acceptable. Before you board your dog at a member kennel, ask about titers.

Before you vaccinate, call any facilities to which you may take your dog. Some boarding kennels are now recognizing titer tests. If you do need to vaccinate, remember that it takes your dog three weeks to build immunity.

Because not everything's cut and dried in this world, suppose that Buddy is one of those dogs who have adverse side effects from vaccinations, and as a result, you adamantly refuse to vaccinate him. But now you can't find a boarding kennel that will honor your wishes. What then? Well, you're going to have to find someone to come in and dog sit for you while you're away. If you can't find a reliable local pet sitter, try Pet Sitters International (www.petsit.com), which is a country-wide organization that has trained pet sitters in most areas of the country. The local obedience organization also may be able to help you.

Vaccinating a healthy dog stresses his immune system, whether or not you see a reaction. And boarding a dog also is stressful — even at the nicest boarding kennels. Under stress, Buddy is vulnerable to picking up disease. It can affect his training and his ability to handle stress especially at dog shows.

Uncovering the rise in doggy hypothyroidism

Providing poor nutrition, overvaccinating, and neutering or spaying a puppy too early can cause a disease called hypothyroidism. *Hypothyroidism* refers to an underactive thyroid gland, which causes physical as well as behavioral abnormalities. It's difficult to successfully train a dog who has hypothyroidism. When a dog has hypothyroidism, his ability to learn and retain information is severely curtailed. This lack of learning ability is frustrating for both dog and handler. Very few veterinarians have that much knowledge about this disease, which is perhaps the most common disease in dogs.

Rarely seen until the 1970s, this condition has become more prevalent because the way of managing dogs has changed in the last 50 years. More than 50 percent of young dogs today show some signs of hypothyroidism. As the dog ages, the percentage increases.

The thyroid gland is part of the endocrine gland system. This system not only controls many of the hormones in the body, but it also controls the brain's ability to deal with stress. It certainly affects his behavior. In a study done at the University of Southampton in England, it was found that more than 50 percent of dogs turned over to a humane society because of aggression problems were suffering from hypothyroidism.

The physical manifestations of hypothyroidism can show from as young as 5 months of age onward. This disease is most commonly diagnosed at around 4 years of age, but dogs 8 years and older also have hypothyroidism, which correlates to the aging process. Dogs with this disease may show the following signs:

- Heart disorders
- Lack of control over body temperature — the dog is either too cold or too hot under otherwise normal conditions
- Oily, smelly, scaly skin and blackened skin on the belly and under the arms
- Some kinds of paralysis

✔ Seizures

✔ Thinning of the hair on each side of the body, usually around the rib cage and on the tail and inside the back legs (see Figure 4-4)

✔ Unexplained weight gain

Figure 4-4:
Thinning
hair due
to hypo-
thyroidism.

Behavioral manifestations of hypothyroidism may include

✔ Unexplained aggression toward people or other dogs

✔ Being picked on by other dogs

✔ Difficulty learning

✔ Fear and anxiety, including separation anxiety and fear of thunderstorms

✔ *Lick granulomas,* where the dog licks constantly at one spot, usually on a leg, and goes down to the bone

✔ Obsessive-compulsive behavior, such as spinning and extreme hyperactivity

✔ Overreaction to stressful situations

✔ Self-mutilation

The preceding behaviors were reported in a 1997 English study, and nearly all the abnormal behaviors disappeared when thyroid medication was administered.

How can you tell if Buddy has a thyroid-related problem? If he's exhibiting any of the physical signs or behaviors listed in this section, make an appointment with your vet as soon as possible. This condition often is overlooked by veterinarians as was the case in the photograph shown in Figure 4-4. If you want to reassure yourself that Buddy doesn't have hypothyroidism, ask your vet to do a blood test and ask for a complete thyroid panel. The results can tell you whether Buddy needs medication. All laboratory reports indicate a low and high normal reading for each test done. High readings are uncommon in adult dogs. Low normal readings need to be supplemented.

The bone crusher: "Oh, my aching back"

Performance events, especially agility, are athletic activities for a dog. So you really shouldn't be surprised that various parts of performing dogs' bodies may go out of whack. After all, human athletes have troubles all the time. Because the dogs' performances are affected, many competitors routinely take their dogs in for chiropractic adjustments. Agility competitors have found that it can shave seconds off a dogs' performance if he is in perfect alignment. It makes sense — if the spine is straight, the dog can move more quickly and easily. Even if your dog isn't a performing dog, remember that simply playing ball or Frisbee with Buddy can have the same effect as performance events.

To keep your dog in tip-top shape, have a chiropractor examine him. Buddy may need an alignment. To find an animal chiropractor in your area, visit the American Holistic Veterinary Medical Associations Web site at www.ahvma.org.

Having a chiropractor look at your puppy during his first year of life to make sure that everything is in order is a good idea. Vigorous play, especially with other dogs, can cause all manner of misalignments, which can then interfere with proper growth.

Quelling fear, anxiety, and other conditions with homeopathy

Many dogs experience fear or anxiety under different conditions. For example, anxiety can occur when Buddy

- ✔ Encounters situations that he perceives as stressful
- ✔ Goes on a trip away from home
- ✔ Has a reaction to a vaccine
- ✔ Senses and experiences thunderstorms
- ✔ Visits the vet

We've been quite successful in dealing with this sort of anxiety with homeopathic remedies. We even carry a small homeopathic emergency kit with us wherever we go, just in case. You can find it on www.volhard.com. (We also provide information on anxiety and handling other special situations in Chapter 17.)

Homeopathy relies on the energy of natural substances, which come from plants or minerals. Homeopathic remedies come in pellet, granular, or liquid form. Popular until the discovery of antibiotics, homeopathy fell out of favor during the middle of the 20th century. Today, it's enjoying resurgence all over the world, and many vets in Europe are trained both in traditional medicine and homeopathy.

Because the homeopathic remedies are so diluted, they're safe to use and don't cause side effects. You can find many of these remedies in large supermarkets and health food stores.

The following list includes a few common homeopathic remedies and the problems they treat. We find these remedies helpful and use them frequently.

- **Aconite:** Fright, anxiety, and fear of thunderstorms
- **Apis:** Bee stings and any shiny swellings
- **Arnica:** Bruising from falls and dog bites and recuperation from any operation
- **Belladonna:** Heat stroke, hot, red ears, and hot spots
- **Carbo Veg:** Bloating or gas (settles the stomach if used 15 minutes before eating)
- **Chamomilla:** Vomiting of yellow bile and teething problems
- **Ferrum Phos:** Stops bleeding
- **Hydrophobinum (or Lyssin):** Reactions to rabies vaccine
- **Hypericum:** Stops pain to nerve endings after injury or operations
- **Ignatia:** Grief, insecurity, stress, or sadness
- **Ledum:** Tick, insect, or spider bites
- **Nux Vomica:** Any kind of poisoning; recuperation after anesthesia
- **Phosphorus:** Sound sensitivity
- **Rhus Tox (poison ivy):** Rheumatism and itchy, oozing rashes
- **Sulphur:** Skin conditions and mange
- **Thuja:** Reactions to vaccines
- **Rescue Remedy:** Stress or trauma (We always carry it when we travel with our dogs.)

Many holistic vets are trained in homeopathy, and you probably can find one in your area without difficulty. To find a holistic vet in your area, go to the American Holistic Veterinary Medical Association's Web site at www. ahvma.org.

Treating chronic conditions with acupuncture

Many vets today use acupuncture for a variety of chronic conditions. Acupuncture specializes in putting the body back into balance. Among its many applications, acupuncture is particularly effective with allergies, skin disorders, ear problems, incontinence in old dogs, and the aches and pains that come with age. It also can be effective for structural problems and chronic diseases of major organs, such as the heart, kidneys, liver, lungs, and stomach.

We advise seeking the help of an acupuncture veterinarian for dogs who are in performance events and for those who are middle-aged or older. Treatments can make an older dog feel like a puppy again. To find a veterinarian in your area who's trained in acupuncture, contact the American Holistic Veterinary Medical Association's Web site www.ahvma.org.

If your dog gets poisoned

Here's one resource that you need to have on your fridge door just in case Buddy gets into something he shouldn't have: the Animal Poison Control center. You can call the center for 24-hour emergency information. The center has 20 full-time veterinary toxicologists on-call to work with you on an emergency with your dog. The number is 888-426-4435. For more information, you also can check out the Web site at www.aspca.org/pet-care/ poison-control.

Chapter 5

Gearing Up for Training Success

Dog training is no different from any other activity — you need the right equipment for the job. Many choices are available to you, and in this chapter, we address the factors that determine what training equipment to use under what circumstances.

Just because it's a collar or a leash doesn't mean you can use it to train your dog. In Chapter 1, we discuss how a mother dog teaches her puppies to stop doing something she doesn't want them to do. She uses a *correction,* something the puppies perceive as unpleasant, to get them to stop. This unpleasant experience teaches the puppies responsibility for their own behavior. A puppy says to himself, "If I use my teeth on Mommy, I'll get nailed. If I don't, mommy will lick my face." So puppy chooses not to use his teeth on Mommy. That, at any rate, is the gist of what we think is the puppy's thought process.

Teaching your dog responsibility for his own behavior is the key to training. Therefore, the dog has to perceive the correction as unpleasant so he can avoid it. (See Chapter 1 for training descriptions and definitions.) If he doesn't perceive the correction as unpleasant, he has nothing to avoid, and the objectionable behavior continues. Therein lies the importance of the correct training equipment.

As a general rule, we use a correction with a collar and leash to deal with undesired behaviors the dog does on his own, such as chasing a cat. We use treats to teach the desired behaviors that the dog wouldn't do on his own, such as sit on command.

Choosing the Right Training Leash and Collar

The type of training collar and leash you need depends on a number of factors, including the following:

- Your dog's Personality Profile (see Chapter 2)
- Your dog's touch sensitivity or threshold of discomfort
- Your dog's size and weight in relation to your size and weight
- The equipment's effectiveness
- Your dog's safety
- Your aptitude for training your dog

Training isn't a matter of strength but finesse. For you, Buddy's teacher, it doesn't have to be a heavy aerobic workout. Also, in selecting training equipment, keep in mind the circumstances. A dog's *touch sensitivity,* or threshold of discomfort, increases proportionally with the interest the dog has in what appeals to him (see Chapter 2 for more info about understanding your dog's mind). For example, when you train Buddy in your backyard, where he has fewer distractions, a buckle collar may be sufficient to get him to respond. When he's out in the real world and wants to chase a squirrel or another dog, you may have to use a training collar to get him to mind.

In the following sections, we provide information to help you choose the best leash and collar for your dog.

Deciding on a leash

Leashes come in an assortment of styles, materials, widths, and lengths. The following are the most common materials:

- **Cotton web:** Cotton web leashes are readily available in pet stores and through catalogs and Web sites, and they come in a variety of colors (see Figure 5-1). We get ours from Handcraft Collars (www.handcraft collars.com).

A good training leash is a 6-foot cotton web leash — it's easy on the hands, easily manipulated, and just the right length. It's also the most economical. For the average-size or larger dog, such as a Labrador, we use a cotton web leash that's ½-inch wide. For toy dogs, such as a Yorkshire Terrier, we use a leash that's ¼-inch wide.

✔ **Nylon:** A nylon leash is another good one for training. Looking a lot like the cotton web leash, the nylon type also is economical and can be easily manipulated, which is an important factor for the training method we use. However, nylon isn't as easy on your hands as cotton web, especially with larger dogs.

Figure 5-1:
Cotton web
leash.

✔ **Leather:** Leather leashes also are quite popular, although they're more expensive than cotton web and nylon leashes. They're usually bulkier than cotton web or nylon but don't readily lend themselves to our approach to training.

✔ **Chain:** We've never quite understood the purpose of chain leashes or why anyone would want to use them, but they do exist. Chain leashes often are used with large dogs, but they're heavy, unwieldy, and hard on the hands. For example, if you wanted to fold the leash neatly into one hand or the other, as required by the training techniques we teach in this book, you wouldn't be able to do so without considerable discomfort. It's definitely not a leash you can use for training Buddy.

Selecting a collar

Collars come in a dazzling assortment of styles, colors, and materials. When training your dog, you need two types of collars:

✔ **A training collar:** The purpose of a *training collar* is for you to be able to guide your dog when he's on leash and, if necessary, to check your dog. (A *check* is a crisp snap on the leash, followed by an immediate release of tension.) A check is used mainly for *abstention training,* which is when you want your dog to stop doing something that he wants to do but that you don't want him to do, such as chasing a cat or a jogger. (See Chapter 1 for more on abstention training.) The check creates an unpleasant experience for the dog, which he can avoid by stopping the unwanted behavior (similar to a mother dog snapping at a puppy). Several different types of training collars are available; we discuss them later in this section. We rely on two types: the snap-around collar and the pinch collar.

- ✔ **A buckle collar:** When not training, your dog should wear a buckle collar with ID tags attached. The collar can be leather, nylon, or cotton web. Buckle collars come in an assortment of colors and styles and are made of fabric or leather. Collars made of fabric usually have plastic clasps; the leather ones have metal clasps. If your dog weighs more than 50 pounds and hasn't yet been trained, you're better off using a leather collar with a metal clasp — a plastic clasp may break when your dog tries to go after a cyclist or other moving object.

You must use the two types of collars — training collars and buckle collars — correctly. Remove the training collar when you aren't training your dog or when you can't supervise him. And don't try to use a buckle collar to train. For the untrained dog, buckle collars are virtually useless. Picture yourself trying to hang on as a fully-grown Rottweiler decides to take off after a cat. Trying to control that dog with a buckle collar would definitely be a heavy aerobic workout.

We describe the advantages and disadvantages of different training collars in the following sections.

Nylon snap-around collars

The *snap-around collar* is our first-choice collar because of its effectiveness and versatility. It works well with dogs of all sizes with an average discomfort threshold. For dogs with high discomfort thresholds, consider the pinch collar (see the later section "Pinch or prong collars" for more). The nylon snap-around collar has a metal clasp that enables you to fasten the collar around the dog's neck. That way, you can fit the collar high on your dog's neck where you have the most control. This collar also has a stationary *dead ring* opposite the clasp that can be used when you aren't training and a loose or floating *live ring* that should be used when you are training. Refer to Figure 5-2 to see this collar and its rings.

A snap-around collar should fit high on your dog's neck, just below his ears, as snug as a turtleneck sweater, for maximum control (see Figure 5-3). To get a good fit, measure the circumference of your dog's neck directly behind his ears with sewing tape or a piece of string that you can then measure with a ruler. For more information, see the DVD set *Living with your Dog,* which is available from www.volhard.com.

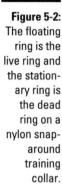

Figure 5-2:
The floating ring is the live ring and the stationary ring is the dead ring on a nylon snap-around training collar.

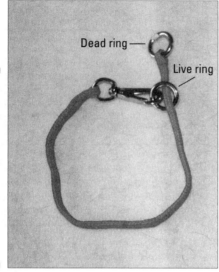

Dead ring —

Live ring

Correct snap-around collar placement for most dogs.

Figure 5-3:
Correct snap-around collar placement.

Table 5-1 presents some advantages and disadvantages to a snap-around collar.

Table 5-1	Pros and Cons of Nylon Snap-Around Collars	
Advantages	*Disadvantages*
Fairly inexpensive	A puppy will grow out of it quickly, and you may have to purchase others
Can be fitted exactly to your dog's neck	Not as easy to put on as a slip-on collar
Very effective	
Quite safe	

Some dogs don't respond to a check on a snap-around collar — that is, the check doesn't create an unpleasant experience for the dog and change his behavior. The dog may be touch insensitive and have a high discomfort threshold. Or, the dog's size and weight in relation to your size and weight may be such that he doesn't feel your check. When that happens, you may need to consider a pinch collar, which we discuss in the following section.

Take the training collar off your dog when he isn't being trained and whenever he isn't under your direct supervision so he doesn't accidentally get it caught on something and choke him. Also, don't attach any tags to the training collar. When you're not training your dog, use a buckle collar to which you've attached his tags.

For more than 40 years, we've used the same source for our snap-around collars — Handcraft Collars — because of the quality and durability. The collars from Handcraft come in half-inch increments. To purchase a collar, go to www.handcraftcollars.com.

Pinch or prong collars

The names *pinch collar* and *prong collar* describe the same piece of equipment. "Pinch" refers to the effect it has on the dog, and "prong" refers to its appearance. For old-time trainers, the pinch collar was the only collar to use for training. A pinch collar certainly is an effective and efficient training tool (see Figure 5-4). Those who use one for the first time often refer to it as power steering. We jokingly call it the *religious collar* because it makes an instant convert out of the dog.

According to our vet, who's also a certified animal chiropractor, the pinch collar is generally the safest training collar. From our perspective, it's also an effective training collar for strong, rambunctious dogs with a high threshold of discomfort. Table 5-2 offers some of the highlights and lowlights of using the pinch collar.

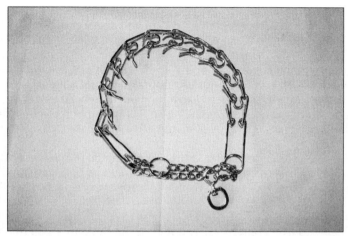

Figure 5-4:
A pinch
collar.

Table 5-2	Pros and Cons of Pinch Collars
Advantages	*Disadvantages*
Readily available in pet stores and through catalogs	Looks like a medieval instrument of torture
Very effective	Twice as expensive as a snap-on collar
Can be fit to the exact size of the dog's neck	
Very safe — it's self-limiting in that it constricts very little and not to the point where the dog's air can be cut off	

Pinch collars come in four sizes: large, medium, small, and micro. We've never used or recommended the large size, because it appears to have been made for elephants. For a large, strong, and rambunctious dog, the medium size is more than adequate. For Golden Retriever–sized or smaller dogs, the small size is sufficient. For toy dogs, use the micro version, which must be ordered. Amazon.com carries the micro size as well as other sizes. Also visit www.opentip.com and leerburg.com/prong.htm#micro.

Any collar or piece of training equipment can be misused or abused. The intent of the user is the key to achieving a harmonious relationship through training. The pinch collar rubs some people the wrong way, because it looks like a medieval instrument of torture. People's perception of a given piece of equipment, however, is immaterial. What counts is the dog's perception, and your dog will tell you. Does your check have the desired effect on the dog's behavior? Are you putting your dog in a position where you can sincerely praise him for the correct response, or are you angry with him and calling him names? Yes, dogs have feelings, too!

When using a pinch collar, put it on your dog about two hours before training him and leave it on him for about two hours afterwards. If you put it on immediately before training and then take it off immediately after you finish, he'll quickly become "collar wise," meaning he'll only respond to commands when the collar is on. The same applies to any other collar that's used to train a dog.

For many dogs, the pinch collar is the most humane training collar, especially if it saves them from a one-way trip to a shelter. The pinch collar isn't the right solution for every training problem or for every dog, but it's the right solution under certain circumstances.

If you decide to use a pinch collar, put it on the same way you put on the snap-around collar (see Chapter 7 for instruction). Simply expand or contract the collar by adding or removing links, respectively.

Chain or nylon slip-on collars

A *slip-on collar,* also called a *choke* or *choker collar,* usually made of chain or fabric, is one that slips over the dog's head. Because such a collar has to fit over the dog's head, it has the tendency to slide down the dog's neck. The strongest part of a dog's body is where the neck joins the shoulder blades. The farther the collar slides down the neck, the more difficult controlling the dog becomes and the less effective the collar is as a training tool. Table 5-3 lists the pros and cons of this type of collar.

Table 5-3	Pros and Cons of Slip-On Collars
Advantages	**Disadvantages**
Readily available in pet stores and through catalogs	Not very effective
Inexpensive	Great potential for damaging the dog's trachea and neck

Slip-on collars, when improperly used, pose a danger to your dog's trachea and spine. Avoid them! Animal chiropractors have made observations of spinal misalignment caused by this collar. Because slip-on collars aren't very effective to begin with and have a poor safety record, we recommend you save your money and get something that works, such as the nylon snap-around collar or the pinch.

Clara's story

When we met Clara, she was in her mid-60s. She lived in a large house outside of town, fairly isolated, although she could see some of her neighbors. We discovered that Clara had had a number of dogs during her life and after her last dog died, had acquired a German Shepherd puppy. Clara felt that she needed a dog that would protect her. She named the puppy Ursa. Whenever we talked, Clara would extol Ursa's virtues — how sweet she was, how easy she was to train, how well she played with the grandchildren, and how many tricks she'd learned.

As time went by, we found out more about Clara. She'd had back surgery with steel rods implanted, and she frequently had to wear a neck brace. She then told us that she had to put Ursa on a pinch collar to walk her. Clara said, "She just got too strong for me. Every time we went for a walk, she would sniff the ground where the deer had been and she would pull so hard that I didn't think I could hold her. So, I put her on a pinch collar to control her and now, after two weeks, I can walk her on her regular collar and she no longer pulls me off my feet. Without the pinch collar to help me, who knows what I would have done. I even thought that I might have to give her up, a thought I couldn't bear. Who knows what would have happened to her?"

Now when we meet Clara, she often has Ursa with her, and according to Clara, the dog is a saint. She said, "Instead of being frustrated and angry with her, I tell her what a good girl she is. I'm happy, and she is happy."

If you do decide to use a slip-on collar, put it on by taking the live ring, the one that pulls the collar tighter, and pass it over the dog's neck from left to right. In this position, the weight of the dead ring will automatically release the collar when pressure is released from the live ring. When worn the other way, the pressure from the live ring won't release promptly. You know when the collar is correct because it looks like a "P."

Readying a Reward: Treats Are Your Training Buddies

Other than your ingenuity and intellect (and the proper equipment), treats are another powerful training tool you can use. Treats are most effective when Buddy is hungry rather than after he has just eaten a meal. Fortunately, most dogs are food motivated.

You can use treats in one of two ways:

- ✓ **As a reward for a desired response:** When you use a treat as a reward, you keep the treat hidden from the dog, so he doesn't know whether he's going to get it. For example, you say "Down," and Buddy lies down. He may get a treat, or he may not.

  When conditioning your dog to a particular command, the treat has to *immediately* follow the desired behavior so the dog understands that he's being rewarded for that particular response. Don't fumble around for a treat and give it to him when he's offering a different behavior. If you're teaching Buddy to sit on command and he gets up just as you give him the treat, you're rewarding Buddy for getting up, not what you wanted at all.

- ✓ **As a lure or inducement to obtain a desired response:** When you use a treat as a lure, the treat is in the open. You can use it to entice the dog to obey a particular command, such as lie down, and when he does, he gets the treat. When a treat is used in this way, it's within the dog's control whether he gets the treat.

Because you're going to use treats both as a reward and as an inducement, you need to decide where to carry them. Some people use fanny packs, some a trouser pocket, and still others a shirt pocket. All these options are fine so long as you can reach them quickly to reward the desired response. Having a few in the palm of your hand when working on a particular exercise isn't a bad idea. The key is to use the treat *before* the dog does something you don't intend to reward. If you can't get to the treat quickly, Buddy may do something you don't want to reward — and you'll have lost the moment to reinforce the appropriate behavior. We make a habit of having some treats with us at all times.

In the following sections, we show you what types of treats are best for training and what to do when your dog isn't excited about food treats.

Picking the ideal tasty treat

We like to use dry treats that we can keep in a pocket for easy reach. When you use something moist or soggy that has to be carried in a plastic bag, by the time you fish it out to give to your dog he has forgotten what it's for. Many dry and semidry treats are available. To maintain your dog's health, avoid treats high in salt or sugar. Experiment to find out what your dog likes and responds to. Trying to train a dog with treats he doesn't like is pointless.

The ideal treat is dry and no bigger than ¼ inch (even smaller for toy dogs). The bigger the treat, the longer it takes Buddy to consume it, which will break his concentration from what you're teaching him. Our favorites are called Elec-tro-bytes, which are dry, small, can be broken in small pieces for puppies or toy dogs, and don't make your pocket smell for days afterwards. They provide valuable replacement nutrition for working dogs or dogs being trained. Look on our Web site (www.volhard.com) for more details.

Dogs also like carrots, broccoli, almost any kind of fruit, and cheese (we use low-sodium string cheese). For a selection of dog treats, check out a pet store such as Petco or PetSmart. Make sure you choose a treat with very few ingredients and preservatives and one that provides good nutrition for your dog. Avoid treats made in China.

Not all human food is safe for dogs. For example, the chemical agents found in chocolate that make it good and tasty to us are harmful for dogs. So keep chocolate away from Buddy. Also avoid macadamia nuts and onions, which can cause abdominal pain and nausea. Grapes and raisins from nonorganic sources and candy that contains xylitol as a sugar substitute can cause nausea, liver failure, and seizures.

Opting for toys when food treats don't work

Some dogs don't respond as well to treats as they do to other objects, such as balls, Frisbees, large stones, or sticks. In that case, use whatever turns your dog on — as long as it doesn't become a hindrance in your training. Your Buddy also may respond to verbal praise or petting as a motivator. You also can use a clicker (see Chapter 1).

Our German Shepherd, Katharina, wouldn't take treats in training. She would, however, respond to a stick or a toy, so that's what we used.

Other Equipment to Consider

In the following sections, we discuss a variety of options that are available to control dogs. You'll be familiar with some of them; others will be new to you. Some are training tools and others are management tools. The difference between the two is that a training tool teaches the dog to assume the responsibility for his behavior, whereas a management tool doesn't; it simply manages the dog's behavior. For example, a crate is a management tool — it controls the dog's movements.

We don't recommend any of the items listed in this section and don't use them ourselves. However, they have been used successfully in special circumstances by our students. They're listed here solely to provide you with information of the options available to you.

Using head halters

The *head halter*, such as the popular Gentle Leader, is an adaptation from the head halters used for horses. It works on the premise that where the dog's head goes, eventually the rest of the body has to follow.

Whereas the pinch collar looks downright menacing, the head halter looks quite inviting and user-friendly. Interestingly, your dog's reaction (and he's the one that counts) is likely to be quite the opposite. He'll readily accept a pinch collar but many vigorously and vociferously object to the head halter, at least initially. This reaction is probably caused by the "muzzling" effect the dog feels — you're taking biting, his principal means of defense, away from him.

The following list describes the principal advantages of the head halter after your dog has learned to accept the effect it has on him:

- ✔ **It's calming and tranquilizing.** This collar is helpful with nervous, timid, shy, or hyperactive dogs.

- ✔ **It's equalizing.** A head halter helps smaller handlers with larger dogs, senior citizens, and handicapped handlers control their dogs.

- ✔ **It's helpful with muzzling.** This collar helps with inappropriate sniffing behavior, whining or barking, some forms of aggression, and play biting or nibbling.

- ✔ **It's readily available at pet stores and through catalogs.** You also can find these halters on the Web by searching for them with your favorite browser.

Table 5-4 provides some additional advantages of the head halter as well as some disadvantages.

Table 5-4	Pros and Cons of the Head Halter
Advantages	*Disadvantages*
Readily available in pet stores and through catalogs	Greatest potential for serious damage to your dog's neck
Not very expensive	Transition tool only
Minimum strength required to use it	The dog doesn't learn to accept responsibility for his behavior. When the halter is removed, the dog reverts to previous behavior.

Because this halter controls the head, a strong pull by the dog or the owner can do serious damage to the dog's neck. In this regard, it isn't quite the same principle as the head halter for horses. Because most people are smaller than horses, the halter is used to control the horse's head from below. In contrast, most people are taller than their dogs, and any pull or tug is going to be upward and, at times, simultaneously to the side. Tugging the dog's neck in this way creates great potential for injury. In relation to a person, a horse's neck also is correspondingly stronger than a dog's. We also feel that the halter can and often does have a depressing effect on the dog. The irony here is that this highly marketable tool has great potential for damage, while the torturous-looking pinch collar is the safest.

Going for a body harness

Body harnesses, which are attached around the chest and back of a dog, are perfectly fine for dogs who don't pull or for small dogs whose pulling isn't terribly objectionable. But for a medium-sized or large dog that pulls, harnesses aren't a good idea because you give up the control you're trying to achieve. The dog literally leans into the harness and happily drags you wherever he wants to go. Harnesses are effective if your dog has a neck injury.

Another option for a dog that pulls is a "No-Pull" harness (see Figure 5-5). These harnesses are specifically designed to control pulling by applying pressure to calming points under the armpits when the dog pulls. No-Pull harnesses are an excellent management tool (not a training tool) for dogs with delicate necks, such as sight hounds, and for dogs who have experienced a neck injury. You can order one of these harnesses at www.pullersplace.com.

Figure 5-5:
A dog in a
No-Pull
harness.

Exploring electronic and other training and management equipment

Electricity has long been used to contain livestock (mainly cattle) as well as horses. Its application to dogs as a training tool and for containment purposes is of more recent origin. Electronic devices became popular with the training of sporting dogs to retrieve birds their owners had shot. The owners needed to be able to control their dogs over distances up to half a mile. Since that time, the concept of controlling the dog through the use of electricity has spawned the many devices that we describe in this section.

Today's electronic devices don't pose much of a risk for the dog, and we aren't aware of any instances where a device's failure has injured a dog. The main risk to the dog is an owner's lack of knowledge of how to use a particular device properly.

A trainer is an individual who has knowledge of all these training devices and knows when and how to use them when the situation arises. For the beginner or impatient owner without education in a device's proper application, it's far too easy to use the device incorrectly. For example, a remote-trainer is frequently used as a means of punishment rather than a teaching tool.

Electric fences

Many housing developments have covenants against fences. That's a problem when you have a dog you want to keep confined. Tying a dog out on a line, except for brief periods, isn't a humane option.

Never fear, technology is here, and the *electric fence* (or *invisible fence*) is the answer. Here's how the system works: A wire is buried around the boundary of the area in which the dog is to be contained. Initially, the area is marked with little flags to provide the dog with a clear visual stimulus. The dog wears a collar that's designed to vibrate or beep when the dog approaches the boundary. When the dog gets too close, he receives a shock. The intensity of the shock can be adjusted. After the dog has learned to respect the location of the boundary, the flags are removed.

Electric fences are best for neighborhoods that don't allow fences and in farm communities where the dog needs to be prevented from visiting the neighbor, who is worried about the dog bothering his livestock.

All in all, the system works well for the majority of dogs, but it isn't foolproof. Here are a few of the problems you may encounter:

- ✔ It doesn't keep other dogs or animals out of the fenced area because they aren't connected to the system. If you have a female dog that isn't spayed, you could run into a problem when she's in season and an unaltered male comes to visit with breeding on his mind. It can't keep children out of your yard either.

✔ Some dogs, in a state of high excitement, will "burn" through the fence. Then they find themselves on the outside of the fence and are afraid to come back in — or they may simply run away.

✔ Some dogs develop aggressive tendencies toward people on the other side of the boundary.

✔ Some dogs quickly become "collar-wise" and disregard the fence when not wearing the collar. Should that happen, he has to wear the collar every time you let him out.

✔ Costs of the systems vary and depend on the size of the enclosure. The least expensive systems are found in pet stores, but in this situation, the owner must learn how to use them. A more expensive option is to use a company that installs the fence and sends a trainer who does the initial training of the dog and instructs the owner on how to use it.

As a result of these problems, you need to keep an eye on him when he's out in the yard. Don't leave him for prolonged periods without supervision.

Shock collars

A *shock collar* is a plastic collar with a small box attached. The side of the collar that faces the dog has two small prongs that fit snugly against the dog's neck. The handler has a hand-held control that has settings that go from low to high electrical stimulation. The euphemisms for this type of collar are the *e-collar* and the *remote trainer*. The word "shock" is often replaced with "stimulation." In simple terms, the electrical stimulation replaces the check on the collar. Remote trainers are most successful for controlling dogs at a distance.

We don't recommend that beginners use these collars. Their use takes knowledge of training and dogs. When used incorrectly, these collars can severely traumatize a dog. Seek a professional trainer if you're considering such a collar.

This collar's origins date back to the 1960s, when they were primarily used for gun dogs. They gave the trainer the ability to communicate with the dog over long distances. The main problems with the early collars were their reliability and their limitations in terms of controlling the amount of stimulation — even at the lowest setting, the shock administered was needlessly intense.

Within the different makes of remote trainers, you find enormous quality differences — essentially, you get what you pay for. The three features influencing the price of a remote-trainer are rechargeable versus replaceable batteries, range, and flexibility. The more sophisticated collars provide the most flexibility in adjusting the intensity of the stimulation, its length, and its range (up to 1 mile). Of course, these high-end collars are the most expensive, ranging from $200 to $500. They may include a tone feature, to which some dogs respond without the need for stimulation.

Generally, such collars aren't carried in retail stores and have to be ordered online. The following are some of the manufacturers of these collars: Dogtra, Innotek, PetSafe, and Tri-Tronics. You can purchase the products at the manufacturers' Web sites or at www.gundogsonline.com or www.amazon.com.

We don't recommend that you experiment with an electronic collar to train your dog — it requires a great deal of expertise and experience. But if you insist on using any kind of electronic collar, try it out on yourself first so you know what it feels like to your dog. Whatever you do, don't point the control at your dog or wave it at him in a threatening motion — he'll associate the stimulation with you, and that's not what you want. Keep the control out of your dog's sight.

Vibration collars

The *vibration collar* works much the same as a remote trainer or shock collar (see the preceding section), but it relies mainly on vibration (rather than electric stimulation) at different levels of intensity to communicate with the dog. The vibration is more annoying than unpleasant, but for many dogs it's just as effective as a remote trainer.

We haven't used this collar, but some of our students have had success with them for dogs with low drives (see Chapter 2). Dogs with high numbers in their Personality Profile aren't likely to respond to it. However, the vibration collar works well with deaf dogs. Cost varies from $30 to $150. They're available from www.amazon.com.

Bark collars

To deal with excessive barking, you have several different *bark collars* to choose from. Your options are: a mild shock, a mechanism that sprays a liquid (usually citronella), vibration, or ultrasound (a loud noise only the dog can hear). The collars use either a microphone or vibration to set the collar off. The more sophisticated ones use both to prevent loud noises or the barking of another dog from setting off the collar. They range in price from $30 to $60 and are available from the manufacturers listed in the preceding section.

If Buddy is an uncontrollable barker, you may want to consider a bark collar — it's a lot cheaper than being evicted.

Locating your runaway with a GPS collar

The latest entries into the e-collar arsenal are GPS tracking and locator collars. You use these collars to locate your pet if he has run away or been stolen. You can even look at a map online that shows you the exact location of your pet. And here you thought you were the only one with the fancy electronic devices. While such collars can locate your pet, if you need a GPS to keep track of your dog, you may want to review your method of training and oversight. These collars aren't cheap — anywhere from $500 to $2,000.

Citronella collars

Citronella collars are used as bark collars (as noted in the preceding section), but they also are used to deter chasing. When activated by the owner, the collar emits a puff of citronella in the direction of the dog's nose. For example, if a dog chases a car, just before he gets there the owner presses the button and the dog gets a whiff of citronella. The expectation is that the dog considers the puff of citronella unpleasant enough to stop chasing things. While not an electronic device, it works on the same principle. Because electric collars aren't allowed in England, for example, they're the collar of choice.

In a 1996 study at the Animal Behavior Clinic of Cornell University Veterinary School, the citronella collar was found to be more effective to control nuisance barking than the electric bark collar.

Prices range from $45 to $60, and they come in scented and unscented versions. Both are available through www.amazon.com.

Scat mats

Don't want your dog taking his daily nap on your favorite armchair or couch while you're at work? The *scat mat,* with which you cover that coveted piece of furniture, may be your answer. When Buddy jumps on it, the scat mat gives him a slightly unpleasant shock, which will stop him from jumping on the furniture. The mat also can be used to prevent Buddy from entering another room in the house. No special collar is required.

The customary sizes of scat mats are 30 inches long by 16 inches wide or 48 inches long by 20 inches wide. They can be extended by plugging two together. They're either battery powered or can be plugged into a wall outlet. You can find scat mats at most of the larger pet stores for $10 to $75, depending on the size.

Indoor containment systems

Do you want to stop counter surfing or jumping on the kitchen table? If so, consider buying an indoor containment system. It consists of a 6-inch disc and a collar for your dog. You place the disc in the center of the countertop or table, and then you adjust the setting for intensity and the distance you want Buddy to stay away. When Buddy gets too close, he receives a mild shock.

The system is battery operated and prevents a dog from jumping on counters or coffee tables. It works on the same principle as the invisible fence (see the earlier section on this product). These systems are carried by most pet store chains, and they generally cost around $40.

Dear friends of ours acquired an English Staffordshire Bullterrier. Meigs is the most adorable butterball on four legs — one solid muscle with incredible leaping ability. He's affectionately referred to as "a sack of cement on four pogo sticks." Even as a puppy he exhibited aspirations of ascending the coffee table. As early as 9 months of age, he was able to jump on the kitchen table from a dead standstill. Very cute, but hardly acceptable. The indoor containment system took care of it.

The Pet Convincer

The Pet Convincer is a powerful substitute to yelling or screaming at your dog to control unwanted behaviors. Although the Pet Convincer is a shortcut to patient training, it's nevertheless an effective deterrent to those behaviors dog owners find most annoying and most difficult to deal with: for example, when Buddy goes ballistic when someone comes to the door, when he can't be dissuaded from jumping on people, when he barks incessantly, and so on. It also can be used when taking your dog for a walk. It can protect your dog from being bothered by another dog. It also works well for joggers and cyclists to ward off potentially unfriendly dogs.

This hand-held device, powered by a replaceable CO_2 cartridge, releases a blast of air. The blast of air, whose intensity is controlled with a trigger, is intended to stop the undesirable behavior. The noise of the blast acts as a deterrent. No doubt it will work better than screaming at the dog. You also have a good chance of the "correction" carrying over to the next time the dog encounters the problematic situation, such as someone coming to the door. You can purchase this product at www.petconvincer.com for $35.

This training tool should never be used in an enclosed space, such as a car. When triggered it must be directed away from the dog's face.

Part II
Performing Puppy Preliminaries

The 5th Wave   By Rich Tennant

"You know, you're never going to get that dog to do his business in your remote control dump truck."

In this part . . .

In this part, we guide you through your puppy's developmental periods to help you understand his physical, behavioral, and emotional needs. You'll be amazed at how quickly he learns. The first few weeks are the most productive in terms of how much you can teach him. So the longer you wait to get started, the slower your progress will be. After helping you understand your puppy's growth periods, we provide training tips to help you survive your puppy's antics. We also include a chapter on housetraining, which is an important part of raising a puppy. Crate training, which can be a big help in housetraining, also is covered.

Chapter 6

Surviving Your Puppy's Growth Periods

In This Chapter

▶ Discovering your puppy's growth periods

▶ Handling an adolescent puppy

▶ Knowing whether to spay and neuter your pup and when to do it

▶ Helping your puppy grow up

*E*veryone wants a super puppy, one that's well behaved and listens to every word you say — a Lassie or perhaps even a Beethoven. Of course, heredity plays a role, but so does early upbringing and environment. From birth until maturity, your dog goes through a number of developmental periods. The many scientists and behaviorists who've studied dog behavior over the last century have made important discoveries about a puppy's developmental periods and how they relate to his ability to grow into a well-adjusted pet. What happens or doesn't happen during these periods has a lasting effect on how your dog turns out, his ability to learn, his outlook on life, his behavior, and how he responds to your efforts to train him.

In this chapter, we explain the developmental periods your pooch will go through and how to begin training him according to the stage he's in. We also discuss how spaying and neutering can affect your dog and his trainability.

Understanding Your Puppy's Early Development

Puppies go through distinct critical periods in the first 12 weeks of life. What happens during this time influences not only their temperament but also their health and overall development. In the following sections, we discuss each of the puppy periods your pet will go through so you can begin training him appropriately.

Birth to 7 weeks

The first puppy period is from birth to 49 days. During this time, the puppy needs his mother and the interaction with his littermates. He also needs to have interaction with humans. All these interactions are important because they lay the foundation for the puppy's future with his human family and what he may encounter as he grows.

Be wary of obtaining a puppy who has been taken away from his mother prior to 7 weeks of age, because it not only deprives the puppy of important behavioral lessons but also can affect the puppy's future health. For example, the puppy obtains antibodies to many diseases by feeding from his mother. Every sip of milk is like a vaccine that protects the puppy for many weeks after he leaves the litter and is placed in his new home.

Between 3 to 7 weeks of age, the mother teaches her puppies basic doggy manners. She communicates to the puppies what's acceptable and what's unacceptable behavior. For instance, after the puppies' teeth have come in, nursing them becomes a painful experience, so she teaches them to take it easy. She does whatever it takes, such as growling, snarling, and even snapping, and she continues this lesson throughout the weaning process when she wants the puppies to leave her alone. After just a few repetitions, the puppies get the message and respond to a mere look or a curled lip from mother. The puppy learns dog language — or lip reading, as we call it — and bite inhibition, an important lesson for when he goes home with his new human family.

The ability of puppies to learn at an early age is amazing. Using models built to scale, experienced trainers have taught puppies between 3 and 7 weeks of age a variety of complex tasks required for working as assistance dogs. These include turning light switches on and off, opening and closing doors, and retrieving objects.

Besides learning from their mothers, puppies also learn from each other. While playing, tempers may flare because one puppy bites another too hard. The puppies discover from these exchanges what it feels like to be bitten and, at the same time, to inhibit biting during play. (See Figure 6-1.)

Puppies separated from their canine families before they've had the opportunity for these experiences with mother and littermates tend to identify more with humans than with other dogs. To simplify, they don't know they're dogs, and they tend to have their own set of problems, such as the following:

- ✔ Aggression toward other dogs
- ✔ Difficulty with housetraining
- ✔ Separation anxiety

 ✔ Excessive barking

 ✔ Mouthing and biting their owners

 ✔ Nervousness

 ✔ An unhealthy attachment to humans

Figure 6-1:
Puppies
discover
valuable
lessons
while
playing.

Photograph by Jane Kelso

At about the 49th day of life, when the puppy's brain is neurologically complete, that special attachment between the dog and his new human owner, called *bonding,* takes place. Bonding is one of the reasons that the 49th day is the ideal time for puppies to leave the nest for their new homes.

Bonding to people becomes increasingly difficult the longer a puppy remains with his mother or littermates. The dog also becomes more difficult to train. In addition, with delay, the puppy has the potential to experience built-in behavior problems, such as the following:

 ✔ The pup may grow up being too dog oriented.

 ✔ The pup probably won't care much about people.

 ✔ The pup may be difficult to teach to accept responsibility for his own behavior.

 ✔ The pup may be more difficult to train, including housetraining (see Chapter 8 for more information).

Getting to know everyone: Weeks 7–12

Your dog is a social animal. To become an acceptable pet, the pup needs to interact with you and your family as well as with other humans and dogs during the 7th through 12th weeks of life. If denied these opportunities, your dog's behavior around other people or dogs may be unpredictable — your dog may be fearful or perhaps even aggressive. For example, unless regularly exposed to children during this period, a dog may be uncomfortable or untrustworthy around them.

Socializing your puppy is critical if you want him to become a friendly adult dog. When your puppy is developing, expose him to as many different people as possible, including children and older people of all shapes, sexes, and sizes. Let him meet new dogs, too. These early experiences will pay off big time when your dog grows up.

Your puppy needs the chance to meet and have positive experiences with those persons and activities that will play a role in his life. The following are just a few examples:

- ✔ **You're a grandparent whose grandchildren occasionally visit:** Have your puppy meet children as often as you can.

- ✔ **You live by yourself but have friends that visit you:** Make an effort to let your puppy meet other people, particularly members of the opposite sex.

- ✔ **You plan to take your dog on family outings or vacations:** Introduce riding in a car.

You can set up all these encounters by taking him to the local park. Most people love to meet puppies. And he can get used to the ride on the way there!

A common way for people to greet a puppy or an adult dog is to pat it on top of the head, just as they do with children (though the cheek pinch is even worse). Puppies and adult dogs don't like this form of greeting any better than kids do. Patting a dog on the head encourages jumping, the very behavior most owners don't want. Instead, stand up straight or kneel down, and then greet the puppy with a smile and a hello. Put the palm of your hand on his chest and calmly stroke it in a massaging motion. Doing so will calm him. When meeting a puppy or dog for the first time, slowly put the palm of your hand toward him and let him smell you.

Socialization with other dogs is equally important to socialization with humans and should be the norm rather than the exception. Puppies learn from other dogs but can only do so if they have a chance to spend time with them. Make it a point of introducing your young dog to other puppies and adult dogs on a regular basis. Many communities now have dog parks where dogs can interact and play together. If you plan to take your puppy to obedience class or dog shows or to use him in a breeding program, he definitely needs to have the chance to interact with other dogs (see Chapter 13). Time spent now is well worth the effort — it will build his confidence and make your job training him that much easier.

Socialization is important for Buddy at this time, but so is training him. Begin training your puppy as soon as you get him. The puppy will learn whether you teach him or not, so you may as well teach him what he needs to know. Start teaching the exercises listed in Chapter 9 as well as the Touch command described in Chapter 10. The exercise to get started in Chapter 1 also can be helpful. At this age it's much easier to physically manipulate the puppy than after he has grown into an unruly teenager.

 During this development period your puppy will follow your every footstep. Encourage this behavior by rewarding the puppy with an occasional treat, some petting, or a kind word. Taking advantage of your puppy's willingness to follow will make teaching the Come command that much easier (head to Chapter 10 for more details on this command).

Suddenly he's afraid: Weeks 8–12

Weeks 8 through 12 are called the *fear imprint period.* During this period, any painful or particularly frightening experience leaves a more lasting impression on your pup than if it occurred at any other time in his life. If the experience is sufficiently traumatic, it could literally ruin your pup for life.

 During the fear imprint period, avoid exposing the puppy to traumatic experiences. When you need to take your puppy to the veterinarian, have the doctor give him a treat before, during, and after the examination to make the visit a pleasant experience. Although you need to stay away from stressful situations, do continue to train your puppy in a positive and nonpunitive way.

 During the first year's growth, you may see fear reactions at other times. Don't respond by dragging your puppy to the object that caused the fear. On the other hand, don't pet or reassure the dog either — you may create the impression that you approve of this behavior. Rather, distract the puppy with a toy or a treat to get his mind off whatever scared him and go on to something pleasant. Practice some of the commands you've already taught him so he can focus on a positive experience. After a short time — sometimes up to two weeks — the fearful behavior will disappear.

Now he wants to leave home: Beyond 12 weeks

Sometime between 4 and 8 months, your puppy begins to realize that there's a big, wide world out there. Up to now, every time you called, Buddy probably willingly came to you. But now he may prefer to wander off and investigate alone. Buddy is maturing and cutting the apron strings, which is normal. He's not being spiteful or disobedient; he's just becoming an adolescent.

While he's going through this phase, keep Buddy on a leash or in a confined area until he has learned to come when called. Otherwise, not coming when called becomes a pattern — annoying to you and dangerous to Buddy. After this activity becomes a habit, breaking it is difficult; prevention is the best cure. Teaching your dog to come when called (before he has developed the habit of running away) is easy. Practice calling him in the house, out in the yard, and at random times. Have a treat in your pocket to reinforce the behavior you want. (For more on teaching the Come command, check out Chapter 10.)

When you need to gather a wandering Buddy, don't, under any circumstances, play the game of chasing him. Instead, call his name in an excited tone of voice. If that doesn't work, run the other way and get Buddy to chase you. You also can kneel on the ground and pretend you've found something extremely interesting, hoping Buddy's curiosity brings him to you. If you have to, approach him slowly in an upright position, using a nonthreatening tone of voice until you can calmly take hold of his collar.

Your puppy also goes through teething during this period and needs to chew anything and everything. Dogs, like children, can't help it. Puppies have the irritating habit of tackling many shoes, but only one from each pair. If one of your favorite shoes is demolished, try to control yourself. Look at it as a lesson to keep your possessions out of reach. Scolding won't stop the need to chew, but it may cause your pet to fear you.

Your job is to provide acceptable outlets for this need, such as chew bones and toys. Our dogs' favorites are beef soup bones that you can get at the supermarket. A dog can't easily break them and they provide hours of entertainment. They also keep your dog's teeth clean. Kong toys (www.kong company.com) are another favorite, especially the hard rubber ones that are virtually indestructible and can be stuffed with peanut butter or kibble. They come in different sizes appropriate to the size of your dog and can keep most dogs busy for hours. Just be sure they're large enough that he can't accidentally swallow one.

Stay away from soft and fuzzy toys. Chances are, your dog will destroy them and may ingest a part of them. We personally don't like rawhide chew toys that have been treated with chemicals or items that become soft and gooey while chewing because the dog can swallow them and get them stuck in his intestines. If you do provide these toys for your pet, be sure to supervise him so he doesn't ingest pieces.

When Buddy is going through this stage, you may want to consider crating him when he's left alone. Doing so keeps him and your possessions safe, and both of you will be happy. Crating him during this growth spurt helps with his housetraining, too. With all the chewing he does during his teething, accidents sometimes happen (chewing stimulates bowel movements in puppies). See Chapter 8 for more on housetraining.

The Terrible Twos: Managing the Adolescent from 4 months to 2 years

The adolescent stage of your dog's life, depending on the breed, takes place anywhere from 4 months to 2 years and culminates in sexual maturity. Generally, the smaller the dog, the sooner he matures. Larger dogs enter (and end) adolescence later in life.

Adolescence is a time when your cute little puppy can turn into a teenage monster. He starts to lose his baby teeth and his soft, fuzzy puppy coat. He goes through growth spurts and looks gangly either up in the rear or down in front; he's entering an ugly-duckling stage.

Depending on the size of the dog, 40 to 70 percent of adult growth is achieved by 7 months of age. If you haven't done so already, you'd better start training now, before the dog gets so big that you can't manage him. As Buddy begins to mature, he starts to display some puzzling behaviors as well as some perfectly normal but objectionable ones.

Because adolescence can be such a tricky time in a pup's life (and yours!), in the following sections, we provide some information to help make the transition as smooth as possible.

Surviving the juvenile flakies

We use the term *juvenile flakies* because it most accurately describes what's technically known as a second fear imprint period (refer to the earlier section "Suddenly he's afraid: Weeks 8–12" for more information on this period). Juvenile flakies are apprehension or fear behaviors that usually are short lived. They're caused by temporary calcium deficiencies and hormone development related to a puppy's periodic growth spurts.

Being patient with the flakies

One day, when our Dachshund, Manfred, was 6 months old, he came into the kitchen after having been outside in the yard. There he noticed on the floor, near his water bowl, a brown paper grocery bag. He flattened, looked as though he'd seen a ghost, and tried to run back out into the yard.

If Manfred was going through a growth spurt at this time, which is normal at 6 months, he could've been experiencing a temporary calcium deficiency, which in turn would produce his fear reaction.

He'd seen brown paper grocery bags many times before, but this one was going to get him. We reminded ourselves that he was going through the flakies and ignored the behavior. A few hours later, the behavior disappeared.

The timing of this event (or events) isn't as clearly defined as it is with the first fear imprint period, and it coincides with growth spurts; hence, it may occur more than once as the dog matures. Even though he may have been outgoing and confident before, your puppy now may be reluctant to approach someone or something new and unfamiliar. He also may suddenly be afraid of familiar people and things.

If you happen to observe a similar situation with your puppy, don't try to drag him up to the object in an effort to "teach" the puppy to accept it. If you make a big deal out of it, you create the impression that he has a good reason to be afraid of whatever triggered the reaction. Leave the puppy alone, ignore the behavior, and it will pass.

Fear of the new or unfamiliar is rooted in evolution. In a wild pack, after the pups become 8 to 10 months of age, they're allowed to go on a hunt. The first lesson they have to learn is to stay with the pack; if they wander off, they may get lost or into trouble. Apprehension or fear of the familiar also is caused by growth spurts. At this point in a puppy's life, hormones start to surge. Hormones can affect the calcium uptake in the body, and, coupled with growth, can be a difficult time for the growing puppy.

Determining what to do when puppy discovers sex

Sometime during this 4-month to 2-year period, depending on the size of your dog, the puppy will discover sex, and you'll be the first to know about it.

Our Landseer Newfoundland, Evo, has always enjoyed playing with other dogs. He's generally well behaved and gets along with people and all the dogs he meets. When Evo was almost 2, he fell in love. We took him to a training facility where we were to meet up with friends who had just adopted an 11-month-old female Labrador Retriever named Indy. Evo was very sweet with her, and at first they played nicely together, chasing and batting at each other with their paws. All of a sudden, a strange look came over Evo's face, and with his face crinkled up he jumped on Indy's back and with his front paws clasped her firmly around her chest. We realized that his puppy days were over.

Sex is sex in any language! Evo was a bit of a late developer because he lives with spayed females and hadn't yet had the pleasure of being involved with an unspayed female. We handled Evo by going up to him, putting his lead on, and taking him away from Indy. He wanted to go back to her and tried several times, but we occupied his mind with training and he soon forgot all about her.

When Buddy experiences a surge of hormones during training, do some heeling or retrieving to get him back into the proper frame of mind.

Blame it on the hormones: Understanding how hormones affect behavior

During the period from 4 months to a year, the male puppy's hormones surge to four times his adult level, and this surge can have important effects on his behavior. You usually can tell when he's entering this phase. The most obvious sign is that he stops listening to you. He also may try to dominate other dogs in the household or ones he meets outside. Fortunately, after this enormous surge, his hormones ultimately return to normal.

At this hormonal turning point, many pet owners discover that their dogs become difficult to handle, so they seek professional help or enroll them in obedience classes. These are appropriate ways to help Buddy make his way through this time and restore harmony to the relationship. This stage also is a good time to consider neutering the dog.

Hormones drive behavior, which means that the intensity of behaviors increases in direct proportion to the amount of hormones coursing through his system. So if you want your male puppy to become calmer and not to assert himself quite so much, neutering him is a good idea.

A sad fact of life

The majority of dogs in animal shelters are delivered to those shelters at around 8 months of age, when they're no longer "cute" and have "stopped listening." Millions of dogs are killed annually because their owners didn't want to spend 10 to 15 minutes a day training them when they were young.

Although female puppies going through puberty may show similar traits, more often they show greater dependency on their owners. They follow their owners around, looking at them constantly, as if to say, "Something is happening to my body, but I don't know what. Tell me what to do." However, keep in mind that females are just as apt to show mounting behavior as males.

If you don't want to neuter or spay your pet, the necessity for training and protection increases. The freedom that the male puppy had before now becomes limited. The better trained he is, the easier this transition will be, but it requires a real commitment on your part. The female, in turn, needs to be protected during her heat cycle, which usually occurs every 6 months and lasts around 21 days. Her attraction is so potent that you may discover unwanted suitors around your house, some of whom may have come from miles away.

Our first experience with a female in season involved our Landseer Newfoundland, Heidi. When we came home from work, we found a good-sized Basset Hound on our front stoop, patiently waiting for Heidi. As we approached, he made it perfectly clear that he was taking a proprietary attitude toward Heidi as well as to the house. We had to enter the house through the back door. We then managed to subdue the little fellow with a few dog biscuits just long enough to check his collar. We were surprised to learn that the horny hound had traveled close to three miles to visit.

Meeting the mature adult when your dog finally grows up

No matter how much you wish that cute little puppy could remain as is, your pup is going to grow up. It happens anywhere from 1 to 4 years, depending on the breed. Smaller breeds will mature faster than larger breeds. If you trained Buddy as a younger dog, he'll now become the perfect pet you always wanted. Figure 6-2 shows a pup on the way to adulthood.

Figure 6-2:
Yes, your pup will grow up.

Spaying or Neutering to Help with Behavior and Training

Unless you intend to exhibit your dog in dog shows to get a championship or to breed the dog, you need to seriously consider neutering or spaying. Doing so can improve behavior and ease of training.

When an intact male becomes aware of a female in season anywhere in the immediate area, chances are he'll be oblivious to any commands you have taught him. View such situations as training opportunities — to remind Buddy that you still expect him to obey. After all, what better distraction is there? If you find you have difficulty controlling Buddy under such circumstances, see Chapter 5 for information on training equipment and Chapter 3 for more on the "adrenaline effect."

In the following sections, we show you both the pros and cons of spaying or neutering your pooch, including the effect the procedures have on your pet.

Heeding the advantages

For both males and females, the advantages of altering your pet generally outweigh the disadvantages. For the male, the advantages of altering include the following:

- ✔ Keeps him calm and less stressed around a female in season
- ✔ Reduces the tendency to roam
- ✔ Diminishes mounting behavior
- ✔ Makes training easier
- ✔ Improves overall disposition, especially toward other dogs
- ✔ Reduces risk of prostate problems developing in the older male
- ✔ Helps to prevent marking behavior in the house

In short, he'll be easier to live with and easier to train. Neutering also curbs the urge to roam or run away. So if the front door is left open by accident, he won't go miles to find a female in season, like our friend the Basset (see the earlier section "Blame it on the hormones: Understanding how hormones affect behavior" to read about our experience with a roaming pooch).

It isn't true that dogs that have been altered lose their protective instincts — it depends on the age when the dog was altered. Generally, dogs altered after a year of age retain their protective instincts.

If you spay your female, she, too, will stay closer to home. Perhaps even more important are these benefits:

- ✔ You won't have to deal with the mess that goes with having her in season.
- ✔ You won't have to worry about unwanted visitors camping on your property and lifting a leg against any vertical surface.
- ✔ You won't have to worry about accidental puppies, which are next to impossible to place in good homes.
- ✔ You may have a happier, healthier dog with fewer violent mood swings and less chance of getting tumors of the mammary glands and infections of the uterus.

Finally, and most important in the context of training, she'll be more even-keeled, a distinct benefit.

Acknowledging the disadvantages

Altering changes the hormone level in a dog's body. Some dogs that are altered develop hormonal deficiencies that can produce arthritis and bone disease and can affect joint and bladder function. The ability to manage stress, cognitive function, weight gain, and tooth and ligament stability are all associated with hormonal deficiencies, according to studies stated in *Animal Wellness Magazine* (February 2010).

The most common deficiency seen is hypothyroidism. It's thought that around 70 percent of all pure-bred dogs have hypothyroidism. Detected in dogs as young as 6 months of age and all the way up to the age of 8 and beyond, hypothyroidism requires a special blood test for diagnosis.

Hypothyroidism can cause these problems:

✔ Dull, oily, thinning, and smelly coats

✔ Increased shedding

✔ Separation anxiety

✔ Skin problems

✔ A tendency to gain weight

Regardless of these disadvantages, we recommend altering a dog that isn't going to be bred simply because altered dogs are so much easier to live with. See the preceding section for the advantages of altering.

Knowing when to spay or neuter

If you decide to alter your dog, think about having the surgery after 7 months of age for both sexes.

Depending on the breed and size of the female, she'll go into her first season any time after 7 months of age. For a Yorkshire Terrier, it's apt to be sooner, and for a giant breed, it's likely to be later, sometimes as late as 18 months of age. If you have your females spayed, wait until after her first season and until about halfway before her second season is due.

If you want a dog to show more adult behaviors and take more responsibility — like being a protector or guard dog, training for competitive events, or working for a living — think about altering males or females between 1 and 2 years of age.

A dog that hasn't been neutered until after a year of age, or a female that has gone through two seasons, is generally easier to train for competitive events such as obedience or agility trials. Dogs have become fully grown by that time, are emotionally mature, have learned more adult behaviors, and can accept more responsibility.

To breed or not to breed your dog? That's the question

Don't even contemplate breeding your dog unless

✔ Your dog is purebred and registered.

✔ You didn't get your dog from an animal shelter or pet store.

✔ You have at least a three-generation pedigree for your dog.

✔ Your dog has at least four titled dogs, such as conformation or working titles, in the last three generations.

✔ Your dog is certified free of genetic disorders applicable to the breed.

✔ Your dog conforms to the standard for its breed.

✔ Your dog has a stable temperament.

Breeding dogs for the purpose of exposing your children to the miracle of birth is *not* a good idea. The world already has enough dogs that don't have homes, and finding homes for your puppies will be much more difficult than you think, if not impossible. Rent a DVD if you want your children to understand the birthing process.

Chapter 7

Starting Puppy on the Right Paw

● ●

In This Chapter

▶ Gathering supplies for your puppy's arrival

▶ Introducing your puppy to his new home

▶ Laying the groundwork for training

▶ Looking at health issues that interfere with training

● ●

*W*hile anticipating your new puppy's arrival, you've probably thought about the day-to-day care this tiny ball of fur will need. You may even have made a list of necessities to purchase: food and water bowls, a leash, grooming aids, and so on. But the necessities don't stop there. You also need to think about laying the groundwork for training. Everything you do from now on teaches your puppy to be the perfect pet you have always wanted.

Teaching your puppy is about more than getting a response to a command; it's also about raising a dog you can live with and take anywhere and who can be a joy as a companion for many years. This chapter guides you through the first weeks and shows how your training relationship starts on day one.

Preparing for Puppy's Arrival

A little advance preparation for the exciting day makes your puppy's home-coming go smoothly. Before Buddy comes home, you need to gather the following (see Figure 7-1):

✔ A crate and crate pad

✔ The food you intend to feed and the dishes you're going to use

✔ A collar and leash

✔ Toys

Figure 7-1:
Items you
need before
your puppy
comes
home.

You can get almost everything you need at a pet supply store, whether in person or online (such as at www.petedge.com or www.petco.com). Ordering online makes for convenient shopping, or you may prefer to check out your options at the store.

In the following sections, we provide info on each of the items you need to gather before welcoming puppy into your home.

Puppy's home at home: Readying a crate

The idea of putting your dog in a crate may seem like a form of punishment. Surely no dog wants to be confined to a crate when he could have free rein of the house, right?

But humans and dogs have very different perceptions of crates. When a crate is used correctly, a dog certainly doesn't perceive it as punishment. Quite the contrary — a crate serves as a den and a place of comfort, safety, security, and warmth. Puppies, as well as many adult dogs, sleep most of the day, and many prefer the comfort of their den. For your peace of mind, as well as your puppy's, get a crate. We show you why to use one and how to set it up in the following sections.

Understanding the advantages of a crate

Consider a few of the many advantages to crate training your dog:

- ✔ **A crate is a babysitter.** When you're busy and can't keep an eye on Buddy but want to make sure he doesn't get into trouble, you can put him in his crate. You can relax, and so can he.

- ✔ **It helps Buddy begin housetraining.** Using a crate is ideal for getting Buddy on a schedule for housetraining (see Chapter 8).

- ✔ **It prepares him for being crated at the vet's office.** Few dogs are fortunate enough to go through life without ever having to be hospitalized. Buddy's first experience with a crate shouldn't be in a crate at the veterinary hospital — the added stress from being crated for the first time can slow his recovery.

- ✔ **A crate helps with bed rest.** Crate training pays off when you have to keep your dog quiet and calm, such as after being altered or after an injury.

- ✔ **It makes driving safe.** Driving any distance, even around the block, with your dog loose in the car is tempting fate. An emergency stop could fling your pet around the car like a pinball. Having Buddy in a crate protects you and him.

- ✔ **It relaxes him on vacation.** When we go on vacation, we like to take our dog. His crate is his home away from home, and we can leave him in a hotel room knowing that he won't be unhappy or stressed — and that he won't tear up the room.

- ✔ **A crate gives Buddy his own special place.** It's a place where he can get away from the hustle and bustle of family life and hide out when the kids (or other pets) become too much for him.

Selecting the best crate for your puppy

Get a crate that's big enough to accommodate your puppy when he becomes an adult dog. Select one that's large enough for your dog to turn around, stand up, or lie down in comfortably (see Figure 7-2).

If you expect that your puppy will become a much bigger adult dog, buy a crate that comes with a divider that enables you to increase the size of the crate as he grows. The most versatile crates have two doors, one on the side and one at the end. You'll appreciate this flexibility, especially when you have to move the crate from room to room.

If you plan to travel with your dog, get a crate that collapses easily and is portable so you can take it with you. Or consider investing in a second crate for the car. Lugging a crate from the house to the car and back again quickly gets old.

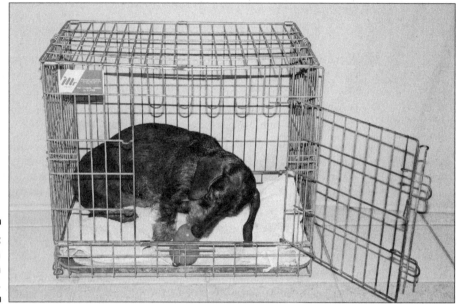

Figure 7-2:
A crate is a
comfy den
for your dog.

Crates come with a crate pan, for which you need a crate pad — you don't want your growing puppy to constantly be on a hard surface; it's tough on growing joints. Get a crate pad with a removable cover that you can clean in the washing machine. Finally, toss a blanket into the crate to keep Buddy warm. (See Chapter 8 for more on crate training your puppy.)

Positioning the crate in your home

Establish an area where your puppy will spend the majority of his time — a place where he won't feel isolated from his new family. The kitchen, family room, or whatever room is most used in the house (but still contains a quiet area) is an ideal place where Buddy can eat and take frequent naps. Head to the later section "Deciding where your puppy should sleep" for more information.

Make sure Buddy's crate is available to him when he wants to nap or take some time out. He'll use it on his own, so make sure he always has access to it. Depending on where it is, your dog will spend much of his sleeping time in his crate.

Never use your dog's crate as a form of punishment. If you do, he'll begin to dislike the crate, and it will lose its usefulness to you. You don't want Buddy to develop negative feelings about his crate. You want him to like his private den.

Driving Miss Bailey: Travel crate alternatives

The safest way to transport your dog in a vehicle is in his crate. A loose dog in a car is a danger to you and your dog — having Buddy in a crate protects both of you.

For some vehicles, such as sedans, crates are too large or cumbersome. Patty found the solution for her Yellow Lab, Bailey: a harness designed for dogs that's secured by the seatbelt,

not unlike a car seat for a child (check out the accompanying figure). Bailey can ride comfortably on the rear seat, either sitting up or lying down.

In a station wagon or SUV, another alternative is a dog barrier that separates the cargo area from the main cabin. Talk to your car dealer about this option.

Puppy's menu: Selecting a proper diet and set of dishes

Choosing a food for your growing puppy isn't easy — you've got too many choices. All of our puppies and our student's puppies are raised on Natural Diet Foundation, or NDF2; you can find the details in Chapter 4 and at www. volhard.com. This is one of the easiest methods of feeding a high-quality diet, which is important for your puppy's growth and health. What you feed your puppy will determine the ease or difficulty you'll have in training Buddy. The better the diet, the easier it is to train him. Turn to Chapter 4 to look over our recommendations and choose an option.

After you settle on a diet for Buddy, be sure to pick out a set of dishes — one for food and one for water. Try to avoid brightly painted or cutesie ceramic dog dishes. Many companies use lead in the manufacturing process of these dishes; over time the lead can leak into the food in the dish. Stick with stainless-steel dishes instead. They come in various sizes and are easy to keep clean. These dishes will last your puppy a lifetime.

Puppy's "clothes"

For your puppy's everyday collar, you need a flat, fabric, adjustable buckle collar that can be made bigger as he grows. Also get a 6-foot-long soft fabric leash for training and walking. For training, Buddy needs a snap-around collar. We use the collars and leashes from www.handcraftcollars.com, a site that offers high-quality products that last a long time. For more on collars, leashes, and other gear, check out Chapter 5.

Puppy's toys

Toys are a wonderful way to amuse Buddy for hours at a time and keep him from attacking your prized possessions. They also can be used in training for dogs who aren't that interested in food (see Chapter 5). You need a variety of them, including the following:

- **Several large plush toys:** Puppies love to play with soft toys and carry them around. However, avoid stuffed animal toys if you have a puppy who likes to rip and tear them apart. They often contain stuffing and squeakers that puppies consider edible. Also beware of the following:

    - Toys that have hard eyes or studs that your puppy *will* pull off — and can swallow.

    - Toys that resemble shoes or your clothes. It's difficult for puppy to understand the difference between his toys and your stuff.

- **Interactive toys:** Interactive toys are great for puppies because they teach as they amuse. The puppy has to figure out how to get the treat, and it gives him something to work on that provides a reward at the end. Such toys are especially important when a puppy is teething. Here are some options:

- **Hard rubber toys:** The Kong Company specializes in hard rubber toys that can be filled with treats or peanut butter to keep dogs occupied. Kong toys come in different sizes, colors, and strengths. The colors identify the strength of the toy; black is virtually indestructible and is the favorite retrieving toy of our Lab.

- **Softer treat holders:** Planet Dog makes a line of interactive toys that come in different shapes and sizes and can be stuffed with treats. Some puppies prefer these to the harder toys because they're made of a softer rubber compound. See `www.pullers place.com`.

- **The Buster Cube:** This is the all-time favorite toy of one of our Dachshunds. We put some treats inside the cube and watch her go at it. She has learned how to roll the cube so treats randomly fall out. Note that on a hardwood floor, the cube is a bit noisy. The Buster Cube is made of cleanable, high-impact plastic. The Small Cube measures 3⅛ inches square, and the Large Cube is 4½ inches square.

Some toys cost a fortune to buy new, but you often can buy them for a fraction of the original cost at your local thrift store.

Bringing Puppy Home — Now What?

You've brought your bundle of fur home, so now what do you do? First off you have to get him acclimated to his new home and surroundings, including introducing him to any children or resident pets. You also have to get his potty habits started and find a good place for him to sleep. We show you how to do all of this in the following sections.

Before reaching 16 weeks of age, you puppy will follow you wherever you go (see Chapter 6). This tendency provides you with endless training opportunities. Although he won't understand what you're saying to him, you can use this behavior to teach him the Touch command (see Chapter 10). The Touch command is an effective foundation for future training.

Getting Buddy situated in his new home

Puppies love to explore new areas, but giving Buddy the run of the house, especially right away, can be overwhelming for him and can lead to trouble. Instead, prepare a specific room or area where he can get his bearings. Placing a baby gate across the entrance to that area can help keep him confined. Carry him into the house and place him in this safe area. In most households, the kitchen would be a good area because it has an easy-to-clean floor when puppy has an accident. Let him sniff around and get used to his new home. Have plenty of safe toys scattered around for him to play with.

The more activity the puppy has, the more he will have to relieve himself. Confining him to an area at first will greatly aid in his housetraining.

The first time you feed your puppy, place his food in his crate to introduce him to his den and establish the idea that the crate is where good things happen (see the earlier section "Puppy's home at home: Readying a crate"). Leave the door open when you feed him so he doesn't feel confined. Check out Chapter 8 for more information about getting your puppy used to staying in his crate.

Introducing puppies and kids

Teaching dogs and children to coexist can go well or badly depending on the boundaries you set. While small children generally can get along well with dogs — especially if their parents are comfortable around dogs — parents do have to make the effort to teach their children how interact correctly with the puppy. Specifically, parents have to do the following:

✔ They must be watchful that children don't pinch, pull out fur, twist ears, fall on, or chase the puppy.

✔ They need to monitor interactions between the children and the puppy. Children tend to run, squeal, and wear loose clothing, all of which incite the puppy's prey drive and encourage nipping. It is a parent's responsibility to discourage both behaviors.

✔ They should teach the children to be calm around the puppy and to gently pet Buddy.

✔ They must stop children from carrying the puppy, because they may drop him.

Tolerance for playing with children varies within and among breeds. Early exposure also is a factor. Dogs between the ages of 7 and 12 weeks that are exposed to well-behaved children generally get along well with kids. The most important thing a parent can teach the child is to have respect for the puppy, thereby fostering a harmonious relationship (see Figure 7-3).

Parents do both the child and the dog a favor if they insist that children keep their hands at their sides or cross them across their chest when around puppies or dogs they don't know. Of course, children also must be taught that they should *never* go up to a strange dog and try to pet him. Only after permission is sought from the owner is this acceptable.

Figure 7-3:
A har-
monious
relationship.

A *bolt hole,* or safe place where the dog can retreat and not be bothered by a child, is essential. When Buddy has had enough play and tries to hide under the bed, it's not a good idea to try to pull him out by the tail.

When our niece visited with her 2-year-old daughter, the toddler was entranced by the dogs, as they were with her. As the visit progressed and they got to know each other, the baby eventually began hanging on to a Labrador's tail as he pulled her around. She also loved to hug the dogs. The dogs tolerated this well, with tails wagging. When she decided to try to ride one like a horse, how- ever, that crossed the line — he went into his crate. Undeterred, the toddler followed him and tried to get into the crate with him — this isn't a good idea even with the most tolerant of dogs. We settled the matter by closing the crate.

The moral of the story is that the bolt hole, whatever and wherever it may be, has to be available to the dog when he has had enough. Look at it like locking the bathroom door! For more on puppies and dogs, see *Puppies For Dummies,* 2nd Edition, by Sarah Hodgson.

Meeting resident pets

When you already have a dog and Buddy is a new addition to your house- hold, you need to stage the introduction. You can't assume that the resident dog will automatically accept Buddy.

We introduce a new member of the family to an older dog by first placing them both on leash. We take the older dog outside to the front of the house, which is neutral territory. We then carry the puppy from the car to the front and let the two meet on leash. Let your older dog sniff the puppy from top to toe. Puppies at this age often turn upside down and pee. In dog language this is a sign of great respect.

When the older dog has satisfied his curiosity, let him invite the puppy into the house. You need to keep an eye on the interaction between the two. Above all, make as much fuss over the older dog as you do over the puppy. You don't want to create the impression that he's being replaced. If the introduction goes badly, alternate between crating the resident dog and the puppy until they get used to each other. For introductions to a resident cat, see Chapter 1.

Tending to his potty needs

Housetraining your puppy can be a challenge, but it doesn't have to be a nightmare. We devote Chapter 8 to the topic, so flip ahead for expert advice on establishing a schedule.

Here's what you need to keep in mind when you first bring your puppy home:

- ✔ Establish a toilet area in your yard, and take Buddy there after he wakes up, shortly after he eats or drinks, and after he has played or chewed.

- ✔ When you see Buddy sniffing and circling, take note! He's letting you know that he's looking for a place to go. When you see this behavior, take him out to his toilet area so he doesn't have an accident in the house.

- ✔ After 8 p.m., remove his water dish so he has a better chance of lasting through the night without having to potty.

Deciding where your puppy should sleep

We can't stress enough the importance of sleep for your growing puppy. After all, he's a baby and needs lots of sleep to grow properly, digest his food, and stay calm. Puppies that don't get enough sleep often get overstimulated and bite at hands, have more accidents, and get whiny. Establish a schedule in which your puppy is crated in a quiet place for a couple hours after morning playtime and again after subsequent play periods during the day.

If he gets whiny when you crate him, put a few small treats into one of the Planet Dog balls or a Kong toy. Playing with these toys will use up the excess energy and help him fall asleep quickly.

At night, you have some choices for where your puppy will spend his sleeping time. Puppies hate to be alone, so if you isolate the puppy from you, the first week or so he will scream louder and louder until you can't stand it any longer. He's preprogrammed to do so; he's telling his mother that he's lost and to come find him.

A few words about vaccinations

Many breeders vaccinate their puppies before they go to their new homes. Research is showing, however, that puppies from a healthy, well-cared-for mother don't need vaccines until they're 12 weeks old because they retain immunity from their mothers. One of the newer vaccines on the market is the Intervet Canine Distemper-Adenovirus Type 2-Parvo Vaccine. The vaccine is given at 12 weeks, with a booster at 16 weeks, and is guaranteed for three years of immunity.

A small number of puppies show allergic reactions to vaccines. If you notice swelling, limping, nausea, or diarrhea after a vaccination, consult your veterinarian immediately. Some puppies seem under the weather for a couple days after vaccination. If your puppy gets a little irritable or has accidents in the house, be patient. If you've started your training, let it go for the same amount of time. Puppies don't learn when they're stressed. The homeopathic remedy Thuja works well to counteract vaccine reactions (see Chapter 4).

If for any reason you have to leave your puppy in a boarding kennel during these early months and vaccinations are required, make sure the vaccine is given three weeks prior to his visit. The immune system takes this long to build antibodies to parvovirus and distemper. Refer to Chapter 4 for more information on vaccinations.

The best idea is to have a crate by the side of your bed, using it as a bedside table (see Figure 7-4). Put the puppy in the crate when you go to bed, and he'll be happy to snuggle down knowing you're close by. If he gets anxious, you can put your fingers through the crate to reassure him that you're there and he isn't alone.

Figure 7-4:
A crate as a bedside table.

If your puppy is part of a multidog household, you can leave all the animals together in the same sleeping area so the puppy has company. Make sure the crate has a soft blanket and large soft toy in it so the puppy stays warm.

Starting Buddy's Education

Puppies love to learn, and they'll learn with or without you. Naturally, you want to teach Buddy what *you* want him to learn. The lessons puppies learn between 7 and 12 weeks of age they'll retain for a lifetime. At this age, Buddy is still easy to physically control. The older he gets and the larger he grows, the more difficult the task becomes — and the more unpleasant it gets for your dog. The best time to start is now. In the following sections, we show you the most important exercises to start with when educating your puppy.

Name recognition

One of the first exercises you want to tackle is name recognition. As obvious as it seems, we meet an amazing number of dogs who don't respond to their names. Training by giving a command to a dog who doesn't respond to his name has little chance for success.

Start with the puppy close by in a distraction-free environment. Say his name and, with a treat, lure him to look at your face. Start with the treat directly in front of his nose and let him follow it with his eyes to your face before you give him the treat. When he does, say "Good dog" and give him the treat. Repeat three to five times.

Review this over the course of several sessions. As he catches on and looks at you when you say his name, start increasing the level of difficulty by calling his name from farther away and, ultimately, when he's distracted.

At the same time, you can start on the Touch command (see Chapter 10), which is the start of the Come exercise. It took our latest Dachshund puppy, Fritz, three days to respond to the command, which we taught him off leash and in the form of a game.

Getting your puppy used to his duds

Prior to starting your training, Buddy will need to get used to wearing his buckle collar. Put this collar on Buddy after his nap, take him outside to relieve himself, and let him eat with his collar on. At first he may scratch at it, because he isn't used to having something around his neck. As he gets used to wearing his collar, the scratching will stop.

After he's comfortable with his collar, introduce Buddy to his leash. Attach the leash to his collar and let him drag it around the room. You need to keep an eye on him so the leash doesn't get entangled. Don't pick up the leash just yet.

When he's comfortable with the leash tagging along behind him, your next step is to get Buddy used to walking on leash while you're holding it. At this age, if you try to get your puppy away from home using your leash, he may resist. He doesn't want to leave home, and you'll wind up dragging him, giving him a negative feeling about his leash. Instead, pick him up and carry him a short distance from the house. At that point, he'll happily lead you back. After several repetitions he'll get used to his leash. Make it fun for your puppy and give him the occasional treat to motivate him to keep moving.

When you're ready to start doing some training with your puppy, you have to put the snap-around collar on him. Start with you and your dog facing each other. Then follow these steps to place the snap-around collar on your dog:

1. **Take the two rings in your right hand.**

   See Figure 7-5a.

2. **Place the collar under your dog's neck and bring the ends up to the top of his neck, directly behind the ears.**

   Figure 7-5b shows the proper placement of the collar in this step. *Remember:* When you begin to put on the collar, the dog flexes his neck muscles, expanding the circumference of the neck by as much as a half inch, creating the impression that the collar is much tighter than it actually is (similar to the effect produced by a horse taking in air as it's being saddled).

3. **Attach the clasp to the floating ring.**

   Refer to Chapter 5 to identify which ring is the floating ring. The smooth side of the clasp needs to be next to the dog's skin. See Figure 7-5c to see what this step should look like.

4. **Attach your leash to the stationary ring, and you're ready to go.**

   Check out Figure 7-5d to see where to attach your leash.

After you get the collar on your dog, you may get the impression that it's much too tight and that you can barely get it around Buddy's neck. We suggest that after the first time you put the collar on, you wait for five minutes. After the dog has relaxed, you then can test for correct snugness. You need to be able to slip two fingers between the collar and your dog's neck (one finger if you have a toy dog). If your fingers won't fit, the collar is too tight; if you can get three or more fingers through, the collar is too loose. One way to make the collar smaller is to tie a knot in it and then attach it as you normally would.

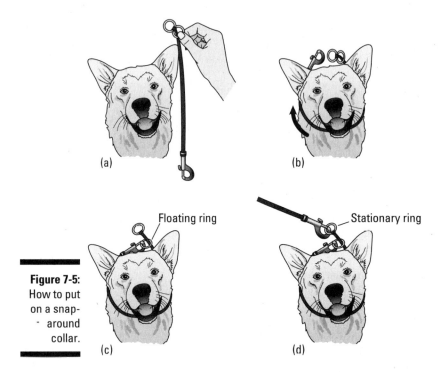

(a)   (b)

Floating ring   Stationary ring

Figure 7-5:
How to put
on a snap-
around
collar.

(c)   (d)

Training for grooming

You can do much of the routine care a dog needs yourself without having to lay out a small fortune for someone else to do it for you. Examples are brushing, bathing, trimming nails, cleaning ears, and brushing teeth. If you start the grooming training when puppy first comes home, Buddy will accept it and you'll have a puppy that you can groom for the rest of his life. Start now while Buddy is small; this way you can manage to pick him up and put him on a table. The most successful time to introduce grooming is after puppy has had a playtime or has exercised.

The equipment you need for grooming depends on the kind of dog you have, because the type of dog you have dictates generally how much grooming he needs. Even shorthaired dogs require some brushing. Regular grooming saves on vacuuming.

For more information on how to make your puppy look his best, see *Dog Grooming For Dummies* by Margaret H. Bonham.

Brushing your puppy

Instead of trying to groom Buddy with both of you struggling on the floor, start by putting him on a table. Grooming on a table is comfortable for you and has a calming effect on your dog. If you have a longhaired breed, he'll need to get used to spending a lot of time on a table. If you have a large-breed dog, you may need the assistance of a family member to get him on the table.

Any solid table will do, but you need to place a towel on it to prevent the puppy from slipping. Lift Buddy onto the table and give him a treat. Gently stroke him all over his body. When he relaxes on the table, bring out your soft-bristle brush and let him smell it. Put a treat on the table, and when he's occupied with it, gently brush his body, mimicking what you did when you stroked him. (Figure 7-6 shows how to groom a puppy.) Give a treat each time you brush another body part. Doing so will keep him occupied, so he won't try to play with the brush. If you follow this routine daily, Buddy will look forward to his grooming sessions.

Even if your puppy is shorthaired, you need to brush him at least once a week, if not more. Brushing is essential in stimulating the skin; it keeps the skin healthy by bringing blood to the surface. Short hair is more difficult to vacuum up than long hair.

When a pup reaches 3 to 5 months, he'll start to lose his puppy coat. It starts on the tail, goes up the spine, and then falls out each side of his body. Before it sheds out, his coat gets dull; the fur is dead and is making room for the adult coat to come in. Keeping puppy brushed helps keep dog fur off the floor and your clothes.

Figure 7-6:
Grooming a puppy on a table.

Bathing your puppy

Even in the best of households, puppies get into things that smell. We walk our dogs at a horse farm, and horse poop is a favorite for rolling. No one wants to spend time with a smelly puppy, so Buddy needs to learn to be bathed.

Various opinions exist concerning how often a dog should be bathed. The simple answer is that you should give Buddy a bath when he smells like a dog or has rolled in something stinky. Heaven forbid he should have an encounter with a skunk.

You can use the bathtub or the shower, or you can bathe him outside, weather permitting (see Figure 7-7). When you first put Buddy into the bathtub or shower, let him calm down before you turn on the water. When you finally turn it on, go slowly and let him look at it. (The water should be quite warm but not hot.) If you're using a sprayer, spray away from him first so he can get used to the sound and sight of the spray. Then, starting at his neck and shoulders, wet his body down to his back legs and tail. Continually tell him what a good boy he is. Keep your voice light and encouraging.

Figure 7-7:
Bathing
your puppy.

If your puppy is too bouncy, have a collar on him so you can control him with one hand. Or have a family member hold him by the collar while you bathe him.

After you wet the puppy down, rub shampoo all over. (Use a coconut oil–based shampoo that has the correct pH for puppy skin and doesn't take the oil out of his coat.) Avoid Buddy's head; bathe only from the neck down. You don't want to get water in his eyes or ears; doing so will scare him. Rinse him carefully, making sure no soap is left in the fur. Lift puppy out of the sink or shower and put him on the same towel-covered table you're using for grooming. With a treat held just above his nose, have him sit and then gently rub him dry with a towel. (See Figure 7-8.) While he's on the table, you can wash his face with a wet facecloth, but be sure to stay away from his eyes. After his bath, keep him in a warm area until he's completely dry.

Figure 7-8:
Drying
puppy after
a bath.

Trimming nails

Your puppy's nails need trimming when you can hear him coming on a hardwood floor. Trimming his nails isn't as difficult as it sounds. First, get him accustomed to having his nails touched. To do so, wait until he's relaxed and then play with his feet, touching each nail. You also can do this during your grooming sessions.

After you have your puppy used to having his nails and toes touched, put Buddy on the table you're using to groom. Put him in a position in which he's comfortable, whether that be sitting or laying down. Using a nail clipper, cut just the tip of one nail. Chances are, the puppy will squeak, not so much out of discomfort, but because it's a new experience. Give him a treat. When he's comfortable with having one nail done, try doing just one foot. Remember to clip the little dewclaws on the side of his front legs. Do the same thing for four days, and you'll have all the nails trimmed.

You also can use a grinder, such as a Dremel tool, to grind his nails or to smooth out the edges after you've trimmed them. This type of tool makes quite a bit of noise, so it pays off to spend a little time letting Buddy see the grinder and smell it when it's turned off and when it's turned on, without using it on his nails. Some puppies are sound sensitive, so we don't suggest using it for these pups. Have Buddy lie down on the grooming table, treats between his paws, and just try one nail at a time. Over a few days you can get all the nails done.

You may need a family member or friend to help you hold the puppy suffi-ciently still so you can clip his nails.

Cleaning ears

Part of your weekly grooming needs include cleaning your puppy's ears. Prick-eared dogs, such as German Shepherds or Corgis, don't need ear clean-ing as frequently as floppy-eared dogs, who seem to vacuum up dirt with their hanging ears. The earflaps of my Dachshunds and Labradors need weekly cleaning.

To get started, have Buddy sit or lay down on the grooming table and gently play with his ears. Lift up the ears flaps on the floppy-eared dog or stroke the prick ear before you start to clean it. Give Buddy a treat and tell him what a good boy he is.

When you and Buddy are both ready to start cleaning, combine in a spray bottle a mixture of half apple cider vinegar and half water. Spray a small amount onto a cotton ball and gently clean the part of the ear that you can see. If you don't know what you're doing, going farther into the ear canal is dangerous — leave that deep cleaning to your vet.

Cleaning the pearly whites

The last part of your weekly grooming session is to check Buddy's teeth. Buddy's mouth is the gateway to his overall health. First, get him used to his mouth being handled. Gently lift his lips on each side of his mouth and touch his teeth. At first, most puppies fight having their mouths handled. But be patient; Buddy will get used to the feeling.

With Buddy on the grooming table, put your arm around his neck and shoul-ders. After he's comfortably positioned, lift his lips on each side. Give him a treat. Then you're ready to wet a cotton ball with warm water and gently wipe his teeth. Give him another treat. By following this process, you're train-ing Buddy to accept his mouth and teeth being touched.

As he grows older, you can introduce a soft toothbrush, which should be used weekly when he's an adult. A human toothbrush is suitable, but a dog toothpaste (which is flavored for his palate) makes the process more enjoy-able for Buddy.

Training Buddy to accept this routine is one of the most important things you can do for him, because as an adult, Buddy's teeth can get coated with tartar that will inflame his gums. Gum disease produces bacteria that have been implicated in heart disease, stroke, and some cancers.

Solving Perplexing Puppy Problems

In this section, we deal with some of the more commonly asked questions we get in our puppy classes about health conditions that interfere with house-training and training in general. Check out this list of behaviors:

- ✔ **My puppy pees small amounts frequently even though I take him outside regularly.** The stress of leaving his mother and littermates along with a long journey to his new home can cause a puppy to get an infection called *cystitis*. It's an inflammation of the bladder, making the puppy think he has to urinate frequently. What you see is puppy straining and producing a few drops of urine. Don't ignore this symptom and think it will get better — it won't. Cystitis can wreak havoc with your housetraining efforts, so be sure to make an appointment with your veterinarian.

- ✔ **My puppy doesn't want to eat his food.** Find out what your breeder fed the puppy before he left home. Try to get some of that food and see if merely the change in diet has affected his appetite. Also take a look at Chapter 4 for dietary suggestions.

  A puppy on medication may have an upset tummy and not feel like eating. Try feeding small meals often. If your puppy is on certain antibiotics, the lack of appetite generally disappears after the medication is stopped. If all else fails, you can drop goat's milk and honey ($^1/_2$ cup of goat's milk to 1 teaspoon honey) into the side of his mouth with an eyedropper, to get him going. After he starts to eat, he'll generally continue. Stop training until he feels better.

  When a puppy is teething (anywhere from 4 to 6 months, depending on the breed), his mouth gets sore. Food can get stuck in the teeth, so you'll often see puppy running his face along the floor or against the couch. Gently put your index finger into the puppy's mouth to clear out anything that's stuck. Provide lots of toys and bones to gnaw on during this teething period. Buddy has to chew to loosen the baby teeth. If he has baby teeth that aren't coming out, an occurrence that's common in toy dogs, take him to your veterinarian. Again, stop training until your puppy feels better.

- ✔ **My puppy has to take pills, and I don't know how to give them.** As a matter of course, teach your puppy to take food off a spoon. Put a little of his favorite food on the end of a teaspoon and encourage him to eat it. At first he'll want to lick it off, but after several repetitions, he'll open his mouth. You can then scrape the food onto the back of his front teeth. Do this on a regular basis, and your puppy will readily take food from a spoon.

  Now when you have to give him a pill, you can hide it in some food on the spoon and he'll willingly take it. You can put the pill into peanut butter, butter, sour cream, yogurt, meat, or anything your dog likes.

✔ **My puppy eats stools when outside.** Various causes are attributed to this habit, but it's usually a sign that the food you're feeding your puppy isn't suitable for him. Pups eat stools to get undigested nutrients they're lacking in their own food. One way to stop the behavior is to keep the yard picked up. You also may want to take a look at the feeding suggestions in Chapter 4.

Some dogs are partial to horse poop or cat poop. This behavior is objectionable to you, but it won't do Buddy any harm. With the Leave It command, you should be able to stop it.

✔ **My puppy constantly bites me when I handle him.** When the puppy mouths you too hard, yell "Ouch" in a loud tone of voice. Then distract the puppy with a toy. In most instances, it takes only a couple times for the puppy to catch on that this isn't acceptable behavior. Some puppies are more persistent than others, in which case you may have to take Buddy gently by the scruff of the neck and lift his front paws off the ground.

Our own Lab, Annabelle, constantly bit our hands when she first came to us, sometimes drawing blood. We then noticed that she had cystitis; after we treated the condition, her biting behavior stopped. Such behavior also may occur just after vaccinations.

✔ **Should I worm my puppy frequently?** Don't worm your puppy without first taking a fecal sample to your veterinarian to be tested. If your puppy has worms, your veterinarian will give you the appropriate medicine for that particular worm. Stay away from wormers in supermarkets or pet stores. Having your puppy ingest too many chemicals at a young age is dangerous, upsets his stomach, and makes him feel unwell. If you do find that he has worms and isn't feeling well, stop training until he feels better.

✔ **Is it safe to use flea and tick products with my puppy?** Ask the advice of your veterinarian on how to deal with ticks and fleas. You'll find many products on the market, but you need to make sure that if you choose to use one it's safe and nontoxic to your puppy.

Ticks can carry Lyme disease, for which there's a vaccine. If you live in an area where ticks are prevalent, be vigilant with your puppy, especially in wooded areas. The most common symptoms of Lyme disease include muscle aches and fatigue. If he does come down with Lyme disease, your dog won't feel much like training, so give him a few days off.

Chapter 8

Honing In on Housetraining

As with any training, some dogs catch on more readily to housetraining than others. As a general rule, most dogs don't present a problem, provided that you do your part. To speed along the process, we strongly recommend that you use a crate or similar means of confinement.

Initially, you may recoil from this concept as cruel and inhumane. Nothing could be further from the truth. Using a crate to housetrain your puppy is the most humane and effective way to get the job done. It's also the easiest way, because of the dog's natural desire to keep his den clean. You'll discover that Buddy likes his crate and that you can enjoy your peace of mind.

This chapter covers the keys to successful housetraining:

✔ Appropriately using a crate or X-pen

✔ Setting a schedule for feeding and exercising, and sticking to that schedule even on weekends — at least until your dog is housetrained and mature

✔ Practicing vigilance, vigilance, and vigilance until your dog is trained

If you've obtained an adult dog from a shelter or other source, he may not be housetrained. For example, if he was tied on a chain outside, he most certainly won't be. The rules for housetraining an adult dog are the same as for a puppy, but the process likely will go much more quickly. The adult dog's ability to control elimination is obviously much better than a puppy's.

For a great deal more information on this subject, see *Housetraining For Dummies,* 2nd Edition, by Susan McCullough (Wiley).

Helping Buddy Get Used to His Crate

Crate training your dog provides peace of mind for you and a safe place for your dog when he needs some peace and quiet and wants to get away from the hubbub of family life. For your dog, a crate is his den where he can relax, take naps, and not be bothered. A crate is his home away from home when you travel, and it provides safety for both of you when he's with you in the car.

To help get Buddy comfortable with his crate, lure him into it with a treat, close the door, tell him what a good puppy he is, and then let him out again. Each time you do this, leave him in the crate a little longer with the door closed, still giving him a treat and telling him how great he is. Finally, put him in his crate, give him a treat, and then leave the room — first for 5 minutes, then 10 minutes, then 15 minutes, and so on. Each time you return to let him out, tell him how good he was before you open the door.

In the rare instances in which a puppy violently objects to being crated, use an X-pen instead. If you have acquired an older dog or a rescue, you may encounter a dog that objects to being crated, more than likely because he has a negative association with a crate. An X-pen should solve that problem.

You also can feed Buddy in the crate. Place his bowl in front of the crate and let him eat. The next time you feed him, place the food just inside the crate. With every successive meal, put the bowl farther inside the crate until it's at the far end. With each successive feeding, increase the length of time you leave him in his crate with the door closed. Take a look at Figure 8-1 to see a dog enjoying a meal in his crate.

Use this opportunity to teach him the Crate command. As you put his meal into the crate, say "Crate." It won't take long before he'll go into his crate on command, especially if he's rewarded with a treat or meal. Thereafter, you can put him on a random reward schedule.

Be sure to give Buddy something fun to keep him occupied when you leave. Interactive toys stuffed with treats, or a Kong with treats inside, are a wonderful way to make the crate fun.

How long can you ultimately leave Buddy in his crate unattended? That depends on your dog and your schedule. Adult dogs can stay in a crate for up to four to six hours. Puppies can't last that long, though. Over the course of a 24-hour period, puppies have to eliminate more frequently than adult dogs. A puppy's ability to control elimination increases with age, at the rate of about one hour per month. Until he's 6 months of age, don't expect a puppy to last for more than four hours during the day without having to eliminate.

When sleeping, most puppies can last through the night. If you have a female puppy and you notice frequent urinary accidents, it could be a sign of a bladder infection called *cystitis.* A trip to the vet can confirm this condition.

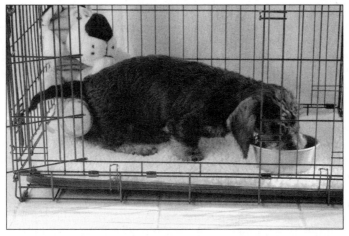

Figure 8-1:
Feeding
a puppy in
a crate.

Establishing a Daily Feeding and Elimination Schedule

Dogs thrive on a regular routine, and you'll come to love it, too: A strict schedule is one of your greatest assets in housetraining. By feeding and exercising Buddy at about the same time every day, you're teaching him to relieve himself at about the same time every day. After the two of you have established a schedule, you can project when he'll need to relieve himself and help him to be in the right spot at the right time.

From 7 weeks to 4 months of age, puppies need to be fed four times a day. Set a time to feed the puppy that's convenient for you, and aim to feed at the same time every day. Depending on your schedule, you may establish a comfortable routine of feeding at 8 a.m., noon, 4 p.m., and 8 p.m. This schedule works well if you go to bed around 11 p.m. and can take the puppy out before you retire for the night. Adjust the schedule to the time you normally get up in the morning.

For a puppy age 4 to 7 months, three daily meals are appropriate. From then on, feed twice a day. Feeding frequent small meals keeps your puppy calm, helps him grow evenly, and controls the time when he relieves himself. Also give your puppy a dog biscuit before bedtime to help him sleep through the night.

Feed the right amount. Loose stools are a sign of overfeeding; straining and dry stools are signs of underfeeding or a poor diet. Be sure to keep Buddy's diet constant and feed the same brand of food at every meal. Abrupt changes in food may cause digestive upsets that won't help your housetraining efforts. See Chapter 4 for more on your feeding options.

For the sake of convenience, you may be tempted to put Buddy's meal in a large bowl and leave it for him to nibble on as he sees fit, a practice called *self-feeding.* Although self-feeding is convenient, for purposes of housetraining, don't do it: You won't be able to keep track of when and how much Buddy eats. You won't be able to time his intake with his need to eliminate. Don't prolong mealtimes, either: After ten minutes, pick up the dish and put it away.

Make fresh water available at all times during the day. If Buddy will be in his crate for more than two hours, leave a dish of fresh water in the crate. You also can attach a little water bucket to the inside of the crate. After 8 p.m., remove his water dish so he can last through the night without having to make a trip outside.

If you're following a regular feeding routine, you're promoting a regular elimination routine, too. Puppies' biological clocks are astonishingly consistent — to see for yourself, write down the times your puppy relieves himself. A puppy usually has a bowel movement several times a day and urinates perhaps six to eight times.

Take Buddy to his toilet area after waking up, shortly after eating or drinking, and after he has played or chewed. Of course, you need to be aware of his unique elimination needs, too. Some puppies need to eliminate more than once in a relatively short period of time. When Fritz, our Dachshund, was a puppy, we immediately took him out when he woke up in the morning. He dutifully relieved himself and came back into the house. Half an hour later, however, he needed to go again. After that, he was good to go for several hours.

When you see your puppy sniffing and circling, take note! He's letting you know that he's looking for a place to go. Take him out to his toilet area so he doesn't have an accident in the house. Use the same door each time you go outside, saying, "Time to go out." At around 11 to 12 weeks, your puppy will ask to go outside by going to the door you have been using.

Designating a Regular Toilet Area

Start by selecting a toilet area. Always take Buddy to that spot when you want him to eliminate. If possible, pick a place in a straight line from the house. You can carry your puppy or put him on leash. Stand still, be patient, and let him sniff around and concentrate on what he's doing. When he's done, tell him what a clever puppy he is and play with him for a few minutes.

Don't take him directly back inside: You don't want to give him the idea that he gets to go outside only to do his business, because he'll learn to delay the process just to stay outside. There will be occasions when you don't have time to play with him; in those instances, just take him back inside.

Witnessing the act of your puppy relieving himself outside, followed by allowing playtime, is perhaps one of the most important parts of housetraining. The first sign of not spending enough time outside with your puppy is that he comes back inside and has an accident. Letting the puppy out by himself isn't good enough — you have to go with him until his schedule has been developed.

Where you live dictates your housetraining strategies. In a city, where dogs have to be curbed to relieve themselves, you need to keep Buddy on leash. If you have a fenced yard and don't mind where he goes, you can let him off leash. If you want him kept to a particular spot, keep him on leash.

No matter where you live — in the city, in a neighborhood, or in the country — you also need to pick up after him. Even in your own yard, unless you have oodles of land, you need to pick up after him, for obvious sanitary reasons. And don't let him do his business in a neighbor's yard — not even in the yard of that crotchety neighbor who yelled at your children.

You also may want to teach Buddy a command, such as Hurry Up, so you can speed up the process when necessary. Time the command to just before he starts and then lavishly praise when he has finished. After several repetitions, Buddy will associate the command with having to eliminate. The Hurry Up command is useful when you're traveling with your dog, and it gets him used to eliminating on leash.

Colette, a star housetraining pupil

First thing in the morning, Mary takes her 12-week-old poodle puppy, Colette, out of her crate and straight outside to her toilet area. Fifteen minutes after Colette's morning meal, Mary lets her out again. Mary then crates Colette and leaves for work.

On her lunch break, Mary goes home to let Colette out to relieve herself, and she plays with her for a few minutes. She then feeds her and, just to make sure, takes her out once more. For the afternoon, Mary crates Colette again until she returns. When she gets home, she walks and feeds Colette and allows her to spend the rest of the evening in the house where Mary can keep an eye on her. Before bedtime, Colette goes out to her toilet area one more time and is then crated for the night.

When Colette turns 7 months old, Mary will drop the noontime feeding and walk. From that age on, most dogs need to go out only immediately upon waking (or soon afterward) in the morning, once during the late afternoon, and once again before bedtime.

Special care is required when it's raining or is cold because many dogs, particularly those with short hair, don't like to go out in the wet anymore than you do. Make sure the puppy actually eliminates before you bring him back into the house.

Handling Accidents Appropriately

No matter how conscientious and vigilant you are, your puppy will have accidents. Housetraining accidents may be simple mistakes or may indicate a physical problem. The key to remember is that, as a general rule, dogs want to be clean. Also remember that accidents are just that — accidents. Your dog didn't do it on purpose.

When Buddy has an accident in the house, don't call him to you to punish him. It's too late. If you do punish your dog under these circumstances, it won't help your housetraining efforts, and you'll make him wary of wanting to come to you (thus hampering his learning of the Come command later).

A popular misconception is that the dog knows "what he did" because he looks "guilty." Absolutely not so! He has that look because, from prior experience, he knows that when you happen to come across a mess, you get mad at him. He has learned to associate a mess with your response. He hasn't made — and can't make — the connection between having made the mess in the first place and your anger. Discipline after the fact is the quickest way to undermine the relationship you're trying to build with your dog.

Dogs are smart, but they don't associate what happened some time ago with belated consequences. When you come home from work and yell at your dog for having an accident in the living room, all you're doing is letting him know that you are angry. Swatting your dog with a rolled-up newspaper is cruel and only makes him afraid of you and rolled-up newspapers. Rubbing his nose in it is unsanitary and disgusting. Dogs may become housetrained in spite of such antics, but certainly not because of them.

Depending on the situation, you should handle accidents in different ways. Consider the following:

- ✔ **When you come upon a belated accident:** Keep calm and put your dog out of sight so he can't watch you clean up (seeing you clean up attracts him to the spot). Use white vinegar or an enzyme stain remover. Don't use ammonia-based cleaners, because the ammonia doesn't neutralize the odor and the puppy will be attracted to the same spot.

✔ **When you catch your dog in the act:** If you see Buddy squatting in the living room, sharply call his name and clap your hands. If he stops, take him to his toilet area. If he doesn't, let him finish and don't get mad. Don't try to drag him out, because that will make your clean-up job that much more difficult. Until your puppy is reliable, don't let him have the run of the house unsupervised.

Regressions in housetraining do occur, especially during teething or just after vaccinations. Regressions after 6 months of age may be a sign that your dog is ill. If accidents persist, take him to your vet for a checkup.

When we travel with one or more of our dogs, we make it a point to keep to the regular feeding schedule and exercise routine as closely as possible. Sticking to customary daily rhythm prevents digestive upsets that can lead to accidents.

Dealing with Different Situations

Dogs are kept in various living conditions. Many live with their owners in apartments, others in suburban settings, and still others on large pieces of property. Their owners may work and be away for long periods, or they have someone at home with them for most of the day. Whatever the situation, the necessary adjustments need to be made.

What to do about an apartment dog

Many dogs live in apartments, and their owners have to jump through a variety of hoops, including taking elevators and stairs, to get their dogs outside. Moreover, if the owner is mobility impaired, taking the dog outside may be a real challenge.

Presumably, an apartment dog is a small dog. In any event, the easiest way to housetrain an apartment dog is to first follow the regimen by using a crate or an X-pen (see the following section).

You also can find portable indoor dog potties: rectangular, three-layer systems topped with antibacterial artificial grass. A grate or tray under the grass makes cleanup easy. These are ideal for small dogs as an aid in housetraining. You use the same basic housetraining techniques as noted earlier in the chapter, except that the dog doesn't go outside. They're similar to cat litter boxes. These indoor dog potties are discussed in further detail in *Housetraining For Dummies,* 2nd Edition, by Susan McCullough (Wiley).

When you're away for most of the day: Using an exercise pen for housetraining

Although a puppy can last in his crate for the night when he's asleep, you can't leave a puppy in his crate for purposes of housetraining for longer than four hours at a time during the day. Your puppy will soil his crate, which definitely isn't a habit you want to establish.

If your schedule doesn't allow you to keep an eye on Buddy during the day or come home to let the puppy out in time, the alternative is an exercise pen, or X-pen. An X-pen (see Figure 8-2) is intelligent confinement and uses the same principle as a crate, except that it's bigger and has no top. An X-pen also can be used outdoors.

Figure 8-2:
An X-pen is another form of containment.

First, you need to acquire an X-pen that's appropriate for the size of your dog. For a dog the size of a Labrador, the X-pen needs to be 10 square feet. For a smaller dog, 6 square feet should be plenty. Set up the X-pen where the puppy will be confined during your absence. If your dog is a super athlete who either climbs over or jumps out of the X-pen, you have to cover the pen with a piece of plywood or pegboard.

To get your dog comfortable in his X-pen, follow the same procedure as you did when introducing him to his crate (see "Helping Buddy Get Used to His Crate," earlier in this chapter). When Buddy is feeling at home in the X-pen and you're ready to leave him for the day, cover one-third of the area with newspapers (no, Buddy isn't going to read the sports section). Buddy will get the hint and eliminate on the newspaper. Cover one-third of the remaining area with a blanket, adding some interactive toys or a biscuit. Finally, leave one-third uncovered.

As he gets older and his ability to control the elimination process improves, gradually reduce the area covered with paper until you can remove it altogether. Because a dog's natural desire is to keep his "den" clean, the process should be completed by the time he is 4 to 6 months of age.

Buddy needs to have access to water during the day, so put his water dish on the uncovered area in the corner of the X-pen close to his bed (some water is bound to splash out, and the uncovered floor is easy to clean). Leave while he's occupied with his toys or the biscuit. Don't make a big deal out of leaving — simply leave.

Some people try to rig up confinement areas by blocking off parts of a room. Theoretically, this works, but it does permit Buddy to chew the baseboard, corners of cabinets, or anything else he can get his teeth on. You may want to confine your dog to part of a room with baby gates. This option works well for some people and some dogs, but remember, it's no holds barrier for whatever items Buddy can access. Lots of chew toys are a must!

Whatever barrier you decide to try, don't use an accordion-type gate — he could stick his head through it and possibly strangle himself. Also, leaving a dog on a concrete surface isn't a good idea. Something about concrete impedes housetraining; many dogs don't understand why it can't be used as a toilet area. Concrete also wreaks havoc on the elbows of large breeds.

You'll find that, in the long run, your least expensive option — as is so often the case — is the right way from the start. Don't be penny-wise and pound-foolish by scrimping on the essentials at the risk of jeopardizing more expensive items. Splurging for an X-pen now will probably save you money on your home improvement budget down the road.

Doing your doody

Being a good dog neighbor means not letting Buddy deface the property of others, including pottying in their yards. When Buddy's got to go, use only areas specifically designed for dog elimination. Even diehard dog lovers object to other dogs leaving their droppings on their lawn, the streets, and similar unsuitable areas. They also object to having their shrubbery or other vertical objects on their property doused by Buddy when he lifts his leg. If Buddy must potty in someone's yard, you need to be ready for poop-scooping duty. After all, part of responsible dog ownership is cleaning up after your dog. Don't let Buddy become the curse of your neighborhood. Do unto others . . . .

Part III
Tackling Training Basics

The 5th Wave   By Rich Tennant

"Down, Skippy, down!! Mike has tried so hard
to socialize this dog so we can have people
over without being embarrassed, but evidently
he needs a few more lessons."

In this part . . .

The chapters in this part deal with the basic commands every well-behaved dog needs to learn — Sit, Down, Stay, Leave It, and Come — as well as door manners and walking on leash without pulling. These commands aren't difficult to teach, but they're important for your safety and his.

Also included is a chapter on dealing with common doggie don'ts, such as jumping on people, counter surfing, incessant barking, and similar nuisance behaviors.

Chapter 9

Mastering Some Fundamentals: Sit, Down, Stay, and Leave It

For the most part, basic training deals with teaching your dog to stop doing what *he* wants to do and instead do what *you* want him to do. The exercises in this chapter are called *impulse control exercises* — they teach Buddy a little self-control.

When teaching Buddy these exercises, say your commands in a quiet tone of voice. Your dog's hearing is about 80 times better than yours, and quiet commands will teach your dog to be attentive to you. Commands also shouldn't be posed as questions. It is "Sit!" and not "Sit?" Your verbal praise needs to be upbeat and sincere.

Your training sessions should be short — ideally two 10- to 15-minute sessions a day. And be sure to finish on a happy, positive note. Doing so is critical because you want Buddy to look forward to these sessions and to get excited when you take out his training collar and leash.

Sit! Good Boy

The Sit command gives you a wonderfully easy way to control Buddy when you need it most. It's also one of the basic commands that you and your dog can quickly accomplish. We show you everything you need to know in the following sections.

The Sit is one of the most useful exercises you can teach Buddy. You can use it for all of these things:

- When you walk in the street and stop at the curb or a traffic light
- When you meet your neighbor and want to catch up on neighborhood news
- Before Buddy goes up and down stairs
- Before he goes through doors
- When guests arrive and you don't want Buddy to jump on them

Getting Buddy into a sitting position

We provide two ways to begin teaching Buddy to sit. Sitting with a treat works for most dogs, but you also need a method to make Buddy sit when a treat doesn't work. Spend some time teaching this exercise in different locations so Buddy can generalize this exercise.

To teach Buddy to sit using a treat, follow these steps:

1. **Show Buddy a small, bite-sized treat; hold it just a little in front of his eyes, slightly above his head. Say "Sit" as you bring your hand an inch or so above his eyes and over his head, to lure him into the sitting position.**

   When using this method of teaching your dog to sit, notice the position your hand is in compared to the dog's head. If your hand is held too high, your dog will jump up; if it's too low, he won't sit. Hold your hand about an inch or so above his head. (Figure 9-1 shows the proper position.)

2. **When he sits, give him the treat and tell him what a good puppy he is.**

   Some dogs catch on to this idea so quickly that they sit in front of their owners whenever they want a treat.

   Tell him without petting him. If you pet him at the same time as you praise him, he'll probably get up, but what you really want him to do is sit. *Praising* is verbal, such as saying "Good" or "Good dog" in a pleasant tone of voice. *Rewarding* is giving the dog a treat for a correct response while he's still in position. For example, if your dog gets up after you've told him to sit, and you then give him a treat, you're rewarding his getting up, not the sit.

If Buddy isn't interested in treats or doesn't respond on his own, you need to physically place him in a sit. Here's how:

1. **With Buddy on your left, kneel next to him, with both of you facing in the same direction.**

   If Buddy is a small dog, you can put him on a table.

2. **Place your right hand against his chest and your left hand on top of his shoulders. Say "Sit" and run your left hand over his back, all the way down to his knees, and with equal pressure of both hands, collapsing him into a sit.**

3. **Keep your hands in place to the count of five and verbally praise Buddy, saying "Good dog."**

   Buddy literally sits in your hand.

4. **Release him with "Okay," or whatever word you prefer.**

Practice making your dog sit five times in a row each training session.

Figure 9-1:
Sitting with
a treat.

Sitting on command

When your dog understands sit, you can start to teach him to obey your command. Here's how to do it:

1. **With Buddy on your left side, and with you standing facing in the same direction, put a treat in your right hand, kept at your side.**

2. **Depending on the size of your dog, put one or two fingers of your left hand through his collar at the top of his neck, palm facing up, and say "Sit."**

   If he sits, give him a treat and tell him how good he is while taking your hand out of the collar. If he doesn't sit, pull up on his collar and wait until he sits; then praise and reward him with a treat. You should praise in a quiet tone of voice so Buddy doesn't get excited and jump up.

3. **Practice until Buddy sits on command without having to pull up on or touch the collar.**

As your dog demonstrates that he has mastered sitting on command, start to reward the desired response every other time. Finally, reward him on a *random* basis — every now and then give him a treat after he sits on command. A random reward is the most powerful reinforcement of what your dog has learned. It's based on the premise that hope springs eternal. To make the random reward work, all you have to do is keep using it!

Now when Buddy wants to greet you by jumping up, tell him "Sit." When he does, praise him, scratch him *under* the chin (dogs don't like being patted on the head), and then release him. Following this simple method consistently, you can change your dog's greeting behavior from trying to jump on you to sitting to being petted. For more information, see the DVD set *Living with your Dog,* which is available from www.volhard.com.

Introducing Down Commands

The Down exercise is divided into three parts:

- ✔ **The Long Down:** This is an exercise that's taught for impulse control. It's an exercise that can be taught as soon as you bring puppy home. It's designed to teach the puppy that you're in charge in a nonthreatening way. Puppies taught this exercise right from the start fit into the family routine and train much more easily. It's taught at a different time than the obedience exercises. We suggest teaching it in the evening when puppy is just about to go to sleep.

- ✔ **The Down:** This obedience command means "lie down now" and should be taught in each of your daily training sessions.

- ✔ **Go Lie Down:** This is a natural extension of Down. This exercise is used when you sit down for dinner or perhaps when you want to work on the computer and don't want to interact with the dog.

Each of these is taught separately, and with the Long Down at a different time than the training session. We explain all three in the following sections.

Warming up with the Long Down exercise

One of the best impulse control exercises is the Long Down. Practice the Long Down under the following conditions:

✔ When your dog is tired

✔ After he has been exercised

✔ When interruptions are unlikely

✔ When you aren't tired

If the situation allows it, you can watch television or read, as long as you don't move.

First, practice placing your dog in the Down position (see Figure 9-2):

1. **With Buddy sitting on your left, use a treat to get him to sit. Kneel next to him, with both of you facing in the same direction.**

2. **Reaching over his back, place your left hand behind his left foreleg; place the right hand behind the right foreleg.**

Figure 9-2:
Lifting your dog to the begging position.

3. **Keep your thumbs up so as not to squeeze Buddy's legs, which is something he may not like and may cause him to resist.**

4. **Lift Buddy into the begging position and, without saying anything, lower him to the ground.**

It takes four weeks of practice to get the Long Down established as a routine, but it's well worth the effort. Here's what to do each week:

✔ **Week 1:** Three times during the course of a week, practice the Long Down exercise for 30 minutes at a time as follows:

1. **Sit on the floor beside your dog.**

2. **Without saying anything, place him in the Down position. (See Figure 9-3.)**

3. **If he gets up, put him back without saying anything.**

4. **Keep your hands off of him when he's down.**

5. **Stay still.**

6. **After 30 minutes, release him, even if he has fallen asleep.**

As a general rule, the more bouncy the dog, the more frequently he'll try to get up and the more important this exercise becomes. Just remain calm, and each time he tries to get up place him back in the Down position. If your dog is particularly bouncy, put him on leash and kneel on the leash so your hands are free to put him back.

Some dogs cooperate relatively quickly, whereas others need more time. If your dog is in the latter group, your first experience with the Long Down (and his) will be the hardest. As he catches on to the idea and gradually (if not grudgingly) accepts the procedure, each successive repetition will go more easily.

✔ **Week 2:** Practice three 30-minute Downs while you sit in a chair next to your dog.

✔ **Week 3:** Practice three 30-minute Downs while you sit across the room from your dog.

✔ **Week 4:** Practice three 30-minute Downs while you move about the room but within sight of your dog.

After week 4, practice a Long Down at least once a month.

Teaching the Down on command

Your dog already knows how to lie down from practicing the Long Down exercise, but he needs to be taught to lie down on command. Down is the command used when you want your dog to lie down in place, right now, and stay there until you release him.

Figure 9-3:
Gently lowering your dog to the Down position.

The following steps can help you teach this command to Buddy (with a small dog, you may want to do this on a table):

1. **With your dog sitting at your left side and both of you facing in the same direction, and with a treat in your right hand, put one or two fingers of your left hand, palm facing you, through his collar at the side of his neck.**

   Show him the treat and lower it straight down and in front of your dog as you apply gentle downward pressure on the collar, at the same time saying "Down."

2. **When he lies down, give him the treat and praise him by telling him what a good puppy he is.**

   Keep your left hand in the collar and your right hand off your dog while telling him how clever he is so he learns he's being praised for lying down.

Practice having your dog lie down at your side five times in a row for five days, or until he does it on command with minimal pressure on the collar. Praise and reward with a treat every time.

When your dog is reliably lying down at your side, you can tell him to "Stay" and then go 2 feet in front of him for 30 seconds. Build up to two minutes over a period of time. If Buddy moves, go back to his side and put two fingers into his collar and apply a small amount of pressure as you say "Down." After Buddy understands, you can build up the time he stays in the Down position.

Make a game out of teaching your dog to lie down on command. Get him eager about a treat, and in an excited tone of voice say, "Down." Then give him his treat. After that, when he lies down on command, you can randomly reward him.

Go lie down, doggy!

The Go Lie Down command is a useful command when you want Buddy to go to a specific spot and remain there for an extended period until you release him. Use the command whenever you don't want Buddy underfoot, such as at mealtimes or when you have visitors and don't want him making a pest of himself.

Select the spot where you want Buddy to hang out — his crate, your bed, his favorite chair, or wherever. Depending on your needs, you also can use a moveable object, such as a dog bed, crate pad, or blanket, so you can change its location as necessary. For the following steps, assume you're going to use a dog bed:

1. **Start by taking your dog to the bed and tell him "Go Lie Down."**

   You may have to coax him with a treat.

2. **When he lies down on the bed, praise, give him the treat, count to five, and release him.**

3. **Repeat until he readily lies down on the bed with the command.**

After he readily goes to his bed on command, follow these steps:

1. **Start 3 feet from the bed, give the command Go Lie Down, and lure him onto the bed with a treat.**

2. **Praise him when he lies down, give him the treat, count to ten, and release him.**

3. **Repeat several times, gradually increasing the time between the praise and the giving of the treat, from a count of 10 to a count of 30.**

   Stop for now — you're getting bored and so is Buddy — and come back to it at another time.

For your next session, review the last progression two or three times and then send Buddy to his bed from 3 feet — but this time you should stand still and simply motion him to go to his bed (along with the Go Lie Down command). He may surprise you and actually go and lie down. If he does, praise him enthusiastically and give him a treat. If he just stands there with a befuddled look on his face, put one finger through his collar, guide him to his bed, and when he lies down, praise and give him a treat. You may have to repeat this process several times until he responds to the command from 3 feet away.

When Buddy responds reliably from 3 feet, gradually and over the course of several sessions, increase the distance from the bed as well as the length of time — up to 30 minutes. If he gets up without being released, just put him back (with your finger through his collar). The Go Lie Down command, although practical, isn't the most exciting exercise. So use common sense, and don't make it drudgery.

You must release Buddy from the spot when he can move again. If you forget, he'll get into the habit of releasing himself, thereby undermining the purpose of the exercise.

Staying in Place

Although the Sit-Stay is used for relatively short periods, the Down-Stay is used for correspondingly longer periods. Traditionally, the Down-Stay also is taught as a safety exercise to get Buddy to stop wherever he is and stay there. For example, suppose Buddy gets loose and finds himself on the other side of the road. He sees you and is just about to cross the road when a car comes. You need a way to get him to stay on the other side of the street until the car has passed by.

The object of the Down-Stay command is to have your dog respond to your command whether he's up close or at a distance. Pointing to the ground won't work from a distance, so you need to train your dog to respond to an oral command. This is where the Down-Stay command comes in — the theory being that the dog is least likely to move in the Down position. You won't find this command terribly difficult to teach.

Doing the Sit-Stay

The Sit-Stay command is one of the most useful exercises you can teach. When you have guests, when your doorbell rings and Buddy rushes barking to the door, when you want Buddy to not dash through open doors, it's the exercise that's not only safe for Buddy but also helps you keep your sanity. It's also useful for stair manners and for stopping him from jumping out of the car when the door is opened (we discuss door and stair manners later in this chapter). Overall, use the Sit-Stay command when you want your dog to remain quietly in one spot.

Teaching the Sit-Stay command

To teach the Sit-Stay command, Buddy needs his training collar and his 6-foot training leash (see Chapter 5 if you need to pick these things out). Before you proceed to another step while teaching the command, make sure Buddy is solid on the previous one. Here are the steps to follow:

1. **With Buddy sitting at your left side, both of you facing in the same direction (called Heel position), put the ring of his collar on top of his neck and attach the leash to the collar.**

   Traditionally, dogs are trained on the left side of the trainer. The custom is said to come from gun dogs: The gun is on the hunter's right, and the dog stays on his left. Service dogs usually are trained on the left as well.

2. **Put the loop of the leash over the thumb of your left hand and fold the leash accordion-style into your hand, with the part of the leash going toward the dog coming out at the bottom of your hand.**

   Hold it as close to the dog's collar as you comfortably can. The farther away from the dog's collar you hold your hand, the less control you have. Apply a little upward tension on the collar — just enough to let him know the tension is there, but not enough to make him uncomfortable.

3. **Say "Stay" and take a step to the right, keeping the tension on the collar. Count to ten, return to Buddy's side, release tension, praise him, and release with "Okay" (or whatever word you choose), taking several steps forward.**

4. **Repeat Step 3, only this time step directly in front of your dog, turn to face him, count to ten, step back to his side, release tension, praise, and release.**

5. **With your dog on your left side, put the ring of the collar under your dog's chin. Neatly fold your leash accordion-style into your left hand, and place it against your belt buckle, allowing 3 feet of slack. (See Figure 9-4.)**

6. **Say "Stay" and then place yourself 3 feet in front of your dog, keeping your left hand at your belt buckle and your right hand at your side, palm open, facing your dog.**

7. **Repeat over the course of several training sessions until your dog is steady on this exercise.**

When you see that Buddy's attention is drifting, he's probably about to move. You can tell that your dog is thinking about moving when he starts to look around and begins to focus on something other than you. Any time you see that lack of attention, reinforce the Stay command. If your dog is thinking about moving or actually tries to move, take a step toward your dog with your right foot and, with your right hand, bring the leash straight up to a point directly above his head. Bring back your right foot and right hand to their original position without repeating the Stay command. Count to 30 and pivot back to your dog's right side. Count to five, praise, and release.

Figure 9-4:
Sit-Stay reinforce-ment.

Until you learn to recognize the signs that Buddy is going to move, chances are you'll be too late in reinforcing the Stay and he will have moved. When that happens, without saying anything, put him back to the spot where he was supposed to stay, stand in front of him, count to ten, return to his side, count to five, and release him.

Administering the Sit-Stay test

The following steps involve testing your dog's understanding of the Sit-Stay, while extending the time and distance during which he's required to stay:

1. **Start with Buddy on your left and hold the leash in your left hand placed against your belt buckle. Place your right hand at your right side, palm facing forward, ready to reinforce as described earlier in the chapter.**

2. **Say "Stay" and go 3 feet in front of him, with no tension on the leash.**

3. **When in front of your dog, slightly rotate your left hand downward, against your body, to apply tension on the leash. Count to 10. Release pressure.**

   Keep your right hand, palm facing up, toward your dog. (See Figure 9-5.)

Figure 9-5:
The Sit-Stay
test.

4. **If Buddy moves to come to you, take a step toward him with your right leg and, with your right hand, bring the leash straight up to a point directly above his head. Don't repeat the Stay command.**

   Test three times for 10 seconds, increasing the tension until you get physical resistance from your dog. Then release the tension. Go back to the side of your dog and release at the end of the exercise.

After you've completed the preceding Sit-Stay test, tell your dog to "Stay" and go 4 feet in front of him with a loose leash. When you're 4 feet from him, your goal is to have him stay for one minute. If he moves, reinforce the stay. When you're 6 feet from him, Buddy should be sufficiently trained so you can leave him for a longer time. Gradually increase your time until you reach three minutes. Go back to the side of the dog and release with praise. If at any time, Buddy breaks his stay, go back a step and repeat until he's reliable. Then proceed to the next step.

Practice the Sit-Stay on a regular basis. After Buddy understands what you want, alternate between the Sit- and Down-Stays every other day (see the earlier section "Teaching the Down on command" for more on the Down-Stay). Start with the Sit-Stay test to refresh Buddy's recollection of what you expect from him.

When Buddy is reliable on leash, try him off leash in a safe place at home. If you have a fenced yard, practice off leash there. When you take Buddy to a different location, start this exercise by reminding Buddy of the Sit-Stay test, before taking him off leash. Always make sure you're practicing in a safe place before you take Buddy off leash. First practice 3 feet in front. Then gradually increase the distance and the time you expect him to stay.

As a part of Buddy's education, he has to learn to stay in either the sitting or the Down position. The Sit-Stay is used for relatively short periods, whereas the Down-Stay is used for longer periods, such as when you're having a meal. If you have practiced the Long Down exercise described in this chapter, teaching the Sit-Stay should go quickly.

How much time should you spend at any given session? We recommend two five-to-ten-minute training sessions a day. Short training sessions tend to keep your dog's interest and wanting more. Remember that the Long Down exercise is practiced separately and for 30 minutes.

Dashing your dog's dashing habits: Door and stair manners

Almost as annoying as unrestrained greeting behavior, but far more danger-ous, is a dog's habit of dashing through doors just because they're open, racing up and down stairs — ahead of or behind you — and jumping in and out of the car without permission. These behaviors are dangerous to your dog because he may find himself in the middle of the road and get run over. These behaviors also are dangerous to *you* because Buddy may knock you over going down the stairs or through the door.

Prevent such potential accidents by teaching Buddy to Stay while you open the door and to wait until you tell him it's okay to go out. For this exercise, Buddy doesn't have to sit, but many dogs will do so on their own after a few repetitions. If you have already taught Buddy the Sit command, use it when you teach him door and stair manners.

Teaching door manners

Teaching door manners doesn't require any prior training and is a good intro-ductory exercise. This exercise is fun to teach because you can see the little wheels in Buddy's brain turning. The dog learns quickly that the only way out of the door is the release word, such as "Okay."

The following sequences assume that you have leashed your dog. If you already did the "Getting Started" exercise in Chapter 1 or taught him the Sit-Stay from earlier in this chapter, teaching Buddy door manners should be a breeze. Here's what to do:

1. **With Buddy on leash and on your left side, hold the leash as close to his collar as is comfortable for you (the closer to the collar you hold the leash, the more control you have).**

There should be no tension on the collar.

2. **Choose a door that opens to the outside (if possible) and approach it right up to the threshold. Say "Stay" and, with your right hand, open the door a crack. When Buddy moves, close the door. Start over: Say "Stay," open the door a little, and, when he moves, close it.**

   If you have an overly enthusiastic dog, you may have to apply a little upward tension on the collar to keep him from moving forward. After several tries, Buddy will look at you as if to say, "Exactly what are we doing here?" The little wheels are turning. Try again, and this time he should stay. When he does, close the door and verbally praise him with "Good dog."

3. **Repeat this process several times, each time opening the door a little wider before closing it again.**

   The entire sequence will take three to five minutes. You can end the session here and pick it up again at another time (after practicing the first three steps, of course), or, if your dog is still interested, continue with the lesson.

4. **Open the door and step over the threshold with your right foot, keeping your left foot planted. When Buddy moves, step back, close the door, and start again. When he's steady, step over the threshold with the right foot and then the left. If he moves, step back, close the door, and try again.**

   As you step over the threshold, you need to let out enough leash so you don't inadvertently pull on it thereby causing Buddy to move. Remember to praise for every correct response. At this point, many dogs will sit on their own when approaching the door. (See Figure 9-6.)

   When Buddy holds the stay after you crossed the threshold, praise, pause, and release him with "Okay"; then let him exit. Remember, praise isn't an invitation to move!

5. **Approach the door, say "Stay," exit, and close the door behind you.**

   You decide when Buddy can follow or when he has to stay. After that, your success depends on consistency on your part. After Buddy has become solid at this exercise, review the entire sequence off leash.

The total time invested is 30 to 45 minutes — well worth it, considering the exercise's application of other situations, such as stairs and the car. The exercise also applies to entering the house, if that's important to you. It makes no difference whether you prefer to go through the doorway first or whether you want the dog to go through first, as long as he stays until you release him. Practice going through doors your dog uses regularly.

Motion means more to dogs than words, so make sure you stand still when releasing your dog. You don't want him to associate your moving with the release. Also, be aware that dogs have an acute sense of time. Let's say you usually wait for two seconds before you release him. He then starts to anticipate and releases himself after one second, defeating the purpose of the exercise. You need to vary the length of time between opening the door and the release so he learns to wait for you to release him.

Figure 9-6:
Practicing
door
manners.

Teaching stair manners

If you have stairs, start teaching Buddy to stay at the bottom while you go up. First tell him "Stay." When he tries to follow, put him back and start again. Practice until you can go all the way up the stairs with him waiting at the bottom before you release him to follow. Repeat the same procedure for going down the stairs.

After Buddy has been trained to wait at one end of the stairs, you'll discover that he'll anticipate the release. He'll jump the gun and get up just as you're thinking about releasing him. Before long, he'll stay only briefly and then release himself. Put him back and start all over. To us, few things are more irritating, and potentially dangerous, than the dog rushing past us as we are descending stairs, especially if we're carrying something.

REMEMBER

All this sounds like an awful lot of work. In the beginning, it does take a little time, but you'll be surprised by how quickly the routine becomes a habit for Buddy. The best part is that you're teaching Buddy to look to your for direction. Also, we think it's important that each member of the family is consistent in following the directions. It makes it easier for Buddy to understand if each family member enforces the same rules.

Leave It: Getting Your Dog to Leave Stuff Alone

When we take our dogs for a walk in the woods or fields, we aren't too thrilled when one wants to ingest horse manure or goose droppings. Nor are we fond of having to extricate such delicacies from a dog's mouth. To tell you the truth, we'd prefer if they didn't pick up *anything* from the ground they perceive as potentially edible. At a dog park in our area, several dogs became seriously ill after ingesting chunks of poison-laced hot dogs. The Leave It command is a good start for such situations.

Teaching this command is a wonderful opportunity to find out more about how your dog's thought processes work. Depending on how quickly Buddy catches on, you may want to practice this exercise over the course of several sessions. Keep the sessions short — no more than five minutes at a time — and follow these steps (you can either sit or stand):

1. **In your left hand, hold a treat between your index and middle fingers and cover it with your thumb. Hold your hand pressed against your leg.**

2. **With your palm facing up, show Buddy the treat. When he tries to pry it loose, say "Leave It," close your hand into a fist, and turn it so that your palm now faces down.**

   Figure 9-7 shows a dog learning the Leave It command.

Figure 9-7: Working on the Leave It command.

3. **Observe your dog's reaction.**

   He may stare fixedly at the back of your hand, he may try to get to the treat by nuzzling or nibbling your hand, or he may start barking.

Ignore all these behaviors and *do not* repeat the command. You're looking for the first break in his attention away from your hand. Most dogs at this point will look either to the right or to the left.

4. **The instant Buddy breaks his attention away from your hand, say "Good" and give him a treat.**

   The most difficult part of teaching this exercise is for you to remain silent and not to repeat the command. Be patient and wait for the correct response.

5. **Repeat preceding steps until your dog looks away from your hand or makes eye contact with you when you give the command.**

   You're teaching Buddy that looking away or at you — and not at your hand — is rewarded with a treat.

   Your dog may think that you're teaching him to turn his head — he will quickly turn away and then look at your hand again. He wants to speed up the process of getting his treat and is now trying to train you. Be sure to wait until he looks away or at you before you praise and reward.

6. **To find out whether Buddy is responding to the command or to the turning of your hand, repeat Step 1 without turning your hand.**

   If he responds, praise and reward. If he doesn't, close your hand into a fist and wait for the break in attention. Repeat until he responds to only the command.

7. **Make yourself comfortable on the floor. Show him a treat, put it on the floor and cover it with your hand. When his attention is on your hand or he tries to get to the treat, say "Leave It." Wait for the break in attention, and then praise and reward him.**

8. **Repeat Step 7, but now cover the treat with just your index finger. Then try the step while placing the treat between your index and middle finger.**

   If you're successful, place the treat 1 inch in front of your hand. Here you need to be watchful: Buddy may be faster at getting to the treat than you can cover it.

9. **Put Buddy on leash and stand next to him, neatly fold the leash into your left hand, and hold your hand as close to his collar as is comfortable without tension on the leash. You need to make sure that the amount of slack in the leash is short enough that his mouth can't reach the floor.**

10. **Hold the treat in your right hand and show it to Buddy. Then casually drop the treat and say "Leave It." If he responds, praise him, pick up the treat and give him another treat from your pocket (not the one you told him to leave alone). If he doesn't, pull straight up on the leash, pick up the treat, and try again. Give the command immediately after letting go of the treat and before he wants to make a dive for it. Repeat until he obeys the command.**

Test Buddy's response by taking off the leash, dropping a treat, and saying "Leave It." If he makes a dive for it, don't attempt to beat him to it or yell "No." He's telling you that he needs more work on leash.

Now for the big test. Select a food item that's readily visible to you in the grass or on the ground, such as some crackers or a few kernels of popcorn. Go outside and drop four or five pieces of food in the area where you're taking Buddy for his big test. Put some of your regular treats in your pocket, and take Buddy for a walk on leash in the area where you left the food. As soon as his nose goes to the food, say, "Leave It." If he responds, praise enthusiastically, pick up the treat, and reward with a different treat from your pocket. (Don't reward Buddy with the object he has been told to leave alone.) If he doesn't, check straight up on the leash. Repeat until he ignores the food on command. When several tries don't produce the desired result, you need to review the training equipment you are using (see Chapter 5).

If Buddy manages to snag a cracker or kernel of popcorn, you're too slow on the uptake. Practice walking around the food-contaminated area until he ignores the food on command.

Buddy should now know and respond to the Leave It command. Test him off leash to see whether he has mastered this command or needs more work. Still, as with any other command, you need to review it with him periodically on leash.

If your dog is anything like ours, he won't be far when you're in the kitchen preparing a meal. His presence there is a wonderful training opportunity. Casually drop a piece of food on the floor — maybe a small piece of bread or cheese, a little broccoli or carrot, or anything else he likes. When he tries to nab it, say "Leave It." If he does, pick up the food and reward him with something else. If he does nab the food, consider it a freebie and put Buddy on leash and try again.

After Buddy is reliable with Leave It at home, take him out into the real world. Take him to the park and test his response on leash by tossing a treat in front of him. When he tries to get it, say "Leave It." If he responds correctly, reward him with a treat from your pocket (not with the treat you told him to leave alone). If he doesn't respond correctly, he's telling you he needs more training. In this case, you need to review the command under similar circumstances at another time, but on leash so you can reinforce it.

Teaching Buddy a reliable response to Leave It also transfers to other situations, such as with jumping on people and resource guarding. You also can use Leave It for excessive barking. Remember to reward correct responses with praise and a treat.

Chapter 10

Canine Cruise Control: Walking on Leash and Coming When Called

· ·

· ·

*T*aking your dog for a nice, long walk is balm for the soul and good exercise for both of you — provided he doesn't drag you down the street. Teaching Buddy to walk on a loose leash makes your strolls a pleasure rather than a chore.

Even better, from the dog's perspective, is a good run in the park or the woods. For this privilege, however, Buddy has to learn to come when called. You can teach him to respond to the Come command by playing the Recall Game.

In the following sections, we provide you with everything you need to know in order to have a pleasant walk or romp in the park, including how to end Buddy's pulling and how to get him familiar with the Come command.

Walking Your Dog

Studies have shown that people who regularly walk their dogs get more exercise than those who go to the gym. It's common sense that if you accompany Buddy on daily outings, you'll benefit, too. These outings should be a real pleasure for both of you, but if Buddy pulls on the leash, they become an unpleasant chore.

To end the pulling, you need to teach Buddy to walk on a loose leash. For that job, you need the right equipment. You have several options for the type of collar you need. Your choices are a training collar or a pinch collar (see Chapter 5 for descriptions of these). Buddy's response to the collar you choose is the determining factor, along with his Personality Profile and discomfort threshold (see Chapters 2 and 3). For a leash, our preference is a 6-foot cotton web leash.

The goal is to teach Buddy that it is *his* responsibility to pay attention to you, not the other way around. Even though he may be several feet ahead of you eagerly pursuing a scent, he must be aware of where you are without straining on the end of the leash. He doesn't have to pay 100 percent attention to you — just enough to "keep an eye" on you.

Dogs pull on a leash because they're more interested in the sights and scents in their environment than in you. Your job is to teach Buddy to become aware of your existence at the other end of the leash and respect your presence.

Born to pull: Teaching Buddy to respect the leash

To teach Buddy not to pull, you need his collar and his leash. Take Buddy to an area that's familiar to him and where there are no distractions — your backyard or a quiet street are good places.

1. **Put the loop of the leash over the thumb of your left hand and make a fist around the leash.**

   Figure 10-1 shows you how this should look.

2. **Place your right hand directly under your left hand and make a fist around the leash. Hold the leash in both hands as though it were a baseball bat. Plant both hands firmly against your belt buckle.**

Figure 10-1:
How to hold
the leash.

3. **Say "Let's Go," or any other command you choose, and start walking.**

4. **Just before Buddy gets to the end of the leash, say "Let's Go." Without turning your head to look at him, make an about-turn to your right and walk in the opposite direction.**

   Make sure you keep *both* hands planted against your belt buckle. When Buddy fails to follow, he'll experience a tug on the leash.

   As a safety precaution, don't put your entire hand through the loop of the leash or wrap it around your hand. If your dog catches you unaware and makes a dash, he could cause you to fall. By having just the loop of the leash over your thumb, you can just let go, and the loop will slide off.

5. **As Buddy scampers to catch up with you, tell him what a clever boy he is. Before you know it, he'll be ahead of you again, and you'll have to repeat the procedure.**

   When you make your turn, do it with determination. Make your turn, and keep walking in the new direction. Don't look back, and don't worry about Buddy; he'll quickly catch up. Remember to praise and reward him when he does. After several repetitions, Buddy should respond to the Let's Go and quickly turn on the command. When he does, stop the session.

   The first few times you try this, you'll likely be a little late — Buddy will already be leaning into his collar, and at that point you're engaged in a wrestling match. Concentrate on Buddy, and learn to anticipate when you have to make the turn. Always give him a chance to respond by saying "Let's Go" *before* you make the turn.

6. **Practice this sequence over the course of several sessions until Buddy responds reliably to the Let's Go command.**

   Keep the sessions short — no more than five to ten minutes.

Most dogs quickly learn to respect the leash and, with an occasional reminder, become a pleasure to take for a walk. Some dogs, on the other hand, don't seem to get it. If Buddy seems particularly dense about this simple concept, you may need to consider a change of equipment. If you started with a buckle collar and it's not working, try a training collar or a prong collar (see Chapter 5). And be sure to put Buddy in a position where you can praise him. Your dog, in turn, will thank you for maintaining a positive attitude. For more information, see the DVD set *Living with your Dog*, which is available from www.volhard.com.

When Buddy responds reliably to the Let's Go command in a distraction-free environment, you're ready for the next sequence. Remember, the goal is to teach Buddy that it is his responsibility to pay attention to *you*. Here are the steps to the next sequence:

1. **Start your session, still without distractions, by reviewing his response to Let's Go with two or three about-turns.**

2. **Eliminate the Let's Go command as you make your turn.**

   The first several tries, Buddy will likely experience a tug on the leash before he turns to follow you. After several turns, however, he'll catch on and respond to your turn. When he does, praise lavishly and stop for that session. Review this sequence for several sessions.

3. **When he's comfortable with the routine and follows you without hesitation when you make a turn, you can move on to introducing distractions.**

   Check out the next section for details on adding distractions.

Making it real: Adding distractions

In the real world, Buddy will encounter all manner of distractions — children, people, squirrels and birds, cyclists and joggers, cars, and, of course, other dogs. Your job is to teach him that you're still the center of attention, no matter what else is out there.

For this sequence, you need a distracter — a member of your family or anyone willing to stand still long enough. The distracter's job is just that: to distract Buddy with any object that may interest him. Food usually works. Of course, the distracter doesn't let Buddy have the object, because that would defeat the purpose of the exercise. Figure 10-2 shows a distracter at work.

The distracter holds the object — for our purposes you can assume that it's food — close to his body, without waving it about or talking to Buddy. Because this is a new exercise for Buddy, you start at the beginning: You reintroduce the Let's Go command.

From a distance of about 10 feet, approach the distracter. When Buddy is engrossed in the food, say "Let's Go" and make your turn. When Buddy fails to respond, he experiences a tug on the leash. Repeat the procedure until Buddy responds by following you on command. When he does, praise lavishly and end the session. At your next session, review the previous sequence; when Buddy responds correctly, stop the session. After that, follow the same sequence but eliminate the command.

Buddy should now have a pretty good idea of what to do, so you're ready to take him to new places. Chances are, on a walk in the park, you'll meet a number of new distractions, including other dogs. Exposing Buddy to variety of new circumstance is a golden teaching opportunity. Practice in those settings what you have taught him.

Figure 10-2:
Teaching
Let's Go
with
distractions.

To find out if Buddy has learned his lesson, try the ultimate test: Give the Let's Go command off leash. Take him to a safe area, preferably fenced, and remove his leash. Let him wander around a bit and then say "Let's Go." Turn your back toward him and walk away. If he comes to you, enthusiastically praise. If not, you have a little more practicing to do.

Winning the Game of Coming When Called

One of the greatest joys of owning a dog is going for a walk in the park or in the woods and letting him run, knowing he'll come when called. A dog that doesn't come when called is a prisoner of his leash and, if he gets loose, is a danger to himself and others.

Some breeds take longer to train than others. With sufficient reinforcement around distractions (and the correct equipment), the majority of dogs can be trained to come when called. Using a pinch collar may be necessary. (See Chapter 5 for more on training gear.)

Follow these basic rules to encourage your dog to come to you when you call him:

✔ **Exercise, exercise, exercise.** Many dogs don't come when called because they don't get enough exercise. At every chance they get, they run off and make the most of this unexpected freedom by staying out for hours at a time.

Consider what your dog was bred to do, and that background tells you how much exercise he needs. Just putting Buddy out in the backyard isn't good enough. You have to participate. Think of it this way: Exercise is as good for you as it is for your dog. A good source for exercise requirements is *The Roger Caras Dog Book: A Complete Guide to Every AKC Breed,* 3rd Edition (M. Evans & Co.).

✔ **When your dog comes to you, be nice to him.** One of the quickest ways to teach your dog not to come to you is to call him to punish him or to do something the dog perceives as unpleasant. Most dogs consider it unpleasant to be called when their owners are leaving them alone in the house or giving them a pill. In these circumstances, go and get Buddy instead of calling him to you.

Another example of teaching your dog not to come is taking him for a run in the park and calling him to you when it's time to go home. Repeating this sequence several times teaches the dog that the party is over. Soon he may become reluctant to return to you when called because he isn't ready to end the fun. You can prevent this kind of unintentional training by calling him to you several times during his outing, sometimes giving him a treat and other times offering just a word of praise. Then let him romp again.

✔ **Teach him the Come command as soon as you get him.** Ideally, you acquired your dog as a puppy, which is the best time to teach him to come when called. Start right away. But remember, sometime between 4 and 8 months of age your puppy begins to realize there's a big, wide world out there (see Chapter 6). While he's going through this stage, keep him on leash so he doesn't learn that he can ignore you when you call him.

✔ **When in doubt, keep him on leash.** Learn to anticipate when your dog is likely not to come. You may be tempting fate by trying to call him after he has spotted a cat, another dog, or a jogger. Of course, sometimes you'll goof and let him go just as another dog appears out of nowhere.

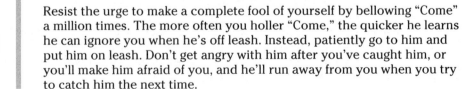

Resist the urge to make a complete fool of yourself by bellowing "Come" a million times. The more often you holler "Come," the quicker he learns he can ignore you when he's off leash. Instead, patiently go to him and put him on leash. Don't get angry with him after you've caught him, or you'll make him afraid of you, and he'll run away from you when you try to catch him the next time.

✔ **Make sure your dog always comes to you and lets you touch his collar before you reward.** Touching his collar prevents the dog from developing the annoying habit of playing "catch" — coming toward you and then dancing around you, just out of reach. Teach him to let you touch his collar before you offer him a treat or praise. We discuss the Touch command later in this chapter.

Teaching the Come command

It's best to teach the Come command by playing the Recall Game with your dog. The Recall Game is taught with two people, one hungry dog, one 6-foot leash, plenty of small treats, and two whistles (optional). Some people prefer to train their dogs to come to a whistle instead of using the verbal command Come. Some people train their dog to do both.

What works best depends on the dog, and you may want to experiment. Consider trying the verbal command first, because at times you may need to call your dog but don't have your whistle. You can then repeat the steps using a whistle, which goes very quickly because Buddy already has some understanding of what he's supposed to do.

For this exercise, you need to be inside the house, with your dog on a 6-foot leash. You and your partner sit on the floor 6 feet apart, facing each other. Your partner gently restrains the dog while you hold the end of the leash. Figure 10-3 shows the Recall Game in action.

Figure 10-3:
Learning Come with the Recall Game.

Here's how to play the Recall Game and teach your dog the Come command:

1. **Call your dog by saying "Buddy, Come," and use the leash to guide him to you.**

   Avoid the temptation to reach for your dog.

2. **When Buddy comes to you, put your hand through his collar, give him a treat, pet him, and praise him enthusiastically.**

   You can — and should — pet Buddy when he reaches you so that coming to you is a pleasant experience for him. This situation is different from teaching the Sit or Down commands in Chapter 9, when you want him to remain in place and petting him would cause him to get up.

3. **Hold onto Buddy's collar and pass the leash to your partner, who says, "Buddy, Come," guides the dog in, puts his hand through the collar, gives him a treat, and praises the dog.**

   Keep working on this exercise until your dog responds on his own to being called and no longer needs to be guided in with the leash.

4. **Repeat the exercise with Buddy off leash, gradually increasing the distance between you and your partner to 12 feet.**

5. **Have your partner hold Buddy by the collar while you go into another room, and then call your dog.**

6. **When he finds you, put your hand through the collar, give him a treat, and praise him.**

   If he can't find you, *slowly* go to him, take him by the collar, and bring him to the spot where you called. Reward and praise.

7. **Have your partner go into another room and then call the dog.**

8. **Repeat the exercise until Buddy doesn't hesitate in finding you or your partner in any room of the house.**

9. **Take Buddy outside to a confined area, such as a fenced yard, tennis court, park, or school yard, and repeat Steps 1, 2, and 3.**

Now you're ready to practice by yourself. With Buddy on leash, take him for a walk. Let him sniff around, and when he isn't paying any attention to you, call him. When he gets to you, give him a treat and make a big fuss over him. If he doesn't come, firmly tug on the leash toward you and then reward and praise him. Repeat until he comes to you every time you call him. After Buddy is trained, you don't have to reward him with a treat every time, but do so randomly.

Adding distractions

Most dogs need to be trained to come in the face of distractions, such as other dogs, children, joggers, food, or friendly strangers. Think about the most irresistible situations for your dog, and then practice under those circumstances.

Put a 12-foot leash on your dog (you can tie two 6-foot leashes together), and take him to an area where he's likely to encounter his favorite distraction. When he spots it (jogger, bicycle, other dog, or whatever), let him become thoroughly engrossed, and then call him. More than likely, he'll ignore you. Give a sharp tug on the leash and guide him back to you. Praise and pet him enthusiastically. Repeat three times per session until the dog turns and comes to you immediately when you call. If he doesn't, you may have to change your training equipment.

Some dogs quickly learn to avoid the distraction by staying close to you, which is fine. Tell him what a clever fellow he is, and then try with a different distraction at another time.

Repeat in different locations with as many different distractions as you can find. Try it with someone offering your dog a tidbit as a distraction (the distracter doesn't let Buddy have the treat, though), someone petting him, and anything else that may distract him. Use your imagination. Your goal is to have Buddy respond reliably every time you call. Until he's steady on leash, he most certainly won't come off leash.

Advancing to off-leash distractions

How you approach adding off-leash distractions depends on your individual circumstances. For example, take your dog to an area where you aren't likely to encounter distractions in the form of other dogs or people. Let him off leash, and allow him to become involved in a smell in the grass or a tree. Keep the distance between you and him about 10 feet. Call him, and if he responds, praise enthusiastically and reward. If he doesn't, avoid the temptation to call him again. Don't worry; he heard you but chose to ignore you. Instead, slowly walk up to him, firmly take him by his collar, under his chin, palm up, and trot backward to the spot where you called him. Then praise and reward.

When he's reliable with this exercise, try him in an area with other distractions. If he doesn't respond, practice for the correct response with the 12-foot leash before you try him off leash again.

Can you now trust him to come to you in an unconfined area? That depends on how well you've done your homework and what your dog may encounter in the "real" world. Understanding your dog and what interests him helps you know when he's likely not to respond to the Come command.

Let common sense be your guide. For example, when you're traveling and have to let him out to relieve himself at a busy interstate rest stop, you'd be foolhardy to let him run loose. When in doubt, keep him on leash.

Adding the Touch command

In their efforts to get their dogs to come to them, many owners inadvertently teach their dogs just the opposite: the game of "keep away." It goes something like this: Owner calls dog; dog comes; owner leans over with outstretched arms, leash in hand, and tries to grab dog. Dog starts dancing in front of owner just out of reach. Frustrated owner advances toward dog, making matters worse. Not a pretty sight. The Touch command fixes the problem or prevents it from happening in the first place. Refer to Figure 10-4 to see the command in progress.

A dear friend of ours, Desmond O'Neill, who for many years has been the training supervisor at a well-known guide dog school, introduced us to the Touch command. Guide dogs are taught to touch the blind owner's hand on command. Now the owner knows where the dog is and can leash the dog or put his harness on. We modified the exercise somewhat and teach it to get a dog to come from a short distance for the same goal: to put a leash on the dog without teaching him the game of "keep away."

Here are the steps to introduce Buddy to the Touch command:

1. **Leash your dog and hold the leash in your left hand. Have a treat in your right hand. Say "Let's Go" (or your chosen command phrase) and start walking.**

   It doesn't matter whether he walks next to you, a little ahead of you, or pulling on the leash.

2. **After about six to ten steps, say "Touch," give a little tug on the leash, and trot backward for six to ten steps with your right hand held away from your right side so Buddy can see it.**

3. **Stop and face Buddy at a 45-degree angle, placing your right foot back and your left foot forward. Place your right hand against your right leg and give Buddy the treat when he reaches your right hand. With your left hand, reach down and take hold of Buddy's collar.**

Figure 10-4:
Teaching
the Touch
command.

Repeat the preceding steps three to four times over the course of several sessions until Buddy reliably turns on the command and comes to your hand.

4. **Find a helper (family member or friend) to distract Buddy. Make sure the helper has a treat and start as in Step 1. Approach your helper from about ten steps. As Buddy approaches the helper, the helper offers him a treat but doesn't let Buddy have it. Now say "Touch"; when Buddy doesn't respond, give him a little tug on the leash, trot backward, and finish the sequence as in Step 3.**

Repeat until Buddy responds to only the command.

5. **Start all over, with Buddy off leash.**

First select a location relatively free of distractions. When he's reliably responding to the command, reintroduce your helper as in Step 4. Buddy's response will tell you whether he needs more repetitions on leash.

Teach new commands in a distraction-free environment. Only when Buddy is reliably responding can you introduce distractions.

We like to use the Touch command during outings with a group of friends and dogs, all of which are off leash, just as a refresher and to let Buddy know that we still expect a response when he's having fun.

Chapter 11

Dealing with Common Doggie Don'ts

Does your dog have what you think is a behavior problem? Does Buddy bark incessantly, but otherwise behave like a model dog? Does he jump on people when he first meets them, but is perfectly well behaved the rest of the time? Does Buddy chew on your favorite possessions when left unattended?

Dogs can exhibit one or two irritating habits that aren't necessarily "behavior" problems. Some can be solved with very little training; others require more time and effort on your part.

The first line of defense is some basic training (see Chapter 9). So-called "behavior problems" are more difficult in isolation than they are when Buddy knows basic commands. You'll find dealing with undesired behaviors easier to handle after you've established a line of communication with Buddy.

If you haven't done the Long Down exercise, you may want to start there. The purpose of the Long Down exercise is to teach Buddy in a nonviolent way that you are in charge. For this reason, it's the foundation of all further training. Training your dog is next to impossible unless he accepts that you are the one who makes decisions. It takes four weeks to get the Long Down established as a routine. But, as soon as you have it, it can go a long way toward helping you establish your role as the leader. For more information, see the DVD set *Living with your Dog,* which is available from www.volhard.com.

The majority of "doggy don'ts" are relationship problems rather than behavior problems. These behaviors often are the result of insufficient exercise, time spent with the dog, or training. In this chapter, we discuss some of the most common doggie don'ts and provide you with some workable solutions.

Preventing Bad Habits

Many dogs form bad habits or behavior problems that have a common cause or a combination of causes. In order of importance, they include the following:

- ✔ Boredom and frustration due to insufficient exercise
- ✔ Mental stagnation due to insufficient quality time with you
- ✔ Loneliness caused by too much isolation from human companionship
- ✔ Nutrition and health-related problems

Loneliness is perhaps the most difficult problem to overcome. By necessity, many dogs are left alone at home anywhere from eight to ten hours a day with absolutely nothing to do except get into mischief. Fortunately, in addition to spending quality time with your dog, you can do some things to help him overcome his loneliness.

Before addressing behavior problems specifically, in the following sections, we give you our general prescription for good behavior.

Good exercise

Exercise needs vary depending on the size and energy level of your dog. Many dogs need a great deal more exercise than their owners realize. Bull Terriers are a good example. If the owner of an English Bull Terrier lives in an apartment in a large city, and the dog doesn't get enough free-running exercise, he's bound to develop behavior problems. These problems can range from tail spinning, which is a neurotic behavior, to ripping up furniture. This kind of dog would show none of these behaviors if he lived in a household where adequate exercise, both mental and physical, was provided.

Dog trainers have a maxim: "Tired dogs have happy owners." After all, dogs that have adequate exercise and can expend their energy through running, retrieving, playing, and training rarely show objectionable behaviors. Dogs denied those simple needs frequently redirect their energy into unacceptable behaviors. Figure 11-1 shows a well-exercised pet.

Figure 11-1:
Tired dogs have happy owners.

When your dog engages in behaviors that you consider objectionable, it can be a vexing problem. Sometimes the behavior is instinctive, such as digging. Sometimes it occurs out of boredom. However, it's never because the dog is ornery. Before you attempt to deal with the behavior, you need to find out the cause. The easiest way to stop a behavior is by addressing the need that brought it about in the first place rather than by trying to correct the behavior itself. And if there's one single cause for behavior problems, it's the lack of adequate exercise.

Good company

Many years ago, we labeled a set of behaviors we used to see in our obedience classes as *single-dog syndrome*. These dogs would run away from their owners more frequently than those dogs living in multidog households. They'd growl around their food bowls, be picky eaters, be possessive about toys, and be much more unruly than dogs living in homes with other dogs. In other words, dog ownership may be easier if you have two dogs.

If you can't bear the thought of being a two-dog household, good company is even more important. "Good company" means not only that you act as a companion to your dog but also that your dog shares the company of other dogs as frequently as possible. Some possibilities include taking regular walks in parks where he can meet other dogs, joining a dog club where dog activities are offered, or putting your puppy into doggie daycare several days a week. Socialization of your pet is a continuing process. If you're able, get another dog to be Buddy's companion. Dogs are pack animals and thrive in the company of other dogs.

Good health

Keeping Buddy in good health isn't nearly as easy as it was 50 years ago. It seems that with the advance of science in so many dog-related fields, dogs should be healthier than ever. This isn't the case, however. Too often through poor breeding practices, poor nutrition, and overvaccination, a dog's health has been threatened like never before.

Owning a dog who has constant health problems — from minor conditions like skin irritations, fleas, smelly coat, and ear infections to more serious conditions that affect his internal organs, such as the kidneys, heart, liver, and thyroid — is no fun! Not feeling well can cause your dog to develop behavior problems. Health-related conditions often are confused with behavior problems. Buddy may have eaten something that upset his stomach, causing a house-soiling accident. He may have a musculoskeletal disorder, making changes of position painful and causing irritability and sometimes snapping. These concerns obviously aren't amenable to training solutions — and certainly not to discipline. For more on your dog's health, see Chapter 4.

Good nutrition

The saying "You are what you eat" applies equally to dogs as it does to people. Properly feeding your dog makes the difference between sickness and health, and it has a profound effect on his behavior. And with the abundance of dog foods on the market, figuring out what's best for your pet can be difficult.

There are several ways to correctly feed your dog:

- ✔ Select a commercial kibble that has two animal proteins in the first three ingredients. You can add some fresh, raw meat and vegetables to the kibble. Kibble stays in the stomach for 15 to 16 hours before it's digested, but adding a good protein source (raw hamburger, chopped stewing steak, canned fish, cooked chicken, or raw lamb) and rotating some fresh vegetables like carrots, broccoli, parsnips, or green beans to your dog's kibble on a daily basis, cuts down the digestion time by several hours. These foods work by providing the correct digestive enzymes for Buddy's stomach to break down his food. Feeding only cooked kibble to Buddy provides little nutrition because cooking eliminates most of the vitamins and minerals and changes the chemical composition of both fats and protein. You don't want Buddy's stomach full of dry food all day; it can cause all sorts of digestive problems, one of which is bloat that can be life threatening.

> ✔ Buy a dehydrated version of a natural diet dog food, to which you add some water and raw meat. (See www.volhard.com for our dehydrated formula.)

> ✔ Make your own dog food. Chapter 4 provides guidance if you want to go this route.

Your choice depends on your level of comfort and the time you have to devote to your dog. If you have doubts about what you're feeding your dog and want more information on your dog's nutritional needs, see Chapter 4. You also can read *The Holistic Guide for a Healthy Dog,* 2nd edition, by Wendy Volhard and Kerry Brown, DVM (Howell Book House). For more information on the ingredients of dog food, read *Pet Food Politics: The Chihuahua in the Coal Mine* by Marion Nestle, who's the Paulette Goddard Professor of Nutrition, Food Studies, and Public Health and Professor of Sociology at New York University (University of California Press) or *Food Pets Die For: Shocking Facts About Pet Food* by Ann N. Martin (New Sage Press).

Good training

Behavior problems don't arise because your dog is ornery or spiteful, and discipline is rarely the answer. Instead, mental stagnation often can be a cause of unwanted behavior. Training your dog on a regular basis, or having him do something for you, makes your dog feel useful and provides the mental stimulation he needs. (To get started with basic training, see Chapter 9.)

Use your imagination to get your dog to help around the house. You'll be surprised by how useful he can become. If you've taught Buddy to retrieve, he can help you bring in groceries from the car. He can carry a package of frozen food, a cereal box, or whatever you think he can hold in his mouth. Encourage him to take it into the kitchen. You can use Buddy to take the dirty laundry to the washing machine. He can carry his leash out to the car. (Chapter 15 shows how to teach a dog to retrieve.) Retrieving and carrying is regarded by Buddy as a reward — he loves to work — so giving him a treat each time isn't necessary. Remember to give him lavish praise, however.

Handling Your Dog's Objectionable Behavior

Like beauty, objectionable behavior is in the eye of the beholder. Playful nipping or biting may be acceptable to some and not to others. Moreover, different degrees of objectionable behavior exist. After all, getting on the couch in your absence isn't nearly as serious an offense as destroying it.

Having worked with dogs for a lifetime, we're perhaps more tolerant of irritating behaviors than most. We also know that dogs like to please and that most behaviors can be changed with a little good training. Knowing a dog's Personality Profile (see Chapter 2) helps you understand why your dog does the irritating things that he does. What we find objectionable, however, is when we visit friends and their untrained dogs jump up at us and scratch us in the process. Other critical negative behavior patterns include dogs who

- Don't come when called, which is dangerous (see Chapter 10 for more on the Come command)
- Don't stay when told (head to Chapter 9 to find out how to teach Stay)
- Chase cats, squirrels, joggers, bicyclists, or worse yet, cars (see how to manage prey drive behaviors in Chapter 16)
- Bark incessantly (discussed later in this chapter)

All these irritating behaviors can be eliminated with the investment of a mere ten minutes a day, five times a week for about four weeks. After that, brush ups several times a week in different locations for the rest of the dog's life, keep the behaviors you want sharp. Training is a lifetime process. It's such a small amount of time and energy to have a wonderful dog to be proud of. Trained dogs are free dogs — you can take them anywhere, and they're always welcome.

When you believe your dog has a behavior problem, you have the following options:

- You can tolerate the behavior.
- You can train your dog in an effort to change the behavior.
- You can find a new home for the dog.
- You can take your dog to the shelter, but do know that this could be a one-way trip for him.

We discuss each of these topics in the following sections.

Tolerating your dog's behavior problems

Considering the amount of time and energy that may be required to turn Buddy into the pet you always wanted, you may decide it's easier to live with his annoying antics than it is to try to change him. You tolerate him the way he is, because you don't have the time, the energy, or the inclination to put in the required effort to change him.

One tool that aids in tolerating any kind of inappropriate behavior is a crate. Leaving Buddy in a crate when you're at work saves you from worrying about housetraining, chewing, and digging. When properly trained to stay in a crate,

Buddy will think of it as his "den." He'll always be safe (and feel safe) in his crate. With a crate, he can go anywhere with you, from the car to a friend's house. Today lightweight crates can be bought for even the largest of dogs. You can even take him on holiday with you. He'll also be comfortable any time you have to leave him at the vet, where dogs are kept in crates during treatment. (See Chapter 8 for more on training with a crate.)

Behaviors you shouldn't tolerate are those that threaten your safety or the safety of others, such as biting people or aggression. True aggression is defined as unpredictable — without warning — and unprovoked biting (see Chapter 16 for more). You also shouldn't tolerate behaviors that threaten the safety of your dog, such as chasing cars (see Chapter 16) or stealing and gulping your possessions (check out the later section "Contending with Chewing — The Nonfood Variety" to curb this behavior).

Trying to solve your dog's behavior problems

You've decided that you can't live with your dog's irritating behaviors and that you're going to work with him so he'll be the pet you expected and always wanted. You understand that doing so will require an investment of time (ten minutes a day, five times a week), effort, and perhaps even expert help. But you're willing to work to achieve your goal — a long-lasting, mutually rewarding relationship. Good for you! This book can help.

Going directly to the source

If you want to stop a negative or annoying behavior, you must deal with the need that brought it about in the first place. When your dog goes through teething, for example, you need to provide him with suitable chew toys. When your dog has an accident in the house, ask yourself whether you left him inside too long or whether the dog is ill (and in that case, a trip to the vet is in order). If your dog is left alone in the yard and continuously barks out of boredom, don't leave him out there. When your dog needs more exercise than you can give him, consider a dogwalker or daycare.

Every behavior has a timeframe and a certain amount of energy attached to it. This energy needs to be expended in a normal and natural way. By trying to suppress this energy, or not giving it enough time to dissipate, you help cause a majority of behavior problems.

By using the Personality Profile in Chapter 2, you can find out where your dog's energies lie. For example, is he high in prey drive? These dogs need more exercise than dogs in other drives. They're attracted to anything that moves quickly and want to chase it. Finding an outlet for these behaviors, such as playing ball, throwing sticks, or hiding toys and having Buddy find them, goes a long way to exhausting the energies of this drive.

Obedience training, in and of itself, isn't necessarily the answer to your problems. Still, when you train your dog, you're spending meaningful time with him, which in many cases is half the battle. Much depends on the cause of the problem (refer to the earlier section "Preventing Bad Habits" for more information).

For most people, dog ownership is a compromise between tolerating and working with their dogs. Many people find certain behaviors objectionable but don't want to do anything about them. As long as the joys of dog ownership outweigh the headaches, people usually put up with these behaviors.

When all else fails: Finding a new home for your dog

Sometimes a dog's temperament may be unsuitable to an owner's lifestyle. A shy dog, or a dog with physical limitations, for example, may never develop into a great playmate for active children. A dog that doesn't like to be left alone isn't suitable for someone who's gone all day. A dog may require a great deal more exercise than the owner is able to give him and, as a result, is developing behavior problems. Although some behaviors can be modified with training, others can't — the effort required would simply be too stressful for the dog (and, perhaps, the owner).

In instances like these, the dog and the owner are mismatched, and they need to divorce. Whatever the reason, under some circumstances, placement into a new home where the dog's needs can be met is advisable and is in the best interest of both the dog and the owner.

We recall an incident involving an English Bull Terrier who was left alone too much and started tail spinning. The behavior escalated to the point that the dog became completely neurotic. At that point, we suggested a new home and found one for the dog on a farm. The dog now had unlimited daily exercise, and within a few weeks the tail-spinning behavior had completely disappeared.

If all reclamation efforts have failed — you can't live with this dog, and he can't be placed elsewhere — your final option is to take him to a shelter or to the veterinarian to have him put to sleep. This option isn't to be considered lightly, and you should only follow through if you've really tried to work it out and truly have no other alternatives. If you choose to take him to a shelter, don't kid yourself; most shelters are overwhelmed by the number of unwanted dogs and are able to find new homes for only a small percentage of these orphans. The rest of the dogs are euthanized.

Teaching Buddy to Keep All Four on the Floor

In many instances, dogs are systematically rewarded for jumping on people. When a dog was a cute puppy, for example, he received much oohing and aahing; everyone was petting him and getting him all excited. Naturally he would jump up to get all that attention. As Buddy got older, relatives and friends would reinforce the behavior with lively petting, especially on top of the head, causing the dog to jump up. He quickly learned to anticipate this greeting ritual and to jump on anybody and everybody that came through the door. Figure 11-2 shows a dog jumping for attention.

Figure 11-2:
Does your dog jump on people?

Now that he's a 50-pound (or more!) energetic and enthusiastic 1-year-old, these assaults are no longer acceptable. Establishing a line of meaningful communication with the dog is your first approach. However, if the behavior has become severely habituated, you may have to take the lead. Both situations are explained in the following sections.

Trying out some basic approaches

Several different approaches are advocated to stop jumping behavior. Some of them work with some dogs, but unfortunately not with all. Even though we don't think these approaches work (and we don't like them), they may be worth a try if you're so inclined.

Before you try any of the following suggestions, keep in mind that Buddy is jumping on you to say hello and to greet you. His intention is good, so temper your method to suit his personality and don't overdo it.

Here are the most common approaches:

- ✔ **The knee approach:** As Buddy tries to jump on you, knee him in the chest. We don't recommend you use this approach because it can injure your dog, especially a small one.

- ✔ **The fly swatter approach:** As Buddy tries to jump on you, whack him (gently) on the top of the head with a fly swatter. However, if you do this on a frequent basis, you'll have a dog that cringes when he gets close to you. You're spoiling the very relationship you're trying to create.

- ✔ **The plastic bag approach:** As Buddy approaches you, snap a plastic bag, which will startle him but won't hurt him. But, of course, this can make him afraid of plastic bags!

- ✔ **The spray bottle approach:** Fill a spray bottle with water, and then spray him with it when he tries to jump on you. Spray him in the face, and tell him to sit. (You can read about the Sit command in Chapter 9.)

- ✔ **The cold shoulder approach:** Ignore your dog and turn your back on him for a few minutes until he has calmed down. You also can face your dog with your arms crossed across your chest. Keep still until he stops jumping. Don't push him away, though. Even pushing the dog away from you is a form of attention for your dog and reinforces the undesired behavior.

One of the many drawbacks to some of these solutions is that you need the appropriate paraphernalia readily at hand. They also disrupt the relationship you have with your dog. It's better to follow the directions in the following section.

Using Sit and Stay

If none of the approaches you try works, teach Buddy to sit on command and follow it up with the Sit-Stay exercise (see Chapter 9). After he's reliable with the Sit-Stay, enlist a helper and follow these steps:

1. **Before your helper comes to the door, instruct her to avoid eye contact with Buddy and to ignore him when the door is opened.**

2. **Have the helper ring the door bell or knock.**

3. **Leash Buddy, tell him to "Sit" and "Stay," and then open the door.**

   Chances are, Buddy will get up to greet your helper. Reinforce the Stay command by checking straight up on the leash to make Buddy sit again. If he doesn't respond, review the training equipment you're using (see Chapter 5).

    Buddy's response to a check depends on the extent to which he's distracted and his discomfort threshold. (See Chapter 3 for more information.)

4. **Repeat the preceding steps until Buddy holds the Stay position on a *loose* leash when you open the door, which may take several repetitions.**

   As soon as he's successful, stop the session.

5. **Before the next session, remind your helper to ignore Buddy and to avoid making eye contact with him. Start the steps from the beginning and invite your helper into the house.**

   When Buddy stays, quietly tell him what a good boy he is and end the session. If he doesn't stay, reinforce the sit with a check of the leash.

You need to maintain this routine until Buddy sits politely when someone comes to the door. When he reliably sits and stays, you can try the exercise off leash. His response will tell you whether he needs more training. *Remember:* Training is often a matter of who's more persistent: you or your dog.

Putting an End to Counter Surfing

Buddy is *counter surfing* when he puts both front feet on the counter to snatch anything edible within reach. When you're present, you can physically remove him. If you've taught him the Leave It command (head to Chapter 9), you can use it to derail his efforts as he's thinking of jumping onto the counter. In either case, you have to be there.

If, however, you aren't present, anything left on the counter is fair game. Unless you're a meticulous housekeeper who makes sure that the counter is always clear of edibles when no one is in the kitchen, you're sure to have a counter-surfing Buddy going after the leftovers that remain on the counter. Check out Figure 11-3 to see a counter surfing dog.

If you just can't seem to keep the counters clear when no one's in the kitchen, one deterrent is to place a fly swatter at an angle on the counter so that when Buddy makes his ascent, it falls off and (hopefully) startles him. Even though this tactic is successful with some dogs, others simply ignore the falling swatter. In addition, you have to remember to put the fly swatter on the counter — and at that point, you may as well remove all food items.

Figure 11-3: Meigs showing early signs of counter surfing.

One little trick that helps Buddy think you're psychic, and to reinforce your Leave It command, is to place a mirror in such a way that you can see the counter from another room. You can bait the countertop with something very tasty, go into the other room, and wait for Buddy to jump up. When you say "Leave It," Buddy will be amazed at your ability to catch him in the act. And for the persistent and dedicated counter surfer, you may consider an indoor containment system to solve the problem (see Chapter 5).

Quieting the Incessant Barker

On the one hand, few things are more reassuring than knowing that your dog will sound the alarm when a stranger approaches. On the other hand, few things are more nerve racking than a dog's incessant barking. Dogs bark for three reasons:

- ✔ In response to a stimulus
- ✔ Because they're bored and want attention — any attention — even if that attention involves the owner being nasty to the dog (scolding or physically punishing)
- ✔ When someone comes to the door

Therein lies the dilemma: You want the dog to bark but only when you think he should. We cover each of these situations in the following sections.

One way to stop a barking dog is an electronic bark collar, which causes a slight electric shock every time he barks. Another way is a citronella collar, which sprays some citronella in the direction of the dog's nose when he barks. These tools work well in a single-dog household. (See Chapter 5 for more info on these collars.)

Barking as a response to a stimulus

Your dog is outside in the yard, and some people walk by, perhaps with a dog on leash, so Buddy barks. Barking is a natural response of defending his territory. After the potential intruders have passed, he's quiet again. People and dogs passing are the stimulus that causes barking, and after they have been removed, your dog stops.

If the people had stopped by the fence for a conversation, your dog would have continued to bark. To get him to stop, you have to remove the stimulus from the dog or the dog from the stimulus. If you live in a busy area where people pass by frequently, you may have to change your dog's environment. In other words, you may not be able to leave him in the yard for prolonged periods. Putting up a dog run is one alternative, if you want your dog to be outside, or putting him in a crate in the house can successfully remove him from the stimulus.

Barking for attention

Sometimes it's as if your dog is barking for no apparent reason. However, even though the motivation isn't apparent to you, your dog always has a reason for barking. It can be due to any or all of the following:

- Anxiety
- Boredom
- Seeking attention because he's lonely

Although Buddy's barking may be unacceptable to you, to him it's the only way he can express his unhappiness and frustration.

 Theoretically, none of the preceding reasons is difficult to overcome if you work to eliminate the potential causes. Spend more time exercising your dog. Spend more time training your dog. Don't leave your dog alone so long, and don't leave him alone so often.

As a practical matter, however, overcoming these reasons isn't that easy. Most people work for a living and must leave their dogs at home alone for prolonged periods. If you live in an apartment, your dog certainly can't bark all day. The stress on the dog is horrendous, not to mention the fact that your neighbors will soon begin to despise you and your noisy dog. (Chapter 17 can help if you suspect that your dog's barking is due to separation anxiety.)

Barking when someone comes to the door

Most dogs bark when someone comes to the door. While you may appreciate being alerted that someone has comes to the door, you probably want Buddy to stop when you tell him "Thank you. I've got it from here." Some dogs don't stop, however, which is pretty embarrassing. Whatever the owners have tried, nothing seems to work.

For this situation, our favorite tool is a clicker (see Chapter 5). Here's how to train Buddy using a clicker:

1. **Acclimate Buddy to the clicker.**

   With plenty of small treats at hand, make yourself comfortable in your favorite chair with Buddy just hanging out. Click and give Buddy a treat. Repeat several times until he associates the click with getting a treat.

   The timing of the click is important — it has to come when he's quiet, followed by the treat.

2. **Recruit a helper to come to the door. When your helper comes to the door and Buddy starts barking, listen for the brief intervals when he stops barking. The instant he stops, say "Thank you" or whatever command you want to use, click, and give him a treat.**

   Continue until Buddy realizes that being quiet is more rewarding than barking. Stop the session here.

3. **Repeat the process over the course of several sessions until Buddy reliably responds to the command you have chosen.**

For more information on clicker training, see Karen Pryor's books *Reaching the Animal Mind: Clicker Training and What It Teaches Us about All Animals* (Scribner) and *Click! Dog Training System* (Barnes & Noble).

Contending with Chewing — The Nonfood Variety

The principal reasons that dogs chew are physiological and psychological. The first is understandable; it could be that a puppy is teething. The second isn't so understandable. Both are a nuisance. In the following sections, we explain both reasons and provide some guidance if you're having problems with chewing.

Dogs that chew objects can be showing a nutritional deficiency, so you may want to change his diet and perhaps visit the vet for some blood work. We were made honorary members of the Bull Terrier Club of America for saving so many Bull Terriers who ate television remote controls. After suggesting a properly balanced natural diet to the owners (see Chapter 4), the dogs were nutritionally satisfied and showed no interest in chewing again.

I'm teething! Examining the physiological need to chew

As part of the teething process, puppies need to chew. They can't help it. To get through this period, provide your dog with a soft and a hard chew toy as well as a canvas field dummy. Real bones (soup bones are ideal) are great hard toys. Hard rubber Kong toys (www.kongcompany.com) with some peanut butter inserted into the center also will keep a dog amused for a long time. Don't give him anything he can destroy or ingest unless they're food items. Carrots, apples, dog biscuits, or ice cubes are great to relieve the monotony; otherwise, he may select other interesting things to chew on, such as those new shoes you left lying around.

When your dog is going through his period of physiological chewing, make sure he doesn't have access to your personal articles, such as shoes, socks, and towels. Think of it as good training for you not to leave things lying around the house. And don't forget that a lonely dog may chew up anything in his path. So make sure your dog gets enough attention from you — and that he gets some strong chew toys! When you can't supervise him, crate him (see Chapter 8).

I'm bored! Recognizing the psychological reasons that dogs chew

Chewing that takes place after a dog has gone through teething is usually a manifestation of anxiety, boredom, or loneliness. This oral habit has nothing to do with being spiteful. If your dog attacks the furniture, baseboards, and walls, tips over the garbage can, or engages in other destructive chewing activities, don't become angry. Instead, recognize that you probably aren't providing him the stimulation he needs and give him some solid chew toys.

Use a crate to confine Buddy when you can't supervise him. Confining him saves you lots of money, and you won't lose your temper and get mad at the poor fellow. Even more important, he can't get into things that are a potential danger to him.

We want to emphasize that confinement is a problem-solving approach of last resort. Ideally, the dog isn't left alone so long and so often that he feels the need to chew in order to relieve his boredom. Your dog doesn't need you to entertain him all the time, but extended periods of being alone can make your pet neurotic.

Dealing with a Digger

One of the favorite pastimes of our Dachshunds is digging, or "landscaping" as we call it. They engage in this activity at every opportunity and with great zest. Because Dachshunds were bred to go after badgers that burrow into hillsides, this behavior is instinctive. Does that mean we have to put up with a yard that looks like a minefield? Not at all, but we do have to assume the responsibility for

- ✔ Expending the digging energy, which involves exercising Buddy
- ✔ Providing an outlet for it, which means giving your dog a place where he can dig to his heart's content
- ✔ Supervising the little darlings to make sure they don't get into trouble

The good news is that most so-called behavior problems are under your direct control; the bad news is that you have to get involved. The cure to digging is rather simple: Don't leave your dog unattended in the yard for lengthy periods. Of course, you can always cover your yard with Astroturf or green cement!

Recognize that digging is part of prey drive (see Chapter 2 for more on the drives). Because it's part of prey drive, all the tips we give you about exhausting the behavior apply here. You can't make a dog dig until he's exhausted, but you can tire out your dog by playing ball or running with him so that he's too tired to dig!

Or, if you have Wirehaired Dachshunds, like we have, you can provide a place where it's safe for them to dig and where they don't excavate craters in the lawn. Put up a small fenced area for them where they can dig. In our case, we walk them in the woods and allow them to dig there. Interestingly, our little guys dig under specific grasses to get at the roots and dirt. It obviously satisfies some need, and we attribute the fact that they've never had worms to this daily intake of Virginia clay. A small amount of dirt has a way of cleansing the large intestines, which is a favorite place for worms to attach. Be careful not to let your dog dig in earth that has had pesticides or fertilizers used on it.

Understanding the reasons for digging

Although some breeds, such as the small terriers, have a true propensity for digging, all dogs do it to some extent at one time or another. Take a look at some of the more common and sometimes comical reasons for digging:

✔ To participate in *allelomimetic behavior*, or mimicking. In training, this practice is useful, but it may spell trouble for your gardening efforts. You plant, your dog digs up.

Maybe you should do your gardening in secret and out of sight of your dog.

✔ To make nests for real or imaginary puppies. This reason applies to female dogs.

✔ To bury or dig up a bone.

✔ To see what's there, because it's fun, or to find a cool spot to lie down.

✔ To relieve boredom, isolation, or frustration.

If you think you have a championship digger who's digging for mice, moles, or other vermin in the ground, consider getting him involved in Earthdog trials, which we explain in Chapter 21.

Managing Marking Behavior

Marking is a way for your dog to leave his calling card by depositing a small amount of urine in a particular spot, marking it as his territory. The frequency with which dogs can accomplish marking never ceases to amaze us. Male dogs invariably prefer vertical surfaces, hence the fire hydrant. Males tend to engage in this behavior with more determination than females.

Behaviorists explain that marking is a dog's way of establishing his territory, and it provides a means to find his way back home. They also claim that dogs are able to tell the rank order, gender, and age — puppy or adult dog — by smelling the urine of another dog.

Those people who take their dogs for regular walks through the neighborhood quickly discover that marking is a ritual, with favorite spots that have to be watered. It's a way for the dog to maintain his rank in the order of the pack, which consists of all the other dogs in the neighborhood or territory that come across his route.

Adult male dogs lift a leg, as do some females. For the male dog, the object is to leave his calling card higher than the previous calling card. This can lead to some comical results, as when a Dachshund or a Yorkshire Terrier tries to cover the calling card of an Irish Wolfhound or Great Dane. It's a contest.

Annoying as this behavior can be, it's perfectly natural and normal. At times, it also can be embarrassing, such as when Buddy lifts his leg on a person's leg (which is a not-so-uncommon occurrence). What he's trying to communicate here we'll leave to others to explain.

When this behavior is expressed inside the house, it becomes a problem. Fortunately, this behavior is rare, but it does happen. Here are the circumstances requiring special vigilance:

✔ When you have more than one animal in your house — another dog (or several others) or a cat

✔ When taking Buddy to a friend's or relative's house for a visit, especially if that individual also has a dog or a cat

✔ When you've redecorated the house with new furniture or curtains

✔ When you've moved to a new house

Distract your dog if you see that he's about to mark in an inappropriate spot. Call his name, and take him to a place where he can eliminate. When you take Buddy to someone else's home, keep an eye on him. At the slightest sign that he's even thinking about it, interrupt his thought by clapping your hands and calling him to you. Take him outside and wait until he's had a chance to relieve himself. If this behavior persists, you need to go back to basic housetraining principles, such as the crate or X-pen, until you can trust him again. (See Chapter 8 for more on housetraining.)

Part IV
Taking Training to the Next Level

The 5th Wave   By Rich Tennant

"It's not officially part of the obedience test, but I thought as long as I'm training him how to do things..."

In this part . . .

This part introduces you to the world of American Kennel Club (AKC) obedience events, from basic to more advanced exercises. You and your dog can strive for titles awarded by the AKC, and we show you how to train for them. For example, to demonstrate that you have taught your puppy elementary manners, you can participate in the S.T.A.R. Puppy or the Canine Good Citizen programs. We also take you from firming up your dog's understanding of basic exercises to teaching him some advanced obedience, including those exercises necessary for the Companion Dog title. You also may want your dog to learn how to retrieve, so we include a chapter that helps you teach him this exercise.

Chapter 12

Participating in AKC S.T.A.R. Puppy and Canine Good Citizen Programs

. . . .

In This Chapter

▶ Looking at the S.T.A.R. Puppy Program and its requirements

▶ Understanding what it takes to be a Canine Good Citizen

. . . .

*T*he American Kennel Club (AKC) administers and oversees, among others, a multitude of performance events with varying degrees of difficulty. These events are designed to demonstrate different levels of training. A good place to start is the AKC S.T.A.R. Puppy Program. The next level of training is the Canine Good Citizen Program (CGC), which builds on the S.T.A.R. Puppy Program.

These programs are based on the premise that *all* dogs should be trained. They're also outreach programs designed to motivate dog owners and encourage them to go further in training their dogs. The Canine Good Citizen Program, in particular, is a window of opportunity to a variety of dog sports. If you want your dog to become a therapy dog, many of the therapy dog organizations require that your dog has successfully gone through this program as well.

Ideally, every dog should be trained to become a Canine Good Citizen. The more dogs that are good citizens, the better the chances dog owners have of counteracting the growing antidog sentiment in many communities. Irresponsible dog ownership has been the cause for this sentiment, so only responsible pet ownership can reverse it.

This chapter shows you what you and your dog can do to prepare for both tests. When you and your dog earn a Canine Good Citizen Certificate, you have accomplished more than millions of other dog owners. Are you ready for the challenge?

Starting on the Right Paw with the AKC S.T.A.R. Puppy Program

The AKC S.T.A.R. Puppy Program is a great way to get your puppy on the right track behaviorally. S.T.A.R. stands for Socialization, Training, Activity, and Responsibility. Many kennel clubs and obedience training clubs, as well as private organizations, offer this program. Figure 12-1 shows an AKC S.T.A.R. puppy.

According to the AKC, "Training classes teach you how to best communicate with your puppy. Organized training classes also provide an opportunity for your dog to socialize with other dogs. . . . AKC S.T.A.R. Puppy training is a natural lead in to the AKC Canine Good Citizen Program."

After you have completed a basic 6-week training class (taught by an AKC Approved Canine Good Citizen Evaluator) with your puppy (up to 1 year old), he's eligible to be enrolled in the AKC S.T.A.R. Puppy Program upon passing a test. This test is conducted as the classes are being taught, and at the end of the classes the instructor gives the test results (which are contained on a form) to the dog owner. They can then enroll themselves into the AKC S.T.A.R. Puppy Program by contacting the AKC. The test consists of 20 items — six rate the owner's behavior (based on the pledge all the owner's must take), five rate the puppy's behavior, and the remaining nine judge the Pre-Canine Good Citizen Behaviors that were taught in the class. For more information on this program, visit www.akc.org/starpuppy.

Figure 12-1: Your dog can become an AKC S.T.A.R. puppy, too.

In the following sections, we further explain the main aspects of this program, including the owner's pledge, the training classes, and the requirements necessary to pass the program.

Getting to know the Responsible Dog Owner's Pledge

The S.T.A.R. Puppy Program includes a Responsible Dog Owner's Pledge. The owner is judged on this pledge as the course progresses. The owner pledges to be responsible for the following:

- His dog's health needs, such as routine veterinary care, proper nutrition, daily exercise, and regular grooming
- His dog's safety, such as controlling his dog, keeping the dog on leash in public, and providing identification and adequate supervision when his dog and children are together
- His dog's manners, including preventing his dog from infringing on the rights of others by not letting his dog run loose in the neighborhood and picking up his dog's waste in public areas
- His dog's quality of life, such as basic training and giving his dog attention and playtime

You can read the full Responsible Dog Owner's Pledge by visiting www.akc.org/starpuppy/test_items_pledge.cfm.

Attending puppy training with your pooch and earning his S.T.A.R. medal

The training part of the S.T.A.R. program requires you and your puppy to attend a six-week obedience class. During the class, the puppy has to do the following:

- Be free of aggression toward people during the class
- Be free of aggression toward other puppies in class
- Tolerate the collar or body harness of his owner's choice
- Show that his owner can hug or hold him (depending on size)
- Allow the owner to take away his treat or toy

After you attend the six-week training course, you and your pup should be ready to graduate from the program! At this time, he should be able to demonstrate basic manners. Specifically, at the conclusion of the training class, the puppy has to demonstrate that he will do all the following:

- ✔ Allow (in any position) petting by a person other than the owner
- ✔ Allow the owner to handle and briefly examine him (ears and feet, for example)
- ✔ Walk on a leash, following his owner in a straight line for 15 steps
- ✔ Walk on a leash past other people who are 5 feet away
- ✔ Sit on command (owner may use a food lure)
- ✔ Down on command (owner may use a food lure)
- ✔ Come to owner from 5 feet when his name is called
- ✔ React appropriately to distractions presented 15 feet away
- ✔ Stay on leash with another person (owner walks ten steps away and returns)

When he passes his exam, he'll be eligible to receive the AKC S.T.A.R. Puppy Medal. You'll get a copy of your dog's AKC Puppy Test, which you then send to the AKC with $10. You'll then receive the medal and a package of information.

These tasks may seem difficult to you at first, but don't worry. You learn everything you need to know in the training class. Plus the chapters in this book devoted to training can help you bone up on all these areas.

Using the AKC Canine Good Citizen Program to Build on Your Pup's Skills

The Canine Good Citizen (CGC) test uses a series of exercises that checks the dog's ability to behave in an acceptable manner in public. Open to all dogs 6 months of age or older, its purpose is to demonstrate that the dog, as a companion for all people, can be a respected community member and can be trained and conditioned to always behave in the home, in public places, and in the presence of other dogs in a manner that reflects credit on the dog. The fee for taking the test is usually $15, plus $5 if the owner wants an AKC certificate.

To become a Canine Good Citizen, your dog must demonstrate, by means of a short test, that he meets certain requirements. In the following sections, we explain the requirements for passing the Canine Good Citizen test as well as how to train for each of those requirements.

Many dog organizations offer CGC training classes; your local kennel club will know the particulars. You can locate your local kennel club in the phonebook, or you can ask your vet, a dog groomer, or any obedience school for more information. You also can get more information at www.akc.org/events/cgc.

Exercise requirements: What to expect during the test

To become a Canine Good Citizen, a dog must pass a test that demonstrates his ability to behave in an acceptable manner in public. The test is scored on a pass/fail basis, and in order to qualify for a Canine Good Citizen certificate, the dog must pass ten tests regarding the following exercises:

- Accepting a friendly stranger
- Sitting politely for petting
- Having a clean appearance and behaving during grooming
- Walking on a loose leash
- Walking through a crowd
- Sitting, downing, and staying in place
- Coming when called
- Reacting appropriately to another dog
- Reacting appropriately to distractions
- Succeeding at supervised separation

These are practical exercises that determine the amount of control you have over your dog. During the test, you can repeat commands several times and encourage and praise your dog. Repeating commands too often, however, demonstrates a lack of control and causes you to fail. You're also not permitted to give food to your dog during the test. All tests are done on leash, and dogs need to wear a well-fitting buckle or slip collar made of leather, fabric, or chain. Other collars, such as head halters or harnesses, aren't permitted. The leash can be either fabric or leather.

Organizations offering the Canine Good Citizen test have considerable leeway in determining the order in which to give the tests. We outline the most common order in the following sections. Usually three evaluators conduct the test. The first evaluator conducts Tests 1 through 3, the second one conducts Tests 4 through 9, and the third one conducts Test 10.

An automatic failure results when a dog eliminates during testing, except during Test 10, provided it's held outdoors. Any dog that growls, snaps, bites, attacks, or attempts to attack a person or another dog isn't a good citizen and must be dismissed from the test. A dog that fails one of the tests is often permitted to try again after the last participant finished. Sometimes they pass the second time, but not often.

We discuss each test briefly in the following sections, including what to expect during the test.

Test 1: Accepting a friendly stranger

This test demonstrates that the dog allows a friendly stranger to approach and speak to the owner in a natural, everyday situation.

The evaluator approaches the dog and owner and greets the owner in a friendly manner, ignoring the dog. The evaluator and owner shake hands and exchange pleasantries. The dog must show no sign of resentment, aggression, or shyness. The dog may not break position, jump on the evaluator, or try to go to the evaluator. If the owner has to hold the dog to control it, the dog fails the exercise.

Test 2: Sitting politely for petting

This test demonstrates that the dog allows a friendly stranger to touch him while he's out for a walk with the owner (see Figure 12-2). With the dog sitting at the owner's side (either side is permissible) throughout the exercise, the evaluator pets the dog on the head and body only. The owner may talk to the dog throughout the exercise.

After petting, the evaluator then circles the dog and owner, completing the test. The dog must not show shyness or resentment. The dog may stand while being petted, but he must not struggle or pull away to avoid the petting. He also shouldn't lunge at or jump on the evaluator.

Test 3: Having a clean appearance and behaving during grooming

This test demonstrates that the dog welcomes being groomed and examined and permits a stranger, such as a vet, groomer, or friend of the owner, to do so. It also demonstrates the owner's care, concern, and responsibility.

For the appearance and grooming test, make sure Buddy looks his best. If he needs a bath before the test, give him one.

The evaluator examines the dog to determine whether he's clean and groomed. The dog must appear to be in healthy condition — proper weight, clean, healthy, and alert. Bring the comb or brush you commonly use on Buddy. The evaluator lightly combs or brushes the dog and, in a natural manner, lightly examines the ears and gently picks up each front foot.

Figure 12-2:
Sitting
politely for
petting.

The dog doesn't need to hold a specific position during the examination, and the owner may talk to the dog, praise him, and give him encouragement throughout. A dog that requires restraining during this examination fails the test.

Test 4: Walking on a loose leash

The fourth test demonstrates that the owner is in control of his dog. The dog's position should leave no doubt that he's attentive to the owner and is responding to the owner's changes of direction.

An *occasional* tight leash is permissible, but constant straining or pulling on the leash is unacceptable. Similarly, excessive sniffing of the floor or ground, indicating that the dog isn't attentive to the owner, also is unacceptable.

During this test, you must make a left turn, a right turn, and an about-turn, with at least one stop in between and another at the end. You may talk to the dog along the way to praise or command him in a normal tone of voice.

Test 5: Walking through a crowd

This test demonstrates that the dog can move about politely in pedestrian traffic and is under control in public places. The test is a great incentive to train Buddy around distractions.

The dog and owner walk around and closely pass several people (at least three). The dog may show some interest in the strangers but must continue to walk with the owner, without evidence of overexuberance, shyness, or resentment. The owner may talk to the dog and encourage or praise the dog throughout the test. The dog shouldn't strain at the leash, jump on people in the crowd, or try to hide behind his owner.

Children may act as members of the crowd in this test as well as in the reaction to distractions test that's discussed later in this chapter. Another leashed, well-behaved dog also may be in the crowd.

Test 6: Staying in place

This test demonstrates that the dog responds to the owner's Sit and Down commands. During the test, the dog needs to remain in the place commanded by the owner.

Prior to this test, the dog's leash is replaced with a 20-foot line. The owner may take a reasonable amount of time and use more than one command to make the dog sit and then lay down. The evaluator must determine whether the dog has responded to the owner's commands. The owner may not force the dog into either position but may touch the dog to offer gentle guidance.

When instructed by the evaluator, the owner tells the dog to "Stay" and, with the 20-foot line in hand, walks forward the length of the line, turns, and returns to the dog at a natural pace (the 20-foot line isn't removed or dropped). The dog must remain in the place in which he was left (though the dog may change position, such as stand up), until the evaluator instructs the owner to release the dog. The dog may be released from the front or the side.

Test 7: Coming when called

This test demonstrates that the dog comes when the owner calls him. The dog remains on the 20-foot line that was used in Test 6. The owner walks 10 feet from the dog, turns to face the dog, and calls the dog. The owner may use body language and encouragement when calling the dog. When leaving the dog, the owner may tell the dog to "Stay" or "Wait," or he may just walk away from the dog. The dog may be left in the Sit, Down, or Stand position. If the dog attempts to follow the owner, the evaluator may distract the dog (for example, by petting) until the owner is 10 feet away.

The point of the test is to determine whether the dog comes when called and whether he stays, and the exercise is completed when the dog comes to the owner and the owner attaches the dog's own leash.

Test 8: Reacting appropriately to another dog

This test demonstrates that the dog can behave politely around other dogs. During the test, two owners and their dogs approach each other from a distance of about 10 yards, stop, shake hands and exchange pleasantries, and continue on for about 5 yards.

The dogs should show no more than casual interest in each other. If either dog goes to the other dog or its owner, he fails. See Figure 12-3 to see how the dogs should behave during a greeting.

Figure 12-3:
Reacting appropriately to another dog.

Test 9: Reacting appropriately to distractions

This test demonstrates that the dog is confident at all times when faced with common distracting situations. The evaluator selects two from the following list. (*Note:* Because some dogs are sensitive to sound and others to visual distractions, most tests involve one sound and one visual distraction.)

- A person using crutches, a wheelchair, or a walker
- A sudden closing or opening of a door
- The dropping of a large book, pan, folded chair, or the like, no closer than 5 feet behind the dog
- A jogger running in front of the dog
- A person pushing a shopping cart or pulling a crate dolly passing 5 to 10 feet away
- A person on a bicycle passing at least 10 feet away

Cat lovers are in luck: Cats aren't used as a distraction in this test.

The owner may talk to the dog and praise him during this test. In a similar situation in real life, you probably would talk in an encouraging way to your dog. The dog may express a natural interest and curiosity and may appear slightly startled but shouldn't panic, try to run away, or show aggressiveness. An isolated bark (one) is acceptable, but continued barking causes the dog to fail.

Test 10: Succeeding at supervised separation

This test demonstrates that the dog can be left with another person and maintain its training and good manners while the owner goes out of sight. Evaluators say to the owner something like, "Would you like me to watch your dog?" The owner then fastens the dog to a 6-foot line, such as the dog's leash, gives the end of the leash to an evaluator, and goes to a place out of sight of the dog for three minutes. The dog shouldn't continually bark, whine, howl, pace unnecessarily, or show anything other than mild agitation or nervousness. This test isn't a Stay exercise; dogs may stand, sit, lie down, and change positions during this test. Dogs are tested individually, not as a group, and more than one dog can be tested at a time.

Preparing to take the test

If you've done the basic training, you're already halfway to being ready for the Canine Good Citizen test. The exercises you need to work on are those that add distractions, including the following:

- ✔ Accepting a friendly stranger
- ✔ Sitting politely for petting
- ✔ Having a clean appearance and behaving during grooming
- ✔ Reacting appropriately to another dog
- ✔ Reacting appropriately to distractions
- ✔ Succeeding at supervised separation

We discuss how to prepare for each of these in the following sections.

Because Buddy's ability to Sit-Stay is so critical to success on many of the tests, make sure that he has this exercise down pat. (See Chapter 9 to find out how to teach Buddy this command.)

Training for accepting a friendly stranger and sitting politely for petting

Start by teaching your dog to Sit for Examination (refer to Chapter 14 for more on how to complete this exercise) and build from there. The Sit command (Chapter 9) is the cornerstone for all the distraction tests. You need a helper for these training exercises.

If you've scored your dog for fight or flight (see Chapter 2), remember that this score determines his response to another person, in this case the helper. For example, if the helper is a stranger and your dog is high in fight, he may show signs of protectiveness. On the other hand, if Buddy is low in fight and high in flight behaviors, he may try to hide behind you or show signs of shyness when the helper approaches.

The aim of the following exercise is for your dog to allow the approach of a stranger who also then touches the dog. For the majority of dogs, this exercise isn't particularly difficult, but it does require a little practice. Follow these steps:

1. **With Buddy sitting at your side, begin as you do for the Sit-Stay.**

   If you need help with this step, check out Chapter 9.

2. **Say "Stay" and have your helper approach your dog from 6 feet at a 45-degree angle to your left.**

3. **Ask the helper to approach the dog in a friendly and nonthreatening manner, without hovering over the dog.**

   As the helper approaches the dog, have the helper show Buddy the palm of his left hand and continue to walk by. If Buddy stays, praise and release. If your dog wants to get up, pull the leash straight up with your left hand, say "Stay," and then try again.

   Buddy's response determines how close the helper gets in the beginning. If he becomes apprehensive about the helper's approach and tries to move, have the person walk past Buddy at a distance of 2 feet without making eye contact or looking at him. Buddy may perceive eye contact as threatening. As Buddy gets used to that maneuver, have the helper offer him treat, placed on the open palm, as he walks by, still without making eye contact with the dog. It doesn't matter whether Buddy takes the treat — it's the gesture that counts. When your dog accepts the helper walking past and offering a treat, stop for this session.

At your next session, first follow the preceding steps and then move on to these:

1. **Have the helper first offer a treat and then lightly touch Buddy on the head, still without making eye contact, as he continues past the dog.**

2. **Ask the helper to attempt to look at Buddy as he touches Buddy and goes past.**

   For this particular test, the eye contact in connection with the examination is the most difficult part of the exercise, and it may require several sessions before the dog is steady.

Training for appearance and grooming

You can introduce the appearance and grooming exercise as soon as your dog accepts being touched by a stranger. Have your helper lightly comb or brush Buddy with you at his side or directly in front. The helper examines the ears and picks up each front foot. If your dog finds this task difficult, have the helper give the dog a treat as he touches a foot. Condition the dog with praise and treats to accept having his feet handled.

The appearance and grooming test is one of the most frequently failed tests, mainly because the dog won't permit the evaluator to handle his feet. If you make a point of handling your dog's feet when he's a puppy (and have your friends do it too), he won't be upset by this action as an adult.

If your puppy or dog doesn't like his feet being touched, try teaching him the tricks Shake and High Five. (See Chapter 23.) He'll soon understand that allowing his front foot to be touched can be fun and is rewarded.

Training for reacting appropriately to another dog

Your dog may stand or sit for this test. He's less likely, however, to try to initiate contact with the other dog from a sit. Practice this exercise with someone who also has a well-trained dog. With your dogs at your sides, approach each other from a distance of about 20 feet and stop close enough to each other that you can shake hands. As you stop, tell Buddy to "Sit" and "Stay."

If your dog wants to say hello to the other dog, reinforce the Stay command. Be sure you instruct your training partner not to let his dog come to say hello to Buddy.

Training for reacting appropriately to distractions

Take a look at the list of distractions in the section "Test 9: Reacting appropriately to distractions" earlier in this chapter. If you think that your dog may be unduly startled by any one of these distractions, you need to practice and condition him to ignore that distraction.

Because your dog's Personality Profile (see Chapter 2) determines how he reacts to a particular distraction, expose him to different distractions to see how he deals with them. Some dogs take it all in stride and others require several exposures to become accustomed to the distraction. The best foundation is a solid Sit-Stay.

Training for succeeding at supervised separation

Although this test doesn't directly deal with distractions, it does evaluate a dog's response to the unforeseen, so it resembles the other tests. It shows that the dog can be left with someone else, which demonstrates training and good manners.

To train your dog to be successful at supervised separation, leave your dog in either the Sit or Down position when you're separated from him. He doesn't need to hold that position until you return; he simply has to refrain from vocalizing or pacing unnecessarily. By having Buddy focus on staying in place, you reduce the likelihood that he'll bark or howl or become overly agitated. Dogs prefer to have direction and not being left to hang out and make their own decisions.

Becoming familiar with the do's and don'ts of taking the test

Your attitude and state of mind are the most important influence on the Canine Good Citizen test's outcome. If you're excessively nervous, your dog will become nervous, too. Owners under stress sometimes behave in ways they would never dream of doing any other time. If you do act differently, your dog will notice and be confused to the point where he may fail. Maintain a positive outlook and rely on your training. The following hints can help you prepare for and participate in the Canine Good Citizen test.

Here's what you should *do* when preparing for the test:

- ✔ Practice the entire test with a helper and friends before you actually enter a test. Doing so is more for your benefit than Buddy's. As you become familiar with the test, you'll lose some of your nervousness. It also can identify Buddy's weak areas and give you additional time to work on them.

- ✔ Give your dog a bath and thoroughly groom him before the test.

- ✔ Use the correct equipment for the test — a well-fitting buckle or slip collar of leather, fabric, or chain, and a leather or fabric leash.

- ✔ Exercise Buddy before you take the test. If your dog eliminates at any time during testing, he fails.

- ✔ Warm up your dog before taking the test so that both of you are as relaxed as possible under the circumstances.

- ✔ Use a second command for any exercise, if necessary.

- ✔ Talk to your dog during an exercise to keep attention on you, if necessary.

- ✔ Ask the evaluator for an explanation if you don't understand a procedure or an instruction.

✔ Maintain a loose leash throughout the entire test, even between exercises, to the extent possible. Although an occasional tightening of the leash generally isn't considered a failure, it does become a judgment call for the evaluator in assessing your control over your dog. Don't put yourself or the evaluator in that position.

✔ Conduct yourself in a sportsmanlike manner at all times.

✔ Keep in mind the purpose of the Canine Good Citizen and become an ambassador of goodwill and good manners for all dogs.

Here are some things you definitely *don't* want to do when preparing for or taking the test:

✔ **Lose your temper or attitude if your dog fails an exercise.** If you berate your dog, you sour him on the entire experience. You may feel a certain amount of disappointment and frustration, but you need to control those feelings. The more you work with your dog, the more attuned he is to your feelings. He'll associate them with the circumstances and not the failure of an exercise.

✔ **Change your attitude toward your dog after he has failed an exercise.** Your remedy shouldn't be to make the dog feel anxious. Instead, review your training, work on the difficult exercise, and try again. If you undermine your dog's confidence, training will take longer and become a less rewarding experience than if you realize that your job is to support and encourage your dog at every step of the way.

If you take the time to participate in the Canine Good Citizen test, you obviously want Buddy to pass. Even if he doesn't, you can still feel good about yourself and Buddy. You're making an effort to train your dog to be a model member of the community. In that small way, you're doing a service to all dogs and their owners.

Chapter 13

Training for Fun and Competition

*I*f you and Buddy enjoy working together, the sky is the limit — you can participate in many performance events. Doing so is a lot of fun, and you meet lots of nice people. We must warn you, though: After you get started, you can become addicted to these events, and your life will never be the same.

Almost every weekend of the year, you can go to some event and show off what the two of you have accomplished. Dog events are categorized as either *conformation shows,* where your dog is judged on his appearance, or as *performance trials,* where you and your dog are judged on your abilities. The shows can be held together or separately.

Different organizations have licensed shows, including those in which *designer breeds,* such as the Goldendoodle or Labradoodle, and mixed breeds can participate. In this book, we concentrate on the shows held under the auspices of the American Kennel Club (AKC), the oldest and largest organization to license such events. To participate in an AKC-licensed performance event, such as Agility, Obedience, and Rally, your dog must be registered with the AKC. More than 80 percent of the participants in these events are women.

The AKC awards three basic obedience titles:

- Companion Dog, or C.D., from the Novice class
- Companion Dog Excellent, or C.D.X., from the Open class
- Utility Dog, or U.D., from the Utility class

The level of difficulty increases with each class, from basic control and retrieving and jumping to responding to signals and directional signals. The classes are designed so that any dog can participate successfully and earn titles. After your dog has earned a Utility Dog title, you're then eligible to compete for the special obedience titles of Obedience Trial Champion and Utility Dog Excellent. We don't go into detail about these advanced competitions, but if you want more information visit www.akc.org.

All three classes and all levels of competition have one exercise in common: heeling. This means that you and Buddy need a firm foundation and have to practice, practice, practice. And even if you aren't planning to compete, teaching Buddy to heel is still important.

In this chapter, we take a look at the AKC Novice class and its goal, the Companion Dog title. We show you the six required exercises and the points needed to earn the title. In Chapter 14, we review the remaining exercises you and your dog need to complete the Companion Dog title.

You can get your own copy of the Obedience Regulations by contacting the American Kennel Club at 5580 Centerview Drive, Suite 200, Raleigh, NC 27606-3390 (919-233-9767 or www.akc.org). Getting your own copy of the regulations is a piece o' cake, so go ahead and get them. Knowing the rules is a good idea so you know what's expected from you and your dog.

Understanding the System: Your Road Map to the Companion Dog Title

If you're interested in helping your dog earn the Companion Dog title, you need to know the ropes on how to get started. This section provides the info you need.

If you've already been to a dog show and seen a performance trial, or watched one on TV, you probably thought, "My dog could never do that." Perhaps, but remember that every one of the participants began with training their first dog.

The Rally class

The name *rally* comes from the use of directional signs, similar to a Road Rally for cars. In the Rally class, the dog and owner complete a course following a series of 10 to 20 signs, depending on the level. Each sign, called a *station,* instructs the owner on each exercise the dog has to perform. For example, the sign may say "Forward," "About-turn," or "Halt."

After the judge has given the first Forward, the owner-and-dog team moves continuously from one sign to the next on their own instead of waiting for the judge's command for each exercise (as in all the other obedience classes). Unlimited communication from owner to dog is permitted, but the owner may not touch the dog and physical guidance is penalized.

This class is fun because you can give all the extra help your dog may need in the form of commands, encouragement, and praise. It's also fast paced, because you move from one sign to the next without any interruption, which makes it very exciting for the dog.

The starting score is 200, and deductions are made for any errors on the part of the dog performing the designated exercise at a station, or for not completing a required exercise. Scoring is more lenient than traditional obedience, but judges should see a sense of teamwork between the dog and owner. You'll encounter approximately 40 different stations, representing all the basic obedience exercises and maneuvers. To earn an AKC Rally title, the dog must achieve three qualifying scores under at least two different judges.

The Rally class has the following different levels:

- Novice
- Advanced
- Excellent
- Rally Advanced Excellent

In the Rally Novice class, all exercises are done on leash, and there are 10 to 15 stations. In the Rally Advanced class, all the exercises, which include one jump, are done off leash, and there are 12 to 17 stations. The Rally Excellent class is also done off leash and includes two jumps and 15 to 20 stations. Finally, the Rally Advanced Excellent title requires the dog to qualify ten times in both the Rally Advanced Class and the Rally Excellent Class at the same trial.

To begin, you and Buddy can enter either the Pre-Novice or the Novice class. The required exercises for both classes demonstrate the usefulness of the purebred dog as a companion, and they help you prepare for obtaining the Companion Dog title. In the following sections, we explain each of these classes and their requirements and characteristics.

You also can enter the Rally class (see the nearby sidebar "The Rally class" for more details).

Requirements for Pre-Novice

The Pre-Novice is a nonregular class, like the AKC S.T.A.R. Puppy and Canine Good Citizen programs (see Chapter 12), and serves as an introduction to the world of obedience events. (*Nonregular classes* are those in which participation doesn't earn AKC titles.) Seven nonregular classes are available: Graduate Novice, Graduate Open, Brace (two dogs handled by one person), Veterans (for dogs at least 7 years of age), Versatility, Team (four dogs and four owners), and Pre-Novice.

For the Pre-Novice class, no minimum point score is required for a qualifying score, and whoever has the highest score wins the class. Pre-Novice is ideal for people or dogs who have never participated in a dog show before.

The cornerstones of the Pre-Novice class, and of all the other obedience classes, are having a dog that does the following:

- ✔ Pays attention to you
- ✔ Knows how to heel

Later in this chapter, we concentrate on these two concepts.

The Pre-Novice class consists of six exercises, each with a specific point value. Your dog must respond to the first command, so you're penalized for any additional commands. All the exercises are performed on leash. Before each exercise, the judge asks, "Are you ready?" You say that you are, and the judge then gives the command, such as "Forward" for the Heel On Leash (see the later section "Let's Dance, Buddy: Heel On Leash") and Figure 8 exercises (see the later section, "Putting a Twist on Things: Teaching the Figure 8") or "Stand your dog and leave when ready" for the Stand for Examination (see Chapter 14). These exercises are always done in the order in which they're listed in Table 13-1.

Table 13-1	The Pre-Novice Class
Required Exercises	*Available Points*
Heel On Leash	45
Figure 8	25
Stand for Examination	30
Recall	40
Long Sit (1 minute)	30
Long Down (3 minutes)	30
Maximum Total Score	**200**

For more information on dog organizations

For more information on dogs and dog competitions, check out the following organizations and their respective Web sites:

✔ **American Kennel Club** (www.akc.org): The official American Kennel Club Web site offers information on almost everything to do with dogs. You can get the profiles of different breeds, find out how to register your dog, and get answers to questions about registration. You can find out about dogs in competition and what titles dogs can earn. This Web page tells you about pedigrees and, if you have a purebred dog, how to get a three-generation pedigree from the AKC. It offers reproductions from the Dog Museum, where many famous pieces of art and old books are housed, and it has archives of articles that have appeared recently, together with information about how the AKC works.

✔ **United Kennel Club** (www.ukcdogs.com): The UKC is the second oldest and second largest all-breed dog registry in the United States. Founded in 1898 by Chauncey Z. Bennett, the registry has always supported the idea of the "total dog," meaning a dog that looks and performs equally well. With 250,000 registrations annually, the performance programs of the UKC include conformation shows; obedience trials; agility trials; coonhound field trials; water races; night hunts and bench shows; hunting tests for the retrieving breeds; beagle events, including hunts and bench shows; and cur, feist, squirrel, and coon events. The UKC world of dogs is a working world. That's the way Bennett designed it, and that's the way it remains today.

✔ **Continental Kennel Club** (www.continentalkennelclub.com): A new and innovative kennel club that's embracing tradition while adjusting to the needs of dog owners worldwide.

The exercises listed in Table 13-1 are an extension of those required for the Canine Good Citizen certificate and are a preview of those required for the Novice class (which we discuss in the upcoming section "The Novice class: What's expected from you and Buddy").

The Novice class: What's expected from you and Buddy

The Novice class consists of six exercises, each with a specific point value (see Table 13-2). The six exercises are always done in the order listed in the table, and they're all pack behavior exercises. For a qualifying score, you and Buddy have to earn more than 50 percent of the available points for each exercise and a final score of more than 170 out of a possible 200.

A qualifying score at an obedience trial is called a *leg.* Your dog needs three legs to earn the AKC Companion Dog title.

Table 13-2	The Novice Class
Required Exercises	**Available Points**
Exercise 1: Heel On Leash and Figure 8	40
Exercise 2: Stand for Examination	30
Exercise 3: Heel Free	40
Exercise 4: Recall	30
Exercise 5: Sit-Stay (1 minute)	30
Exercise 6: Down-Stay (3 minutes)	30
Maximum Total Score	**200**

Like the Pre-Novice class exercises, the Novice class exercises are an extension of those required for the Canine Good Citizen test (see Chapter 12). The Stand for Examination exercise, for example, is a form of temperament test similar to the "accepting a friendly stranger" and the "sitting politely for petting" exercises in the Canine Good Citizen test.

However, some important differences and additions exist in the Novice class exercises:

✔ Buddy has to respond to the first command.

✔ Walking on a loose leash (see Chapter 12) is now called Heeling, and it consists of both heeling on and off leash and includes a Figure 8 on leash. (Refer to the later section "Putting a Twist on Things: Teaching the Figure 8" for more information.) It's also more exacting.

✔ The temperament test requires the dog to stand and is performed off leash with you standing 6 feet in front of your dog. When you're in position, the judge will approach your dog from in front and touch Buddy's head, body, and hindquarters.

✔ The Come When Called (see Chapter 8) is now referred to as the Recall. It's performed off leash and requires Buddy to Stay, Come on command, Sit in front of you, and then go to Heel position on command.

✔ The Sit and Down-Stay are done off leash for one and three minutes, respectively.

The Novice class is tailor-made for the dog who's highest in pack drive behaviors. For the dog who's highest in prey drive behaviors, this class is a little more challenging because of his distractibility around sights, sounds, and smells. (See Chapter 2 for what the different behaviors mean.)

Dog show tidbits

The term *dog shows* is all encompassing. It can be a *breed show,* where the dogs are judged solely on conformation standards — how closely they meet the standard for their breed. It can be a show that includes a breed show as well as performance competitions, such as obedience, agility, and rally, or it may just include performance events. To participate in a dog show, participants have to register about three weeks before the event.

When you look at the Novice class exercises in Table 13-2, you see that 120 points depend on your dog being able to stay — for the Stand for Examination, the Recall, the Sit, and the Down-Stay. So you can see how important the Stay exercise is. (You can find out more about helping Buddy with the Stay command in Chapter 9.)

First Things First: Teaching the Ready! Command

The first exercise in either the Pre-Novice or the Novice class is the Heel On Leash, and we like to teach our dogs a command that tells them that the two of us are going to heel together. The command we've chosen is Ready! Notice that the command includes an exclamation mark and not a question mark. You say it in a quiet and yet excited tone of voice — almost a whisper. The reason we've chosen this command is simple: In an obedience trial, the judge asks, "Are you ready?" before she says "Forward" (or any other order).

When the judge asks you the question, naturally, you're expected to give some indication that the two of you are ready to go. We use the answer "Ready!" and Buddy snaps to attention and is all set to go. The judge then says "Forward," at which point you say, "Buddy, Heel!" and start to move.

No doubt you're wondering why all this is necessary when Buddy is supposed to respond to the Heel command and move with you when you do. The reason is that when you give the Heel command, you want to make sure that Buddy's attention is on you and not something else that may have attracted his attention. Otherwise, he may just sit there like a bump on a log, totally engrossed in what's going on in the next ring, and when you start to walk, he has to play catch-up.

To avoid this scenario, teach Buddy the Ready! command. In addition, you need to decide on your leadoff leg — the one that tells the dog when he's expected to go with you. If you're right-handed, you'll be more comfortable making your leadoff leg your right, but you can start on either leg, as long as you're consistent. Experiment and see which one works better.

In the following sections, we show you how to get Buddy positioned next to you on the leash before starting the process of teaching him the Ready! command.

Using Control Position

Before you start teaching Buddy the Ready! command, you must get him positioned in such a way that helps him succeed. You need to hold the leash in *Control Position,* which makes it easier for you to remind Buddy of his responsibility to pay attention to you and stay in Heel position when he permits himself to become distracted (see Figure 13-1).

Figure 13-1:
Using
Control
Position.

To hold the leash in Control Position, follow these steps:

1. **Attach the leash to your dog's training collar.**

2. **Position both rings of the collar under his chin.**

3. **Put the loop of the leash over the thumb of your right hand.**

4. **Neatly fold the leash, accordion-style, into your right hand, with the part going to the dog coming out from under your little finger.**

5. **Place your right hand against the front of your leg, palm facing your leg.**

6. **With your left hand, grasp the leash in front of your left leg, palm facing your leg.**

Keep both hands below your waist at all times and your elbows relaxed and close to your body. Take up enough slack in the leash so that the leash snap is parallel with the ground.

Working through the sequences of the Ready! command

Most commands you teach your dog consist of several steps, called *sequences.* Each sequence adds to the dog's understanding of the command. The following sections show you the six sequences you use to teach the Ready! command.

Focusing Buddy's attention on you

The goal of Sequence 1 is to systematically teach your dog to focus on you and pay attention. Here are the steps to take:

1. **Attach the leash to the training collar and sit your dog at Heel position.**

   Your dog is in *Heel position* when the area from his head to his shoulder is in line with your left hip, with both of you facing in the same direction.

2. **Hold the leash in Control Position and look at your dog, keeping your left shoulder absolutely straight.**

   Don't forget to smile and relax. (We discuss the Control Position in the earlier section "Using Control Position.")

3. **Say your dog's name, release with an enthusiastic "Okay," and take five steps forward at a trot, keeping your hands in Control Position.**

Don't worry about what Buddy is doing; just concentrate on your part.

4. **Repeat several times.**

Introducing Buddy to the Ready! command

With Sequence 2, you introduce your dog to the Ready! command. Practice the exercise we present in this section over the course of several sessions.

When teaching this command, hold your hands in Control Position, and keep your shoulders absolutely straight. You want to use body language to communicate forward motion to your dog. Dropping your left shoulder or pointing it back communicates just the opposite.

Follow these steps to introduce the Ready! command:

1. **Attach the leash to the training collar, and sit your dog at Heel position.**

2. **Hold the leash in Control Position and look at your dog, keeping your left shoulder absolutely straight.**

3. **Quietly and in an excited tone of voice, say "Ready!"**

4. **Say "Buddy, Heel," move out briskly for five paces, and release.**

Wait until you finish giving the command before you move. Otherwise, you're teaching your dog to move on his name, which isn't a good idea.

5. **Repeat this sequence several times.**

Ignore what Buddy is doing in this exercise. Concentrate on your part of keeping your hands in position and starting and releasing on the leadoff leg. Be sure to keep the exercise fun and exciting for your dog.

Getting Buddy to respond to Ready!

The goal of Sequence 3 is to teach your dog to respond to the Ready! command. Here's what to do:

1. **Attach the leash to the training collar, and sit your dog at Heel position.**

2. **Hold the leash in Control Position and look at your dog, keeping your left shoulder absolutely straight.**

3. **Quietly and in an excited tone of voice, say, "Ready!"**

4. **Say "Buddy, Heel," start at a fast pace as quickly as you can for ten paces, and release.**

5. **Repeat several times.**

Here are a couple helpful hints for you as you do this sequence the first few times:

- ✔ **Wait until you've finished the command before you start to run.** It would hardly be fair to your dog to take off without having told him what you want. You may feel a little tension on the leash before Buddy understands that you want him to move with you.

- ✔ **Resist the temptation to let your left hand trail out behind you when you feel a little tension on the leash, and resist the urge to let your left shoulder drop.** Hook the thumb of your left hand under your waistband and lock it in place, and concentrate on keeping that left shoulder straight.

After four to five tries, you'll notice that Buddy is actually responding when you say "Ready!" and is becoming more attentive to the command.

Rewarding Buddy's response

Sequence 4 rewards dogs that respond to the Ready! command and helps those that are a little slow to pick up on it. Check out these steps:

1. **With your dog sitting at a Heel position, neatly fold the leash into your left hand, which should be placed at your belt buckle.**

2. **Hold a treat in your right hand, placing your hand at your right side.**

3. **Look at your dog, smile, and say "Ready!"**

4. **Do one of the following:**

    - If he looks at you, tell him how clever he is, give him the treat, and release.

    - If he doesn't look at you, put the treat in front of his nose, and move the treat in the direction of your face. When he follows the treat, tell him how clever he is, give him the treat, and release.

5. **Repeat until your dog responds without hesitation to the Ready! command.**

Reinforcing the Ready! command

Sometimes Buddy will be distracted to such an extent that he won't respond to the Ready! command. For those occasions, you need to be able to reinforce the command so he knows that when you say the magic word he has to pay attention no matter what's out there. Perform the following Sequence 5 steps to reinforce the Ready! command:

1. **Attach the leash to the training collar, and sit your dog at Heel position.**

2. **Hold the leash in Control Position and look at your dog, keeping your left shoulder absolutely straight.**

3. **Give the Ready! command.**

4. **Do one of the following:**

    • If Buddy looks up at you expectantly, praise and then release.

    • If he doesn't look up at you, check the leash in the direction you want him to focus — usually up toward your face. When he looks up, praise and release.

    Nagging your dog with ineffective checks isn't a good training technique. Get a response the first time so you can praise and release him. If you repeatedly don't get a response, review the prior sequences.

5. **Repeat until your dog is rock solid on responding to the Ready! command.**

Convincing Buddy to ignore distractions

Sequence 6 is the review progression for the entire Ready! exercise. The goal of this sequence is to help your dog ignore distractions. During this sequence, you start working with a helper who will try to distract your dog. Your helper can be a friend or family member. The three main distractions are

✔ **Visual, or first degree:** Helper approaches and just stands there.

✔ **Auditory, or second degree:** Helper approaches and tries to distract Buddy with "Hello, puppy! Want to come and visit?" or whatever else comes to mind. Note that the name of the dog isn't used.

✔ **Object of attraction, or third degree:** Helper approaches and offers Buddy a toy or a treat.

When performing the following steps, practice with first degree until your dog ignores the distracter. Then move on to second degree and third degree, respectively.

1. **Neatly fold the leash into your right hand, and place your left hand around the leash directly under your right hand, as though you're holding a baseball bat.**

   Allow about 2 inches of slack in the leash and place both hands against your belt buckle.

2. **Give the Ready! command.**

3. **Have the helper approach in a nonthreatening manner.**

   When you're working on distraction training, have the helper approach your dog at a 45-degree angle and not straight on from the front or the side. Straight-on approaches are considered confrontational to some dogs. The helper starts to approach the dog from 10 feet away and stops 2 feet from the dog.

4. **Do one of the following:**

   • If your dog keeps his attention focused on you, praise and release.

   • If he permits himself to become distracted, reinforce, praise, and release.

Review this exercise with Buddy on a regular basis.

Heeling Despite Distractions

After you've taught Buddy to pay attention to you on command, and while he's sitting at the Heel position (see the earlier section "Working through the sequences of the Ready! command"), you have to teach him to pay attention during heeling. Up to now, most of your heeling has probably been done in areas relatively free of distractions, perhaps even in the same location. The time has come to expand Buddy's horizons. You need to get him out to new places.

For Buddy, any new location is a form of distraction training. Everything looks different, and more important, everything smells different. When you take him to a new place, let him acclimate himself first — take in the sights and smells. Give him a chance to relieve himself as well.

When you participate in an obedience trial, defecating or urinating in the ring is an automatic nonqualification (NQ), so you need to teach Buddy that when he's working it's not the time or place for bathroom breaks.

The following sections provide the info you need to make sure your dog is successful when heeling around distractions.

Helping your dog heel in new places

In a location new to your dog, and after he has had a chance to look around a bit and relieve himself, do some heeling with particular emphasis on having your dog pay attention to you. Anytime his attention wanders — he may want to sniff the ground or just look around — remind him with a little check that he has to pay attention to you. When he does, tell him what a good boy he is, and then release him with "Okay."

Check the leash in the direction you want your dog to focus — somewhere on you. Depending on his size, this can be your ankle, lower leg, upper leg, torso, or face. Focusing on your face would be ideal, and some dogs learn it quickly; others are structurally unable to.

When you release Buddy, take five steps straight forward at a trot. Keep both hands on the leash. You want to get him excited about heeling with you. If he gets too excited and starts to run ahead, release him with somewhat less enthusiasm. After any check to refocus the dog's attention on you, release him. Doing so makes it fun for your dog to watch you.

Using a distracter while you're heeling

The purpose of heeling with distractions is for your dog to ignore them, concentrate on what he's supposed to do, and focus his attention on you. Exactly how he accomplishes this goal isn't important, so long as he does. Dogs have excellent peripheral vision and can heel perfectly well without directly looking at you.

You now need a helper to assist you. Heel your dog past your helper, who can be standing, sitting, or squatting while smiling invitingly at your dog. If your dog permits himself to become distracted, check him to refocus his attention on you. When he does refocus on you, praise and release with "Okay." Repeat until your dog ignores your helper and instead pays attention to you as you pass the distracter.

After your dog has learned to ignore your helper, have the distracter talk to your dog (the dog's name is not used) and then offer him a treat. You want to teach your dog to ignore such distractions and remain attentive to you. When he does, be sure to praise and release him. After Buddy has caught on to the concept that he has to pay attention to you no matter what, use the release less frequently.

Let's Dance, Buddy: Heel On Leash

Heeling is like dancing with your dog. And *you* have to lead. If you know anything about dancing, you know that you have the tougher job. The dog will follow only your lead, so you need to give him the necessary cues to change direction or pace. ***Remember:*** The Heel On Leash is a requirement for both Pre-Novice and Novice classes (refer to the earlier section "Understanding the System: Your Road Map to the Companion Dog Title" for more on these classes).

Heeling is a pack drive exercise (see Chapter 2). Before giving the command to heel, put your dog into pack drive by smiling at him and gently touching him on the side of his face. In an obedience trial, you can do this before you respond to the judge that you're ready, but not after.

In the earlier section "Heeling Despite Distractions," we show you how to teach Buddy to heel around distractions. In order to master the Heel On Leash, you need to review that exercise on a frequent basis. In addition, you need to work on perfecting turns and changes of pace. We discuss the Automatic Sit as well as those turns and changes of pace in the following sections.

Under the AKC Obedience Regulations, the judge of an obedience trial will call a heeling pattern for you. The pattern has to include — in addition to normal pace — a fast pace, a slow pace, and a right, left, and about-turn. That pattern is the bare minimum. A simple heeling pattern may look something like this: forward, fast, normal, left turn, about-turn, halt, forward, right turn, slow, normal, about-turn, halt.

If you have your dog's attention, and if you don't accidentally confuse him with incorrect cues, your obedience trial should go reasonably well. Still, you need to look at each of the maneuvers in this section as separate exercises that you and Buddy have to practice — sort of like the steps of a particular dance.

If you need to check your dog, release with "Okay" after the check. And when your dog is doing something correctly, or is trying, be sure to reward him with a treat or praise.

Once a week, test your dog's understanding of heeling by doing a little pattern with him that's similar to what you'd perform in the ring. Just remember that in the ring, you're not allowed to check your dog, and you can't have any tension on the leash. The only true test is when your dog is off leash, but using the umbilical cord technique gives you a good idea of what you need to practice. (Chapter 14 explains the umbilical cord technique in further detail.) The purpose of testing your dog's understanding of heeling is to see what you need to practice. Most of your time should be spent practicing. Test every fourth or fifth session.

The halt

When you *halt,* Buddy is expected to sit at Heel position without any command or signal from you. This maneuver is called the *Automatic Sit,* because the cue for the dog to sit is when you stop. Under the Obedience Regulations, you're penalized if you use a command or signal to get the dog to sit. The dog has to do it on his own.

To teach Buddy the Automatic Sit, follow these steps:

1. **Put the rings of the training collar on top of your dog's neck.**

2. **As you come to a halt, check with your left hand straight up.**

   Be careful that you don't inadvertently check toward or across your body, because doing so will cause your dog to sit with his rear end away from you and not in a straight line. As a result, you and your dog will be penalized.

3. **Practice two or three Automatic Sits with a check, and then try one without a check.**

   Your dog will immediately tell you where you stand with that exercise.

Changes of pace and turns

For the changes of pace and turns, we train dogs to take their cue from the leadoff leg. We use three techniques to teach this concept:

- ✔ The release
- ✔ An object of attraction, which can be a treat or favorite toy
- ✔ A check

Changing pace

This section contains a changing pace example: Suppose you want to teach your dog to stay with you as you change pace from slow to normal. Perform these steps:

1. **Release your dog with "Okay" from a slow pace on your leadoff leg.**

   The idea of this step is to get your dog all excited about accelerating with you from slow to normal pace.

2. **As you go from slow to normal, use a treat to draw the dog forward as the leadoff leg makes the transition.**

   Hold the leash in your left hand and the treat in your right. Show the dog the treat just as you're about to make the change, and draw him forward with your right hand as the leadoff leg accelerates into normal pace.

3. **Hold the leash in Control Position and occasionally, and only when necessary, give a little check straight forward at the same time the leadoff leg makes the transition.**

   The check teaches your dog that ultimately it's his responsibility, on or off leash, to accelerate when you change pace. You can read more about the Control Position in the earlier section "Using Control Position."

Most of your repetitions of any of the heeling components should include the release or a treat.

Making turns

Your dog needs to learn three different turns: right turn, left turn, and about-turn. When making any of these turns, try to keep your feet close together so your dog can keep up with you.

For the right and about-turns, Buddy needs to learn to accelerate and stay close to your side as you make the turns. You can teach him by using these techniques:

- ✔ The release as you come out of the turn
- ✔ A treat to guide him around the turn
- ✔ A little check coming out of the turn, if necessary

When you use a treat, do the following:

- ✔ Neatly fold the leash into your left hand, and place it against your right hip. Doing so keeps your shoulder facing in the proper direction.
- ✔ Hold the treat in your right hand at your side.
- ✔ Just before you make the turn, show your dog the treat, and use it to guide him around the turn.
- ✔ Hold the treat as close to your left leg as you can so your dog learns to make nice, tight turns.

For the left turn, Buddy first needs to slow down (so you don't trip over him) and then accelerate again. Draw back on the leash just before you make the turn, and then use the same techniques that you use for the right and about-turns.

You don't have to practice these maneuvers in succession as long as you do two or three of each during a training session.

Putting a Twist on Things: Teaching the Figure 8

The *Figure 8* is a fun exercise. In the ring, it's done around two people, called *stewards,* who stand 8 feet apart and act as posts. You and your dog start equidistant from the two posts and walk twice completely around and between them. In practice, you can use chairs as posts. In order to stay in Heel position, your dog has to speed up on the outside turn and slow down on the inside turn, while you maintain an even brisk pace throughout.

One lament we frequently hear is, "He does fine at home, but take him anywhere and forget it!" To solve this problem, make a point to seek out new locations for training, at first without distractions and then with distractions, to see how Buddy does.

Until your dog masters this exercise, he'll have a tendency to forge or crowd on the inside turn and to lag or go wide on the outside turn. When teaching the exercise, use your body as your main communication tool. By rotating the upper part of your body back toward your dog, or forward away from your dog, you cause him to slow down or speed up, respectively. Your left shoulder will be the cue for your dog, indicating what you want him to do. When the left shoulder points back, your dog will slow down; when it points forward, he'll speed up. Just as dogs communicate with each other through body language, so can you.

Go ahead and try it. It's almost the same motion as the twist, only from the waist up. Rotate the upper part of your body first to the left and then to the right. You'll use this motion to control your dog's momentum.

In the following sections, we introduce a set of sequences to show how to get started on training Buddy for a successful Figure 8 exercise. **Remember:** The Figure 8 is a requirement for both Pre-Novice and Novice classes (refer to the earlier section "Understanding the System: Your Road Map to the Companion Dog Title" for more on these classes).

Preparing Buddy for the Figure 8

Before you begin practicing going around posts, use the steps in this Sequence 1 section to teach Buddy that he has to speed up his pace when you circle to the right and slow down when you circle to the left.

For the inside turn in which you circle to the left, follow these steps:

1. **Start with your dog sitting at the Heel position, with your leash in Control Position.**

   You can read more about Control Position in the earlier section "Using Control Position."

2. **Say "Buddy, Heel," and walk a circle to the left, about 4 feet in diameter, at a slow pace.**

3. **Twist to the left as you walk.**

4. **Release your dog with "Okay" after you've completed the circle.**

After two or three tries, you'll notice how your dog responds to your body cues. If nothing happens, exaggerate your body motion.

For the outside turn in which you circle to the right, use the following steps:

1. **Start with your dog sitting at the Heel position, with the leash neatly folded into your left hand.**

2. **Put your left hand against your right hip.**

   Doing so keeps your left shoulder facing forward.

3. **Have a treat in your right hand.**

4. **Say "Buddy, Heel," and walk in a circle to the right, about 4 feet in diameter, at your normal brisk pace.**

5. **Use the treat, which is held just in front of his nose, to guide your dog around, and give him the treat after you've completed the circle.**

The Obedience Regulations are quite specific about the position of your hands. For the Heel On Leash, you can hold the leash in either hand or in both, as long as they're in a natural position. For the Heel Free, your arms can swing naturally at your side, or you can swing your right arm naturally at your side and place your left hand against your belt buckle.

When making the outside turn, you're looking for a visible effort on the part of your dog to accelerate. Repeat these steps several times so you become comfortable with the maneuver. Then try going at a trot.

Introducing Buddy to the actual Figure 8

The Sequence 2 goal is to teach your dog the Figure 8. Following is the review progression for this exercise:

1. **Place two chairs about 12 feet apart.**

2. **Start with your dog sitting at the Heel position, 2 feet from the center-line, equidistant between the chairs.**

3. **Neatly fold the leash into your left hand, and place it against your belt buckle; hold a treat in your right hand.**

4. **Say "Buddy, Heel," and start to walk at a slow pace around the chair on your left, rotating the upper part of your body to the left.**

5. **When you get to the center between the two chairs, show your dog the treat and guide him around the chair on your right at a trot, keeping your left shoulder facing forward.**

6. **Stop at the center, and sit your dog; then praise and release with "Okay."**

   Buddy should now be sitting without a command or correction.

Hold the treat at your right side and out of Buddy's sight until you get to the center and want him to speed up. Then hold it as close as you can to your left leg so he learns to stay close to your side. Don't show the treat to him on the inside turn, or he'll try to get to the treat instead of slowing down. Your success in keeping Buddy at Heel position without crowding or lagging depends on how well you use your shoulders to communicate with him.

Doing the perfect Figure 8

Sequence 3's goal is the perfect Figure 8 — the way you have to execute it in an obedience trial. Figure 13-2 shows a dog working a Figure 8. Here's how to do it:

1. **Practice the review progression (see the preceding section), making two complete Figure 8s.**

2. **Start from the center and complete one Figure 8 at normal pace, using your shoulders to cue your dog.**

   Stop in the center. Buddy should now sit on his own without any further help from you. Repeat the review progression often to maintain your dog's enthusiasm.

3. **Over the course of several sessions, put the chairs closer together in 1-foot increments until they're 8 feet apart.**

4. **Practice a Figure 8 with the umbilical cord technique, concentrating on the direction of your shoulders.**

   Keep your left hand on your belt buckle. We discuss the umbilical cord technique in Chapter 14.

5. **Try a Figure 8 off leash.**

   Although the Figure 8 is done on leash in the Novice class, practicing it off leash is a good test. You'll quickly see where your dog needs more practice.

Figure 13-2:
The perfect
Figure 8.

At one point or another, you may have to use a little check going into the out-side turn to impress on Buddy how important it is to you that he speed up.

Your Dog Isn't an Elephant: Reinforcing Training

True or false? After my dog is trained, I'll never have to practice his lessons again.

Answer: False.

Your dog doesn't have the memory of an elephant, so you need to review his lessons on a regular basis. For example, if you've used the Recall Game (see Chapter 10) to teach Buddy to come when called, you need to reward him with a treat on a variable schedule when he responds to your call and comes to you. If you get lax, the association between the command and the reward will weaken. You can tell when this begins to happen: First, Buddy doesn't come immediately. He may take a detour or lift his leg just one more time. Then, you have to call him again. Finally, he ignores you when you implore him to come.

The principle of *successive nonreinforced repetitions* sounds more complicated than it is. These repetitions are responses to a command without any reinforcement, such as not giving your dog a treat when he comes to you after you've called him.

Every time your dog responds to a command without reinforcement, which can be a reward or a check, depending on how you have taught the dog the command, it's a nonreinforced repetition. The number of these repetitions is finite and depends on the extent to which the behavior is in harmony with the dog's instincts or drives. After a Labrador Retriever has been trained to retrieve, he'll happily fetch almost indefinitely without any reinforcement. An Afghan Hound, on the other hand, will probably retrieve only a few times without reinforcement. The Labrador was bred to retrieve; the Afghan wasn't.

Every command you've taught your dog needs to be reinforced on a random basis, or the association between the command and the reinforcement weakens.

Several years ago, we had an excellent demonstration of this principle when we visited friends in Newfoundland, who have two delightful Whippets. Every morning, our friends take a short ride to the local park for their own daily walk and to let the dogs run. Naturally, we joined them.

The park covers about 100 acres, with wonderful walking trails, plenty of wildlife, and a large pond inhabited by a variety of fowl. After we were inside the park, much to our surprise, our friends let the dogs loose. When we say surprised, it's because Whippets are sight hounds — they're extremely high in prey drive and love to chase anything that moves. They're also incredibly fast and can cover great distances in seconds. We were wondering how our friends would get these dogs back.

To make a long story short, when the dogs ranged a little too far or started chasing something, our friends called them back. To our amazement, the dogs came instantly every time, and every time they got a treat. The response was reinforced!

Any taught response needs to be reinforced. You needn't worry about the exact number of nonreinforced repetitions your dog will retain of a given behavior. All you need to know is that they're finite. To keep him sharp, randomly reinforce — whether you think he needs it or not.

Making excuses and blaming the dog is easy, but your dog isn't an elephant and needs occasional reminders.

Chapter 14

Completing the Companion Dog Title

. . . .

In This Chapter

▶ Doing the Stand for Examination exercise

▶ Working toward Heeling Off Leash

▶ Perfecting the Recall exercise

▶ Excelling at the group exercises

. . . .

C hapter 13 introduces the American Kennel Club (AKC) Novice class and
its goal — the Companion Dog title. The chapter is an overview of the
six required exercises for the title and the points needed to earn that title.
It also provides the nitty-gritty details for successfully completing the first
exercise — heeling on and off leash. This chapter covers the remainder of the
exercises for the Companion Dog title:

✔ Stand for Examination

✔ Heeling Off Leash

✔ Recall

✔ Group Exercises

  • Long Sit

  • Long Down

The benefits of earning the Companion Dog title are knowing that you have a
well-trained dog, that the two of you can work together as a team, and that you
are spending quality time together. It's also a great feeling of accomplishment.

During a training session, practice different exercises, and vary the order.
Start with some brisk heeling as a warm-up, including fast starts and changes
of pace. Keep training interesting and fun for both of you.

Dog shows are held indoors and outdoors in all kinds of weather conditions. If the dog show you're attending is outdoors and it's raining, the judge will have on rain gear, which may include a big, floppy hat or poncho — something your dog may not have experienced before. Don't be caught unprepared: Practice under those unpleasant conditions and wear different items your dog may see.

You're Getting a Check-Up: Preparing for the Stand for Examination

The *Stand for Examination* is a requirement for the Novice class, but it's also a practical and useful command to teach your dog in general. Brushing, grooming, and wiping feet, as well as visiting the vet, are certainly a lot easier with a dog who has been trained to stand still than it is with one who's in perpetual motion.

In the ring, Stand for Examination looks something like this:

1. You give your leash to the steward, and the judge says, "Stand your dog and leave when ready."

2. You stand your dog in Heel position (see Chapter 13), say "Stay," walk 6 feet straight forward in front of your dog, turn around, and stand facing the dog.

3. The judge approaches your dog from in front and touches your dog's head, body, and hindquarters with one hand. The judge then says, "Back to your dog."

4. You walk around behind your dog and return to the Heel position.

When you begin teaching this exercise to your dog, you can stand, kneel on your right knee or both knees, or have the dog on a table, depending on his size. You want to avoid leaning over him, because if you do, he'll want to move away from you — especially if he's low in defense fight behaviors (see Chapter 2 for more on personality).

To prepare Buddy for the Stand for Examination exercise, you need to teach him a number of sequences — seven to be exact. First you need to teach him to stand on command, although you may physically place him into a stand. Then you need to teach him to stand still, and finally you teach the examination part of the exercise. We review each of the seven sequences in the following sections.

Introducing the Stand command

Your Sequence 1 goal is to teach your dog the Stand command. Here's how it works:

1. **Start with Buddy sitting at your left side, off leash, with both of you facing the same direction.**

2. **Put the thumb of your right hand in the collar under his chin, fingers pointing to the floor, palm open and flat against his chest.**

3. **Apply a little downward pressure on the collar, say "Stand," and at the same time, apply backward pressure on his *stifles* (the joint of the hind leg between the thigh and the second thigh — the dog's knees) with the back of your left hand.**

   Figure 14-1 shows how your hands should be placed in this step.

4. **Keep both hands still and in place — the right hand through the collar and the left hand against his stifles — and count to ten.**

5. **Praise and release with "Okay."**

Repeat this exercise three to five times per session over the course of several sessions.

Figure 14-1:
This well-behaved pooch stands for examination.

Teaching Buddy to stand still

Sequence 2's goal is to teach Buddy to stand still while your hands are still holding him in place. Buddy will have to stand still when the judge examines him. Follow these steps:

1. **Place your dog into a Stand (see the preceding section).**

2. **With both hands on your dog, keep him standing still to the count of 30.**

3. **Over the course of several sessions, increase the time you keep him standing still to one minute. Praise and release.**

Showing Buddy how to stand still without holding him in position

Your Sequence 3 goal is to get your dog to stand still without holding him in position. Check out these steps:

1. **Place Buddy into a Stand.**

2. **Take your left hand away from his stifles.**

3. **Count to 30, and reposition him if he moves.**

4. **Praise and then release.**

   Praise is a verbal thing — not a petting thing. When you praise Buddy, be sure that he remains in position. Praise tells him he's doing something correctly and isn't an invitation to move. Don't confuse verbal praise with the release.

5. **When he's steady without you holding onto him with your left hand in Step 3, take your right hand out of the collar.**

It will take Buddy several sessions to master this sequence.

Working on the Stand-Stay command

Sequence 4's goal is to teach Buddy the Stand-Stay. Here's how to do it:

1. **Stand your dog as described in the earlier section "Introducing the Stand command."**

2. **Take both hands off your dog and stand up, keeping your shoulders square.**

3. **Say "Stay."**

4. **Count to 30, praise, and release.**

5. **Practice until you can stand next to him for one minute without him moving.**

Learning the Stand-Stay command (or Sit or Down-Stay) isn't exciting for your dog, so follow the exercise with something he enjoys. After the release, play ball or throw a stick. Give him something to look forward to.

Leaving Buddy in a Stand-Stay

In Sequence 5, you progress by leaving Buddy in a Stand-Stay position. These steps show you how:

1. **Stand in Heel position next to your sitting dog.**

2. **Put the thumb of your right hand through the collar as in Sequence 1 (see "Introducing the Stand command" earlier in this chapter).**

   Depending on the size of your dog, you may have to bend at the knees to avoid leaning over him.

3. **With a little downward pressure on the collar, say "Stand."**

   He should now stand without you having to touch his stifles. If he doesn't, physically assist him by placing your left hand against his stifles.

4. **Take your right hand out of the collar and stand up straight.**

5. **Say "Stay," and step directly in front of him.**

6. **Count to 30, step back to a Heel position, praise, and release.**

   Reposition Buddy if he moves.

7. **Gradually increase the distance you leave him to 6 feet in front.**

8. **From now on when you leave him, go 6 feet straight forward, turn and face him (don't back away from him), count to 30, go back, praise, and release.**

Getting Buddy familiar with the Return

After you leave Buddy in a Stand-Stay, you, of course, have to return. And when you return, you have to do so by walking around and behind your dog to Heel position. Introducing the Return is your Sequence 6 goal. The following steps can help:

1. **Stand your dog and go 6 feet in front of him (see the preceding section).**

2. **Go back to your dog, put two fingers of your left hand on his withers (the highest part of the back between the shoulder blades) to steady him, and walk around behind him to the Heel position.**

3. **Pause, making sure he doesn't move; then praise and release.**

4. **When he understands that you're going to come around behind him, avoid touching him as you return to the Heel position.**

   In an obedience trial you aren't allowed to touch the dog upon your return.

Preparing Buddy for the actual examination

Sequence 7's goal is to teach Buddy the examination part of the exercise. For this sequence, you need a helper. At this time, the helper can be a family member. Eventually, however, Buddy has to be examined by a stranger, and because the judge can be either male or female, you need to practice with both men and women.

To introduce your dog to this exercise, start with the Sit for Examination, which is almost identical to the Sitting Politely for Petting exercise in the Canine Good Citizen test (see Chapter 12). Do the following:

1. **Put the rings of the collar on top of the dog's neck.**

2. **Attach your leash to the collar.**

3. **Sit your dog at the Heel position.**

4. **Neatly fold the leash into your left hand, hold it above his head, and say "Stay."**

5. **Have your helper approach and offer your dog the palm of his or her hand.**

   If Buddy tries to say hello to the helper, reinforce the Stay command with a check straight up.

6. **Have your helper lightly touch Buddy's head and back.**

7. **Praise and release with "Okay."**

8. **Repeat Steps 1 through 7 until he readily permits the examination.**

   Practice the examination over the course of several sessions.

9. **Repeat the steps off leash with your dog standing at Heel position, then with you standing directly in front, then 3 feet in front, and finally 6 feet in front.**

Before every exercise, the judge asks, "Are you ready?" We answer with "Ready!" for the heeling exercises and "Yes" for everything else, including the Stand for Examination. (Check out Chapter 13 for how to prepare your dog for the Ready! command.)

Heeling Off Leash

Heeling Off Leash is really only an extension of Heeling On Leash, but it isn't quite the same. Buddy knows when he's on leash and when he's off leash. When he's on leash, he may give you the impression that he's perfect. Then you take the leash off, and he acts as though he has no idea what the exercise is all about. The reason is simple — he knows he's off leash.

If this situation happens to you, review Heeling On Leash (refer to Chapter 13), and reinforce the Heel command with a treat or a check when he needs help. For normal pace, he usually doesn't need any reinforcement, but he probably does for changes of pace and turns.

Remember that Heeling Off Leash is the ultimate test of your training. With a little practice, Buddy will get the hang of it. To make sure he understands, 90 percent of your practicing should be done on leash so you can remind him what you expect from him.

You can remind your dog of his responsibility to remain in Heel position by taking him by the collar as you do when heeling with the umbilical cord technique (see the following section).

Transitioning to Heeling Off Leash

To make the transition from Heeling On Leash (which we discuss in Chapter 13) to Heeling Off Leash, we use a technique called the *umbilical cord*. This maneuver lets you and your dog experience the feeling of Heeling Off Leash while he's still attached.

The umbilical cord technique, which we show in Figure 14-2, teaches your dog that it's his responsibility to remain in Heel position. Unless he learns to accept that responsibility, he won't be reliable off leash. You can help the process by being consistent in reminding him of that responsibility. Anytime you make a move to bring him back to Heel position, you must follow through. If Buddy deviates and you reach for the collar, but he corrects himself and you do nothing, Buddy doesn't learn anything.

Here's how the umbilical cord technique works:

1. **With your dog sitting in the Heel position and the leash attached to the collar, take the loop end of the leash in your right hand and pass it around behind you into your left hand.**

2. **With your right hand, unsnap the leash from the collar, pass the snap through the loop of the leash, and reattach it to the collar.**

3. **Pull on the leash to tighten the loop end around your waist at your left side.**

4. **Put your left hand against your belt buckle, and let your right hand swing naturally at your side.**

5. **Say "Buddy, Heel," and start to walk your normal brisk pace.**

   If your dog deviates from Heel position, *slowly* reach for the collar. Put two fingers of your left hand through the collar, palm facing you, at the side of his neck, and bring him back to Heel position. Keep walking, let go of the collar, and tell him what a good dog he is.

Figure 14-2:
Using the
umbilical
cord
technique.

When you reach for your dog, be sure you do it slowly and deliberately so as not to frighten him. Remember, he's still on leash and can't go anywhere. If you start snatching at him, he'll become apprehensive and try to bolt. For Buddy, this lesson is important. He learns to accept you reaching for the collar so you can do it when he's actually off leash.

If you have difficulty getting two fingers through the collar — because your dog is small or has lots of hair around his neck — use the leash snap to bring him back to Heel position. When you get to the off-leash part, put a little hang tag on his collar that you can easily grasp.

At first, keep the time and distance short, so you have a better chance of maintaining your dog's interest and attention. As you train with the umbilical cord technique, gradually increase the number of steps, make a right turn, take another ten steps and halt, praise, and release. Remember to say your dog's name before you make the turn. Start over and incorporate an about-turn, using his name before the turn. Also incorporate changes of pace. (We discuss turns and changes of pace in Chapter 13.)

As you and your dog's proficiency increase, add distractions in the order you did in Chapter 13. You also need to gradually increase the time and distance that you heel your dog before a halt. How much total time should you spend on this exercise? After a two-minute warm-up of heeling in Control Position (see Chapter 13) in a large circle or straight line with plenty of releases, you should spend no more than one to two minutes per training session.

Successfully getting off leash

Whenever you feel like you and Buddy are ready for Heeling Off Leash, get started. If you have any doubt about what Buddy will do, practice in a safe area, such as your backyard. Here are the steps to follow:

1. **Start with a two-minute warm-up in Control Position (see Chapter 13).**

   Walk in a large circle or a straight line. Forget about turns, and concentrate on keeping his attention on you. Now is the time to remind him to pay attention to you. Check, if you have to, and then praise and release with "Okay."

2. **Set up for the umbilical cord technique, heel for 10 to 15 steps, and release.**

   Set up again and heel for about the same distance and halt. (We discuss the umbilical cord technique in the preceding section.)

3. **As you halt, put your right hand against his chest, place him into a sit, and stand up.**

4. **Unclip the leash from his collar, and put the snap into your left pocket so a loop dangles on your side.**

5. **Say "Buddy, Heel," and start at a brisk pace.**

    If you need to reinforce, very slowly reach for his collar, bring him back, let go of the collar, and praise.

6. **Halt after ten steps, and sit your dog.**

7. **Put the leash back on your dog and release him.**

8. **Go on to another exercise or end your session.**

Proficiency comes in small increments and not all at once. Add something new to your off-leash heeling each session, such as a turn (use his name) or a change of pace. Keep it short and snappy, and make it exciting and fun. Over the course of several sessions, both you and Buddy will become increasingly confident and begin to work as a team. Resist the temptation to go beyond his ability to be successful.

When you and your dog are comfortable doing this exercise in an area relatively free of distractions, you can go on to Heeling Off Leash with distractions. Use the same order as you do when Heeling On Leash — that is, making it incrementally more difficult as you progress (see Chapter 13).

Mastering the Recall

The *Recall* exercise is different from the traditional Come command, where you're only concerned about the dog coming to you (see Chapter 10 for more on Come). The Recall consists of these four components, which we discuss in the following sections:

- ✔ Stay
- ✔ Come
- ✔ Front
- ✔ Finish

The Recall is performed from one end of the ring to the other. The judge tells you to leave your dog in a Sit-Stay and to go to the other side of the ring. He or she then tells you to call your dog. You give the Come command, Buddy comes, and he's expected to sit directly in front of you. The judge then says "Finish," and you say "Buddy, Heel," and Buddy goes to the Heel position.

Stay

The first part of the Recall exercise requires your dog to master the Stay command. Chapter 9 covers the basics of this command. We cover training your dog to stay with distraction in "Training for the Group Exercises" section later in this chapter.

Come with distractions

Even though Buddy already knows the Come command, you still need to work on distraction training — for which you need a helper. Leave Buddy in a Sit-Stay, and go 20 feet in front of him. Have your helper position herself equidistant between you and Buddy — about 2 feet from Buddy's anticipated line of travel. Facing Buddy, the helper crouches and smiles.

Call your dog, and as he passes the distracter, release backward. To *release backward,* throw your hands up invitingly and take a few steps back with an enthusiastic "Okay!" Then give him a treat when he gets to you. If he goes to the distracter, smile and very slowly approach Buddy. Put the leash on the dead ring of the training collar and, with a little tension on the leash, show him exactly what he should've done by trotting backward to the spot where you called him. (To find out which ring is the dead ring on your dog's training collar, visit Chapter 5.) Praise and release backward when you and the dog get to the spot where you called him. You may have to show him a few times until he catches on. After he's successful, stop for that session. Figure 14-3 shows a dog coming amid distractions.

If your dog veers from the distracter, use two distracters, separated by about 10 feet, and teach your dog to come between them. As Buddy progresses in his training, work your way through second and third degree distractions (which we discuss in Chapter 13).

The purpose of distraction training is to build your and your dog's confidence that he can do it. It also teaches him to concentrate on what he's supposed to do. If at any time you feel the exercise is too much for him, stop. Come back to it at another session.

Figure 14-3:
Coming with
distractions.

Front

The object of both the Front and the Finish (see the following section) is to teach the dog a position, and you can practice both exercises indoors in the form of a game. The Front is similar to the Automatic Sit at Heel (see Chapter 13) in that the dog is supposed to come to you and sit in front without a command to sit. We like to use a chute to teach the dog exactly where we want him to sit when he comes to us. For a chute, we use plastic rain gutters that are appropriately placed for the size of the dog. They should be about as long as your dog. Place them on the ground, just far enough apart so your dog can sit comfortably in between.

When practicing the Front, keep the upper part of your body erect. If you lean over or toward your dog, he won't come in close enough. If you need to get down to his level, bend at the knees.

The following sections provide a set of sequences that help you teach your dog the Front using a chute. First you familiarize him with the chute and then you coax him into it.

Getting Buddy used to the chute

Sequence 1's goal is to get Buddy familiar with the chute. Making sure he's used to the chute is important because it teaches him to sit straight in front of you. Here's the best way to familiarize Buddy with the chute:

1. **Place the chute pieces on the ground 2 feet apart.**
2. **Walk your dog through the chute a few times.**
3. **Heel your dog into the chute and have him sit in it.**
4. **Repeat Steps 1 through 3 until he readily sits in the chute.**

If Buddy is uncomfortable going into the chute, widen it.

Teaching Buddy to come into the chute and Front

Sequence 2's goal is to teach your dog to come into the chute and perform a straight Front (see Figure 14-4). Try these steps:

1. **Heel your dog up to the chute, and tell him to stay.**
2. **Walk through the chute and face your dog.**
3. **Hold a treat in both hands below your waist and stand straight up.**
4. **Call your dog and, as he comes, bring your hands to your waist — using the treat to make him sit directly in front of you.**

   You want to teach Buddy to sit as close as possible in front of you without touching you. Using treats helps lure him in. Only give him the treat when he sits straight, however. If he doesn't, try again.
5. **Give him the treat, praise, and release backward.**

   See the section "Come with distractions" earlier in this chapter for info on the release backward.
6. **Practice Steps 1 through 5 about five times.**
7. **When your dog masters Steps 1 through 5, leave him on a Stay 3 feet from the entrance of the chute and call him to you for a Front.**
8. **Increase in 2-foot increments the distance that you leave him facing the entrance of the chute, until he's 35 feet from the entrance.**

Once he's comfortable with it, you can use treats to practice this sequence without the chute.

In the ring, you're not allowed to carry food or give second commands. You can give either a command or a signal but not both. The exception is the Stay command, which can be accompanied by a signal.

Ultimately, Buddy has to sit in front of you with your hands hanging naturally at your side, so you need to wean him from seeing you with your hands in front of you. You can still reward him in practice when he does the exercise correctly.

Figure 14-4:
Using
chutes to
teach a
straight
front.

Finish

After your dog comes to you and sits in front, the judge says "Finish." You say "Buddy, Heel," and your dog goes to the Heel position. He can either go directly to Heel position to the left, or go to the right and walk behind you to Heel position. We like to teach both, just to keep the dog guessing.

For both finishes, you can use either a command or a signal. We prefer a signal because the dog more readily understands a signal than a command — and it more clearly indicates to the dog the way we want him to go. Here's a list of the commands and the signals you can use for each Finish:

- ✓ **Finish to the left:** You can use the Heel command, and for the signal you can use your left hand to indicate the direction you want Buddy to go.

- ✓ **Finish to the right:** You can use the Place command, and your right hand to indicate which direction to go.

Your dog's response to the Finish to the right or left tells you which direction is better for him. As a general rule, a long-bodied dog does better going to the right.

In the following sections, we show you the sequences to teach Buddy to Finish on command or signal from either the left or the right.

Introducing a Finish to the left and right

Your Sequence 1 goal is to introduce Buddy to the Finish to the left. Here are the steps:

1. **Sit your dog at Heel position, say "Stay," and step directly in front of him.**

2. **Say "Buddy, Heel," and then take a step back on your left leg, keeping the right leg firmly planted in place, as you guide him with a treat held in your left hand in a semicircle into Heel position.**

   Make the semicircle large enough so that he winds up in the correct position.

3. **Give him the treat, praise, and release with "Okay."**

4. **Repeat Steps 1 through 3 until he enthusiastically and briskly goes to Heel position.**

You'll quickly see that the guidance of your left hand becomes his signal to go to heel.

The Finish to the right uses the same progressions as the Finish to the left, except that you step back on the right leg and guide Buddy around behind you into Heel position. When you're using a treat, you have to switch it behind your back from the right hand into the left. The same applies to the leash.

Teaching a Finish on command or signal

Your Sequence 2 goal is to teach Buddy to Finish on the left on command or on signal. Here's how:

1. **Put the leash on the training collar.**

2. **Neatly fold the leash into your left hand.**

3. **Step in front, say "Buddy, Heel," and step back on your left leg, using the leash to guide him into Heel position.**

   The signal is the same guiding motion you use in Sequence 1 (see the preceding section).

4. **Reward him with a treat, praise, and release.**

5. **Practice Steps 1 through 4 until he goes to Heel position without any tension on the leash.**

6. **Now eliminate the step back on the left leg, and experiment by using either the command or signal.**

Training for the Group Exercises

The group exercises are the last part of the Novice class test for the Companion Dog title. They consist of a Long Sit and a Long Down for one and three minutes, respectively, and they're done off leash in a group. The number of dog/handler teams in a group depends on the number of exhibitors competing in the class and the size of the ring. Here's how the group exercises work:

1. The judge tells the teams to line up on one side of the ring.

2. He or she instructs the handlers to sit their dogs and leave their dogs, whereupon the handlers go to the opposite side of the ring, turn, and face their dogs.

3. After a minute the judge gives the order to return and the handlers go back to their dogs, walking around behind the dogs to Heel position. (See the earlier section "Getting Buddy familiar with the Return" for more on teaching the Return.)

The same procedure is followed for the three-minute Down. A dog that lies down during the Long Sit, sits during the Long Down, or moves out of position, receives a nonqualifying score.

When you're training your dog, change only one variable at a time. When teaching any type of Stay, for example, change the distance or the time but not both together. Increase one, and increase the other when Buddy is steady. (You can read more about the Stay command in Chapter 9.)

Look at the Stay exercises from the perspective of time and distance. Teach Buddy to stay in place for a specific period of time with you about 3 feet in front. Then the first time you increase the distance from your dog, decrease the time you're away from him.

Although you can give a command and/or signal for any Stay exercise, your dog's Personality Profile (see Chapter 2) influences whether you want to use a signal. Any Stay is a pack drive exercise, so you want your dog in pack drive. For dogs low in defense fight behaviors, a Stay signal puts them into defense drive where they're uncomfortable. Using a Stay signal may cause the dog to break the Stay and come to you — or to whine and fidget.

Because he's competing for the Companion Dog title, Buddy already knows the basics of the Sit and Down-Stay (if not, check out Chapter 9). You just need to fill in the missing pieces. In other words, you need to practice

✔ With distractions

✔ Off leash

✔ At the right distance

✔ For the requisite length of time plus one minute

✔ At different locations and on different surfaces

The review progression for any Stay is the Sit-Stay test (see Chapter 9).

Setting up self-generated distractions

To introduce *self-generated distractions* (meaning those you create), put the leash on your dog's training collar with the rings under his chin. Then say and signal Stay, and step 3 feet in front of him. Place your left hand against your belt buckle and hold your right hand ready to reinforce. Jump to the right, the middle, the left, the middle, forward, and backward. Any time Buddy wants to move, reinforce the stay (see Chapter 9). How vigorously you do these distractions depends on Buddy's Personality Profile (refer to Chapter 2) and your physical condition. As he learns, add clapping and cheering. And periodically review these distractions in your training.

Increasing the level of difficulty

Practice with self-generated distractions off leash from about 3 feet and then 6 feet in front of Buddy to increase the level of difficulty of the Sit-Stay and Down-Stay. When Buddy is off leash, and you need to reinforce the Stay, slowly approach him and put him back by placing two fingers of each hand through the collar at the side of his neck. If he's coming to you, put him back from in front — that is, guide him back to the spot where you left him in such a way that you're facing him when you reinforce the Stay. Don't repeat the command.

Whenever you approach your dog, do so in a nonthreatening manner so he doesn't become anxious. You never want your dog to become frightened when you approach him.

Gradually increase the time to two minutes for the Sit-Stay and four minutes for the Down-Stay. Although practical, these are boring exercises for both you and your dog. You usually don't need to practice them every session. Once or twice a week suffices. Afterward, reward your dog with something he enjoys, like throwing a Frisbee or a stick.

Oops: Playing the yo-yo game

Some handlers have unintentionally taught their dogs, or vice versa, what we call the yo-yo game. The scenario goes something like this:

1. Buddy is on a Sit-Stay with his handler standing 30 feet away.

2. Buddy lies down, and the handler approaches to reinforce the Sit-Stay.

3. Buddy sits up by himself, and the handler retreats.

This scenario can, and often does, deteriorate into the yo-yo game. Buddy lies down, the handler approaches, Buddy sits up, and the handler retreats, with Buddy not having learned a blessed thing — except perhaps how many times he can play the game.

Moral of the story? When you make any move to reinforce any command, you *must* follow through, even if Buddy corrects himself before you've had a chance to reinforce the command. After you've started toward him, slowly continue without saying a word and when you get to him, make him lie down from front by putting your thumbs on the side of his neck through the collar and applying downward pressure. When he's in the Down position, reverse the procedure and lift him back up into a Sit. Let go of the collar, turn around, and leave. But always do it with a smile.

When Buddy stays for the requisite length of time, gradually increase the distance you're away from him to 35 feet. Increasing the distance should go quickly, because this exercise isn't new for him. Be sure to also practice in different locations and on different surfaces.

Because Buddy must remain sitting or down until the judge releases the group, it's not unusual for dogs to anticipate breaking the sit or down as soon as the owner returns. A good way to head off this behavior is to occasionally return and then without stopping continue back to your distant position.

Chapter 15

Retrieving

In This Chapter

▶ Following the steps to retrieving success

▶ Refining your dog's retrieve

Many dogs like to retrieve, or at least chase, a variety of objects. For them, it's a self-rewarding activity. They do it because they enjoy it. Some of them actually bring back the ball, Frisbee, or stick just so you can throw it again. They continue as long as it remains fun. When it's no longer fun, they stop. They also retrieve only articles they like. For example, your dog may happily retrieve a stick, but he may turn up his nose when you want him to fetch a ball.

The well-trained dog has been taught to retrieve and has learned to do it for you and not just for himself. Of course, he can have fun in the process as long as he understands that it's not a matter of choice.

To many owners, the distinction between "doing it for him" and "doing it for you" only becomes important when the owner has aspirations of participating in performance events that require retrieving — such as AKC Obedience competition and Flyball, among many others that you can read about in Chapter 21. However, many people like to have their dog retrieve objects even if they aren't involved in events; see the later success story about Sunny. After your dog has been taught to retrieve formally, he can retrieve almost anything.

Our own preference is to systematically teach our dogs to retrieve on command. The system we use requires the dog to do two things: deliver the object to hand versus dropping it at our feet and release the object when told rather than having to pry it out of his jaws.

In this chapter, we take you through the necessary steps to make a reliable retriever out of Buddy. Most dogs, of course, already know many of the different component behaviors of retrieving, but few know them all and can put them together. Even though Buddy may know how to fetch, he may still have trouble giving up the object after he brings it back. So you still need to go through the progressions of teaching him this exercise to make sure he knows all its parts.

There's a practical side to teaching your dog to retrieve. One of our students wanted her Golden Retriever, Sunny, to bring in the morning paper, preferably in readable condition. So we first had her teach Sunny the formal retrieve. We then told her to go out with Sunny, have him pick up the paper, bring it in the house, and reward him with a dog biscuit. It only took Sunny two repetitions until he figured it out. From then on, every morning he dutifully brought in the paper. After several days we got a frantic phone call from Sunny's owner. It seems that Sunny was somewhat of an entrepreneur. In an effort to garner more biscuits, he started retrieving the neighbors' papers as well. Fortunately, that problem was easily fixed — a biscuit only for the first paper. When Sunny realized the "one biscuit only" rule, he stopped bringing home the neighbors' papers.

Go Fetch! Explaining the Steps to Successful Retrieving

The Retrieve sounds simple, but it consists of many separate behaviors that the dog has to learn:

- ✔ Taking the retrieve object
- ✔ Holding it
- ✔ Walking and carrying the object
- ✔ Picking it up off the floor/ground
- ✔ Bringing it back
- ✔ Giving it up

For the dog that already retrieves on his own, teaching him to do it on command is a cinch. For those dogs who don't, you need to have a little more patience. Your dog's willingness to retrieve depends on what your dog was bred to do and how many prey drive behaviors he has (see Chapter 2).

To get started, you need the following equipment:

- ✔ Enthusiastic and patient owner
- ✔ Hungry dog
- ✔ Small can of cat food
- ✔ Metal spoon
- ✔ Wooden dumbbell
- ✔ Chair

The object we use for teaching the Retrieve is a wooden dumbbell. You can buy one at your local pet store or through catalogs. You need to get one that's appropriate for the size of your dog and the shape of his mouth. You want the bells to be big enough so your dog can pick it up off the ground without scraping his chin, and you want the diameter of the bar thick enough so he can comfortably carry it. The bar's length should be such that the bells clear the whiskers on the sides of his face.

You also can purchase plastic dumbbells; they last a lot longer than wooden ones. In the teaching process, however, we have found that dogs take more readily to wooden dumbbells than to plastic ones.

For some reason dogs can't resist cat food; it works well as a reward. Because many dogs aren't fond of retrieving metal objects, use a metal spoon to get them used to the feel of metal. We also let Buddy lick out of and play with the empty can so he learns how to retrieve metal objects. Before you give Buddy the can, make sure that its edges aren't sharp; otherwise he could cut his mouth.

Teaching the Take It command

Although many dogs retrieve a variety of objects on their own, they don't necessarily do so on command. To teach our dogs to retrieve on command, we begin by creating an association with the command and what we want the dog to do — take an object in his mouth. The one object few dogs can resist is food — especially cat food — so that's how we start.

The ideal time to start teaching Buddy to retrieve is when he's hungry, before you feed him.

Follow these steps to get Buddy started on the Take It command:

1. **Place the cat food, spoon, and dumbbell on a chair.**

2. **With Buddy sitting at your left side, face the chair.**

3. **Put a small portion of food on the spoon and offer it to him with the command Take It (or whatever command you want to use).**

   Buddy should take the whole spoon from you; however, some dogs at first may lick at it before they get the idea.

4. **Give the command in an excited and enthusiastic tone of voice to elicit prey drive behavior.**

   Check out Chapter 2 for information on the basic drive behaviors.

5. **Repeat this exercise ten times or until Buddy readily opens his mouth to get the food off the spoon.**

Showing Buddy the Hold It and Give commands

As soon as Buddy has an inkling of what the Take It command means, you're ready to introduce him to his dumbbell. But going from food to a dumbbell is quite a transition, so you need to be patient with him.

When you're teaching Buddy any of the behaviors associated with retrieving, your body posture is important. You want to be at his right side without hovering or leaning over him because that posture would put him into defense drive when you want him in prey drive.

Here are the steps for introducing Buddy to the dumbbell using the Hold It and Give commands:

1. **With Buddy sitting at your left side, again facing the chair, put your left palm lightly on top of his muzzle and place your left index finger behind his left canine tooth. (See Figure 15-1.)**

   Place small dogs on a table for this exercise. Doing so helps you from having to lean over and create a hovering posture. It also saves your back!

Figure 15-1:
Gently opening your dog's mouth.

2. **Gently open his mouth and with your right hand place the dumbbell in his mouth with the command "Take It."**

    Hold the dumbbell by the bell so you can easily put the bar in his mouth.

3. **Rest the thumb of your right hand on top of his muzzle, fingers under his chin, and cup his mouth shut. (See Figure 15-2.)**

    The goal of this progression is for your dog to accept the dumbbell in his mouth voluntarily. It's only an introduction, so you don't want to close his mouth over the dumbbell for longer than one second.

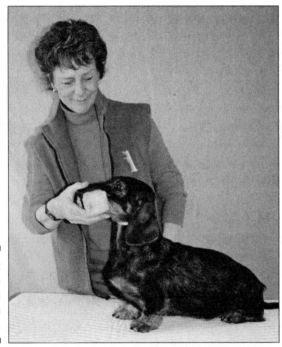

Figure 15-2:
Putting the dumbbell in your dog's mouth.

4. **Praise enthusiastically, immediately say, "Give" (or whatever command you want to use), and take the dumbbell out of his mouth.**

5. **Reward with the cat food.**

6. **Repeat this process ten times each for five sessions.**

After Buddy readily accepts the dumbbell consistently, you can go on to the exercise in the next section.

When we teach one of our dogs to retrieve, we practice this exercise once a day on consecutive days. If you're the ambitious type, you can practice more frequently, as long as your dog remains interested and will actively work for the treat. However, practicing sporadically isn't a good idea because your dog will forget what he has learned during the last session, and you basically have to start all over.

Helping your dog retrieve on command

After Buddy has become accustomed to having the dumbbell in his mouth (see the preceding section), you're ready to tackle the next step. The goal is for Buddy to take the dumbbell voluntarily in his mouth when you give the command. Here's how to do it:

1. **With Buddy sitting at your left side, have the chair with cat food in place, and put two fingers of your left hand through his collar, back to front, palm facing you, at the side of his neck.**

2. **With your right hand, place the bar of the dumbbell directly in front of his mouth, touching the small whiskers.**

3. **Say, "Take It," and when he takes it, briefly cup his mouth shut and tell him how clever he is.**

4. **Say, "Give," take out the dumbbell, and reward with food.**

   At this point in the training, your dog may not yet take the dumbbell but will open his mouth. In that case, just put the dumbbell in his mouth, cup his mouth shut, and so on.

If he sits there like a bump on a log, watch for signs of intention behavior. *Intention behaviors* are those actions that tell you what the dog is thinking (see Chapter 2 for more). They range from the subtle, such as bringing the whiskers forward, to the overt, such as sniffing the dowel, licking his lips, or intently staring at the dumbbell. Buddy is thinking about taking the dumbbell but isn't quite sure he can.

When you see intention behavior from your dog, take your hand out of the collar, open his mouth, put the dumbbell in, and briefly cup his mouth shut. Praise, remove the dumbbell from his mouth, and reward with food. Repeat this process until Buddy readily opens his mouth and accepts the dumbbell on command. Praising him while he has the dumbbell in his mouth is important.

Be patient. Sometimes it can take several minutes before the dog makes a move. If absolutely nothing happens and the little wheels have come to a grinding halt, review the preceding process five times and then try again. Some dogs appear to be particularly dense about taking the dumbbell voluntarily on command, but with enough repetitions, they'll get it.

Learning to hold and reach for the object

Before you proceed with the retrieve part of this exercise, you need to teach Buddy what you want him to do with the dumbbell after he has it in his mouth. You want him to hold the dumbbell in his mouth and not drop it before the Give command. You may think this concept is obvious, but it's not evident to Buddy until you teach it to him.

Your goal is to have Buddy firmly hold the dumbbell until you say "Give." Follow these steps:

1. **Start in the usual position, with Buddy at your left side and the cat food on the chair.**

2. **Put the dumbbell into his mouth and say, "Hold It."**

   To prevent him from mouthing the dumbbell with his back teeth, make sure his head is parallel to the ground. Keep the upper part of your body straight so you don't hover or lean over him.

3. **Hold the back of your right hand under his chin. (See Figure 15-3.)**

   If Buddy decides to drop the dumbbell at this point, he'll open his mouth by dropping his bottom jaw. Keeping the back of your hand under his mouth stops this from happening. If you hold the palm of your hand under his chin, Buddy may construe it as an invitation to drop the dumbbell.

4. **Smile and count to five.**

5. **Praise, remove the dumbbell, and reward him with food.**

Figure 15-3: Holding the back of your hand under the dog's chin.

6. **Repeat these steps 20 times, gradually increasing the time you have him hold the dumbbell in 5-second increments up to 30 seconds.**

If Buddy starts rolling the dumbbell around in his mouth or looks as though he will open his mouth to drop it, give him a *gentle* tap under the chin with "Hold It." Then remove the dumbbell with "Give," praise, and reward.

As soon as Buddy understands that he has to hold the dumbbell, the next sequence is to teach him to reach for it. Use these steps:

1. **With two fingers of your left hand through his collar at the side of his neck, back to front with the palm facing you, hold his dumbbell 2 inches in front of his mouth.**

2. **Say, "Take It."**

3. **If he does, cup his mouth shut with "Hold It," count to five, praise, remove dumbbell with "Give," and reward with food.**

4. **If he doesn't take the dumbbell, gently bring his head forward by the collar toward the dumbbell until he reaches for and takes it. Cup his mouth shut with "Hold It," count to five, praise, remove the dumbbell with "Give," and reward with food.**

5. **Repeat Steps 1 and 2 until your dog voluntarily reaches for and takes the dumbbell.**

   Increase the distance Buddy has to reach for the dumbbell in 2-inch increments to arm's length.

Walking while holding the dumbbell

The next step in the retrieve progressions is teaching Buddy to walk while holding the dumbbell in his mouth. Okay, you're probably saying to yourself, "For Pete's sake, is all this really necessary?" The answer? It depends on the dog. At this point in the training, the majority of dogs understand the concept and can hold the dumbbell in their mouths and walk at the same time. (Hey, even some people have difficulty walking and chewing gum at the same time, so give your dog a break.) If your dog does it, you can skip this step. Still, we've seen dogs, including some of our own, that couldn't make this transition from holding the dumbbell to walking with it at the same time. So they had to be taught to do so. When we devised this approach to teach retrieving, we included the walking-while-holding sequence just to make sure that all eventualities are covered.

Here are the steps to follow to teach Buddy to walk while holding the dumbbell:

1. **With Buddy sitting at your left side, facing the chair with the cat food and spoon from about 6 feet away, put the dumbbell in his mouth with "Take It," followed by "Hold It."**

   Encourage him to walk toward the chair.

2. **To give Buddy confidence, put your right hand under his chin when he starts to move.**

   Your hand stops Buddy from dropping his bottom jaw as he walks, keeps his mouth closed around the dumbbell, and helps him succeed.

3. **When he gets to the chair, praise, remove the dumbbell from his mouth with "Give," and reward him.**

4. **Repeat until Buddy walks with the dumbbell without you holding your hand under his chin.**

   Gradually increase the distance to 20 steps in 5-step increments.

Training Buddy for the pick-up

You and Buddy are getting close to the final progression of teaching him to retrieve. Right now you're ready for the pick-up. Resist the temptation to just throw the dumbbell and expect Buddy to pick it up and bring it back. He may actually do it, but he also may not. He may just chase it and then stand over it, not knowing what to do next. In the long run, make sure that he knows what you expect by teaching him. Here's what to do:

1. **With Buddy sitting at your left side, place the chair with the cat food and spoon *behind* you.**

2. **With your fingers in his collar, hold the dumbbell about 2 inches from Buddy's mouth and say, "Take It."**

3. **When he does, praise enthusiastically, say, "Give," remove the dumbbell from his mouth, and reward.**

   Your goal with Steps 2 and 3 is to lower the dumbbell in 2-inch increments toward the ground and have Buddy retrieve it from your hand.

4. **When you get to the ground, place the bell of the dumbbell on the ground and hold it at a 45-degree angle.**

5. **Say, "Take It," and when Buddy takes the dumbbell, take your hand out of the collar, say, "Hold It," and back up two steps.**

   He'll quickly come to you to get his reward.

6. **Praise, remove, and reward.**

7. **Repeat until he's comfortable picking up the dumbbell with you holding it at that angle.**

Learning to bring it back

Buddy has discovered how to go to the dumbbell and pick it up off the ground while your hand is still on it. You now progress to the stage where he'll pick it up by himself and bring it back to you. Here's how we teach this part:

1. **Place the dumbbell on the ground but keep your hand on it.**

2. **Have Buddy retrieve the dumbbell several times while you have your hand on it.**

3. **Hold your hand first 2 inches, and then 6 inches, and then 12 inches away from the dumbbell until you can place it on the ground and stand up straight.**

4. **Each time he retrieves the dumbbell, back up several steps, praise, remove, and reward.**

5. **If your dog doesn't pick up the dumbbell from the ground, place it into his mouth and back up, praising him.**

You don't reward Buddy when you're helping him learn; you only reward when he does something you have told him to do.

If this sequence becomes an issue and your dog continues to refuse to take the dumbbell, review the prior progressions. Make sure that you follow them religiously and that your dog masters each progression before you go on to the next.

6. **Say, "Stay," and place the dumbbell 1 foot in front of your dog.**

7. **Say, "Take It," and when he brings it back, praise, remove, and reward.**

8. **Repeat by first placing it 3 feet and then 6 feet in front of your dog.**

Your dog will tell you how many times in a row you can ask him to retrieve. If he has many prey drive behaviors, you can get in quite a few repetitions. If not, he'll quickly lose enthusiasm. You're better off stopping after five repetitions and picking the game up again at the next session.

For your dog, picking up a dumbbell that you placed on the ground isn't terribly exciting, and if it weren't for the reward, it would be an absolute bore. Still, this sequence is necessary because you want your dog to learn he has to do it for you and not for himself.

Putting it all together

Now comes the fun part, where you get to throw the dumbbell and Buddy gets to chase it and bring it back. Follow these steps:

1. **Throw the dumbbell a few feet, and at the same time send your dog to the dumbbell with "Take It."**

2. **As soon as he picks up the dumbbell, say "Come" and tell him how terrific he is.**

3. **When he gets back to you, take the dumbbell with "Give" and reward him with a treat.**

Sometimes dogs get carried away by the fun of it all and don't come right back with the dumbbell. They may make a detour, or just run around for the joy of it. If that happens, say, "Come," as soon as he picks up the dumbbell. Then praise and reward him when he gets back to you.

4. **Gradually increase the distance you throw the dumbbell, and as he gains confidence, introduce the Sit in front with "Hold It."**

When he gets back to you say, "Sit" and "Hold It." Because he hasn't done this task before, you may have to hold your hand under his chin to prevent him from dropping the dumbbell. When he's successful, praise, remove, and reward. From then on make him sit and hold the dumbbell every time he gets back to you.

Congratulations! You now have a dog that retrieves on command — at least a dumbbell. To play the game of fetch, however, most people probably use a Frisbee, a ball, or a stick. Few dogs have any difficulty making the transition from the dumbbell to one of these objects. Usually, it's the other way around. The dog will happily retrieve a ball, but will turn his nose up at the dumbbell.

You also can use the Retrieve command to have Buddy bring in the newspaper, carry his leash, and — size permitting — carry your handbag or retrieve lost keys. We taught one of our dogs to open the refrigerator door and retrieve a can of soda. Unfortunately, we were unable to teach the dog to close the fridge door and had to abandon that trick.

Polishing and Perfecting the Retrieve

In this section, we show you how to put all the pieces of the retrieve together. You'll now introduce the Stay command when you throw the dumbbell. After waiting a short time, you'll tell Buddy to "Take It." Some dogs respond well to the voice command; others respond better to a hand signal given with the left hand toward the dumbbell. Practice with Buddy to see which one brings the kind of response you want.

Wait for it: Testing your dog's patience

Buddy has to learn to stay while you throw the dumbbell and until you release him to get it. Making him wait gets him even more excited about getting to his dumbbell. Trying to teach your dog patience is almost like teaching your 2-year-old child patience, but you can do it. Just follow these steps:

1. **Start with Buddy at your left side.**

2. **Put two fingers of your left hand through his collar, say, "Stay," and throw the dumbbell about 15 feet.**

3. **Very, very slowly let go of his collar, count to five, and say, "Take It."**

4. **When he returns with the dumbbell, praise, remove, and reward.**

5. **Repeat these steps until your dog holds the stay without you having to hold him by the collar.**

Give the Take It command in an excited and enthusiastic tone of voice to put the dog into prey drive. Don't use a harsh or threatening tone because that tone may put the dog in the wrong drive and make it more difficult for him to learn. A hand signal also can be given to Buddy if he's high in prey drive. It goes from the left side of your body toward the dumbbell. If at any time your dog needs motivation, throw the dumbbell and at the same time say, "Take It," letting him chase after it.

Retrieving with distractions

After Buddy knows how to retrieve, he's ready for distraction training. Introduce your dog to distractions as follows (you need a helper for this sequence):

1. **Your helper stands about 2 feet from the dumbbell.**

   He or she assumes a friendly posture that's not threatening to the dog.

2. **Send Buddy and as soon as he picks up the dumbbell, enthusiastically praise.**

   Look at the exercise as having been completed as soon as your dog picks up his dumbbell.

3. **As the dog gains confidence, have your helper stand a little closer and then over the dumbbell.**

   Also ask the helper to hide the dumbbell by standing directly in front of it with his back to the dog. You also can use a chair as a distraction by putting the dumbbell under the chair and then on the chair.

Continue to use food rewards for Buddy on a random basis; that is, instead of using them every time and in a predictable pattern, use them only often enough to maintain his motivation.

During distraction training, you may see the following responses or variations thereof:

✔ **He hesitates and fails to retrieve.** He starts going toward the dumbbell but then backs off and fails to retrieve, meaning, "I don't have the confidence to get close enough to the helper to retrieve my dumbbell."

Without saying anything, slowly approach him, put two fingers of your left hand through the collar, back to front, palm facing you, at the side of his neck and take him to the dumbbell. If he picks up the dumbbell, back up, praise, remove the dumbbell and reward; if he doesn't, put the dumbbell in his mouth, back up, then praise, remove, and reward. Don't repeat the command.

Keep trying, and remember your dog's learning style and how many repetitions it takes before he understands. You may find that you have to help him several times before he has the confidence to do it by himself. As soon as he has done it on his own, stop for that session.

✔ **He gives up.** He leaves altogether and doesn't retrieve, saying, in effect, "I can't cope with this." In this case, use the remedy from the preceding response.

✔ **He does nothing.** In other words, he's thinking, "If I don't do anything, maybe all of this will go away." If your dog does nothing, use the same remedy from the first response.

✔ **He becomes distracted.** He permits himself to be distracted, meaning, "I would rather visit than retrieve my dumbbell." If you experience this response, use the remedy from the first response.

✔ **He takes the dumbbell to the distracter.** Slowly approach your dog without saying anything, put the leash on the dead ring of the training collar and, with a little tension on the collar, show him exactly what he was supposed to do by guiding him to you. No extra command is given.

✔ **He anticipates the retrieve without waiting to be told to do so.** In other words, he breaks the stay and tries to retrieve without the command. He's catching on and wants to show you how clever he is.

Without saying anything, slowly approach him, take the dumbbell out of his mouth, put it down where he picked it up, go back to the starting point and then send him. Whatever you do, don't shout "no" or do anything else that would discourage him from retrieving after you have just worked so hard to get him to pick up the dumbbell.

✔ **He does it correctly.** At this point, stop training for that session.

When your dog confidently retrieves with the first level of distractions, introduce the next level. Second-degree distractions, which are visual and auditory, consist of having your helper crouch close to the dumbbell while trying to distract him by saying, "Here puppy, come visit for some petting." The distracter doesn't use your dog's name. After Buddy successfully works his way through the 2nd-degree distraction, you can increase the level of difficulty to the 3rd degree, which uses food or a toy. Have the helper offer Buddy a treat, a ball, or a toy about 1 foot away from the dumbbell. Of course, the helper never lets him have those items. (See Figure 15-4.) If Buddy goes to the distracter or tries to take the food, follow the preceding guidelines until Buddy does it correctly. Then stop for that training session.

Figure 15-4: Retrieving with 3rd-degree distraction.

Distractions add an extra dimension and take training to a higher level. Challenging Buddy to use his head with distraction training helps build your dog's confidence and teaches him to concentrate on what he's doing. This type of training is especially important for the shy dog, providing the confidence he needs to respond correctly under different conditions.

During distraction training, keep in mind that anytime you change the complexity of the exercise, it becomes a new exercise for the dog. If Buddy goes for the food, you would treat his response the same way you did when you first introduced him to distraction training. No, your dog isn't defiant, stubborn, or stupid; he's just confused as to what he should do and has to be helped again.

When using distraction training, giving Buddy a chance to work out the situation for himself is important. Don't be too quick to help him. Be patient, and let him try to figure out on his own how to correctly handle the situation. After he does, you'll be pleasantly surprised by the intensity and reliability with which he responds.

You're now ready to work with different objects you want Buddy to retrieve. When you do, you may have to review the first few sequences. Just because Buddy retrieves one object doesn't necessarily mean he'll retrieve others. He may need to get used to them first. If you would like to see how to teach Buddy to retrieve, go to www.volhard.com to find out how you can get a copy of our Retrieve DVD.

Part V
Dealing with Special Situations

In this part . . .

This part deals with special situations such as managing so-called aggressive behavior, helping your dog cope with thunder and loud noises, and reducing separation anxiety and the incidence of submissive urination, among others. This part also includes a chapter on the needs and training of the older dog as well as a chapter on seeking expert training help.

Chapter 16

Addressing Aggression

The term *aggression* means different things to different people. For example, a passerby may well consider a dog that runs along the fence in his yard barking and snarling furiously aggressive. But if he's your dog, you may consider the behavior to be a perfectly normal reaction: The dog is protecting his territory, which is what you expect from him.

Many dog owners want a certain amount of protectiveness, or "aggression," from their canine companions — but only at the right times and under the right circumstances. For the dog, determining the right time and right circumstance can be a tough call. This chapter helps you sort out how to manage the "aggression" issue in a variety of situations.

Of the many behaviors a dog expresses, perhaps the most misunderstood is aggression. To someone who knows dogs, a growl or baring of the teeth under certain circumstances can be expected. But for someone who's new to dogs, it can be frightening. So, this so-called aggression is the behavior that causes the most angst on the part of the owner. It's often dealt with incorrectly and frequently lands the dog in a shelter to be adopted again or put down. Because aggression can be caused by mismanagement and misunderstanding of dog behavior on the part of the owner, we explain in this chapter what can cause "aggression" in a home and training environment.

Understanding Aggression

The terms *aggression* and *vicious* often are used incorrectly for behaviors that aren't true aggression. Eberhard Trumler, the noted German behaviorist, defines true aggression as "unpredictable and unprovoked biting — without warning — with the intent to draw blood." If we accept this definition, the vast majority of so-called aggressive incidents occur with plenty of warning from the dog and are predictable and/or provoked.

For example, say you're walking your dog when a stranger approaches, causing your dog to start growling, maybe because he's afraid (which would be referred to as *defense flight*) or maybe because he wants to protect you (which would be referred to as *defense fight*). In either case, it isn't true aggression, because the dog is giving you ample warning of his intentions. It's now your job to manage the situation correctly. (Flip to Chapter 2 for more on defense drive.)

To manage the situation, you can cross the street; you can turn around and go the other way; or you can tell your dog to heel and pass the stranger, keeping yourself between the stranger and your dog. Basic training exercises such as Heel and Sit help you manage the situation by giving your dog something on which to focus. Under no circumstances should you make any effort to calm your dog by reassuringly petting him and telling him in a soothing voice, "There, there, it's perfectly okay." Buddy will interpret your soothing as, "That's a good boy. I want you to growl." Well, perhaps you do want him to growl, but if you don't, these kinds of reassurances reinforce the behavior.

In the following sections, we provide information to help you determine what aggressive behavior is and why it occurs.

What is aggressive behavior?

Aggressive behavior can be directed toward any or all of the following:

- ✔ Owner
- ✔ Family
- ✔ Strangers
- ✔ Other dogs and animals

Signs of aggression include the following:

- ✔ Low-toned, deep growling
- ✔ Showing of teeth and staring
- ✔ Ears and whiskers pointing forward with the dog standing tall with his hackles up from his shoulders forward and his tail straight up
- ✔ Actual biting

A good reason to be "aggressive"

A good friend of ours, who was raised on a large farm, recalls an incident involving two of her younger brothers, ages 10 and 8. One morning, the boys announced they were going down to the pond to fish. Off they went with the family dog, Lucy, in tow. A short time later, they returned crying and sobbing: "Lucy won't let us dig for worms. She growled at us and showed her teeth." Because this behavior was uncharacteristic for Lucy, their mother decided to investigate. She found Lucy sitting at the edge of the pond where the boys had tried to dig for worms, intently staring at a rock. As the mother approached, Lucy became agitated and started barking. The mother then called one of the farm hands. With the aid of a rake, he turned over the rock, and they discovered a nest of copperheads.

When the aggressive behavior is directed toward you, ask yourself whether the question of who is Number One has been resolved. Usually it hasn't been, and the dog is convinced that he's Number One or can become Numero Uno. He's not a bad dog; he's just a pack animal and is looking desperately for leadership. If that leadership isn't forthcoming on your part, he'll fill the vacuum. Dogs are quite happy and content when they know their rank order.

Looking at the causes of aggression

Aggressive behavior can be caused by many different factors, including heredity, poor health, or environment. Hereditary aggression, unless selectively bred for, is relatively rare, because it contradicts the whole concept of domestication. Aggressive behavior is more frequently the result of the dog feeling bad or being in discomfort or even pain. In these cases, the dog's action isn't a behavioral problem but a health problem.

The most common cause for dog bites is environmental — the result of a misunderstanding or outright mismanagement of the dog. A misunderstanding can occur when a puppy or dog nips at the owner's hand during play or when the dog is playing retrieve and accidentally bites the hand when his owner tries to get the stick. Most dog owners can recognize when a bite occurred due to a misunderstanding — in this case, the dog will likely be just as horrified as the owner.

Bites occurring because of mismanagement are a different matter. For example, say the kids are playing with Buddy and he has had enough, so he retreats under the bed. When one of the children crawls after Buddy and tries to drag him out, Buddy snaps at the child's hand and may even make contact. This isn't an uncommon scenario, and it certainly isn't aggression. Even though the dog may not have provided any warning, his behavior was predictable — the fact that Buddy retreated should have told the children that he'd had enough. Similarly, when you stick your hand in the crate of a dog that isn't yours, and he growls at you, you should know that you need to remove your hand. If you persist, he has given you ample warning that he may bite.

One scenario we frequently encounter is the dog, when told to get off the couch or bed, growls at the owner. When we ask the owner whether the dog has had any basic training, the answer invariably is "not much" or "none." In this case, the first order of business should be teaching the dog the basic impulse control exercises — Sit and Stay, door and stair manners, the Leave It command (see Chapter 9), and the beginner exercise in Chapter 1. For those who don't want to bother with training their dogs or who simply don't have the time, there's always the Scat Mat or the indoor containment system (see Chapter 5 for more details on these products).

Aggression is a natural and even necessary phenomenon. In the case of unwanted aggression, human mistakes or misunderstandings are the usual cause. The owner may be unintentionally rewarding the undesired behavior, causing it to occur again and again, or the owner may not have socialized the dog properly. Only when you're unable to manage aggression, or don't understand its origin, does it become a problem.

Keeping your dog at home until he has had all his vaccinations at 6 months of age prevents proper socialization with people and other dogs and can be a cause for aggression. During the critical socialization period and early puppyhood, Buddy learns dog language from other dogs allowing him to behave appropriately around them. After Buddy has had his first set of vaccines (for parvovirus and distemper), it's perfectly safe to take him out and about. It's critical that Buddy be taken different places in puppyhood so he learns to accept different environments. Training in different areas is helpful to the puppy because he discovers that his training is enforced not just at home but wherever he finds himself. (Refer to the nearby sidebar "Socializing your pup when he's young" for more information.)

Socializing your pup when he's young

A few years ago, it was brought to our attention that a number of Rottweilers had bitten their veterinarians when taken for their six-month checkups. Apparently, the situation had gotten so bad that many vets didn't want these dogs as clients anymore. At that point, the Rottweiler Club of England consulted us. We found that the same veterinary community that didn't want these dogs as clients anymore had advised the dogs' owners *not* to let the dogs out in public before they had all their vaccinations — that is, until they were 6 months of age. Those owners who followed this advice ended up with completely unsocialized dogs.

This example is a classic case of aggression on a grand scale caused by a lack of understanding of behavior. Socialization is a continuing necessity throughout your dog's life. If you don't socialize Buddy, you *will* have problems as he grows up. Take this advice seriously, and get Buddy into a good puppy class as soon as you can. And continue to take him out so he can mix with other dogs as he continues to mature. (Check out Part II for more about training puppies.)

Managing a Dog's Aggression — Prey, Pack, Fight, and Flight Drives

This section examines the triggers of aggression in the context of the three drives — prey, pack, and defense (which includes fight and flight drives). The triggers are different in each drive, and so is the management. Your dog's Personality Profile (see Chapter 2) tells you the likely triggers so you can predict what Buddy will do under certain circumstances. Discovering how to anticipate your dog's reaction under certain situations is part of managing his behavior.

Other than ignoring or putting up with the behavior, you have three basic options:

- **Expending the energy:** Each behavior has a *timeframe,* or energy, and it can be managed by expending that energy, which means exercise specifically focused on that energy. The exercise can be playing ball, jogging, playing tug-of-war games, or whatever. Basic training is always essential.

- **Suppressing the energy:** This option means that the dog isn't given an outlet for the energy. Suppression can be an effective temporary solution, provided that the dog has periodic opportunities to expend the energy.

Total suppression can be dangerous. Liken it to a bottle of soda that's shaken vigorously. When you take the top off it explodes. So a dog who has been bred to run (for example, a Greyhound or Whippet) but suppressed will run for a long time and may not come back. Working dogs that come from generations of dogs who have worked for a living don't make good pets where their natural behaviors are suppressed. Unless they have an outlet for their intelligence, they can become grumpy, irritable, and obsessive over toys. Some even indulge in self-mutilation. Training and working these dogs regularly is a necessity.

A friend of ours who's a professional trainer recently had a dog in for training because it bit its owners and also ran away. The dog was a Malinois, which is bred to work. When the trainer enquired about the amount of exercise and training this dog was receiving, the answer was practically none. Just a walk around the block twice a day. Our friend easily found the solution by working the dog in his training field. He walked around the perimeter of the field and showed the dog where he had hidden a lot of toys. He brought the dog back to the entrance to the field and told her to find a toy. It took about 20 minutes for the dog to find them all, but the activity had expended the energy and she was calm and happy for the rest of the day. She never showed any tendencies to bite.

✔ **Switching the drive:** When Buddy growls at another dog, for example, he's in defense drive. To manage the situation, switch him into pack drive. Cheerfully say something like "You must be joking" and walk away in the opposite direction.

Depending on the situation, you're going to use a combination of the three options in your management program. In the following sections, we focus on the triggers and management for aggression caused by the three different drives.

Dealing with aggression from dogs high in prey drive

You shouldn't be surprised that *prey behaviors,* those associated with chasing and killing prey, are one of the leading causes for aggression. In a sense, aggression coming from this drive is the most dangerous, because so many different stimuli can trigger it. Dogs high in prey drive are stimulated by sounds, smells, and moving objects. Chapter 2 can help you further recognize a dog who's high in this drive.

Triggers

Anything that moves triggers prey behaviors. Dogs high in prey drive chase cars, bicycles, joggers, cats, other dogs, squirrels, bunnies, you name it. And if they catch up with whatever they're chasing, that's when the problem starts. Running after a car for example, can get your dog killed. Running after a cat can be dangerous if the cat stops, turns, and attacks your dog. He can lose an eye that way. Running after squirrels and other critters also needs to be stopped. Imagine that you're traveling with Buddy and stop at a rest stop that has trees, squirrels, and picnic tables with families enjoying an outing. If Buddy gets loose and chases the squirrel, you can run into trouble. If you're lucky, the squirrel goes up a tree and Buddy doesn't catch it. But the act of chasing can terrify the families and also can lead Buddy to keep going out onto the highway.

Prey drive can be triggered in a training class situation when dogs are moving on the heeling exercise. Some beginner dogs get overly excited and start barking at the other dogs. This behavior makes it impossible for the instructor to guide the students, and it makes the other dogs in the class nervous and excited too. It can be common in under-socialized dogs and some rescue dogs.

To diffuse this situation, it's wise for the instructor to have the owner and dog sit on the sidelines during the moving exercises and have them practice their Sit-Stay (see Chapter 9). If you're the student in this situation, it's a good idea either to sit on the sidelines or put your dog into the car if you can't manage him. Practice at home until the dog has become more confident and can rejoin the class.

Management

Play retrieve games on a regular basis, and make sure your dog gets plenty of exercise. When you take him for a walk and he spots a cat or squirrel, distract him, redirect his attention on you, and go in the opposite direction. The Leave It command (see Chapter 9) may be sufficient, or you may have to give him a check on the leash to refocus his attention on you. Basic training is a must to control this kind of behavior in the long term. See Figure 16-1.

Figure 16-1:
Releasing
energy from
prey drive.

If he doesn't reliably respond to the Come command, don't let him loose in situations where he may take off after something. Better yet, train him to come reliably on command. Whatever you do, don't let Buddy chase cars, joggers, or cyclists.

Handling aggression from dogs high in defense drive

Survival and self-preservation govern defense drive, which consists of both fight and flight behaviors. Defense drive is more complex than pack or prey because the same stimulus that can cause aggression (fight) also can elicit avoidance (flight) behaviors.

After some basic training, dogs with high fight drive are terrific companions and protectors, great competition and show dogs, and a joy to own. As young dogs, they may start bucking for a promotion. You may see signs of aggression toward you when you want the dog to get off the furniture or in similar situations when he doesn't want to do what you tell him.

If a puppy is allowed to grow up doing anything he likes and isn't given parameters for what he can and can't do, he likely won't make a satisfactory pet. After all, he'll develop a sense that he can do anything he pleases.

Full-fledged signs of aggression don't just suddenly occur. He'll start off by giving many warnings, from growling to lip lifting to staring at you. If you condone these behaviors and avoid dealing with them, your dog is on his way to becoming aggressive.

Buddy also may be aggressive toward other dogs. When meeting another dog, he'll try to lord it over the other dog. The classic sign is putting his head over the shoulder of the other dog. The dog of lesser rank lowers his body posture, signaling that he recognizes the other dog's rank.

When two dogs perceive each other as equal in rank, a fight may ensue. Left to their own devices (that is, off leash), chances are they'll decide that discretion is the better part of valor. Both know that there are no percentages to fighting. They slowly separate and go their own ways.

A true dogfight is a harrowing and horrifying experience, and most people prefer not to take the chance that it'll occur. Discover how to read the signs and take the necessary precautions by keeping the dogs apart. Dogs are no different from people: Not all of them get along.

Some owners inadvertently cause dogfights by maintaining a tight leash on the dog. A tight leash alters your dog's body posture, thereby giving an unintended aggression signal to the other dog. Maintain a loose leash when meeting another dog so you don't distort Buddy's body posture. And at the slightest sign of trouble, such as a hard stare from the other dog, a growl, or a snarl, happily call your dog to you and walk away. *Happily* calling is important because you want to defuse the situation and not aggravate it by getting excited. You want to switch the dog from fight drive into pack drive.

A female dog is entitled to tell off a male dog who's making unwanted advances. She may lift her lip, a signal for the male dog to back off. If the male doesn't take the hint, she may growl or snap at him. This behavior isn't aggression but perfectly normal dog behavior.

Taking something out of Buddy's mouth

At some point during your dog ownership, you'll have to remove something from Buddy's mouth. It could be a chicken bone from the garbage, your shoe, or anything else inappropriate. Don't yell at him or chase him. He'll redouble his efforts to eat whatever it is. Try the Leave It command (see Chapter 9). If that doesn't work,

try a trade. Offer him a fair trade, such as a piece of cheese or a treat. As he reaches for it, of course, the chicken bone (or whatever you're after) will drop out of his mouth. Remember, never chase Buddy and corner him. Doing so destroys the very relationship you've been working so hard to achieve.

Triggers

Aggressive behaviors can be set off in a dog with defense drive (fight and flight) by a variety of triggers. Some of the more common ones are

- ✔ Approaching the dog in a threatening manner
- ✔ Hovering or looming over the dog
- ✔ Staring at the dog
- ✔ Teasing the dog
- ✔ Telling him to get off the couch or bed
- ✔ Trying to remove something from his mouth (see the sidebar, "Taking something out of Buddy's mouth")

You can avoid some of these triggers altogether — like teasing him, staring at him, or hovering over him. Just don't do them. Other triggers, though, you need to deal with.

Management

If you've identified that your dog's aggression is triggered by defense drive, you have four ways to manage that aggression. We discuss the methods in the following sections.

Provide exercise and training

One way to manage aggressive behavior is to provide plenty of exercise and training. Exercise physically tires the body, and training tires the brain. In this situation, lack of mental stimulation gets the dog into trouble. Aim for two training sessions a day, each at least ten minutes long. If you keep to the same time schedule, you'll have a happy puppy.

Training doesn't stop just because Buddy grows up. He loves to use his brain all the way into old age. Using his brain helps keep him young. Be inventive in your teaching. Get him to help you around the house — he can take the laundry to the washing machine or help you bring in groceries to the kitchen. He'll love the challenge. Periodically review door and stair manners, getting in and out of the car, and his recall. A short obedience routine is always enjoyed, and teaching him tricks can be fun. (See Chapter 23 for a list of tricks and games you can practice with Buddy.)

Play tug of war

Another way to manage aggression is to expend the energy in the fight drive by playing a good game of tug of war. This game allows the dog to use up his timeframe of wanting to growl, tug, and bite. Instead of trying to suppress the behavior, dissipate its energy. The absence of an outlet for that energy, or efforts to suppress it, only makes matters worse. Figure 16-2 shows a game of tug of war.

Figure 16-2:
The tug of war game.

Put aside ten minutes several times a week to play tug of war at the same time every day. Here's what you do:

1. **Get a pull toy, a piece of sacking, or a knotted sock to use for the game.**

2. **Allow your dog to growl and bite the object and shake it while you're holding it. After a satisfying tug, let Buddy have the toy.**

   Be careful not to tug too hard toward you; you could injure Buddy's mouth or loosen a tooth.

3. **Let him bring the object back to you to play again.**

4. **Be sure to let him win each time by letting him carry it to his bed or wherever he wants to go.**

   Some people object to the approach of letting the dog "win." Win exactly what? You started the game, you ended the game. You made all the decisions.

5. **When you have had enough, walk away from this session with the dog in possession of the toy.**

   Remember that everything belongs to you, especially the affection, attention, and time he seeks from you. If your dog comes after you for more play time, then simply turn your back on him and ignore him. (See Chapter 2 for more.)

The game effectively discharges the energy and the timeframe in that drive. The game should be removed from regular training sessions and done when you and your dog are alone with no distractions. It's his time and his only. You'll be amazed at how satisfying the game is to your dog and at the calming effect it has on him.

Practice the Long Down

A third way to manage high-fight-drive aggression is with the Long Down (see Chapter 9). We can't emphasize enough the importance of this exercise. It's a benign exercise and establishes quite clearly who's in charge (that would be you) in a nonpunitive way. For dogs who express any kind of aggressive behavior, go back to this exercise and do a 30-minute Down. Make this the last thing you do at night, and do it two or three times a week. The Long Down and the tug-of-war game are simple solutions for the good dog who gets too pushy.

Use a muzzle

If your situation has reached the point where you're afraid of your dog, he tries to bite you, or you can't get him into the Down position, use a muzzle. You also may require professional training help (see Chapter 19). Buddy may need to see the chiropractor or veterinarian if his body hurts when you touch it. His aggression may be related to a physical problem. See the nearby sidebar "When aggression in a training situation is due to a physical problem" for more information.

When you're nervous or anxious about what your dog may do when encountering another dog or person, your emotions go straight down the leash, which can cause your dog to react in an aggressive manner. In a sense, your worries become a self-fulfilling prophecy. You can solve this dilemma with the use of a muzzle.

Using a muzzle is a simple solution to a complex problem. It allows you to go out in public with your dog without having to worry about him. A strange thing happens to a dog while wearing a muzzle. After you've taken away his option to bite, he doesn't even try. It's almost as if he's relieved that the decision has been taken away from him. Even better, it gives you peace of mind and allows you to relax. On the other hand, although your dog acts differently, so will people you encounter — a muzzled dog will make people apprehensive. A muzzle should be a last resort and isn't a substitute for seeking professional help.

Training to a muzzle should be done slowly and gently because, at first, many dogs panic from having something around their faces. But with diligence, common sense, and some compassion for the dog, you can train him quite easily to accept it. Here's what you need to do:

1. **Put the muzzle on your dog for a few minutes, and then take it off again.**

2. **Give him a treat, and tell him what a good boy he is.**

3. **Repeat Steps 1 and 2 over the course of several days, gradually increasing the length of time your dog wears the muzzle.**

4. **When he's comfortable wearing the muzzle at home, you can use it when you take him out in public.**

In some European cities, ordinances have been passed that require certain breeds to wear muzzles in public. We've seen many of these dogs happily accompanying their owners on walks. They were well behaved and seemed to be quite comfortable with their muzzles.

Many owners are reluctant to use a muzzle because of the perceived stigma attached to it. You have to make a choice — stigma or peace of mind? Something else to think about: Suppose that your dog actually bites someone. When you have such a simple solution, why take the chance?

Controlling aggression from dogs high in pack drive

Pack drive consists of behaviors associated with reproduction and being part of a group. Believing that a dog high in pack behaviors could be aggressive may be difficult to grasp, but you must accept the fact. This type of dog may

- ✔ Show signs of aggression toward people
- ✔ Attack other dogs with no apparent reason
- ✔ Not stop the attack when the other dog submits

A tug-of-war case in point

When we came up with the *tug-of-war-is-good* concept, we were teaching a class of students who were very advanced in their training. Many of them were training their second or third dogs, and all were experienced competitors. They had chosen dogs with a relatively high fight drive because they knew how well those dogs trained and how good the dogs looked in the show ring — bold and beautiful. But they had to live with the dogs' tendency toward aggressive behavior and always had to be careful in

a class or dog show situation — when the dog was around other dogs.

For the entire eight-week session, they were told to put time aside daily to play tug of war with their dogs. By the third week, we noticed a big difference in the dogs' temperaments. When together in class, the dogs became friendly toward each other, played more, trained better, and were perfectly well behaved when away from home.

Triggers

The problem with this kind of aggression is that few obvious triggers seem to exist. It's frequently observed in dogs that are taken away from their litters and mothers before 7 weeks of age. Between 5 and 7 weeks of age, a puppy learns to inhibit his biting (see Chapter 6). He also learns canine body language at this time. In short, your puppy learns he's a dog. Puppies that haven't learned these lessons tend to be overly protective of their owners and may be aggressive to other people and dogs. They can't interpret body language and haven't learned bite inhibition.

In a household with more than one dog, while one dog is being petted and the other is seeking your attention at the same time, the dog being petted may aggress toward the other dog. This overpossessiveness isn't uncommon from adopted older dogs and rescued dogs.

Lack of adequate socialization with people and other dogs prior to 6 months of age also can cause subsequent aggressive behaviors. We can think of several instances when a female owner has come to us because her dog was aggressive toward men. The cause in each case was lack of socialization or exposure to men. As long as the dog didn't come in close proximity with men, the dog didn't have a problem. A change of circumstances, such as a boyfriend, however, made aggressiveness a problem.

Management

You can solve a lack of socialization with other people by gradually getting the dog used to accepting another person. As always, the job is made easier when the dog has had some basic training and knows simple commands like Sit and Stay (which are described in Chapter 9). Here's what you need to do:

1. **Begin with Buddy sitting at Heel position in Control Position (no tension on the leash and only ½ inch of slack).**

   You can read more about Control Position in Chapter 13.

2. **Have the person walk past the dog from a distance of 6 feet, without looking at the dog.**

3. **Just before he passes the dog, have the person throw Buddy a small piece of a hot dog or another treat.**

4. **Repeat Steps 1 through 3 five times per session — but no more.**

5. **When Buddy shows no signs of aggression at 6 feet, decrease the distance.**

6. **Keep decreasing the distance until Buddy will take a treat, open palm, from the person.**

   The person shouldn't look at the dog. He should pause just long enough to give the dog the treat and then pass.

When aggression in a training situation is due to a physical problem

Demi was a delightful wire-haired Dachshund who was ready to compete for her Companion Dog title (see Chapters 13 and 14 for more on this title). She started to move her feet on the Stand for Examination exercise where all four feet must keep still while the judge is examining the dog. The fidgeting got so bad that when someone approached to examine her she would cower and then try to run away. If the person insisted on touching her, she finally whipped her head around and tried to bite. This wasn't normal behavior for Demi, who usually was a very sweet dog. Her owner took her for a visit with the veterinarian who discovered that Demi had a kidney infection. The kidneys sit just under the lumbar vertebrae in the lower back and every time someone touched that point, it hurt her. So she did the only thing she knew to do — bite to keep from feeling pain. After a short course of antibiotics and a visit to the doggy chiropractor to straighten out that part of her back, she went on to get her Companion Dog title successfully and had no further problems with people touching her back.

Aggression toward other dogs, especially if the aggressor has had a few successes in his career, isn't so simple to resolve. Prevention is the best cure here: Keep your dog on leash, and don't give him a chance to bite another dog when you're away from home.

To calm dogs with aggressive tendencies, get some essential oil of lavender from a health food store. Put just a couple drops on a small cloth, and wipe it onto your dog's muzzle and around his nose. Lavender has a calming effect, and we've had great success with it in class situations where one dog aggresses at another dog. It enables the dog to concentrate on his work. We've also used the oil in a spray bottle (four drops of oil to 8 ounces of water) and sprayed the room before the dogs come in. It really works wonders with the dogs and even calms the owners. Some of our students who have been in agility competition, and have dogs that couldn't concentrate because of the number of dogs and people around them, have found that wiping their dog's muzzles and noses with the oil has made a dramatic improvement in their performances.

Coping with Aggression around the Food Bowl

Your dog may growl when you get close to his food bowl. From his point of view, he's guarding his food — an instinctive and not uncommon reaction. The question is this: Should you try to do anything about it? And if the answer is yes, what do you do?

Some owners unwittingly exacerbate the behavior by trying to take the dog's food bowl from him while he's eating. Doing so definitely isn't a good idea. Why create unnecessary problems? Don't attempt the practice of taking food away from him and then putting it back. Imagine how you'd feel if someone kept taking away your dinner plate and putting it back. In no time at all, you'd become paranoid at the dinner table. That sort of thing creates apprehension and makes the guarding and growling worse.

Our advice for those owners who have this kind of problem is to change the environment. Make sure Buddy is fed in a place where the children or other dogs can't get to his food. A good place to feed him is in his crate. Give him his food and bones in his crate, and give him peace and quiet. And make sure that when he's in there, everyone leaves him alone. Head to Chapter 8 to see how to train your dog to a crate. Follow the directions and the food bowl aggression problem will be solved.

A lot of conflicting advice is available about the subject of feeding Buddy. We can tell you that in the 40 years we've bred, shown, owned, and taught thousands of people how to live with their dogs successfully, following the preceding advice has worked. We can't stress enough that it's important to leave Buddy alone when you feed him. Give him a place where he can be quiet and enjoy — and more importantly — digest his food, without the stress of kids, people, or other animals around his food bowl. Respect his space. If you insist on putting your hands in his food or taking it away, you'll train your dog to be neurotic. It will totally destroy the very relationship you're trying to build, and doing so is one of the first steps in teaching Buddy to become aggressive.

A recent study done in the Netherlands discusses whether the type of food a dog eats can cause behavior problems, in particular, aggression. See the study at `journals.cambridge.org/action/displayFulltext?type=1&fid=1452588&jid=NRR&volumemeld=20&issueld=02&aid=1452580`.

Dealing with Fear-Biters

The term *aggression* for fear-biters is actually a misnomer. These dogs don't aggress — they only defend themselves. When they do bite, it's out of fear; hence they're called *fear-biters*. Anytime this type of dog feels that he's cornered and unable to escape, he may bite. Biting to him is an act of last resort. He'd much rather get away from the situation.

Avoid putting this type of dog in a position where he thinks he has to bite. Use a similar approach to the one described in Chapter 17 for submissive wetting. Fear-biters are most comfortable when they know what's expected of them, as in training. Timid behavior can resurface when they're left to their own devices and not given clear instructions on how to behave.

Getting attacked by another dog

What do you do when you're walking your dog down the street on leash and another dog comes out of nowhere and attacks your dog? You do this:

- ✔ No matter what, *don't* yell or scream. Remember, prey drive is stimulated by sound — especially high-pitched sounds. Screaming just escalates the intensity of a dogfight. Try to keep calm at all times.

- ✔ While you have hold of the leash, your dog is at the mercy of the other dog. Let go so he can either retreat or fend for himself.

- ✔ For your own safety, don't try to separate the dogs, or you may get bitten. In the vast majority of incidents like this, one dog gives up, and the other one walks away.

- ✔ Canvass the neighborhood to find out who the loose dog belongs to. Then visit the person in a friendly way and make them aware that their dog is running loose and scaring (or harming) your dog. Perhaps times can be worked out so that when you walk your dog, the other dog is confined. Under no circumstances should you try to see whether the dog has a collar or tag. You would lean over the dog to do this, which would trigger more aggression. If talking to the owner doesn't work, consider getting a Pet Convincer to take on walks with you (see Chapter 5).

When we trained and exhibited our Yorkshire Terrier, Ty, we got into the habit of being ever vigilant about the intentions of other dogs. We learned to position ourselves between Ty and other dogs so they couldn't make eye contact with each other. Fortunately, we never had any untoward incidents with him.

Dogs high in *flight drive* can appear shy around strangers, other dogs, or new situations. They may hide behind their owners and need space. Keep them a good distance away from people and other dogs, and don't corner them for any reason. Use your body to reassure these dogs; squat down to their level, bending your knees and not hovering over them, and coax them to you with some food. Be patient to gain their confidence, and never, ever grab for them.

What this dog needs is confidence building. Training with quiet insistence and encouragement is one way to achieve a more comfortable dog. To get the dog used to people and other dogs, enroll him in an obedience class. You need to be patient with this dog and figure out how to go slowly. If you try to force an issue, you may wipe out whatever advances you've made.

This dog needs a structured and predictable environment. Walk, feed, and play at certain times of the day so the dog knows what's coming. Dogs have a phenomenal biological clock, and deviations from the time of walking and feeding can make undesirable behaviors resurface.

Rescued dogs — in particular, those who have gone through several homes — often have large numbers of flight behaviors. A tightly controlled schedule greatly helps in their rehabilitation.

Chapter 17

Helping Your Hound Handle Special Situations

In This Chapter

▶ Resolving issues with phobias and other problems

▶ Making your dog happier in uncomfortable situations

Dogs can have a variety of phobias and other problems — some that are related to training and others that aren't. Depending on the severity, these problems can be solved with your help. In this chapter, we list some of the more common ones and the approaches that have worked to solve them.

Fear of Loud Noises and Thunder

Some dogs have keener senses of hearing than others, to the point where loud noises literally hurt their ears. For example, one of our Landseers would leave the room anytime the TV was turned on. Fear of thunder also can be the result of this type of sound sensitivity.

Under ordinary circumstances sound sensitivity isn't a problem, but it can affect a dog's ability to concentrate in the presence of moderate to loud noises. A car backfiring causes this dog to jump out of his skin, whereas it only elicits a curious expression from another dog.

Dogs that experience fear of thunder and lightening become agitated and apprehensive when they sense an approaching storm. They may try to get out of the house, hide under the bed, engage in destructive behaviors, or exhibit other neurotic signs. Attempts to console the dog only reinforce his fears.

One product that claims an 85 percent success rate in controlling these symptoms is the Thundershirt — a pressure wrap that applies a gentle, constant pressure on a dog's torso. For more information, see www.thundershirt.com. The homeopathic remedy Aconite is helpful for some dogs as well. (Chapter 4 provides more information on homeopathic remedies.)

Coping with Separation Anxiety

With *separation-related behaviors,* also called *separation anxiety,* your dog becomes anxious and stressed when you leave him. He's emotionally responding to being physically separated from the person to whom he's attached. Dogs that experience separation anxiety usually are high in pack drive and low in defense (fight) drive. (See Chapter 2 for more information on the many drives your dog may have.)

The most frequent inquiries we get about separation anxiety come from individuals who have just adopted a rescue dog. With these dogs, a certain amount of anxiety on the dog's part is understandable. Everything is new, including the people, surroundings, and routine. We usually advise the owner to give the dog a week or two to settle in before becoming overly concerned.

In some cases, having an overly solicitous owner makes the problem worse. As the owner prepares to leave the house, he or she makes a big fuss over the dog: "Now don't worry. Mommy/daddy will be back soon, but I have to go to work for now. You be a good boy while I'm gone, and I'll bring you a nice treat." Such reassurances only increase the dog's anxiety at the expectation of being left alone.

The owner then makes an equally big fuss upon his or her return: "Poor boy. Did you miss me while I was gone? I missed you too. Were you a good boy?" These utterances increase the dog's excitement in anticipation of the owner's return.

The most typical and obvious signs of separation anxiety are destructive behaviors (destructive chewing, scratching, and in severe cases, self-mutilation), vocalizations (whining, barking, or howling), house soiling, pacing, and excessive drooling.

One solution to Buddy's boredom and loneliness is to get another dog. They can keep each other amused, and two dogs are more than twice the fun of one dog. But be warned that two dogs can also mean double trouble.

If you don't want to get another dog, try the approaches we discuss in the following sections. One of these may be just the trick to getting Buddy more comfortable at home without you.

Testing the desensitizing approach

People are just as much creatures of habit as dogs are, and they tend to follow a specific pattern before leaving the house. This pattern becomes the dog's cue that you're about to depart. Make a list showing your customary routine before leaving the house. For example, you may pick up your bag or briefcase, grab the car keys, put on your coat, turn off the lights, and then reassure and pet the dog.

At odd intervals, several times during the day, go through your routine exactly as you would prior to leaving, and then sit in a chair and read the paper or watch TV, or just putter around the house. By following this procedure, you'll begin to desensitize the dog to the cues that you're about to leave.

When your dog ignores the cues, leave the house without paying any attention to the dog. Leave for about five minutes, and then return. When you return, don't pay any attention to him for about 5 minutes. After that, interact in a normal fashion with your dog.

Repeat this process over the course of several days, staying out for progressively longer periods. Turning on the radio or TV and providing suitable toys for your dog also may help. Whatever you do, make sure to ignore the dog for five minutes after your return. With this process, you want to take the emotional element out of your going and coming so your dog will view the separation as a normal part of a day and not as a reason to become apprehensive.

Trying the D.A.P. approach

Another way to cope with separation anxiety is to use D.A.P. — Dog Appeasing Pheromone — a product developed by vets that mimics the properties of the natural pheromones of the lactating female. After giving birth, a mother dog generates pheromones that give her puppies a sense of well-being and reassurance.

D.A.P. is an electrical plug-in diffuser that dispenses the pheromone, which the dog's sense of smell detects. See Figure 17-1 to take a look at a D.A.P. dispenser. The pheromone reminds the dog of the well-being he felt as a puppy. In clinical trials, D.A.P. was effective in about 75 percent of cases in improving separation-related behaviors. To be effective, the diffuser must be plugged in 24 hours a day. D.A.P., which is odorless to people, is available at pet stores and from pet product catalogs.

Looking at some other options

Consider enrolling your dog in a doggie day care facility where he can meet and play with other dogs while you're away. It may take his mind off wondering where you are. For more on your dog's social needs and the pros and cons of doggie day care, flip to Chapter 3.

For relatively mild cases of separation anxiety, a visit from a pet sitter during the time he's left alone may be enough to allay his anxiety.

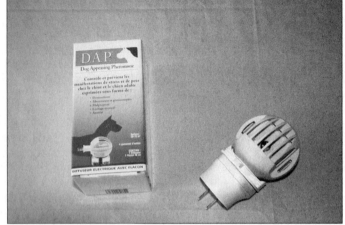

Figure 17-1:
A D.A.P.
dispenser.

Soiling the House

House soiling that occurs after you've housetrained your dog and that isn't marking behavior (see Chapter 11) can have a variety of causes other than separation anxiety. Its usual causes are one or more of the following:

- ✔ **You've left your dog too long without giving him a chance to relieve himself.** As the saying goes, accidents happen, and that's just what it was — an accident. You know your dog's endurance and schedule, so don't blame the dog when for some reason you were unable to adhere to his needs. You may have had to work late, or some other unforeseen event prevented you from getting home on time. As long as it doesn't become a regular occurrence on your part, the behavior won't be a continuing problem.

- ✔ **Your dog may have an upset stomach.** Abrupt dietary changes, such as changing dog foods, are the most common cause for an upset tummy. Any time you change your dog's diet, do so gradually by mixing the new food with his old food over a period of several days so his system can get used to the new food.

  Another cause of upset stomach may be from something he ate that didn't agree with him. Giving treats at holiday times that your dog ordinarily doesn't get, such as turkey and gravy or pizza, can create havoc with his digestive system.

- ✔ **Your dog may have *cystitis*, or a bladder infection.** This condition is more common among female dogs than male dogs and may cause dribbling. Cystitis is an inflammation of the bladder wall that can be caused by a bacterial infection. It makes Buddy feel as if there's constant pressure

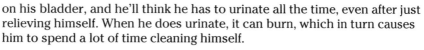

on his bladder, and he'll think he has to urinate all the time, even after just relieving himself. When he does urinate, it can burn, which in turn causes him to spend a lot of time cleaning himself.

Although not very dangerous in and of itself, cystitis can cause all sorts of problems if left unattended, because the bacteria can spread up into the kidneys. If you see any of the preceding symptoms, a trip to your vet is a must. A short course of the appropriate antibiotics cures this inflammation quickly.

✔ **If your dog is older, he may have developed urinary incontinence.** The slackening of the sphincter muscles that holds the urine in the bladder can cause incontinence, which often happens as your dog ages. So many dogs are put to sleep for this perceived problem, which although not easy to live with, can be solved in several ways, including being treated with medication and homeopathic remedies.

Acupuncture, which we discuss in Chapter 4, is probably the best treatment and is very effective. If you can find a vet trained in acupuncture, have your dog go through a series of treatments to solve the problem. Many vets today are trained in acupuncture, and finding one who can help isn't very difficult. A change in diet to a more natural diet also can often solve this problem (see Chapter 4). Finally, you can find many herbal and homeopathic remedies on the market specifically targeted at the kidney and bladder of older dogs. A good holistic vet can help you make the best choice for your dog.

While you're finding a vet to help you, you still have to live with the soiling problem. Put a tablecloth that's plastic on one side and soft on the other under your dog's blanket or bed. Doing so saves the furniture or floor, and both are easy to wash. You also can consider diapers, but only as a last resort because the urine may burn his skin. Don't give up on that old friend — explore the alternatives and see how you can support Buddy in his old age. Chapter 18 provides more information on caring for a senior dog.

Dribbling and Submissive Wetting

Dogs that are high in defense flight and low in defense fight drives are notorious for submissive wetting behavior. (See Chapter 2 for more on your dog's drives.) This behavior usually occurs upon first greeting the dog. He will either squat or roll over on his back and dribble, dating back to his days as a puppy when his mother cleaned him.

When Buddy dribbles, don't scold him, because it only reinforces the behavior and makes it worse. By scolding him, you only make him act even more submissively, which brings on the wetting. Also, don't stand or lean over your dog or try to pick him up, because that, too, makes him act submissively and causes wetting.

Fortunately, submissive wetting isn't difficult to solve. Follow these steps:

1. **When you come home, ignore your dog.**

   Don't approach Buddy; let him come to you instead.

2. **Greet your dog without making eye contact and by offering the palm of your hand.**

   This step is important. The back of the hand transmits negative energy, and the palm of the hand transmits positive energy.

3. **Be quiet, and let him sniff your palm.**

4. **Gently pet him under the chin, not on top of the head.**

   Be sure to pet under the chin rather than on top of the head, because dogs generally don't like being patted on the head. To them, it's much like a child being pinched on the cheeks.

5. **Don't reach for or try to grab the dog.**

   Reaching for or trying to grab him will cause him to be afraid of you and make the problem worse.

When friends visit you, they also can help you manage your dog's wetting behavior. Tell your visitors when they arrive to ignore the dog and let him come to them. Instruct them about offering the palm of the hand and about not trying to pet the dog.

Taking Buddy on the Road

Whenever possible, we take our dogs with us when we travel. We don't like to leave them in boarding kennels, and they're good travelers. Traveling with a well-trained dog is a real pleasure because you know he'll behave himself around people and other dogs.

If you, too, travel with your dog, you need to ensure that Buddy has the opportunity to stretch his legs every few hours, just as you do. The same rules of housetraining apply when you're traveling. If he's still a puppy, be prepared to stop about every two hours. An older dog can last much longer.

In the car, crate Buddy for his and your safety. For reasons not entirely clear to us, many people drive with their dog loose in the car. The problem with this situation occurs when you have to make an emergency stop — Buddy can be thrown, causing injury to him and possibly you and your passengers. If you drive a sedan that can't accommodate a crate appropriate for the size of your dog, at least get a seatbelt halter for Buddy (see Chapters 7 and 8 for more information on crate training and the seatbelt halter).

Start with a review of teaching Buddy door manners (see Chapter 9). After that, apply the same progressions teaching Buddy to enter and exit the car with particular emphasis on exiting. Unless Buddy is crated, hatchback vehicles are a special challenge because you can't see what he's doing.

When given a chance, many dogs love to ride in the car and stick their head out of the window. Don't allow them to do this — it's dangerous! He may get hit by a pebble or stone thrown up by a car in front of you. He also can injure his eyes with flying debris.

When we travel with one or more of our dogs, we make a point to keep to their feeding schedule and exercising routine as closely as possible. Sticking to customary daily rhythm prevents digestive upsets that can lead to accidents.

Getting used to entering the vehicle

First, practice entering the car in the driveway or garage. Put Buddy's training collar on him and attach the leash to the live ring (refer to Chapter 5 to determine which is the live ring). Have him Sit and Stay, and then open the car door. If he moves, reinforce the Stay command. (By now Buddy should sit on command; if he doesn't, head to Chapter 9.) Count to five and then tell him to get into the car with whatever command you have chosen. "Hup" is the one we use. After he's in the car, take off the leash, and close the door. If you're using a crate and he has been trained to get into the crate in the car, follow the same procedure except direct him to jump into his crate. Just remember to close the crate door so it doesn't interfere with closing the car door.

At first, some dogs may be reluctant to jump into the car or crate, in which case you have to lift them in. With several repetitions (and provided Buddy is physically able to jump into the car or crate), he'll do it on his own. Our Dachshunds, although willing, are too small to jump into the car without help. Ramps are great for those dogs who can't physically jump into the car or crate. See Chapter 18 for more information.

Staying put before exiting the vehicle

When taking Buddy on the road, an especially important exercise is teaching Buddy to stay in the vehicle when you open the door from the outside. That way you can leash him before letting him out. When you're using a crate or seatbelt harness in the car, you can skip this sequence.

After Buddy is in the car, get into the car yourself and close the door. Tell Buddy to stay, exit the car, and close your door. From the outside, open the door from which you want Buddy to exit the car and repeat the Stay command.

When Buddy stays, attach the leash to his training collar, count to five, and release him with "Okay" to exit the car.

If Buddy tries to make a move to get out of the car, close the door (being careful you don't slam his tail or any of his limbs in the door!). Repeat opening and closing the door until he stays so you can attach the leash to his training collar. Then count to five and release him with "Okay" to exit the car.

Review these sequences over several sessions until both of you are comfortable with the procedure and the rules. When Buddy reliably holds the Stay in the car, you need to practice around distractions. On a weekend, go to the local park when it's busy with people and dogs. Before you get out of the car, tell him to "Stay." Exit the car, crack open the door through which he will exit, and repeat "Stay." Open the door all the way, and he'll tell you whether he needs more training.

Preparing for your road trip

In preparation for your road trip, you need to train Buddy to ride in the car and to get in and out of it as we describe in the preceding sections. You don't want to be in a position of having to take Buddy out of the car at a busy interstate rest stop for a potty break and have him get loose.

If Buddy is used to relieving himself off leash, you may want to teach him to eliminate on leash on command (we use the Hurry Up command). After all, when you stop during your trip at a busy rest stop and are looking for a few blades of grass, you certainly don't want Buddy off leash.

Make sure you also pack all his possessions needed for the trip, such as his collar and leash, water and food, blankets, bowls, toys, towels to dry him off in case he gets wet, clean-up material if he throws up or has an accident, baggies for multipurpose cleanup and disposal, and any medications he's on. You may want to make a list so you don't forget anything.

If you're planning to visit relatives or friends and Buddy is going to stay in their home, about a week before the trip, start reviewing his basic exercises — Sit and Stay (no jumping up on people), Down, Come (you can use the Touch command), and Leave It. (You can read about all these exercises in Chapters 9 and 10.) Your hosts will be impressed with (and appreciative of) how well behaved Buddy is.

When you arrive at your destination and are finished with the hugs and hellos, immediately take Buddy to an area where he can relieve himself. If necessary, clean up after him. Above all, try to stick to Buddy's daily routine as much as possible, especially his feeding and elimination schedule. It would be most embarrassing if he had an accident in the house.

Easing carsickness

Some dogs get carsick, which manifests itself in excessive drooling or vomiting, and can be attributed to

✔ True motion sickness

✔ A negative association with riding in a car

Dogs that have a tendency to get carsick usually aren't taken for rides very often. And when they're taken for a ride, it's usually to the vet. You can compare his reaction to that of a child who, every time it gets in the car, goes to the doctor for a shot. It doesn't take many repetitions before your dog makes an unpleasant association with your car.

Some dogs get sick in vans because they *can't* see out of the window, and others get sick in cars because they *can* see out of the window. In the latter case, covering the crate may solve the problem.

Whatever the reason for the dog's reaction, you can create a pleasant association with the car. By working with your dog to make car rides a positive experience, you can tell how well he's taking to the car and how much time you need to spend at each sequence.

Throughout the following remedial exercise, maintain a light and happy attitude. Avoid a solicitous tone of voice and phrases such as, "It's all right. Don't worry. Nothing is going to happen to you." These reassurances validate the dog's concerns and reinforce his phobia about the car. Here's what to do:

1. **Open all the car doors and, with the engine off, lure or put Buddy in his crate (see Chapter 8 for crate training), which is in the car. You also can feed him in his crate.**

   After he's in the crate (no matter how he got there), give him a treat, tell him how proud you are of him, and immediately let him out again. Repeat this step until he's comfortable in his crate.

2. **When Buddy is confident getting into the crate, close the doors on one side of the car, with the engine still shut off.**

3. **When he's comfortable with Step 2, tell your dog to get in the crate, give him a treat, and close all the doors.**

   Let him out again, and give him a treat. Repeat until he readily goes into the crate, and you can close all the doors for up to one minute.

4. **Tell your dog to get into the crate, close all the doors, get into the car with him, and start the engine.**

   Give your dog a treat. Turn off the engine, and let him out.

5. **Now it's time for a short drive — no more than once around the block.**

   Increase the length of the rides, always starting and ending with a treat.

When Buddy is comfortable riding in the car, make it a point to take him for a ride on a regular basis. You want the ride to be a pleasant experience for him, like going for a walk in the park — not just the annual trip to the vet.

You need to be careful about leaving Buddy unattended in the car for more than 10 minutes when the outside temperature is greater than 60 degrees and the sun is shining. The temperature inside a car, even with the windows partially open, rises quickly.

If you discover that he truly has motion sickness, give Buddy a ginger cookie when traveling in the car — the ginger will calm his stomach.

Going to Doggie Daycare

Doggie daycare has become almost as popular as daycare for children, and with good reason. The dog isn't left alone at home alone for the entire day with nothing to do (except possibly get into mischief). At doggie daycare he gets to play with other dogs and have a good time for most of the day. When his owners pick up Buddy in the afternoon, he's sufficiently tired and doesn't make any other demands on them except dinner.

Dogs don't have to be trained for daycare, but most likely they'll be evaluated. For their own convenience in handling the dogs, the staff may train the dogs to understand at least the Sit and Stay commands. The environments that daycare facilities offer vary enormously; they may be spa-like or Spartan. Most have an indoor facility, but many also have an outdoor area. Some offer grooming, bathing, and training as well. Some even have swimming pools.

Before committing to a daycare facility, you should have a chance to evaluate the facility and its program, and the facility will have the opportunity to evaluate Buddy. For you, things to look for are cleanliness, supervision, the number of dogs in a given space, indoor and outdoor areas, ratio of staff to the number of dogs, appropriate rest times for the dogs, and how they're housed during this time (they're usually crated). You and Buddy both have to be comfortable with your choice, but his opinion is particularly important. Does he look forward to going to that facility, or does he balk? Pay attention to how *he* feels.

Minding Your Manners at the Dog Park

Many communities have dog parks — designated areas where dogs can run and play off leash. Some parks are fenced, and some aren't. Some municipalities make the park available to the community; other parks are privately operated. Both may restrict entry, either by residency requirements or fees. All dog parks have rules, which are posted at the entrance (if the park is fenced).

The two main rules require you to pick up after your dog and to control him at all times. Unfortunately, both rules often are ignored. It never ceases to amaze us how many so-called "conscientious" dog owners seem to be oblivious to these rules. We're convinced that the main reason for the nation's growing anti-dog sentiment stems from the fact that so many dog owners don't clean up after their dogs and don't keep them under control. The gyrations some owners go through to get their dogs to come to them when it's time to go home are prime-time comedy.

Before you ever take Buddy to a dog park, make sure you have distraction-trained him to come when called. And keep in mind that when you take him to the dog park for the first time, it's best to take off the leash; the vast majority of dogfights occur when one or both dogs are leashed. The "regulars" at the park will have formed a pack, which will rush up to Buddy, the new-comer, to investigate. While perfectly normal, it can be quite an overwhelm-ing experience for Buddy. Fortunately, it rarely results in an altercation as long as everyone stays calm. After the initial greeting ceremony is over, everyone will go his own way.

Almost every park has a bully, so it's your responsibility to keep your eye on Buddy to intervene, if necessary. The owner of the bully is usually singularly oblivious to what his or her dog is doing — and much less interested in cor-recting the undesired behavior. Because bullies "teach" other dogs bullying behaviors, it needs to be corrected by the owner.

Even under the best of circumstances, dog parks contain some hazards. Vets call them "Parvo Parks" because of the various pathogens and parasites to which the dogs are exposed. In rural areas with abundant wildlife, giardiasis (or "beaver fever"), which people can get from infected dogs, has become such problem that a vaccine has been developed. The main symptom is gas-trointestinal distress. Dogs also can pick up the usual kennel cough, hook and whip worm, and various viruses.

We recommend that after visiting a dog park you thoroughly clean your shoes or take them off before you go into the house. (We reserve one pair just for the dog park.) And before letting your dog into the house, thoroughly clean his feet (consult your vet for a safe disinfectant). Moreover, if you regularly visit a dog park, you should get biannual fecal examinations for your dog from your vet.

Keeping Your Canine Calm at the Vet's Office

Most dogs don't like to go to the vet's office, whether it's something serious or just for the semiannual or annual checkup. We experience similar feelings about our own annual physicals.

For the untrained dog, the anxiety level of going to the vet is increased by the owner, who's fidgeting with the dog, telling him not to do this, to quit doing that, to behave himself, to calm down, to sit still, to not visit, and on and on. Because the dog hasn't been trained, he doesn't have a clue what his owner wants, so he has an increase in apprehension.

For the trained dog, the owner's message is reassuring — "Sit," "Down," "Stay," and "Good dog!" are all commands he's used to. Instead of hearing "Don't do whatever you're doing," he hears "Good dog." (See Chapter 9 for basic training.) And keep in mind that the trip in the car to the vet's office also often is traumatic if the dog isn't used to the car. To avoid this problem, check out the earlier section "Taking Buddy on the Road."

Being Patient with the Rescue Dog

We have had several rescue dogs and all of our cats over the years have been rescues. The most difficult rescue dog we had was a feral German Shepherd-looking dog, and the easiest was a Springer Spaniel who was dumped on our property. With patience and persistence, the feral dog became a terrific guard dog, and the Springer was a great obedience dog.

The main problem with rescues isn't that they're inherently different from a puppy you may get from a reputable breeder; the issue is that you don't know their background. Many dogs are brought to the shelter for no other reason than that they have outgrown that cute puppy stage. Others are turned in because they have become unmanageable — read this to mean they suffer from a "lack of basic training." The reasons vary, some legitimate though most not.

Over the years, we have worked with many rescues, the majority of which turned out to be fine pets. After several weeks of getting used to their new homes, most were happy to be where they were. Even so, some came with behavioral "baggage" of unknown causes. The most common is separation anxiety, ranging from mild to severe. (You can read more about this behavioral issue in the earlier section "Coping with Separation Anxiety.") Another one is unexplained aggressive-appearing behavior (see Chapter 16). Many of the quirks of rescues can be solved, but it starts with basic training.

Chapter 18

Teaching an Old Dog New Tricks: Keeping Your Senior Young

....

In This Chapter

▶ Determining what age is old for a dog

▶ Providing Buddy with the training exercises he needs to stay sharp

▶ Paying attention to the dietary and health needs of the older dog

▶ Understanding the importance of grooming an older dog

▶ Introducing Buddy to a new puppy to invigorate him

▶ Considering carts and wheelchairs for your aging pet

....

*O*ld dogs are wonderful to have around. They have known you for so long, have shared so many memories with you, have been there for you through good times and bad, and know your every move. They're precious resources and loving family members, and they deserve the best you can give them. Some good souls also adopt older dogs; these dogs can be wonderful pets as well.

In this chapter, we discuss the best ways to train these senior citizens so they stay healthy, happy, and young at heart. We also provide some reminders about the importance of keeping your older dog well groomed. If you want to introduce a young canine friend to your senior dog, we provide tips on the best ways to do that as well.

Older dogs thrive on knowing their daily routines. They wake up at a certain hour and go to the door to be let out for their morning or evening walk. They like to eat at set meal times. In fact, you often can set your clock by their habits. Adhering to Buddy's customary routine is extra important if he's losing his sight and/or hearing. If he's becoming deaf, remember that he can't hear you when you approach. To avoid startling him, make sure you gently touch him to let him know you're nearby, especially when approaching him from the rear. Old dogs startle quickly, and may get irritable if they're woken up abruptly. Changing Buddy's routine can cause needless anxiety to your old friend.

Old Gray Muzzle: Exploring the Signs of Aging in Dog Years

What does "old" really mean? In the case of dogs, "old" is breed-specific; the aging process is related to the size of the dog. The life expectancy of giant breeds, such as Mastiffs or Newfoundlands, is often only 7 to 8 years, whereas smaller dogs live to well over 15 years. Medium to large dogs live 10 to 13 years.

A number of factors affect life expectancy in dogs. At the top of the list is diet, which shouldn't come as a surprise. A dog's muzzle doesn't have to turn completely grey with age unless there's a genetic component. He'll have some white hairs for sure, but if you feed and supplement Buddy correctly, he can age without looking old at all. (The later section "Taking Care of Your Older Dog's Health and Nutrition Needs" provides some pointers.)

Another factor is spaying and neutering. Recent studies show that spayed females lived longest of dogs dying of all causes, whereas nonspayed females lived longest of dogs dying of natural causes. Although neutering protects your male dog against testicular cancer, neutered males have the shortest lifespan, probably as a result of prostate cancer.

Depending on the breed of your dog, you may see the signs of aging beginning from 7 years on and sometimes even before. Signs are graying of the muzzle, loss of hearing and vision, arthritis and an inability to get around as well, weight gain, and decreased energy. Some of these changes can be delayed by following the simple preventative steps that we suggest in this chapter.

For more information on how to take care of your older pet, see *Senior Dogs For Dummies* by Susan McCullough (Wiley).

Teaching Exercises to Keep Buddy's Mind and Body Sharp

The value of exercise as your dog ages can't be overemphasized. Just as humans have less energy, less muscle mass, and less ability and endurance as they age, dogs experience the same things. Humans can enroll in classes at the gym to keep themselves supple, but your dog relies on you for help.

In the following sections, we show you some exercises for your dog that involve the use of most of Buddy's muscles, tendons, and ligaments. Remember that muscles keep bones in place. So keeping Buddy's muscles flexible will strengthen his skeletal system as well as his heart and lungs, improve his circulation, and help to keep his immune system strong. We also make suggestions to keep his mind sharp. Training your old friend can be fun for you and your dog, and it can add years to his life.

Do be careful that you don't ask too much from Buddy. If you find him stressing or unable to do a certain exercise because it's painful for him, have your veterinarian check him out.

Many of these exercises require you to use treats as motivation. Treats should be small and not too hard and should provide very few calories. Look for treats that have only 3 or 4 ingredients in them. For more information on treats and to find those that we recommend, check out Chapter 5.

Begging

The balancing act in this exercise makes use of most of the muscles along his back as well as stomach and side muscles. Balancing strengthens Buddy's core, or center body muscles, and makes them stronger. How your dog is built will determine whether he's able to achieve perfect balance without help or whether you may have to assist him by holding his front paws. Strong core muscles allow Buddy to run and turn more easily. Here's what to do:

1. **With your dog sitting in front of you, hold a treat about an inch above his nose.**

   You can find out more about the Sit command in Chapter 9.

2. **As he stretches his neck to reach the treat, slowly elevate the treat until Buddy is sitting on his haunches.**

   Getting himself balanced takes a while, so be patient. After he balances himself, give him the treat.

3. **Increase the time that Buddy holds the begging position until he can hold it for about 15 seconds.**

   Repeat four times each session.

Crawling

Crawling stretches the back and neck muscles, which helps Buddy to remain limber and able to look up, down, and to the right and left. Practice this on a soft surface so Buddy doesn't graze his elbows or stifle (knee) joints. This exercise can be done by nearly all breeds of dogs. Follow these steps to help your dog do the crawling exercise:

1. **With a treat in your right hand, have Buddy sit at your left side.**

2. **Put your left-hand palm down on Buddy's shoulders and slowly lower the treat between his front paws. As Buddy follows the treat, slowly, an inch at a time, pull the treat forward with your right hand.**

3. **As he lowers his body, keep your left hand on Buddy's shoulders so he can't get up. He should start to crawl toward the treat.**

Be careful not to apply too much pressure, because it will stop his ability to crawl forward and it may hurt him.

Aim for four crawls and then reward him. Repeat four times during a session, each time starting from the sitting position. As Buddy gets the hang of this exercise, you can increase the number of crawls before rewarding him.

Walking backward

Walking backward strengthens the muscles of Buddy's back legs. As mentioned earlier, muscles keep bones in place. With older dogs, their hips and back legs often become arthritic (especially those spayed or neutered at a very young age). *Arthritis* occurs when bone grinds on bone and inflammation appears, causing pain and discomfort. To help Buddy if he already has some arthritis, or to help prevent it, keeping his back leg muscles in shape is a good idea. (You also may want to check with your veterinarian about getting monthly Adequan shots, which are excellent for relieving arthritis in dogs. Or consider using Myristin, which is an arthritis supplement.) The muscles and nerves in this part of the body control the bladder and rectum. Keeping them strong helps Buddy to avoid incontinence in old age. Try these steps to teach Buddy to walk backward:

1. **With Buddy standing in front of you, take a treat and hold it at his nose level.**

   If you need help with the Stand command, check out Chapter 14.

2. **Slowly take tiny steps toward him, and when he steps backward, reward him.**

   Do it again, aiming for two steps. Reward each increment. Your goal is to reach 25 steps per training session before rewarding. Build up to 100 steps, rewarding every 25 steps. Be careful to keep your hands still and in the same position.

When our vet first recommended this exercise for our Lab, Annabelle, we thought "Wow, that's a lot of steps!" But after Annabelle caught on, it took less than five minutes to complete the 100 steps with dramatic improvement of her mobility. She was rewarded every 25 steps. See Figure 18-1 to see Annabelle in action.

Figure 18-1:
Our
12-year-old
Annabelle
walking
backward.

Doing neck and head stretches

The following head and neck stretching exercises will help keep Buddy's muscles in his head and neck region supple. The nerves to the eyes, ears, and mouth are all contained in this area of the body, so keeping the muscles along his cervical spine stretched will keep his head, neck, mouth, teeth, and gums in good shape. If you start these exercises around the age of 8, they can go a long way to preventing loss of hearing and sight as Buddy ages. If your dog is older than 12 when you start these exercises, he'll probably be stiff in the beginning, so go slowly. If you're persistent and do these exercises with Buddy daily, you'll be surprised at how quickly the flexibility comes back.

Here's how to do it:

1. **With Buddy sitting in front of you, take a treat and slowly lower it between his front legs.**

   Don't let him lie down, but allow him to stretch his neck far enough down to reach the treat. Reward him when he reaches the treat.

2. **Take another treat and slowly move it past his shoulder, first to the right and then to the left, having Buddy stretch his neck as far as he can.**

   Reward each stretch. See Figure 18-2 to see this step in action.

3. **Take the treat and hold it just above his head so he stretches upward.**

   Reward him when he stretches for the treat.

Figure 18-2:
Neck
stretches to
keep Buddy
in shape.

Using the coffee table stretch

The coffee table stretch is an important one to do because it helps stretch Buddy's spine. When his spine is in good shape, he'll move around much more freely and easily. Follow these steps:

1. **Tell Buddy to lie down just a few inches in front of a coffee table.**

   To find out more about the Down command, head to Chapter 9.

2. **Put a treat on the edge of the table. Tell Buddy to stand and stretch forward for the treat.**

   This maneuver helps to stretch his spine. Be careful not to put the treat too far from him, however. You don't want him to walk toward it; rather you want him to stand up from the Down position and stretch. This exercise goes slowly in the beginning because Buddy has to figure out what to do, but be patient.

Walking, sitting, and downing

Walking, sitting, and downing are all great for keeping Buddy in shape. Simple as these activities seem, they go a long way to exercise all the muscles in Buddy's body. They can be done inside around the house, but it's better if you can take him for a ten-minute walk and practice them daily. It makes his daily walks more fun, and it's good for you too. Have a pocket full of treats before you leave! Here are the steps to take:

1. **With Buddy on leash at your left side, walk ten steps forward and say "Sit."**

   If Buddy doesn't sit, use a treat to make him sit. See Chapter 9 for details.

2. **Go ten steps and say "Down."**

   If he doesn't lie down, head to Chapter 9 to see how to teach Buddy the Down command. Each session you can alternate between a sit and a down, two times each. Make sure you make a big fuss of him and reward him by giving him a treat when he's successful.

Swimming

One of the best exercises for Buddy is swimming. It allows him to use his entire body without putting pressure on his aging joints. More and more facilities now have hydrotherapy pools for dogs. These pools have a current that can be adjusted. (Figure 18-3 shows a senior dog trying out a hydrotherapy pool.) If Buddy doesn't know how to swim, look for a facility where a qualified instructor is in the pool with your dog. Start slowly, building up Buddy's stamina to 20 minutes, two to three times per week. Most of swimming facilities insist that Buddy wear a life jacket, and they have a selection for you to choose from that will fit him. This is a good safety requirement.

You can find facilities close to you by using your favorite Web browser to search for hydrotherapy pools for dogs. Be sure to enter your town and state in the keywords. Visit the facility before you book an appointment for Buddy to swim. You want to make sure that the facility is clean and that a qualified person will be swimming with your dog. Avoid pools that are dirty or where dogs are left to swim around by themselves. Also avoid those where the dogs are tethered across the pool to make them swim in place. This setup is only used at pools in veterinary facilities where qualified instructors are supervising the swimming and monitoring the heart rate of the dogs.

Another possibility is taking Buddy to a local lake or pond. You need to check the body of water thoroughly before you allow Buddy to swim in it though. Many ponds and lakes are in rural areas and serve as a runoff for farm fields. These farm fields are heavily fertilized, and the runoff goes into the pond or lake. Also, the bacterial count in most ponds is very high, especially around the muddy edges. If you find that Buddy is scratching and he gets runny eyes after swimming in one of these areas, don't take him back. Bathe him immediately and take him to your veterinarian to determine whether he has picked up a staph infection.

If you have your own swimming pool, and it has steps where Buddy can get in and out, let him have the occasional swim. However, be aware that the chlorine in the pool can irritate his eyes, making them red and runny. Also, keep in mind that dogs not used to swimming can tear the liner of the pool.

Figure 18-3: Meigs swimming in the hydro-therapy pool.

Applying mental stimulation

Treat dispensers are a great way to keep any dog amused and mentally sharp. These toys range from puzzles to simple rubber toys with holes for treats. Most rely on the concept of putting a treat in the toy and letting the dog figure out how to get the treat. Whether pushing around the toys with their noses, or using their paws, these can be great fun for dogs. Our only objection to some of them is that they can be really noisy when pushed around on a hardwood floor.

Buster Cubes, which you can read more about at www.bustercubes.com, are popular for this type of play. More complex interactive toys and puzzles can be found at www.bestfriendsgeneralstore.com.

Playing games indoors also can be helpful for stimulating your dog mentally. For a number of years, we lived in upstate New York in an area aptly named the Snowbelt. With an average annual snowfall of 250 inches, this area afforded us few outdoor training opportunities for a good four months of the year.

To exercise our dogs' minds, we would play the Find It game, which is really easy to do. Follow these steps:

1. **Show your dog his favorite toy, leave him on a Sit-Stay, and place the toy close to the door of the room.**

   To read about the Sit-Stay, check out Chapter 9.

2. **Return to your dog and point to the toy with your left hand while telling him to find it and bring it back to you.**

   After he has learned Find It, start placing the toy around the corner and send him to fetch it. Gradually increase the level of difficulty by putting the toy in different places around the house. Dogs love this game, and it keeps them mentally stimulated.

Last, but not least, take Buddy to a new area to walk once a week. Make sure it's safe to let him off leash and to do all the normal doggie things like smelling and wandering around. If you have a friend who has a dog that's a friend of Buddy's, make a date so the dogs can walk together. These weekly walks will give Buddy something to look forward to, and both dogs will be content. Being mentally stimulated and being allowed to be a dog are two of the kindest things you can do for your old friend.

Taking Care of Your Older Dog's Health and Nutrition Needs

To understand why good nutrition is vital to the health and well-being of your dog (which in turn affects his ability to learn and your ability to train him), you need to think of Buddy's body as a machine that has an engine. For the engine to work correctly, all the component parts of the engine must be in good order. It must be given the correct fuel (think food), for example; if the fuel given is of the wrong blend, the engine may splutter and lose power. If the fuel is totally incorrect, the engine may stop working altogether. As your dog ages, his engine needs to be given the very best fuel you can afford. In the following sections, we provide you with information regarding feeding your senior pup and keeping him healthy with supplements.

In many instances, older dogs take less of a medication than is indicated by their weight. If your senior friend has to be put on medication for any reason, watch for side effects. If you notice adverse reactions, your vet will either reduce the dose or change the medication. If Buddy is on thyroid medication, for example, his dose may need to be reduced as he ages (but not always).

Maintaining Buddy's slim and trim figure with a satisfying diet

How much and what kind of food you feed Buddy as he ages depends on you. You are in charge of how much and what Buddy eats. Keeping Buddy slim to the point you can feel his ribs (but not see them) is your contribution to keeping him healthy. Studies show that a decrease in caloric intake can add years to Buddy's life. Vets report that more than 50 percent of all older dogs they see are grossly overweight. Just as obesity in humans creates all sorts of health hazards, the same applies to Buddy. Heart disease, diabetes, cancer, and joint problems are all associated with Buddy being overweight.

Buddy has an uncanny knowledge of what's good for him and what isn't. If he becomes a picky eater on the food you're currently feeding, head to Chapter 4 and review some healthy alternatives. If Buddy isn't getting the exercise he needs and he's overweight, you need to cut down the amount of food you're feeding. Try decreasing his food by about 10 percent for a week and see if that helps. Add in some fresh raw foods to satisfy his hunger. If he maintains weight, you're putting in more calories than he's burning on a daily basis. Cut back 25 percent and see whether that doesn't trim him down.

Be careful not to give treats that are loaded with calories. Use fresh vegetables like pieces of carrot, cucumber, or broccoli instead. Raw fruits can be used in moderation. Apples are favorites with our dogs, but we peel them first to remove the skin, which harbors the insecticide sprays used in growing them.

Here's one of our favorite sayings: "If your dog is overweight, *you're* not getting enough exercise." Get your dog moving to help keep his weight in check. Take him for walks and play games with him. Refer to the earlier section "Teaching Exercises to Keep Buddy's Mind and Body Sharp" for some tips.

If you haven't switched to a balanced, raw food or supplemented commercial diet, now may be the time to do so. In terms of prolonging Buddy's life, a balanced, raw food diet is the best you can feed. Raw food is easy to digest, and you control Buddy's caloric intake with this type of diet. It provides all the nutrients needed in old age and breaks down and converts to energy.

The diet we recommend is called NDF2. All you have to do is to add water and the meat your dog likes best. This diet is used by a lot of the top-winning show and working dogs in the country. If you watch the Westminster Dog Show, you will see many dogs that are fed this way. Chapter 4 provides information on all these diet options.

So-called "lite" or weight management dog foods for older dogs, according to a study by Tufts University of 100 commercially available foods, have shown a wide variance of calories recommended. In fact, many of them recommend more calories than an older dog requires. With most of these foods, pets would actually gain weight when the owners adhered to the feeding directions on the labels. These foods generally are full of indigestible grains. These make Buddy's body work harder to break down the food in his stomach that doesn't give him energy. And often poor Buddy experiences gas when on these foods. Not what we recommend for your old friend.

If you must use a dry kibble for your dog, at least add some fresh foods and supplements so his digestion works better and he feels better. If you feed Buddy correctly, he'll feel like a puppy again.

Making life easier with supplements

As Buddy ages, he'll need some supplements so he can digest and break down his food and medications. For example, chances are high that he'll need a supplement to support his aging joints. You'll also want to use supplements to boost his immune system and improve his cognitive abilities.

The $5 billion a year supplement industry produces thousands of products. It's overwhelming to the average dog owner and almost impossible to make an informed choice. We've made the job easier by listing in the following sections the supplements we have used successfully over the years. Unless otherwise noted, these products are available through www.volhard.com.

Digestive enzymes

To readily absorb food and utilize it, senior dogs (those over the age of 8) need to be supplemented with digestive enzymes. Enzymes help practically all body systems function better. Digestive enzymes specifically break down food particles for storage in the liver or muscles and are used when the body needs them. They're naturally secreted along the digestive tract and help the nutrients in food to be absorbed into the bloodstream.

As Buddy ages, the production of these enzymes slows down and the food he eats isn't as well absorbed and turned into energy. Supplemental digestive enzymes are particularly useful for dogs who experience digestive upsets, such as vomiting and diarrhea, and who have gas and have problems with weight control. Digestive enzymes also help older dogs that are on medication; they make it easier to absorb and cause it to work better.

Immune booster

To rebuild the immune system, the Immune Booster supplement is a vitamin/ mineral mix that contains colostrum. *Colostrum* is the yellowish fluid that's secreted by the mammary glands of mammals after they have given birth. It contains high levels of proteins and immune factors that help to protect the newborn from infection. Sources used in supplements generally come from either cows or pigs. Colostrum helps to boost the body's immune system, burns fat, and builds lean muscle. It's especially useful in healing the body, so use for any dog who has experienced surgery, illness, or trauma of any kind. It can be used before and after vaccination. Colostrum works quickly, and we recommend its use for only three weeks.

Myristin (arthritis formula)

Cetyl myristoleate is a unique fatty acid ester incorporated into the fat layers of cell membranes. It's often referred to as the WD-40 for joints because of its lubricating qualities. Myristin helps to reduce pain and inflammation caused by bone grinding against bone. It helps over a period of a month or so to rebuild the synovial fluid that stops bones rubbing together. We recommend this arthritis formula for dogs with weak rear ends, dogs who limp, and all older dogs experiencing arthritis. We have used this for close to 15 years and find it to be the best of its kind on the market.

System saver

The System Saver supplement is an herbal anti-inflammatory that contains frankincense, green tea, turmeric, and orange peel flavonoids. It's effective for use with hip dysplasia, arthritis, tendonitis, dermatitis, autoimmune and degenerative disorders, and inflammatory bowel and respiratory diseases that haven't responded to traditional medications. It has shown amazing results in skin problems that have genetic tendencies and that are impossible to cure otherwise.

RNA

Ribonucleic acid (RNA) is one of the substances used successfully for aging and degenerative diseases. By taking a capsule twice a day, RNA has been found to increase skin elasticity and to energize the body. It is antiviral and has cognitive enhancing effects. We have used RNA for many years with our older dogs and have found that their ability to heal is enhanced, their cognitive abilities don't diminish with age, and they don't lose their hearing or sight.

We carried out an experiment with our 16-year-old Dachshund male some years ago who had eaten some moldy treats. He was extremely ill and his blood work showed elevated liver enzymes, elevated kidney reading, and elevated lipase and triglyceride levels. Within three months of using RNA and without changing anything else, everything normalized and he lived to be more than 18 years old.

Caution: Old dogs can easily be overdosed

Evo, our Newfoundland had stubbed his toe. He was 13 years old and getting frail. Our holistic veterinarian suggested an antibiotic plus the homeopathic remedy Nat Sulph, which is specific for nail beds. For the first couple of days Evo was fine, but then he stopped eating, was lethargic, and was constantly rubbing his head with his paws. He looked close to death's door. In reading the instructions on the antibiotic, we noticed the side effects included the symptoms

Evo displayed. We reduced the dose, and he immediately improved. We continued with the homeopathic remedy and the situation resolved itself.

Was this anyone's fault? Was Evo allergic to the antibiotic? We don't think so. It was simply that he was frail, old, and didn't have the kind of energy to deal with such a high dose of antibiotics.

The idea behind using RNA is that you provide the cells with an abundance of their basic building materials to repair any damage caused by aging. Available through the Vitamin Research Products Web site at www.vrp.com.

Keeping up with Grooming

Grooming Buddy as he gets older is critical to his well-being. If he feels well, he'll be easier to train. Simple things like keeping his nails short, his coat brushed out, and his ears and teeth clean make him feel good.

As Buddy ages, it's not as easy as it was for him to take part in self-grooming. Older dogs aren't as flexible as they used to be. So reaching their rear ends or tummies to clean may not be possible for some dogs, especially if they're overweight. As a result, their fur can get matted easily. Look under Buddy's arms to make sure that his freedom of movement isn't curtailed by mats.

Here's a rundown of the things you should get in the habit of doing for Buddy every week:

- ✔ **Put some time aside to give him a really good brush from top to toe.** Brushing stimulates the skin by bringing blood to the surface and keeps it healthy by removing dead fur. Just because you have a smooth-haired dog or one that goes to the groomer every six weeks doesn't mean that a weekly brush isn't necessary. Pay particular attention to the rear, the underside of the tail, and the back of the hind legs. Look for any discharge from the genitals and any fur mats that may make it uncomfortable for your older dog to get up and down easily. He may get some feces stuck on the fur around his rectum or urine on his back legs, but frequent washing of this part of his body will prevent skin burns. We suggest using a coconut oil shampoo, which is gentle and doesn't take the oil out of his coat. Trimming the hair around these areas makes it easier to keep clean for the both of you.

✔ **Check your dog's ears for any odor and clean them.** If they have a musty odor, your dog may have a yeast infection, which can be painful. And if it isn't treated, it can cause deafness. If you see black discharge, he may have ear mites. Talk to your vet about what he recommends to clear the infection. As a weekly cleanser you can use apple cider vinegar and water (half and half) on a cotton ball and wipe out the ears. Or, as long as Buddy has no sore spots, rubbing alcohol on a cotton ball does a great job for overall cleansing.

Be sure not to poke around too far in the ear — just clean the part you can easily see. Avoid using cotton swabs and sticking your finger into the ear canal. Not only is this painful for Buddy but you can damage the ear.

✔ **Trim his nails regularly.** Buddy's nails don't get the wear and tear they did when he was young, so they don't wear down as easily. Allowing nails on the front feet to get too long forces the dog to walk on his nails and pushes his weight onto his shoulders, weakening them. As a rule of thumb, when you can hear your dog's nails clicking along the floor when he walks, they're too long. If you feel you can't trim his nails by yourself, take your dog to the groomer or your vet for a trim on a regular basis. (See Chapter 7 for tips on getting a dog used to this practice.) Figure 18-4 shows a well-groomed set of nails. You'll notice that it's difficult to see the nails on Annabelle's foot. If you can see the nails sticking out, they're likely too long.

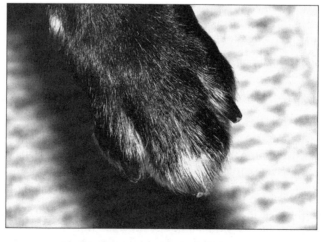

Figure 18-4:
Keeping
your
senior's
nails short
is a must.

✔ **Check Buddy's teeth.** Buddy's mouth is the gateway to his overall health. When his teeth get coated with tartar, his gums will become inflamed. Gum disease produces bacteria, which drains into his stomach and has been implicated in heart attacks, strokes, and some cancers. To clean his teeth, you can use a toothbrush and some doggie toothpaste. Both are available at any pet store. An effective tartar remover is a gel called Petzlife (available at `petzlife.com`), which you rub onto Buddy's teeth daily. Petzlife also puts out an oral mist that you spray on his teeth. Both products work to dissolve the tartar in one month. This product is a good alternative to putting Buddy under anesthesia at the veterinarian for a teeth cleaning.

If your dog's teeth are badly stained and he has inflamed gums, the only alternative is to take your dog to the veterinarian and have him put under anesthesia to have his teeth professionally cleaned. Anesthesia is dangerous for Buddy at any age, but he could have an adverse reaction if he's older. But sometimes you just can't avoid a professional veterinary teeth cleaning. Make sure that Buddy's blood panel is taken before he's put under the anesthesia. This panel will indicate the health of his liver (which has to detoxify the anesthesia), his kidneys, heart, and so on. It will tell you whether it's safe for Buddy to have this procedure done. After his teeth are cleaned, use oral brushing or gel products on a regular basis.

Bringing Home a Puppy to Help Rejuvenate Buddy

Bringing up a young dog and teaching him life's lessons in the presence of your older dog can help Buddy stay young. Plus, puppies brought up with older dogs are easy to train because they usually mimic the older dog's behavior.

Don't wait too long to introduce a puppy to Buddy. Bring him in when your older dog is young enough to enjoy him. If your dog has been fed, trained, and exercised well, he really won't age that much until he's 11 or 12. This is an ideal time to bring in the puppy. Buddy can still get around okay, teach the puppy manners, and enjoy his new companion's company. If your dog is showing signs of aging at 8 or so, don't wait any longer. Do it now, because the older dog, if he isn't feeling well, won't enjoy a puppy under foot.

Introducing a puppy into a household that has an older dog can be handled as we suggest in Chapter 7. The main thing to remember is that it's Buddy's house, and he has to invite the youngster to come in. Introductions are best done on neutral territory, such as the front lawn, the sidewalk, or somewhere away from the house. Let both dogs sniff each other all over. Buddy knows by smelling the puppy that he isn't a small grown dog but rather something tiny that needs help in learning to be a dog. Then tell Buddy to take the puppy home. Let Buddy in the house first and have puppy follow him in. Make sure you always feed, brush, and train Buddy before the puppy. Buddy is number one, and peace will reign if he's treated that way.

Using a crate with the puppy is the best way to stop the puppy from jumping all over Buddy when he's taking his nap (see Chapters 7 and 8). When Buddy is teaching the puppy manners, it's normal for him to growl at times. This growling is okay, so leave him alone to teach the lesson. However, don't let puppy take liberties with Buddy, and crate him when it becomes obvious that Buddy dislikes the attention.

Fritz, our Dachshund puppy, came to us when Annabelle, our Labrador, was 11 years old and beginning to age. Teaching Fritz took years off her life — she gets a lot more exercise trying to keep up with puppy and looks years younger than her chronological age.

Figure 18-5 shows Annabelle with another 6-month-old puppy friend named Felix. Teaching puppies is what Annabelle likes to do, and it keeps her mentally alert and happy.

Figure 18-5:
Playing with
Felix keeps
Annabelle
young.

Looking Into Dog Beds, Ramps, Wheelchairs, and Carts

As Buddy ages, you need to provide a soft bed for him to sleep on so his elbows, knees, and other joints are protected from hard surfaces. A soft bed is especially important if he's becoming arthritic. And if his back legs get weak and he has difficulty getting up and walking, you may need to purchase a product to help him maneuver higher places or simply stay mobile. In the following sections, we provide some information on products that we and our students have used over the years.

Making Buddy cozy: Beds

With a plethora of beds to choose from, you may find it difficult to determine which one is the best one for Buddy. Mostly it's dependent on his size. But also make sure it's soft to protect his joints. We have dog beds all over the house, and at different times of the day the dogs are stretched out on them and enjoying their naps. We buy beds that have a washable outer cover; after all, the bed covers are in the wash weekly. In the dog crates that we use for traveling, we use the sheepskin topped beds with washable covers. They're filled with either a microfiber pad or sponge in a waterproof casing.

You'll find an enormous price difference in beds from different sources. We like to search the Internet to comparison shop before investing in new beds.

The detergent you use to wash your dog beds is important. Many of the popular brands contain chemicals that can cause contact allergies on the skin around the joints of older dogs. Buddy, as he ages, sleeps more than he did as a younger dog and spends more time on his bed. So if your dog gets a red rash where his body contacts the bed, changing your detergent may be in order. We use Dreft, which is made for babies and is hypoallergenic, and our dogs experience no contact allergies.

Making heights more manageable with ramps

Ramps aren't as important for smaller dogs as they are for dogs weighing more than 50 pounds. Small dogs can be lifted onto the couch or bed, into the car, or into the bathtub. However, the larger the dog, the stronger your back has to be. With the giant breeds, it's next to impossible to move them if you're alone.

We advise using a ramp while Buddy is still firm on his feet. Introduce it to him when he reaches 8 or so. We train our dogs to use the ramp for getting into the van and into the bathtub. It's much less stressful for Buddy than trying to get him to jump up with his front legs so you can lift up the rear.

The ramp we like is lightweight and telescopes down to a third of its size. These features make it easy to pack on top of or next to the crates in the car. We got ours from `www.dogramp.com`, and we're pleased with its quality and stability. Dog ramps usually are priced around $100.

Helping the handicapped dog: Wheelchairs and carts

It's heartbreaking to have your beloved dog become paralyzed in the rear and be unable to move. This condition can be caused by disease or trauma or old age. It doesn't mean the end of life for your pet, however. A number of companies have designed wheelchairs or carts with wheels to support the rear end of your pet.

We once had an old German Shepherd who was accidentally given too many vaccines by a well-meaning veterinarian who was merely giving her an annual checkup at age 14. Within 48 hours, our perfectly mobile dog was paralyzed. We never gave up on her, and it was our first introduction to using carts with wheels. The cart was made to her measurements. She lived two more years using her cart and had a very happy life.

Your handicapped dog also can be fitted with a cart made to measure by an orthopedic veterinarian. We like www.k9-carts.com and find their products sturdy and reliable. At this company's Web site you can see a video of how dogs manage to retrieve, run, and go for long walks in their carts, enjoying every moment.

Chapter 19

Supplementing Your Training Efforts with Expert Help

In This Chapter
- ▶ Knowing your training school options
- ▶ Hiring a personal dog trainer
- ▶ Deciding on a dog training camp

*Y*ou have a number of choices when it comes to Buddy's education. You've obviously chosen to train out of a book (good choice!). But a time may come when you need expert help. This chapter outlines your options, including attending obedience training classes, hiring a private trainer, and sending Buddy to camp. Each choice has pros and cons, and your own personality and lifestyle determine your preference.

No matter what decision you make, keep in mind that there are enormous quality differences not only in terms of training effectiveness, but also in how the dogs are treated. Dog training is a completely unregulated area, and anyone — yes, anyone — can proclaim himself a trainer. And keep in mind that teaching skills aren't the same as training skills. To teach people how to train their dogs, an instructor needs good communication and people skills along with a thorough knowledge of dog training.

When you attempt to make a rational choice, remember that many paths lead to a well-trained dog. Beware of experts who say only their way is the right way. Successful dog training depends not so much on the *how,* but on the *why.* Dogs aren't a homogeneous commodity, and the approach to training has to take into account the dog's Personality Profile (see Chapter 2) as well as your own personality.

Going to Obedience Training Class

If you find you need outside help, we recommend an obedience training class where you're instructed how to train your dog. Having taught obedience training classes for 30 years, we're naturally biased in favor of this choice. A basic class usually addresses your most immediate concerns, such as not pulling on the leash, teaching the Sit and Down-Stay commands, and mastering Come. You also can find classes devoted to puppy training and advanced training for performance events when you and Buddy are ready.

When you go to an obedience training class, don't expect the instructor to train your dog. That isn't his job. The purpose of the class is to show *you* what to do, have you try it a few times to make sure you've got it right, and then send you home to practice. Be prepared to attend class at least one a week and practice at home at least five times a week.

We think taking Buddy to school is perhaps one of the best things you can do for the both of you. Here's why:

✔ It gets you out of the house into an atmosphere where you can spend quality time together and strengthen the bond between you and your dog.

✔ Both of you have fun while learning useful things that make living together that much easier.

✔ It's an excellent way for you to meet similar people and for Buddy to socialize with other dogs.

✔ Classes usually are economical and keep your training on track with weekly sessions.

✔ A knowledgeable individual tells you what you may be doing wrong and can help you succeed.

A few drawbacks to consider include these:

✔ Most classes are sequential in nature. So, if you miss a class, you'll fall behind and may have a difficult time catching up. Falling behind is discouraging and may cause you to drop out.

✔ The schedule and location may be inconvenient.

✔ The instructor dictates how, what, and when.

✔ The training method may not be right for you or your dog.

The following sections help you avoid these missteps and find the right training class for you and your dog.

Good obedience training class criteria

Obedience training classes are offered in almost every community. Until fairly recently, obedience and kennel clubs conducted the majority of classes. Today, however, schools or private individuals also teach classes. The difference has nothing to do with the quality of the training; it relates solely to profit motive. Clubs are nonprofit organizations, and the instructors — usually members who have trained and shown their own dogs — generally volunteer their services. Training schools and individuals who hang out their shingles are for-profit organizations. Some of the large pet chain stores also offer obedience training classes.

To locate a class, look in the phone book under an entry such as "Pet and Dog Training" to find out what your community offers. You also can use your favorite Internet browser to search for local dog obedience training classes. You'll likely have several choices.

Call one of the organizations listed to find out where and when the class meets. Ask whether you can observe a beginner class. If you aren't allowed to observe a class, which is highly unusual, forget that organization. When you do go to observe, leave Buddy at home so he doesn't interfere with the class and you aren't distracted.

When you're at the session, ask yourself a few questions about the class you're observing:

- ✔ **What is your first impression of the class?** You're looking for a friendly, pleasant, quiet, and positive atmosphere. The training area should be clean.

- ✔ **Do the dogs seem to have a good time?** You can quickly tell whether the dogs are enjoying themselves or whether they'd rather be at home gnawing on their favorite bone.

- ✔ **How does the instructor deal with the class participants?** You want the instructor to be encouraging and helpful, especially to anyone who seems to be struggling.

- ✔ **How does the instructor deal with the dogs?** You want the instructor to be nice to the dogs, not to yell at them or create anxiety or fear.

- ✔ **Does the instructor appear knowledgeable?** As a student, you aren't likely to be able to tell whether the instructor actually is knowledgeable, but at least he needs to give the appearance of being so.

- ✔ **What is the ratio of instructors to students?** We always aim for a one-to-five ratio, with a limit of 15 students for one instructor with two assistants.

- ✔ **Is the space adequate for the number of dogs?** Insufficient space can cause aggression and frustration in a class situation.

If you don't like what you see and hear, find another organization. If you feel satisfied with what you're seeing, it may be the right class for you and Buddy. But while you're visiting, you need to find out a few more bits of information:

- ✔ **The cost of the class and what is included:** For example, our basic training courses — or Level 1, as we call it — consisted of eight 50-minute sessions and included a training collar and leash, weekly homework sheets, and a resource book authored by us as part of the fee. (You can purchase the book we provide to students at www.volhard.com.) What a particular organization includes in its fee varies. At the very least, you should get a homework sheet as a reminder of what was covered in class and what you need to work on during the upcoming week.

- ✔ **The schedule of classes, the level of classes, the fee, and the length of the program:** For participants' convenience, most obedience training classes are held in the evening or maybe on weekends. A beginner class can run anywhere from four to ten weeks, at a cost of $50 to $200, depending on who teaches it and where you live. Price isn't necessarily an indicator of quality; nor is the length of the program necessarily an indication of how much you learn. Most beginner classes consist of six to eight hourly sessions, at a cost of about $100.

- ✔ **The goal of the program:** What can you expect from your dog after completing the class? This is pretty much under your control, because you're the one who's going to train Buddy. To succeed, you need to be prepared to practice with him five times a week. Two short sessions a day are preferable to one longer session, but for most people that isn't realistic. In a basic obedience training class, most organizations teach Heel On Leash, Stay (in both the Sit and Down positions), and Come. How long your training session should last depends entirely on your aptitude and Buddy's Personality Profile (see Chapter 2). Still, anything longer than 20 minutes is stretching it.

Puppy classes

Taking Buddy to a puppy obedience training class is the best investment you can make in his future. The benefit of taking a puppy to class is that he can socialize with other young dogs and have fun, yet learn manners and the proper way to interact with his own kind. Buddy's brain at this point in his young life is like a sponge, and he'll remember nearly everything you teach him now for the rest of his life. He'll learn all those lessons that will make him an ideal pet.

Look for an organization that offers puppy classes, preferably one that teaches basic control instead of just socialization and games. Nothing is wrong with socialization and games; both are necessary, but at the right time and in the right context. Look for a class where the people are having fun with their dogs and where the instructor is pleasant and professional to the students. Above all, you want to see happy dogs.

You want Buddy to view meeting other dogs as a pleasant but controlled experience, not one of playing and being rowdy. As he grows older, playing and being rowdy is no longer cute and will make him difficult to manage around other dogs.

The ideal puppy class allows the puppies to interact with each other for up to three minutes before the class starts — and for the first two classes only. After that, the puppies are allowed to play for three minutes after class. This way Buddy learns that he must be obedient to you first and that the reward is playing after he has worked — this is a lifetime habit you want to instill while he's young.

 Stay away from classes where you're told that Buddy is too young to learn obedience exercises. This type of organization shows a lack of knowledge of dog behavior.

You can expect your puppy to learn Sit, Down, Stand, Come, and Stay, all on command; he'll also learn to walk on a loose leash. An excellent program, with well-trained instructors, also will have Buddy doing the same exercises off leash as well as on signal. For Buddy, these exercises are easy stuff.

Advanced classes

Most people who go on to advanced training start training their dogs in a beginner class. They then discover that the organization offers more advanced training as well as different activities. For example, you may find that, in addition to obedience training, the organization trains agility and perhaps tracking. Or you may discover that some of the members have therapy dogs and so on. You may get bitten by the training bug, and if you and Buddy enjoy what you're doing, go for it.

 To train for participation in performance events, join an organization that offers training at that level. The organization's instructors can coach you and your dog in the intricacies of the various requirements.

Hiring a Private Trainer

You may have serious time constraints that keep you going to classes with your dog, so you may be considering a private trainer. Private trainers aren't cheap, but using their services is better than not training at all.

You can take private lessons from an instructor, either at your house or at some other location. Under such an arrangement, the instructor teaches you what to do, and you're expected to practice with your dog between sessions. In terms of time and effort, this is one of the most efficient arrangements.

In selecting a private trainer, be choosy. This individual has a great impact on shaping your dog's skills. Ask for references — and call them. You also want to inquire into the trainer's experience. Make sure the trainer's teaching method is how you want your dog trained, too. For instance, you want to steer clear of abusive training methods.

Anyone can declare himself a dog trainer! Look for someone who belongs to one of the following groups:

- ✔ The IACP, or International Association of Canine Professionals (www. dogpro.org)
- ✔ The APDT, or Association of Pet Dog Trainers (www.apdt.com)
- ✔ The NADOI, or The National Association of Dog Obedience Instructors (www.nadoi.org)

These are national organizations that provide continuing education for their members. These organizations don't condone abusive methods of training. Ask how many conferences the trainer has attended, and find out whether he's certified by that organization. Avoid someone who has just begun training dogs. Chances are they haven't had enough experience with different dogs to be helpful.

When you've found a trainer you're comfortable with, find out whether the training will take place at your residence. Most trainers go to the dog's home, which is an advantage because the trainer gets to see where and how Buddy lives, allowing him to tailor a program to meet your special needs. But before you sign on the dotted line, watch how the trainer interacts with Buddy and especially how he works him. Before committing to a long-term arrangement, ask the trainer whether he'll work with Buddy first. If you like what you see, then you can commit to further training sessions.

At some point, you'll have to become involved and learn both the various commands Buddy has learned and how to reinforce these commands. After all, the object is for Buddy to obey you, not just the trainer. You'll be expected to work Buddy under the trainer's direction so you can learn what and how he was taught.

Enjoying the Great Dog Training Camp Adventure

Most doggie camps have a vacation element, where you and Buddy can enjoy each other while an instructor helps you train your dog (see Figure 19-1). If you feel you want to take a week's vacation with Buddy where you can have fun and learn more about dogs, training, or a particular activity, dog camp is the place for you.

Figure 19-1: Happy Labs and owners at a dog training camp.

Dog camps have been around ever since we can remember. When we became serious about training and competing with our dogs, we went to dog camps. They were great fun and invaluable learning experiences. In 1977, we started our own camps, and since then we've conducted more than 100 in the United States, Bermuda, Canada, England, and Puerto Rico. See www.volhard.com for more details.

Most dog camps last from four to five days, and the number of participants can range from 20 to more than 100. Here are a few of the distinguishing features:

- ✔ Some camps are highly structured, with each hour of the day filled with specific activities; others are more loosely organized.

- ✔ Some camps are program driven, with participants learning a particular approach to training; others are activity driven and expose participants to a variety of activities they can do with their dogs.

- ✔ Some camps are designed for a particular activity, such as agility or obedience competition; others are more general.

✔ Some camps require prior training experience; others don't.

✔ Some camps include room and board in the tuition; others include only the camp itself.

✔ Some camps are held in full-fledged conference centers offering every conceivable amenity; others are held in more Spartan settings.

A good starting point for more information about dog training camps is the Internet. Use your favorite Web browser to search for "dog training camps," and you'll find many options.

Part VI
The Part of Tens

The 5th Wave   By Rich Tennant

"Okay, let's get into something a little more theoretical."

In this part . . .

This part is packed with quick lists that you can read in a flash. Here you can find ten training traps and how to avoid them, ten sporting activities that you and Buddy can share together, ten reasons why dogs do some of the things they do, and ten tricks that will amaze and astound. Have fun!

Chapter 20

Ten Training Traps and How to Avoid Them

In This Chapter

▶ Recognizing and becoming aware of training traps

▶ Knowing what to do when a training trap becomes a problem

*O*ne of the definitions of *trap* is "a trick by which someone is misled into acting contrary to their own interest or intentions." This definition pertains to human-to-human interaction and human-to-dog interaction. In the realm of dog training, some of these traps dog owners lay themselves and others the dog lays for them. Sometimes the occurrence of traps doesn't really matter, but all too often it does. So, in this chapter, we explore these training traps, how to recognize them, and how to avoid them.

Procrastinating on Basic Training

As soon as you get your puppy or older dog, you need to immediately start training him. Often owners can think of all kinds of reasons to put off basic training. When it's a puppy, he's too young, cute, or small to begin training. We still hear the old refrain, "Let him have his puppyhood." But, in reality, training doesn't interfere with puppyhood — if anything else, it enhances it. Did your parents wait until you were a teenager before starting any schooling? Of course not. If it helps, think of it this way: Your puppy will start to train you from the day he steps into the house. The same applies when you acquire an older dog. So don't be bashful about training him. Get into the habit of looking at your interactions with Buddy as teaching opportunities.

In addition to housetraining, you can start with crate training, leash training, name recognition, the Long Down exercise, and the Touch command. (You can get more info on housetraining and crate training in Chapter 8.

Information on the other topics can be found in the chapters in Part III.) *Remember:* All these exercises should be taught in an area free of distractions. No other people or dogs should be present. When Buddy understands a command, you can begin to add distractions.

Buying into Attention-Seeking Behavior

Barking for attention, at least for us, is the most annoying form of attention-seeking behavior. The same applies to jumping up on people. The dilemma is that in your efforts to get the dog to stop, you're giving him the attention he seeks. For a dog, negative attention — such as yelling at the dog to stop — is still attention.

When dealing with attention-seeking behavior, remember that everything belongs to *you,* including your attention. You decide when to dispense it and when to withhold it. The first rule is to ignore the dog — turn your back on him and walk away. This approach requires a bit of patience, but most dogs realize quickly that their way doesn't produce the desired results and they will stop.

This advice doesn't mean that you should neglect your dog. Just the opposite — give him plenty of attention by stepping up your basic training regimen. The difference is that you decide when to initiate the interaction and when to end it, not Buddy. And don't forget to determine whether Buddy is barking or jumping up for another reason, such as having to go out.

Forgetting to Release Your Dog from a Stay

The quickest way to undermine your efforts to teach and maintain a reliable Stay is to overlook releasing your dog. You release a dog by saying "You're free" or "Okay." When you forget to release Buddy, he'll begin to release himself, which isn't acceptable. You're the decision-maker, and you decide when he can move, not the other way around.

During the day you have several opportunities to reinforce the Stay command. For example, reinforce Stay when you feed your dog and when entering doorways. (Chapter 9 provides more info on teaching Stay.)

Eliminating Rewards Too Soon

During the teaching of various exercises, most dog owners use rewards like treats and verbal praise. Oftentimes, however, owners stop using treats as the dog masters commands, and then the dog stops obeying those commands. To avoid this behavior, begin to reward correct responses on a random basis after the dog is familiar with a command so he won't know when he's going to be rewarded. Random rewards are powerful motivators because they rely on the principle of "hope springs eternal."

We like to use random rewards for the life of the dog. Compare it to your paycheck — would you continue working if you didn't get paid?

Using Your Dog's Name as a Command

Your dog's name is used to focus his attention on you and is followed by a command, such as "Buddy, Come." His name isn't an all-purpose command to control or direct his behavior. Repeatedly yelling his name in frantic and varying tones of voice without getting a response tells you that you have to get back to basics. It also teaches your dog to ignore you.

When you call your dog's name, ask yourself, "Exactly what am I trying to communicate?" Do you want him to stop doing what he's doing? Do you want him to come to you? Be specific and use a command. For example, use the Come command if you want your dog to come to you. Use the Down command if you want your dog to lie down.

Having to Repeat Commands away from Home

When you give a command and nothing happens, you probably repeat it and hope it will produce the desired result. Repeating commands, however, isn't a good training practice. More often than not, you're systematically teaching your dogs to tune you out. He's telling you in no uncertain terms that he has gaps in his education.

We frequently hear, "Well, he always does it at home," and he probably does. Whatever the command involved, chances are it was taught at home, a location familiar to the dog and usually without distractions. His obeying at home doesn't mean that Buddy will generalize the learned behavior to new and different locations with serious distractions.

To avoid this training trap, you need to review in new locations those commands you've taught him at home. After that, you must review the commands around distractions, such as other dogs. One of the reasons we like obedience classes is that they provide a different place with plenty of other dogs. (Chapter 19 provides more information on obedience training classes.) Buddy will learn to focus on you and to ignore the distractions that come with class.

Are you home free after teaching Buddy in obedience school? Not quite, but training will become much easier. After the first class, the location is familiar to Buddy, and after several classes the dogs will be too. So you still need to practice in new locations with new distractions.

Punishing Your Dog When He Comes to You

The quickest way to cause a problem with the Come command is by punishing your dog, either verbally or physically, when he comes to you. And that's one problem you don't want to create.

The first dog we enrolled in an obedience class was our Landseer Newfoundland, Heidi. A good friend encouraged us to do so, because Heidi would top out at around 140 pounds. As it turned out, we loved the experience and literally "went to the dogs" from there.

We still remember one of the very first remarks by the instructor: "Whenever your dog comes to you, be nice to him." We have modified that admonition to "Whenever your dog comes to you, don't do anything the dog perceives as unpleasant." And what your dog perceives as unpleasant may be entirely different from what you think he perceives as unpleasant. Some dogs don't like to be bathed, in which case you wouldn't call your dog to you to give him a bath. Instead, you simply go get him and bring him to the tub. The same applies to grooming, nail clipping, and giving medications.

The absolute worst thing you can do is to verbally or physically punish your dog when he comes to you after having enjoyed a romp around the neighborhood. No matter how mad or upset you may be, welcome him home with lots of praise. You also need to ask yourself who's at fault. How did Buddy get the opportunity to run loose?

Running After Your Dog

If you want your dog to come to you, chasing after him is counterproductive to your goal. Instead of chasing after your dog, consider some common situations and the solutions:

- ✔ If your dog is chasing a rabbit (or anything else), you need to review teaching your dog to come when called with particular reference to training equipment (see Chapters 5 and 10).

- ✔ If your dog is running from you because he's afraid of you, play the Recall Game that we explain in Chapter 10.

- ✔ If your dog is running from you because he thinks it's a game of chase, run the other way and have him chase you. As soon as he does, stop with your back to him and intently examine the ground as though you've found something of particular interest. Dogs are curious creatures, so he'll want to see what you've found. At that point, slowly take him by the collar and attach the leash. If you try to snatch him too quickly, he'll just bolt again.

Under no circumstances should you ever verbally or physically punish your dog when you finally corral him.

Expecting Too Much Too Quickly

Many dog owners become frustrated with training because they feel the dog isn't progressing quickly enough. But keep in mind that dogs learn the same way that everybody else does — through experience, clear and concise instructions, and repetition. And what the novice trainer has to realize is that she's learning as well and that her aptitude for the task will influence how quickly the dog learns.

Experienced trainers, for example, can train a dog in a fraction of the time that it takes a beginner. In an obedience class, the budding trainer is guided step by step, so basic training is usually accomplished within eight weeks. Consistently applying the techniques in this book will yield similar results. The key is patience, persistence, and, above all, never blaming the dog — he's trying just as hard as you are.

Ignoring the Principle of Consistency

When training your dog, consistency counts, so don't ignore the principle. Otherwise you'll end up with a poorly trained dog. A maxim that trainers use says, "Don't give a command unless you are able to reinforce it." For example, if you tell Buddy to sit and he ignores you, you need to reinforce the command. Show him exactly what you want him to do by placing him into a sit. Failure to do so will result in unreliable responses to the command in the future.

Of course, you'll encounter times when you don't or can't follow that maxim, such as when you're in the shower. Just make a mental note that you need to review Buddy's response to the command.

Consistency results in a pattern of behavior that becomes habitual. Consider the following examples:

- After Buddy has grasped the concept that he has to wait to eat his meal until you've released him (see Chapter 1), he'll dutifully wait until you release him. In fact, after a while, you won't even have to tell him to wait.

- After you've introduced door manners to Buddy (see Chapter 9), you'll see the same results as with waiting for his food. As you approach the door, he'll stay, again without having to be told, when you open the door and leave.

These results can be achieved in several training sessions through consistency. The behaviors are easy to teach because most dogs are quick studies and quickly figure out what is to their advantage. They think, "I don't get to eat/go out unless I stay first."

Chapter 21

Ten Fun and Exciting Sporting Activities

In This Chapter

▶ Sharing in the fun of sporting activities with your dog

▶ Looking at what service dogs can do

*I*n addition to obedience competition (see Part IV), you and your dog can participate in numerous other performance events. Some are for specific breeds, such as herding trials, and others are for all dogs, such as agility. Many are conducted under the auspices of the American Kennel Club (AKC), and some aren't, such as Schutzhund trials. Still others are for one specific breed only, such as the Portuguese Water Dog rescue trials and the Newfoundland Club of America's Water Rescue and Draft Dog events.

The AKC awards more than 50 different performance titles in eight different categories. And other organizations have an almost equal number of titles. In this chapter we discuss the AKC competitions and more, including Flyball competitions and Schutzhund trials. We also include a section on service dogs who work for a living.

Agility Events

Agility is an exciting and exhilarating sport for both owner and dog. The popularity of agility competitions has experienced phenomenal growth over the last ten years, and with good reason: Dogs love it, human participants love it, and it has enormous spectator appeal. Agility competitions began in England and were then introduced in the United States by Charles ("Bud") Kramer in the early 1980s. Kramer was instrumental in its success as an activity in which all dogs could participate. He also developed the increasingly popular Rally class (see Chapter 13). You may have seen agility competitions on one of the television channels that specialize in televising dog events. Refer to Figure 21-1 to see a dog competing in an agility trial.

Figure 21-1:
A dog in action during an agility trial.

Photograph by Carolyn Noteman

The AKC isn't the only organization that sponsors agility trials, but it now has the largest number of trials. Other organizations sponsoring agility trials are the United States Dog Agility Association (USDAA), which started it all, the Australian Shepherd Club of America (ASCA), and the North American Dog Agility Council (NADAC). There are also international agility competitions.

In agility competition, the dogs, under the direction of their owners, negotiate a complex obstacle course that includes walking over a teeter, a 5-foot high A-frame, and a 4-foot high plank with ramps; weaving in and out between a series of poles; jumping over and through objects; and going through tunnels. To compensate for the size differences among dogs and to make the competition fair, seven height divisions exist. You and Buddy can earn nine AKC agility titles as well as titles awarded by other organizations. The original four titles are shown in Table 21-1.

Table 21-1	The Original AKC Agility Titles
Title	*Requirements*
Novice Agility (NA)	Three qualifying scores under two different judges
Open Agility (OA)	Same
Agility Excellent (AX)	Same
Master Agility (MX)	Must have earned the AX title and then qualify ten more times

As with obedience, the level of difficulty increases with each higher class, as does the number of obstacles. Other than the exercises themselves, some significant differences exist between agility trials and obedience trials. We outline the differences in Table 21-2.

Table 21-2	Differences between Agility and Obedience Trials
Agility	**Obedience**
Your dog has to be able to work on both your right and left side.	Your dog works on your left side.
You have minimum time limits during which you and your dog have to complete the course.	There is no time limit (within reason).
The obstacles and the order in which the obstacles are to be negotiated vary.	The exercises and the order of the exercises are always the same.
Continuous communication with your dog is encouraged.	During your dog's performance of an exercise, you can't talk to your dog and can give only one command.

No doubt, part of the appeal of agility competition is its seeming simplicity. Almost any dog in reasonably good physical condition quickly learns the rudiments of the various obstacles. And, almost any owner who's also in reasonably good physical condition can compete in agility. But few things are ever as simple as they appear.

Beginning agility is deceptively simple; it's not as easy as it looks. Because the courses you and your dog have to negotiate are never the same, your ability to communicate with your dog is important. Any lapses in communication invariably result in Buddy's failure to complete the course correctly. You're also competing against the clock and have to make split-second decisions. In addition, you need to memorize the course before you and your dog compete.

Agility is wonderful for dogs with high prey drive and teaches your dog to work with you as a team, turning it into a pack drive game (Chapter 2 describes pack drive in more detail). Dogs that belong to the Herding, Working, Sporting, Toy, and Nonsporting groups all do well in agility. One of the fastest dogs is the Border Collie.

You can see what makes agility so exciting. The two of you really have to be able to work as a team and keep your wits about you. We highly recommend that you try it. You'll be amazed how your dog will take to it. We aren't suggesting that you try to set up an agility course in your backyard — few of us have the wherewithal to do that. Find out from your local dog organizations where agility trials are being held and then take a look. Most communities have a group or an individual who holds classes that meet on a regular basis where you and Buddy can get started. Even if you aren't interested in competing, agility courses are good mental stimulation for Buddy as well as good exercise for both of you.

Tracking Titles

The dog's incredible ability to use his nose and follow a scent is the basis for tracking events. Any dog can participate, and if you enjoy tromping through the great outdoors in solitude with your dog, tracking is for you. Tracking also is potentially the most useful activity you can teach your dog. Many a tracking dog has found a lost person or lost article. And don't forget the important work that dogs in law enforcement do. Dogs who like to use their noses do well in this sport, though almost all dogs can be taught to track.

Your dog's sense of smell is almost infallible. Local law enforcement often uses dogs to sniff out bombs, drugs, and other contraband. Researchers are even using them to detect cancer in a person.

Buddy can earn three tracking titles:

- **Tracking Dog (TD):** The track has to be at least 440 yards, but not more than 500 yards in length. A person lays the track 30 minutes to 2 hours before the event, and it has three to five turns. It doesn't have any cross tracks or obstacles.

- **Tracking Dog Excellent (TDX):** The track has to be at least 800 yards, but not more than 1,000 yards in length. The track has to be not less than three hours and not more than five hours old. It has to have five to seven turns. It must have two cross tracks and two obstacles, such as a different surface or a stream.

- **Variable Surface Tracking (VST):** The track has to be at least 600 yards, but not more than 800 yards in length. Age of track is the same as for the TDX. It has to have four to eight turns. It has to have a minimum of three different surfaces, such as concrete, asphalt, gravel or sand, in addition to vegetation.

The principal differences between the classes are the age of the track and the surface. Your dog has to complete only one track successfully to earn its title, unlike obedience or agility titles, for which three qualifying performances are required.

The basic idea of successful tracking is the dog's ability to follow the track layer's footsteps from beginning to end. A dog that veers too far away from the track and has obviously lost the scent is whistled off and doesn't qualify on that particular occasion.

Field Trials and Hunting Tests

Hunting tests and field trials are popular and test your dog's ability to demonstrate the function for which he was bred. They rival obedience and agility competitions in popularity. These events are for the Pointing breeds, Retrievers, Spaniels, Beagles, Basset Hounds, and, you would never guess, Dachshunds. The tests are divided by type of dog and sometimes by specific breeds. Some of them, such as Beagles, work in groups of two, three, and seven or more. The performance requirements vary, depending on the specific breed and the particular event.

Earthdog Trials

Earthdog tests are for dogs bred to retrieve critters that live in tunnels or dens. The Dachshund, which translated means "badger hound," and the smaller Terriers are eligible to participate in these competitions.

The object is to locate the quarry in a tunnel or den. In the tests, rats (which are caged for their protection) or a mechanical, scented device are used as the target.

Tests are conducted at four different levels:

- First the dog takes an introductory test to see whether he has any aptitude. There's no title for this test, but it's a prerequisite for the later titles.

- After the dog has passed the introductory test, he's eligible to compete for the Junior Earthdog (JE) title.

- Next he competes for the Senior Earthdog (SE) title.

- Last is the Master Earthdog (ME) title.

Naturally, the level of difficulty increases with each title. As the levels progress, the distance from which the dog has to locate the den is increased and the tunnels that the dog has to encounter become more complex.

Earthdog trials are quite a specialized activity and explain the penchant these dogs have for redesigning the backyard. The instinct of Terriers is to discover and root out the critters that live underground. This can lead to monumental "landscaping." Our Dachshunds are forever digging for moles or anything else that may be under the ground. Of course, anything recently planted must be immediately dug up just to make sure nothing edible has been buried.

Lure Coursing

An equally specialized activity is lure coursing, which is for the sight hounds, such as Whippets, Afghans, Saluki, and Italian Greyhounds. These dogs were bred to run down game over great distances. If you have ever seen a sight hound running flat out, you can appreciate how fast-paced and exciting lure coursing is.

In an AKC test an artificial lure is used, which the dogs follow around a course in an open field. Scoring is based on speed (which is blazing), enthusiasm, and endurance. Of course, it helps if the dog is actually chasing the lure and isn't off on a frolic of his own.

The dog can earn three titles: Junior Courser (JC), Senior Courser (SC), and Field Champion (FC).

Schutzhund Training

The word *Schutzhund* means "protection dog." After field trials, Schutzhund training is probably the oldest organized competition. It originated in Germany in the 20th century and is the progenitor of obedience exercises, tracking, and, to some extent, agility. Many of its exercises have been incorporated into today's performance events. It's hugely popular in Europe, but competitions are held worldwide. Although Schutzhund isn't an AKC performance event, it enjoys an avid following in the United States.

Schutzhund training all began when the German Shepherd came to be used as a police dog. Billed as the only true multipurpose dog, the German Shepherd was expected to guard and protect, herd, track, be a guide dog for the blind, and, of course, be good with children. Rigorous breeding programs were designed to cement these traits into the breed. Behavior was bred to behavior so that only those dogs with demonstrated abilities procreated. Looks weren't considered as important as ability.

As a police dog, a dog's main responsibility is to protect his handler. He also has to be able to pursue, capture, or track down suspects. Building searches require great agility, perhaps jumping into windows and negotiating stairs and even ladders. Naturally, he has to know all the obedience exercises.

It wasn't long before competitions began among police units to see who had the most talented and best-trained dog. Dog owners became interested and the sport of Schutzhund was born.

Schutzhund training consists of three parts: protection, obedience, and tracking. To qualify for a title, the dog must pass all three parts. When obedience and tracking were introduced in this country, they were patterned on the requirements for the Schutzhund dog. Agility competitions derived in part from the Schutzhund obedience exercises, which include walking over the A-frame as well as different jumps.

Schutzhund training, which is a rigorous and highly athletic sport and one of the most time consuming of all dog sports, isn't limited to German Shepherds. Other dogs of the guarding, working, and herding breeds, such as Rottweilers and Belgian Malinois, that have the aptitude can participate. Even some of the nonguarding breeds can do it, although you won't see them at the upper levels of competition.

Flyball Competitions

Flyball is a relay race consisting of two teams with four dogs on a team. The course consists of two sets of four hurdles, set up side by side and spaced 10 feet apart. At the end of each set of hurdles sits a box that holds a tennis ball. At the same time, each team sends the first dog to retrieve the ball. The dogs jump the hurdles, retrieve the ball, and return over the hurdles. When the first dog crosses the finish line, the next dog starts, retrieves the ball and so on until all four dogs on each team have completed the course. The team with the fastest time wins, provided no errors were made, such as a dog going around one or more of the hurdles, either coming or going.

Flyball was invented in the 1980s and is a popular, extremely fast-paced competition. For information, visit the North American Flyball Association's Web site at www.flyball.org. Dogs high in prey drive do well in Flyball, although the Poodle in all sizes frequently can be seen in competition.

Freestyle Performances

Canine Freestyle is a choreographed musical program performed by a dog/owner team, sort of like figure skating for pairs. The object is to display the team in a creative, innovative, and original dance. In Freestyle, the performance of every team is different, although the various performances often share basic obedience maneuvers.

Started in the early 1990s as a way to bring some levity to obedience training, Freestyle has caught on like a house afire. Chances are you have seen it on one of the TV shows featuring dog activities. Freestyle is fun to watch and fun to train. Any dog high in pack drive will do well. In competition you see almost all breeds competing. For more information, see The World Canine Freestyle Organization's Web site at www.worldcaninefreestyle.org.

Dock Diving

One of the more recent entries into the field of performance events is Dock Diving. The principle idea is that the dog is trained to jump off a dock into a lake or a 60-foot-long pool of water. (Figure 21-2 shows a dog performing a Dock Dive.) Any dog can participate, but naturally, he has to learn how to swim and must like water. Dock Diving features three events: Big Air, Extreme Vertical, and Speed Retrieve. Here's a rundown of each event:

- ✔ **Big Air:** This is a competition to determine which dog can jump the furthest into the water. The dog is left on a Stay at any point on a 40-foot-long dock and the owner positions herself at the edge of the dock closest to the water. She then tells the dog to jump and encourages the dog by throwing an object that's retrievable, floatable, and nonedible into the water. The top dogs jump distances anywhere from 20 to 28 feet.

- ✔ **Extreme Vertical:** This is a competition to determine how high a dog can jump. A bumper is suspended on a pole, and the dog has to jump to get the bumper. The height is increased with each successful grab. The top dogs are able to reach the bumper at over 7 feet.

- ✔ **Speed Retrieve:** This is a timed event in which the dog has to retrieve an object suspended above the water at the end of a pool. The Speed Retrieve combines speed, jumping, and swimming.

These competitions have enormous spectator appeal and have drawn a huge following. The breeds most commonly seen in competition are Retrievers and German Shepherds. See www.dockdogs.com for more information.

Figure 21-2:
A diving
Dock Dog.

Photograph by Diana Rockwell

Working as a Service Dog

The term "service dog" was first used to describe police dogs and dates back to the beginning of the 20th century. Training for this job started in Germany and the dog was, you guessed it, the German Shepherd. Dogs also were used in the military for various duties, such as guarding, reconnaissance, surveillance, mine detecting, and peace keeping.

Over the years, the tasks of service dogs have multiplied to an astonishing degree. You now can find seizure-detection dogs, cancer-detection dogs, and sugar-level-monitoring dogs, giving new meaning to "Lab" test.

In the following sections, we describe some of the most common service dogs and their duties.

Detection dogs

After man discovered the dog's incredible scenting ability, the detection dog was born. Humans have approximately 10 million olfactory cells, compared to a Labrador Retriever's 220 million and the German Shepherd's 200 million.

Because of their keen senses, dogs are now routinely used to detect drugs and explosives and search for victims buried in the rubble of collapsed buildings and avalanches. The dog has even replaced the pig to hunt for truffles, probably because he isn't as inclined as the pig to eat the truffles he finds.

The most visible use of detection dogs is at international airports where they're used to detect drugs and other contraband, such as large amounts of cash or barred food items. To avoid needless anxiety on the part of passengers, traditional "image" breeds, such as the German Shepherd, Doberman, and Rottweiler, have been replaced by the more benign look of the Beagle, Springer Spaniel, and Golden Retriever as well as similar-sized mixed-breed dogs.

Assistance dogs

Assistance dogs are used to help individuals in need. (See Figure 21-3 for a look at a working assistance dog.) The following list includes the main types of assistance dogs:

- **Guide dogs for the blind:** The use of dogs to assist blind individuals dates back to 1930, when the first training centers were started in England. Seeing-eye organizations tend to have their own breeding programs in order to cement the physical and behavioral traits necessary to become a reliable guide dog. Guide dogs undergo the most extensive training of any of the assistance dogs. The predominant breeds are German Shepherds, Golden Retrievers, and Labradors.

- **Dogs for the deaf and hearing impaired:** These dogs are trained to react to certain noises and to alert their masters. For example, a dog may jump on the bed when the alarm clock goes off, tug at his owner's leg when someone is at the door, or take his owner's hand to alert him to the presence of an unexpected guest.

- **Dogs to assist the physically handicapped:** A good assistance dog for the handicapped can respond to about 50 different commands, such as retrieving objects that are out of reach or have been dropped, opening and closing doors, pulling wheelchairs, or turning light switches on and off. Excellent retrieving skills are a must (see Chapter 15 for how to teach your dog to become a reliable retriever). The majority of these dogs are Golden Retrievers, Labradors, or crossbreeds, such as Labradoodles or Goldendoodles.

- **Therapy dogs:** The main purpose of the therapy dog and his handler is to provide comfort and companionship to patients in hospitals, nursing homes, and other institutions. The training is based on the Canine Good Citizen program (see Chapter 12), with some added requirements. Any well-trained dog with good social behavior skills can become a therapy dog.

In addition to their specialized skills, all assistance dogs play an important therapeutic role for their owners, especially children who have impairments that can cause them to become physically or emotionally withdrawn from society.

Figure 21-3:
You can
recognize
assistance
dogs by
their
jackets.

Companions

Most of you reading this book have a dog that serves as a pet and companion, a living being that's devoted to you, is always happy to see you, and
doesn't argue or complain. What more could you ask for?

Chapter 22

Ten Reasons Dogs Do What They Do

....

In This Chapter

▶ Explaining some of your dog's curious behaviors

▶ Looking at a few behaviors you may wish your dog didn't have

....

*W*ho knows why your dog does some of the things that he does? Or more important, who *wants* to know why your dog does some of the things that he does? Well, if you're curious, this chapter offers answers to a few of these questions.

Why Do Dogs Insist on Jumping on People?

The behavior of dogs jumping on people goes back to the weaning process. As puppies grow, the mother dog begins to feed them standing up so puppies have to stand on their hind legs to feed. Then, as her milk decreases, the puppies jump up to lick at the corner of her mouth, trying to get her to regurgitate her semidigested meal. When she does, it's the puppies' first introduction to solid food.

As dogs grow, jumping becomes more of a greeting behavior, as in, "Hi, good to see you," much like people shake hands when they meet someone. Because the behavior is so instinctive, modifying it is sometimes difficult. Although you're probably pleased that your dog is happy to see you, you'd also probably prefer a more sedate greeting, especially if Buddy is a large dog. Because jumping on people is a friendly gesture from the dog's point of view, we suggest modifying the behavior in a positive way by teaching a reliable Sit command (see Chapter 9).

Why Do Dogs Sniff Parts of Your Anatomy That You'd Prefer They Didn't?

When two dogs meet each other for the first time, they often go through what looks like a choreographed ritual. After some preliminaries, they sniff each other's respective rear ends and genitals. Dogs "see" with their noses and gather important information in this way. They can identify another dog's gender, age, and rank order, information that dictates how they interact with one another.

When meeting a new person, a dog wants to know that same information. Some are confirmed "crotch sniffers," but others are more subtle. Although embarrassing for the owner and the "sniffee," the behavior is harmless enough and easily remedied with the Sit command. (Head to Chapter 9 for information on teaching Buddy to sit on command.)

Why Do Male Dogs Lift Their Legs So Often?

All dogs *mark* their territory by leaving small amounts of urine — the male more so than the female. You can liken the behavior to putting up a fence; it lets other dogs in the neighborhood know he has been there. The scent enables dogs to identify the age, gender, and rank order of every dog that has marked that spot.

When you take Buddy for a walk, he intently investigates various spots and then lifts his leg to deposit a few drops of urine to cover the area, thereby reclaiming his territory. Male dogs have a special fondness for vertical surfaces, such as a tree or the side of a building. Corners of buildings are a special treat. Height of a particular marking is important because it establishes rank. Comical contortions can be the result, such as when a Yorkshire Terrier tries to cover the mark of a Great Dane. Females don't seem to have that need, which explains why they can do their business in a fraction of the time it takes a male. Both males and females also may scratch at the ground and kick the dirt after urinating to spread their scent, thereby claiming a larger amount of territory.

If your male dog starts to mark things in your house, it may be because something new is introduced into the household. The regression in this housetraining may occur when a baby or another pet is added to the family, or even when a new piece of furniture or drapes are added to the household. If this happens to you, refer to Chapter 8 and follow the instructions for training a puppy.

Why Do Dogs Mount Each Other?

Both female and male dogs can display mounting behavior. Even though this behavior is more normally associated with males trying to flirt or breed with a female, it also can be seen male to male, female to female, and female to male. Most people think it's only related to sex, but it also can be a dominance display with dogs of the same gender — the one on top reminding the other who is in charge — or it can be a behavior that's displayed when dogs that know each other well have been separated for some time. The behavior is then a form of bonding, like a hug, meaning, "I missed you."

Instead of discouraging this behavior, we have found it better to leave the dogs alone; they work things out well between themselves. They have to, because they're pack animals and know exactly the message they're trying to convey, usually to bring harmony back to the household or situation.

The time mounting behavior can be construed as abnormal is if a female has some vaginal discharge indicating some sort of infection, which smells as if she's in season. In that case, other dogs won't leave her alone, and a visit to the vet is the appropriate remedy.

Why Do Dogs Like to Chase Things?

Dogs chase things for a variety of different reasons:

- ✔ To chase intruders, be it people or other animals, off their property
- ✔ To chase a potential meal, such as a bird, rabbit, squirrel, or chipmunk
- ✔ To chase just because the object is moving, such as cars, bicycles, or joggers
- ✔ To chase because it's fun

Whatever the reason, chasing usually isn't a good idea because it can endanger the safety of people and the dog. Unless you're prepared to keep Buddy on leash under circumstances where he's likely to chase, you need to train him to come when called, especially around strong distractions. (Chapter 10 provides tips on how to successfully teach the Come command.)

Why Do Dogs Roll in Disgusting Things?

Dogs delight in rolling in the most disgusting stuff, such as dead fish, deer or rabbit droppings, and similar decaying debris. To make matters worse, the urge to roll seems strongest just after Buddy has had a bath. Do dogs *like* to smell putrid?

Behaviorists believe that because the dog is a pack animal, he's merely bringing back to the pack the scent of possible food sources. The pack can then track down a meal. The behavior is instinctive. Most dogs roll at one point or another, some to a greater extent than others. It's just part of being a dog. If you have taught a reliable Leave It command, you can interrupt the behavior. But another solution if you have a constant roller: Keep several bottles of shampoo handy.

Why Do Dogs Eat Weeds or Grass?

Dogs come with many instinctive behaviors. One of those behaviors is the incredible knowledge of what weeds to eat and when. One reason a dog eats grass is to induce vomiting. He may have eaten something that disagrees with him, and the grass goes into the stomach and binds whatever it contains, which is then expelled. It's an adaptive behavior that protects the dog against indigestion and food poisoning. As a result, dogs that have access to the right kinds of grasses, those with wide, serrated edges, rarely get food poisoning.

Dogs have an infallible knowledge of which weeds to eat. These weeds often are the very same that are found in capsules in the health food store to boost immune and other body systems. Should you stop your dog from eating weeds? Absolutely not! He knows much better what he needs than you do. Just make sure you don't expose your dog to areas that have been sprayed with chemicals. If your dog insists on eating a plant that you know is not good for him, use the Leave It command (see Chapter 9).

Dogs also seem to have a sense of the medicinal value of various plants. When one of our Newfoundlands became arthritic, he would seek out the large patch of poison ivy we have on our property. During our daily walks, he would make it a point to stand in that patch for a few minutes, eat the grass that grew there, and then move on. At first we couldn't understand his behavior. We subsequently discovered that *Rhus Tox,* a homeopathic remedy for achy joints and rheumatism, is made from poison ivy.

Why Do Dogs Hump Humans' Legs?

Some believe that humping humans' legs is a sign of dominance, but this is doubtful. Puppies often hump their littermates, a behavior believed to be practice for future sexual encounters. Many dogs continue humping humans' legs or other dogs even after they're spayed or neutered. The explanation is probably as simple as they have learned the behavior feels good.

Why Do Dogs Scoot on Their Rear Ends?

Once in a while, your dog may appear to be sitting and then will suddenly drag himself around on his front paws, with his rear end on the floor. It looks as if he's trying to clean (or scratch!) his rear. This behavior can mean that his anal glands — small scent sacks just inside the rectum — are full and need emptying. When they need emptied, you need to take him to your vet so she can express the glands. With some breeds, these small glands have to be emptied a couple of times a month. With other breeds, you never see this behavior.

Another reason for this behavior is tapeworms. The segments of these worms are pushed out through the rectum and irritate the dog. To rid himself of the segment, he'll scrape his rectum on the carpet or on the grass outside. If you think your dog has worms, visit your vet and let her make a diagnosis.

Why Do Dogs Circle Before Lying Down?

In the wild, dogs had to trample down the grass to make a bed for the night. Even though this tamping down is no longer necessary, the behavior is instinctive. You can still see when your dog makes small circles stomping on his bed. The behavior is harmless — let him be a dog.

You may have to intervene when he's tearing up your bedspread or your couch. If that should happen, you need to deny him access to the bed or couch, or consider covering them with something that you don't mind being destroyed.

Chapter 23

Ten Tricks for Fun and Games

*E*very well-trained dog knows a trick or two that can impress friends and family alike. Tricks you can teach your dog can be simple or complex, depending on your dog's drives and your interest.

One of the more astonishing tricks, at least until you know how it works, requires a reliable retrieve on command. Others require no more than a simple Stay, but to the uninitiated, they're equally astonishing. This chapter offers just a few to get you started.

The trick to teaching successful tricks is sequencing. *Sequencing* means breaking down what you want to teach your dog into components small enough for the dog to master, which lead up to the final product. For example, if you want to teach your dog to shake hands, (and possibly add a High Five), start by taking Buddy's paw in your hand with the command you want to use and then praise and reward him. Next, offer your palm, and so on.

For this chapter, we're indebted to Mary Ann Rombold Zeigenfuse, one of the lead instructors at our annual training camps and the trainer of President George H. W. and Barbara Bush's dog Millie. She wrote *Dog Tricks: Step by Step* (Howell Book House, Inc.), thereby keeping alive the tradition of anyone who has ever had anything to do with the White House, no matter how remote, becoming an author.

Teaching tricks based on your dog's personality

When you decide on the kind of tricks to teach Buddy, keep in mind his Personality Profile (see Chapter 2). Tricks like High Five or Roll Over, for example, are easiest with dogs low in fight behaviors and not so easy with those high in fight behaviors. A dog high in fight behaviors wouldn't stoop so low — it's beneath his dignity.

Dogs high in fight drive can be taught some tricks, but they fall more into the category of games. These dogs have a high confidence level so they're great at the hide game, where you hide from your dog and he has to find you, or bobbing for apples, tug o' war, or jumping through your arms. All of these require confidence and can go a long way to get rid of the energy in that drive.

Tricks learned quickly by dogs low in fight behaviors include

✔ High Five

✔ Roll Over

✔ Play Dead

Tricks learned quickly by dogs high in prey behaviors are

✔ Find Mine, such as keys, wallet, or whatever (dog must know how to retrieve)

✔ Jump through Arms or Hoop

Tricks learned quickly by dogs high in pack behaviors include

✔ Don't Cross This Line or Stay until I Tell You

✔ You Have Food on Your Nose

Shake and High Five

In this section, we show you how to teach Buddy to Shake and then add a High Five for extra flair. This exercise has four sequences. Sequences 1 through 3 teach Shake and Sequence 4 adds the High Five. The object is to teach Buddy to raise one front paw as high as he can on command.

Your goal for Sequence 1 is to introduce your dog to the concept of the exercise: Shake hands. Here's what to do:

1. **Sit your dog in front of you.**

2. **Reduce your body posture by kneeling or squatting in front of your dog so you're not leaning or hovering over him.**

3. **Offer him your palm at mid-chest level and say, "Shake" or "Gimme Five," or whatever command you want to use.**

4. **Take the elbow of his dominant front leg and lift it off the ground about 2 inches.**

   If you don't know your dog's dominant side, he'll quickly show you.

5. **Slide your hand down to the paw and gently shake.**

6. **Praise enthusiastically as you're shaking his paw.**

7. **Reward with a treat and release him with "Okay."**

8. **Repeat this sequence five times over the course of three sessions to get your dog used to the exercise and to hearing the command.**

Your goal for Sequence 2 is for your dog to lift his paw. Follow these steps:

1. **Sit your dog in front of you and reduce your body posture.**

2. **Offer your palm at mid-chest level with the command Shake.**

   Pause. You're looking for some sort of response. If nothing happens, touch his elbow and offer your palm again. Give him the chance to lift his paw.

3. **After he lifts the paw on his own, take the paw, enthusiastically praise, reward, and release.**

4. **If nothing happens after offering your palm and saying "Shake," take his paw, praise, reward, and release.**

Stay with Sequence 2 until your dog is lifting his paw off the ground on command so you can shake it. Move on to Sequence 3 when your dog is ready.

Your goal for Sequence 3 is to put his paw on your palm.

1. **Sit your dog in front of you and reduce your body posture.**

2. **Offer your palm at mid-chest level and say "Shake."**

   At this point, he should put his paw on your palm. When he does, praise enthusiastically, reward, and release.

3. **If nothing happens, go back to Sequence 2.**

Stay with Sequence 3 until your dog readily and without hesitation puts his paw on your palm. Then, if you want to teach your dog to add an impressive High Five to his Shake, you can move on to the last sequence.

Your goal with Sequence 4 is to get your dog to raise his paw as high as he can. Use these steps:

1. **Sit your dog in front of you and reduce your body posture.**

2. **Offer your palm at his chin level and say "Shake."**

   By now your dog should readily and without hesitation put his paw on your palm. When he does, praise, reward, and release. If not, go back to Sequence 3.

3. **Raise your palm, in 2-inch increments, until you have reached your dog's limit. (If you have a Yorkie, you're done.)**

   After several repetitions, your dog will stretch his paw as high as he can. Praise, reward, and release.

The Other One

The Other One trick is an extension of Shake, which you can find in the preceding section. It follows the same sequences, except you want your dog to give you the other paw. What you'll see happening after mastering Shake is that as soon as you offer your palm, your dog will give you his paw without waiting for the command.

You're going to use the same sequences here as in the High Five exercise. The only difference is that you'll point directly at the leg you want the dog to lift, that is, the other one, and you'll use a new command, such as The Other One (or whatever phrase you prefer). Buddy will soon figure out the difference, because he won't get the treat unless he gives you the correct paw. This trick will impress your friends and neighbors with how clever Buddy is.

Roll Over

Roll Over is always a crowd pleaser. It requires the dog to lie on the floor and completely roll over sideways. As a prerequisite, the dog must know how to lie down on command. (See Chapter 9 for more on the Down command.) This trick follows three sequences to get him ready for the final trick.

Your goal with Sequence 1 is to get your dog to roll over with a little help from you. Give these steps a try:

1. **Place your dog into the Down position, either with a command or a treat.**

2. **Reduce your body posture by kneeling or squatting in front of your dog so you're not leaning or hovering over him.**

3. **Hold the treat in such a way that your dog has to look over his shoulder while lying on the ground.**

4. **Say "Roll Over" and slowly make a small circle around his head, keeping the treat close to his nose.**

5. **With your other hand, gently help your dog roll over in the direction you want him to go.**

   When the dog has completely rolled over, enthusiastically praise, reward, and release with "Okay."

6. **Repeat Steps 1 through 5 until your dog is completely relaxed with you helping him roll over.**

Your goal for Sequence 2 is for your dog to roll over on his own. Here's how to accomplish it:

1. **Place your dog into the Down position, either with a command or a treat.**

2. **Reduce your body posture.**

3. **Say "Roll Over" and get him to follow the treat without any help from you.**

   When he does it, praise, reward, and release. If he doesn't respond or needs a lot of help, go back to Sequence 1.

4. **Repeat the steps until your dog rolls over with little guidance from you.**

Your goal in Sequence 3 is to get your dog to roll over on command. As you follow these steps to help Buddy perform the final trick, don't have a treat in your hand, but be prepared to reward immediately when you get the correct response:

1. **Say "Down" and then "Roll Over."**

   The first few times you do this, you may have to use the same hand motion as though you had a treat in it. Praise, reward, and release when your dog does the trick properly.

2. **Reduce the hand motion until he does it on command alone.**

3. **Enthusiastically praise, reward, and release when he performs on command.**

After your dog has mastered the trick, he'll offer this behavior anytime he wants a treat. Unfortunately, you can't reward him for that — if you did, he'd be training you to give him a treat on demand. Instead, go to random rewards when he does the trick on command.

Play Dead

Playing dead is an old favorite and a logical extension of Roll Over. It consists of aiming your index finger and "firing" at your dog with a command such as Bang, and your dog falls on his side or back and plays dead. You teach your dog this trick with three separate sequences.

You can easily teach this trick to dogs low in fight behaviors. If your dog is high in fight behaviors, don't waste your time.

The goal of Sequence 1 is to get your dog to lie down on his side or back. Use these steps:

1. **With a treat in your "gun" hand, put your dog in the Down position.**

2. **Lean over your dog and in a deep tone of voice say "Bang" as you point your index finger at him.**

   If he's high in flight behaviors, he'll roll on his side or back.

3. **Praise and give him a treat while he's in that position and then release him with "Okay."**

   If he doesn't roll on his side or back, use the treat as you did in Steps 3 and 4 for Roll Over. Then praise, reward, and release him.

4. **Repeat this sequence until your dog responds to the Bang command.**

Your goal in Sequence 2 is for your dog to play dead from the sitting or standing position. Here's how to do it:

1. **Get your dog's attention by calling his name.**

2. **Lean over your dog and in a deep tone of voice say "Bang" as you point your index finger at him.**

   If he lies down and plays dead, praise, reward, and release. If he doesn't, show him what you want by placing him in the "dead" position. Praise, reward, and release.

3. **Repeat this sequence until your dog responds to the Bang command from the sitting or standing position.**

Sequence 3 shows you how to teach your dog to play dead at a distance. Follow these steps:

1. **With your dog about 2 feet from you, get his attention by using his name and then give the Bang command as you point your finger at him.**

   If he responds, praise, go to him, reward him, and then release. If he doesn't, show him what you want and start all over.

2. **Practice this sequence as you gradually increase the distance to about 6 feet.**

This last sequence goes quickly because your dog has learned to respond to the Bang command and signal. You can then gradually increase the time between his response and the praise, reward, and release to 30 seconds. After that, start giving the reward on a random basis.

TIP

Using your dog's natural behaviors to your advantage

Teaching Buddy tricks that use his natural tendencies generally makes teaching tricks easier. If your dog has a quirky habit, you may find that you can turn it into a fun trick. When you see a behavior you want to turn into a trick, tell your dog how clever he is and give him a treat.

For example, when you see Buddy do a play bow (front legs down and stretched out in front of him and rear legs standing up), and you want to turn the behavior into a trick, praise him when you see him do it and give him a treat. Next, give the behavior a command, such as Take a Bow. When you see him do it, give the command, praise, and reward. It won't take long before Buddy responds to the command. Another example is Sit Up and Beg, which is a favorite of one of our Dachshunds who sits up and begs any time she wants a treat. She is now rewarded only rarely for the behavior, but that doesn't stop her from trying.

Find Mine

The Find Mine trick is one of the most impressive tricks you can teach Buddy. It combines the Retrieve with the dog's use of his nose to discriminate between different articles. It's a terrific parlor trick that will astound and amaze your friends. We show you three sequences to help you teach Buddy this trick. (To find out more about teaching your dog the Retrieve, check out Chapter 15.)

The goal of Sequence 1 is for your dog to retrieve something of yours, such as your keys. Follow these steps:

1. **Get a leather or plastic key chain and put some keys on it.**

   Using something leather or plastic makes the set of keys easier for the dog to pick up and carry.

2. **Get your dog excited about the keys and throw them a few feet in front of you with the command Find Mine.**

   If he brings them back, praise, reward, and release him with "Okay." If he doesn't, review the first few sequences of teaching the Retrieve (see Chapter 15).

3. **Repeat this sequence until your dog readily brings back your keys.**

A dog's ability to differentiate among scents is far more acute than ours. Dogs can be taught to identify any number of objects by scent, including underground gas leaks.

Your goal in Sequence 2 is for your dog to find your keys. Here's how to do it:

1. **Tell your dog to "Stay" and with him watching you, place the keys in the corner of an armchair or couch.**

   If you haven't yet taught your dog the Stay command, check out Chapter 9.

2. **Go back to your dog and send him to the keys with the Find Mine command.**

   Praise, reward, and release him when he returns with the keys.

3. **Repeat this sequence several times, each time changing the location slightly, so Buddy gets used to looking for the keys.**

Your goal in Sequence 3 is for Buddy to find your keys by using his nose. This sequence is the heart of the trick and the real fun part. Use these steps:

1. **Tell your dog to "Stay" and without him watching, place the keys on the floor, just inside the doorframe of another room.**

2. **Go back to your dog and send him to the keys with the Find Mine command.**

   What you want him to do is to find your keys by retracing your steps and then using his nose to locate the keys.

3. **Enthusiastically praise, reward, and release him when he brings you your keys.**

Over the course of several sessions, make the Find Mine game increasingly difficult. For example, a fairly advanced search would involve you going into one room, coming out again, and going into another room and putting the keys behind a wastebasket. Anytime he gets stuck, help him by showing him where you placed the keys. Remember to praise and reward correct responses; however, you no longer have to reward every time.

For many years, this has been our favorite trick. Like any good trick, it's baffling if you don't understand how it's done, yet it's childishly simple for the dog. It starts with the knowledge that a dog's nose is far more powerful than a human's and that he's able to discriminate between different scents. He can certainly tell the difference between you and anybody else. Armed with this knowledge, you're ready to fleece anyone gullible enough to take on Buddy.

Here's a fun game to play with your dog:

1. **Crumple up a dollar bill, place it on the ground, and have your dog retrieve it with the Find Mine command.**

2. **Have a helper, such as a family member, also crumple up a dollar bill.**

3. **Place the bills on the floor about 6 inches apart and send your dog to the bills with the Find Mine command.**

   At this point, the odds are better than 50 percent that he'll bring back your dollar bill. If he does, praise and reward. If he brings back the wrong one, just take it from him and send him again to get the correct one.

4. **Repeat until you're sure he's using his nose to identify your dollar bill.**

5. **Have your helper add another bill.**

   Each time your dog is successful, have your helper add another bill, until there are a total of ten bills from which to choose. While Buddy is learning this trick, he'll occasionally make a mistake and bring back a wrong bill. Take it from him and send him again with the Find Mine command. Reward every correct response. **_Remember:_** You need to replace any wrong bills that the dog brings back, because they'll now have his saliva on them.

The fun part comes when you change the denomination and get other people involved. Say you have a half dozen visitors. During a lull in the conversation you say, "Did you know that our dog can tell a $20 bill from a $1 bill?" Of course, nobody is going to believe you. So, you take out a $20 and ask if anybody has any ones? Crumple up your $20 and have the others crumple up their singles. Then have Buddy do his number as described in the preceding steps. A variation is to ask for someone else's $20 with the understanding that if your dog retrieves it, you get to keep it. Naturally, you can only handle that $20 and the person who gave it to you can't contribute any singles. Good luck!

Jumping through a Hoop and Your Arms

A hula hoop makes a wonderful prop for this trick, which is suitable for medium- to small-sized dogs. You teach your dog to first jump through the hoop and then through your arms. Start by getting a hoop that's appropriate for your dog's size, and then follow the three sequences we introduce.

The goal of Sequence 1 is to get your dog to jump through the hoop on leash. Here's how to teach him:

1. **Lay the hoop on the ground and take your dog over to examine it.**

   Take your time with this step so Buddy thoroughly smells the hoop and isn't frightened by it.

2. **Put your dog on leash and walk him over the hoop.**

3. **Pick up the hoop and let the bottom edge rest on the ground.**

4. **Thread the leash through the hoop and encourage your dog to jump through by saying "Jump."**

   You can use a treat to get him to walk through the hoop. Repeat until your dog readily goes through the hoop with the Jump command. Praise, reward, and release with "Okay" for successful attempts.

5. **Thread the leash through the hoop and raise it a few inches off the ground.**

   If necessary, use a treat to get him through and then enthusiastically praise. As your dog gains confidence, begin raising the hoop in 2-inch increments until the bottom is eye level in front of him.

The goal of Sequence 2 is to get your dog to jump through the hoop off leash. To accomplish this goal, follow these steps:

1. **Take the leash off and present the hoop in front of your dog with the bottom no higher than the dog's knees.**

2. **Say "Jump" and let the dog jump through.**

   Praise and reward with a treat. Repeat but change the position of the hoop so that the bottom is level with the dog's elbows, and then his shoulder. The maximum height you can raise the hoop depends on the size and athletic ability of your dog.

   Keep in mind that as soon as you get to about shoulder level (the dog's, not yours), you need a surface with good traction on which the dog can take off and land. Wet grass and slippery floors aren't good surfaces for this trick. He may wind up injured or at the very least featured on a funniest home video show.

3. **Teach your dog to jump as you pivot in a circle with the hoop.**

   Pivot slowly at first and then increase speed, but never so fast that the dog loses interest or can't keep up.

With the following Sequence 3 steps, your dog learns to jump through your arms:

1. **Review having your dog jump through the hoop at his shoulder level several times, and then put the hoop away.**

2. **Squat down and let your dog see you put a treat at the spot where he's going to land.**

3. **Make a circle with your arms out to the side.**

   Keep the upper part of your body upright.

4. **Tell your dog to "Jump" and when he does, praise him and tell him how clever he is.**

Going around you to the treat is considered bad form, so you need to pick up the treat before he gets it. Then try again. It won't take him long to figure out that the only way to the treat is through your arms. Stop after he has been successful.

Keep working on Sequence 3 until your dog jumps through your arms every time you make the circle.

Don't Cross This Line

The Don't Cross This Line trick is an extension of door and stair manners (see Chapter 9). Its most useful application is to keep your dog out of one or several rooms in the house, either temporarily or permanently. You use four sequences to teach this trick.

Because Don't Cross This Line is a good review of door and stair manners, remember that you have to release your dog to go through doors or up and down stairs. If you get lax about it, your dog will start releasing himself, thereby defeating the object of the training.

The goal of Sequence 1 is to review door manners on leash. Follow this review:

1. **Use the Stay or Wait Until I Tell You command.**

   Put your dog on leash.

2. **Walk toward the front door, say "Stay," and open it.**

   Make sure the leash is loose and that you aren't holding Buddy back. If he starts to cross the threshold, give him a check on the leash to bring him back in.

3. **Close the door and start all over.**

   Because you may have already taught him to sit at the door before you release him, this review on leash will go quickly.

4. **Repeat the steps until he begins to hesitate crossing the threshold.**

The goal of Sequence 2 is that your dog learns to cross the threshold with your permission. Work on these steps:

1. **Walk toward the front door, say "Stay," and open the door.**

2. **Briefly hesitate and then say, "Okay" and cross over the threshold with your dog.**

With Sequence 3, your goal is to go through the doorway without your dog following you. Here's how to do it:

1. **Approach the door and open it.**

2. **Say "Stay" and go through the doorway.**

   If he tries to follow, pull him back by extending your arm through the door and then close the door on the leash.

3. **Open the door, but don't let him come out until you say "Okay," and then praise him.**

Your goal in Sequence 4 is to review Sequences 1 through 3 coming back into the house.

You can apply this same principle to one or more rooms in the house. As a trick, you can teach it to your dog by drawing a line on the ground and using the line as a threshold. After your dog understands the basic principle, he'll catch on to anything you don't want him to cross.

You Have Food on Your Nose

You Have Food on Your Nose is one cute trick. It involves balancing a piece of food on Buddy's nose until you say "Okay." Some dogs even toss it in the air and catch it on the way down. We introduce four sequences to help you and Buddy master this trick.

Your goal in Sequence 1 is to be able to cup your hand over your dog's muzzle so you can put a piece of food on his nose. If you've taught your dog the Retrieve, he already knows this (see Chapter 15). Follow these steps:

1. **Sit your dog and pet him for a few seconds.**

2. **Cup your hand over his muzzle from the top, just as you do for the Retrieve.**

3. **Kneel or squat in front of your dog and keep your upper body straight.**

   With your other hand hold a piece of food or a treat near your dog's nose and get him to focus on the treat.

4. **Release with "Okay" and give him the treat.**

5. **Repeat until you can cup his muzzle and he focuses on the treat.**

The goal in Sequence 2 is to put the treat on his nose. Work through these steps:

1. **Gently hold his muzzle and put the treat on the dog's nose in front of your thumb.**

2. **Tell him to "Stay" or "Wait," and then release him.**

   The treat will either fall off or get bounced into the air.

The goal of Sequence 3 is to increase the time he balances the treat while you cup his muzzle. Here's how to do it:

1. **Start by holding his muzzle and placing the treat on his nose.**

2. **Say, "Stay" and have your dog balance the treat for ten seconds, and then release him.**

3. **Repeat and increase the time to 20 seconds.**

With the following Sequence 4 steps, your dog should balance the treat without help from you:

1. **Put the treat on his muzzle and then slowly let go of his muzzle, reminding him to "Stay."**

2. **Get him to focus on your index finger by holding it in front of his nose.**

3. **Wait a few seconds and release your dog.**

You can now gradually increase the time your dog holds the treat before you release him as well as gradually increase the distance of your finger from the dog's nose.

What if he drops or tosses the treat before you say "Okay"? Well, if you can't get to the treat before he does, reduce the time and distance until he's reliable again. Then you gradually can increase the time and distance.

Take a Bow

Performers customarily take a bow after a performance to accept the applause of the audience. This trick teaches your dog to take a bow after he has performed the tricks you've taught him.

For this trick your dog has to know the Down and the Stand for Examination commands. Review the progressions for teaching the Down command in Chapter 9 and the progressions for teaching the Stand for Examination command in Chapter 14. We introduce three sequences to help you teach your dog to bow.

The goal of Sequence 1 is to show Buddy what you want him to do. Use these steps:

1. **Stand your dog at Heel position.**

   With a small dog, you can teach this trick on a table. (Check out Chapter 13 for more info.)

2. **Place your left hand, palm facing down, under your dog's belly with a little backward pressure against his hind legs.**

3. **Place your right hand through the collar under his chin.**

4. **Say, "Take a Bow" and apply a little downward pressure on the collar.**

   You want Buddy to lower the front end and remain standing with the rear end. If he can't grasp the concept, use a treat to get him to lower his front end, keeping your left hand in place to keep the rear end standing. When Buddy is successful, praise and release with "Okay."

5. **Practice this sequence until he lowers his front end on command with minimal downward pressure on his collar.**

   Praise enthusiastically after each successful repetition.

The goal of Sequence 2 is for Buddy to lower his front end without your hand through the collar. Follow these steps:

1. **Stand your dog, keeping your left hand under his belly.**

2. **Say, "Take a Bow" and pat the ground in front of him with your right hand.**

   When he lowers his front end, praise and release.

3. **Practice these steps several times until he responds to the command without you patting the ground.**

The goal of these Sequence 3 steps is for Buddy to take a bow on command:

1. **Stand your dog, point to the ground in front of him with your left hand, and say, "Take a Bow."**

   When he does, praise and release. If he tries to lie down, prop up his rear end with your left hand. Practice until you no longer have to prop up his rear.

2. **When he takes a bow on command, say, "Stay" and release him after several seconds.**

   Be prepared for your audience's applause.

Index

Business/Accounting & Bookkeeping

Bookkeeping For Dummies
978-0-7645-9848-7

eBay Business
All-in-One For Dummies,
2nd Edition
978-0-470-38536-4

Job Interviews
For Dummies,
3rd Edition
978-0-470-17748-8

Resumes For Dummies,
5th Edition
978-0-470-08037-5

Stock Investing
For Dummies,
3rd Edition
978-0-470-40114-9

Successful Time
Management
For Dummies
978-0-470-29034-7

Computer Hardware

BlackBerry For Dummies,
3rd Edition
978-0-470-45762-7

Computers For Seniors
For Dummies
978-0-470-24055-7

iPhone For Dummies,
2nd Edition
978-0-470-42342-4

Laptops For Dummies,
3rd Edition
978-0-470-27759-1

Macs For Dummies,
10th Edition
978-0-470-27817-8

Cooking & Entertaining

Cooking Basics
For Dummies,
3rd Edition
978-0-7645-7206-7

Wine For Dummies,
4th Edition
978-0-470-04579-4

Diet & Nutrition

Dieting For Dummies,
2nd Edition
978-0-7645-4149-0

Nutrition For Dummies,
4th Edition
978-0-471-79868-2

Weight Training
For Dummies,
3rd Edition
978-0-471-76845-6

Digital Photography

Digital Photography
For Dummies,
6th Edition
978-0-470-25074-7

Photoshop Elements 7
For Dummies
978-0-470-39700-8

Gardening

Gardening Basics
For Dummies
978-0-470-03749-2

Organic Gardening
For Dummies,
2nd Edition
978-0-470-43067-5

Green/Sustainable

Green Building
& Remodeling
For Dummies
978-0-470-17559-0

Green Cleaning
For Dummies
978-0-470-39106-8

Green IT For Dummies
978-0-470-38688-0

Health

Diabetes For Dummies,
3rd Edition
978-0-470-27086-8

Food Allergies
For Dummies
978-0-470-09584-3

Living Gluten-Free
For Dummies
978-0-471-77383-2

Hobbies/General

Chess For Dummies,
2nd Edition
978-0-7645-8404-6

Drawing For Dummies
978-0-7645-5476-6

Knitting For Dummies,
2nd Edition
978-0-470-28747-7

Organizing For Dummies
978-0-7645-5300-4

SuDoku For Dummies
978-0-470-01892-7

Home Improvement

Energy Efficient Homes
For Dummies
978-0-470-37602-7

Home Theater
For Dummies,
3rd Edition
978-0-470-41189-6

Living the Country Lifestyle
All-in-One For Dummies
978-0-470-43061-3

Solar Power Your Home
For Dummies
978-0-470-17569-9

...et
...ging For Dummies,
. Edition
8-0-470-23017-6

eBay For Dummies,
6th Edition
978-0-470-49741-8

Facebook For Dummies
978-0-470-26273-3

Google Blogger
For Dummies
978-0-470-40742-4

Web Marketing
For Dummies,
2nd Edition
978-0-470-37181-7

WordPress For Dummies,
2nd Edition
978-0-470-40296-2

Language & Foreign Language
French For Dummies
978-0-7645-5193-2

Italian Phrases
For Dummies
978-0-7645-7203-6

Spanish For Dummies
978-0-7645-5194-9

Spanish For Dummies,
Audio Set
978-0-470-09585-0

Macintosh
Mac OS X Snow Leopard
For Dummies
978-0-470-43543-4

Math & Science
Algebra I For Dummies,
2nd Edition
978-0-470-55964-2

Biology For Dummies
978-0-7645-5326-4

Calculus For Dummies
978-0-7645-2498-1

Chemistry For Dummies
978-0-7645-5430-8

Microsoft Office
Excel 2007 For Dummies
978-0-470-03737-9

Office 2007 All-in-One
Desk Reference
For Dummies
978-0-471-78279-7

Music
Guitar For Dummies,
2nd Edition
978-0-7645-9904-0

iPod & iTunes
For Dummies,
6th Edition
978-0-470-39062-7

Piano Exercises
For Dummies
978-0-470-38765-8

Parenting & Education
Parenting For Dummies,
2nd Edition
978-0-7645-5418-6

Type 1 Diabetes
For Dummies
978-0-470-17811-9

Pets
Cats For Dummies,
2nd Edition
978-0-7645-5275-5

Dog Training For Dummies,
2nd Edition
978-0-7645-8418-3

Puppies For Dummies,
2nd Edition
978-0-470-03717-1

Religion & Inspiration
The Bible For Dummies
978-0-7645-5296-0

Catholicism For Dummies
978-0-7645-5391-2

Women in the Bible
For Dummies
978-0-7645-8475-6

Self-Help & Relationship
Anger Management
For Dummies
978-0-470-03715-7

Overcoming Anxiety
For Dummies
978-0-7645-5447-6

Sports
Baseball For Dummies,
3rd Edition
978-0-7645-7537-2

Basketball For Dummies,
2nd Edition
978-0-7645-5248-9

Golf For Dummies,
3rd Edition
978-0-471-76871-5

Web Development
Web Design All-in-One
For Dummies
978-0-470-41796-6

Windows Vista
Windows Vista
For Dummies
978-0-471-75421-3

Available wherever books are sold. For more information or to order direct: U.S. customers visit www.dummies.com or call 1-877-762-2974.
U.K. customers visit www.wileyeurope.com or call (0) 1243 843291. Canadian customers visit www.wiley.ca or call 1-800-567-4797.